Institutional
Environments
and Organizations

Institutional Environments and Organizations

Structural Complexity and Individualism

W. Richard Scott
John W. Meyer
and Associates

SAGE Publications
International Educational and Professional Publisher
Thousand Oaks   London   New Delhi

For information address:

SAGE Publications, Inc.
2455 Teller Road
Thousand Oaks, California 91320

SAGE Publications Ltd.
6 Bonhill Street
London EC2A 4PU
United Kingdom

SAGE Publications India Pvt. Ltd.
M-32 Market
Greater Kailash I
New Delhi 110 048 India

Printed in the United States of America

Library of Congress Cataloging-in-Publication Data

Main entry under title:

Institutional environments and organizations: structural complexity
 and individualism / W. Richard Scott and John W. Meyer with
 collaboration of John Boli . . . [et al.].
  p.   cm.
 Includes bibliographical references and index.
 ISBN 0-8039-5666-5.—ISBN 0-8039-5667-3 (pbk.)
  1. Organizational sociology. 2. Organizational change.
 3. Complex organizations. I. Scott, W. Richard. II. Meyer, John
 W. III. Boli, John, 1948- .
 HM131.I527 1994
 302.3′5—dc20   93-49370

94 95 96 97 98 10 9 8 7 6 5 4 3 2

Sage Production Editor: Diane S. Foster

Contents

Preface

IN 1983, we published a collection of our studies under the title *Organizational Environments: Ritual and Rationality* (with B. Rowan & T. E. Deal, Sage; updated edition, 1992). The studies involved were mainly theoretical and interpretive essays—although some empirical materials were involved—taking an institutional view of modern organizational structure. They were part of a first wave of institutional ideas that emphasized (a) the environmental dependence of much organizational structure, (b) the broadly political and cultural environmental dimensions involved, and (c) the effects of these dependencies on the character of much modern organization—in particular, the sprawling, complex, and often decoupled nature of organizations produced under highly institutionalized regimes.

Since then we and others have pursued these ideas, often with empirical studies of the environment-organization linkage and its effects. We have also expanded our attention to include the aspects of the modern rationalized environments that produce so many consequences—attending to properties of organizational fields, national environments, and even world society, as these are involved in generating and changing organizations.

The products of these efforts are assembled in this book, which collects some of our empirical and theoretical efforts over the last decade in a more-or-less integrated form. The result is a collection of articles, not a tightly coherent text. But the articles relate to and build on one another in pursuit of differing but related strands of the argument. Several of the articles have been previously published, some in rather out-of-the-way places; but several chapters have not previously appeared but are original preparations for this volume. Brief integrative essays introduce each section.

We believe that each article contributes to the volume and also benefits from its connections to the other chapters.

Our work falls in three categories—one that is more theoretical and two that are more empirical. In Part I we first discuss the nature of rationalization in the modern environment—the cultural and organizational changes that have produced extraordinary (and sometimes worldwide) waves of organizing and organizational change. Then in Part I we discuss the linkages between these changing and intensifying contexts and particular organizations and organizing situations. What are the various ways in which institutions have been viewed and what are the mechanisms by which they shape organizational structure?

Part II discusses, more empirically, effects on one major domain of organizational change in recent decades: increases in the complexity of typical organizations and in the scale of organizing on many dimensions. The first chapter discusses a worldwide expansion in formal accounting arrangements. The remaining three chapters discuss the steady expansion of complexity and scale in U.S. public education in this century, relating it to changes in the wider U.S. public order and its controls.

Part III discusses organizational change in response to the long-term rationalization and expansion of individual identity and rights in American (and probably world) society. We discuss the mental health system, the expansion of training programs in organizations, and finally the rise of complex personnel arrangements having the character of constructed "internal labor markets."

Our work has benefited from support from many sources. Some are formal and financial. Work on Chapters 1, 3, and 11 was in part aided by fellowships from the Center for Advanced Study in the Behavioral Sciences (including MacArthur Foundation support). Chapter 2 was prepared with support from the Stockholm Center for Organizational Research, which also assisted our overall efforts to pull the book together. Work on Chapters 6 through 10 was conducted under the auspices of Stanford's Institute for Research on Educational Finance and Governance, with funds from the National Institute of Education. Chapters 11 and 12 were prepared with support from the Spencer Foundation. And work on Chapter 13 was funded by the National Science Foundation. (Further specification of support sources and other types of assistance appears in each chapter's acknowledgments.) In all of these cases, we should point out that our views and analyses are our own, and they do not necessarily reflect the views and positions of our supporting agencies.

Although we have been centrally involved in all the work reported in this book's chapters, we obviously owe special thanks and give acknowledgement to the coauthors of the various chapters; their collaboration is noted in the listed authorships.

Throughout our research, we received much support and encouragement from colleagues associated with Stanford's Center for Organization Research. The help and comments—and sometimes direct research assistance—of many of our colleagues, both faculty and student, in the center are acknowledged in the individual chapters. The importance of the institutional support provided by an exceptional collection of Stanford scholars concerned with organization theory will be obvious to any informed reader of the book.

As noted, several chapters in this volume have been previously published, and we thank the publishers for permission to republish them here. A slightly revised Chapter 1 is taken from Thomas, Meyer, Ramirez, and Boli, *Institutional Structure: Constituting State, Society, and the Individual* (1987), pp. 12-32. Chapter 5 was published in *Theory and Society, 22* (1993), pp. 487-511. Chapter 6 first appeared in *Accounting, Organizations and Society, 11* (1986), pp. 345-356. Chapter 7, somewhat revised, is taken from James and Levin (eds.) (1988), *Comparing Public and Private Schools. Vol. I: Institutions and Organizations,* pp. 128-152. Chapter 8 first appeared in *Administrative Science Quarterly, 32* (1987), pp. 186-201.

Chapter 9 comes from Zucker (ed.) (1988), *Institutional Patterns and Organizations: Culture and Environment,* pp. 139-167. Chapter 10 originally appeared in Scott and Black (eds.) (1986), *The Organization of Mental Health Services: Society and Community Systems,* pp. 15-29. Chapter 11 was first published in Barry Staw and L. L. Cummings (eds.) (1991), *Research in Organizational Behavior* (Vol. 13, pp. 297-326). Finally, Chapter 13 appeared in the *American Journal of Sociology, 99* (1993), pp. 396-427.

W. Richard Scott
John W. Meyer

I. DEVELOPMENTS IN INSTITUTIONAL THEORY

The idea that organizations are deeply and essentially embedded in wider institutional environments rose to prominence in the late 1970s and early 1980s. It was but one of several theories that developed in reaction to prevailing conceptions of organizations as bounded, relatively autonomous, rational actors (for a review, see Scott, 1992). Our own work (Meyer & Scott, 1983b) was part of the initial wave of institutional analysis (see also DiMaggio & Powell, 1983; Meyer & Rowan, 1977; Zucker, 1977).

Since the early period, institutional theory and research have developed rapidly and currently occupy a prominent place in the field of organizational analysis. Substantial collections of the more recent sociological work are available (e.g., Zucker, 1988a; Powell & DiMaggio, 1991), and relevant studies routinely appear in the journals covering the field.

The studies in this book represent the more recent development of our work on institutional analysis. They include both theoretical and empirical contributions, and also reflect on the evolving literature in the area. They deal with the full range of major issues and themes that now come under the heading of institutional theory, and they suggest directions in which we see the field going or argue for directions that it should go.

The Themes of Institutional Analysis

The following core ideas remain at the center for contemporary institutional thinking. They have been elaborated and improved over time but reflect a good deal of thematic consistency. These ideas are reviewed and developed in Part I, and they appear prominently in the various studies reported in Parts II and III.

First, the visible structures and routines that make up organizations are direct reflections and effects of rules and structures built into (or institutionalized within) wider environments. Organizations reflect patterns or templates established in a wider system (see Chapter 1). The rise of such patterns drives the birth (and lowers the mortality) of organizations and also greatly affects their detailed structural content. School, firm, or hospital structures reflect standard forms created in the wider environment: The existence of such organizations depends in good part on the environmental institutionalization of such forms. The emphasis on the importance of these wider cultural and symbolic patterns shaping organizations is somewhat distinctive to the sociological, in contrast to the economic or political science, strands of institutional theory (see Chapter 3).

Second, the dependence of organizations on the patterning built up in wider environments—rather than on a purely internal technical and functional logic—produces organizational forms that are often rather loosely integrated (or decoupled) structures (see Chapters 1 and 3). Stable organizing requires and results from external legitimation and may be quite consistent with a good deal of internal looseness. Local functional requirements are not the central source of organizational structure, and they are not likely to be fully consistent with it. Schools have curricula and categories of students, firms have departments and offices and procedures, and hospitals have treatment programs and specialists that may make cosmopolitan rather than local sense.

Third, the environmental patterns that drive organizing work through linkages and effects that go beyond simple direct control. They have a constitutive, or phenomenological, aspect; and they are made up of meaning systems as well as hard-wired controls (see Berger & Luckmann, 1967, and Chapters 1 and 3). Certainly the direct controls of the state regulate many features of schools, firms, and hospitals (and in various ways determine and accredit their existence). But institutionalized meanings also play important roles in defining what schools, firms, and hospitals are to look like, why they are valuable, and what they are and are not to do. Environmental patterning is not only narrowly legal and economic, but also broadly social and cultural in character and effect.

Fourth, the environmental patterns that create and change organizations can be described as rationalized and rationalizing. Much cultural material, even in modern systems, has limited effect on formal organizations: All sorts of developments in values, tastes, aesthetics, and knowledge affect society in other ways than through organizing. The tendency of modern sociocultural environments toward rationalization—the creation of cultural schemes defining means-ends relationships and standardizing systems of control over activities and actors—are the core elements that create ways of organizing and organizational change. For instance, modernizing cultures may create a value for individual self-esteem with limited organizational effect. But when this value is culturally and legally tied to the rights of citizens, and when it is culturally and scientifically defined as an appropriate and effective instrument for making social action more efficient, organizational templates change, new organizations are created, and older forms transformed. The studies in Part III of this book describe some of the relevant consequences of a rationalized version of individual value for nationwide and perhaps worldwide elaboration of personnel administration—now, re-created as "human resources"—functions in organizations.

Institutionalization processes can occur at various structural levels—from interpersonal and intraorganizational to organizational field to societal and even transsocietal levels (see Chapter 4). Our own recent work emphasizes the broader influences. Our institutional vision is thus of a wider social and cultural world infused with long-term processes of rationalization—scientific and professional, cultural and ideological, political and organizational—that have continually expanded possibilities and necessities for organizing and for expanding and changing organizations. The resultant organizational world is filled with somewhat standardized (and often a bit decoupled) organizations as a matter of both ritual and mundane reality. These organizations spread within and between sectors, within and between societies, and come to cover in a surprisingly standardized way the whole world. We indeed have a "society of organizations," to borrow Perrow's (1991) phrase, but the organizations involved are by no means autonomous actors: They are embedded in every aspect of their structure and functioning. Although organizations may have absorbed society, as Perrow claims, society has no less absorbed organizations. World society itself is now filled with organizational structures (see Chapter 2), and it is constituted of highly organized and isomorphic nation-states (see Chapter 1), almost all of which contain massively expanded internal organizational machinery of the most standardized sorts. There is not only plenty of variation from sector to sector and state to state, but also many trends and features of great consistency.

The Structure of This Book

Part I is devoted to theoretical and conceptual concerns, often transcending the specifics of our empirical work. In this part, we hope to suggest future directions, not simply to integrate our own past research. Chapters 1 and 2 deal with the loose ends at the beginning of any institutional theory: the evolution of the rationalized environment on which organizations and organizing are thought to depend. Our efforts here are to support a vision of cultural rationalization that is far from simply dependent on the interests and power of a few rational actors or groups in a prior world. In contrast to the arguments of DiMaggio (1988, 1991) and others who see the creation of institutions as an occasion for reviving "agency"—the rational actor endowed with a preexisting set of interests to be defended and advanced by creating new cultural rules—we think the most interesting and useful forms of institutional theory depend on showing the collective and cultural character of the development of institutional environments. Rationalization has been a long-term process or set of processes in Western history, and it is by no means simply a product easily reducible to an intellectually comforting set of specifiable prior interests and powers, whether good or evil. To pick the two substantive themes of our empirical work, it is by no means clear what subgroup interests or powers have produced the enormously expanded modern model of the empowered individual and sent it worldwide in a doctrinal binge extending human rights across races, genders, and classes. Neither is it obvious what interests or powers have driven all sorts of rationalistic functions—personnel structures, accounting arrangements, planning departments—into massive numbers of organizations around the world.

Chapters 3, 4, and 5 focus mainly on developing ideas about the core institutional theme: the nature of the linkages between environment and organization. Chapter 3 reviews institutional arguments from several disciplines to reveal both the areas of agreement and disagreement. In general, sociological versions—in particular, the more recent work (see DiMaggio & Powell, 1991)—stress the importance of cultural cognitive models external to specific organizational forms, while earlier sociological work, along with economic and positive choice theorists, emphasize rule systems and normative controls built into organizational structures. The newer sociological approaches—including this volume—stress the constitutive functions of institutions; the earlier sociological and the institutional economic and positive choice theories stress the regulative functions of institutions. These latter groups and, more generally, traditional thinking in the field take for granted the autonomy, rationality, and boundedness of organizations and their internal actors. As a consequence, these analysts have had the greatest difficulty confronting institutional theory on this count. It was not difficult for these traditional scholars to see evidence that cultural beliefs and legal requirements exert direct effects on organizations. But it has been much harder for them, given their presuppositions of a world of "real" actors, agents, and interests to understand that central institutional effects entail not influences on actors but the creation of actors, not changes in incentives but transformations in meaning systems. We devote much effort, in Chapters 3, 4, and 5 to elucidating this question of how institutional effects occur—to reviewing the literature and to putting forward our own arguments. We envisage a rich texture of linkages between highly developed institutional environments and socially constructed actors, both individual and organizational.

In these more theoretical chapters, then, we try to expand the lines of thought included in institutional theory backward into the exploration of the construction of the rationalized environment and forward into the investigation of process links between these environments, organizations, and organizing.

Most of our empirically oriented work, represented in the chapters of Parts II and III, focuses centrally on the core first theme of institutional theory: the direct linkages between aspects of institutional environments and the organizations that are embedded in them. Chapter 6 develops arguments about the types of circumstances—including national polities—that are likely to generate expanded organizational accounting. Chapters 7, 8, and 9 show empirically how the peculiar funding and control contexts of American education produce organizational elaboration and complexity in school and district structures. Chapters 10, 11, and 12 discuss—and present illustrative materials on—the effects of institutionalized American individualism (in law, in the professional ideologies of the social sciences, and in public beliefs) as it creates expanded and complex organizational arrangements dealing with mental health and with broad structures of organizational training. Chapter 13 shows similar impacts of legal changes and professional constructions on the elaboration of the American organizational personnel system.

Beyond simply showing environmental impacts on organizational arrangements (the first institutional theme noted above), these chapters also emphasize the ideological or phenomenological aspects of the linkages (the third theme). Political and professional (and scientific) ideologies are important aspects of the relevant environments. We are not simply concerned with showing the operation of some tight and linear legal or bureaucratic control systems devolving from the state. The political theory or ideology of individualism is involved in and legitimates the decentralized models of schooling, the expanded doctrines of mental health, of organizational training, and of employee rights and citizenship. So too is the mediating role of the sciences and professions as they construct and legitimate elaborate models of rationalistic local organization, and of the expanded and empowered individual contributor to organizations and to society. The projects involved are fundamentally cultural ones and have special standing in the American polity.

The research studies in Parts II and III focus almost entirely on the American organizational context and reflect the peculiarities of the American culture and state—a system that is notorious for generating much organizational activity. The mixture of a relatively weak central state and an expanded public culture and polity continues to prove explosive—providing a hothouse for generating the rationalistic cultural ingredients (and requirements) for organizing at a very rapid rate.

Thus these studies are relevant to our fourth institutionalist theme: the analysis of the rationalistic environment and its expansion and change in the current period. The chapters in Part II address the pressures that produce expansions in organizational complexity—a main theme in the history of modern organization in the United States and elsewhere—as it is produced by a public culture expanding all sorts of collective goods but locating primary responsibility for them in particular organizations. The chapters in Part III address the organizational consequences of the long-term expansion in the status, identity, rights, and powers of the individual, a core myth in practically all forms of modernity and a dominant one in the United States.

Although many of the organizations included in our empirical studies are public, professional service organizations—schools and mental health agencies—our studies also include manufacturing firms and commercial organizations. The themes we stress—the effects of wider cultural systems on organizations and organizing—are by no means limited to the soft (public service) sectors of the world of organizations. Moreover, while our own research is restricted to U.S. organizations, these themes are not confined to the United States; they clearly operate worldwide. Perhaps this simply reflects some decades of American dominance, but it more likely signifies a world with much collective culture but little organizational centralization, paralleling some aspects of the American scene (see Chapter 2). In any event, the phenomena we discuss in Parts II and III have obvious parallel in worldwide trends.

A Final Note

Our efforts, particularly in the more theoretical Part I, have as one aim confronting an issue not well dealt with in modern organization theory—an aim institutional theory is peculiarly well positioned to address. We have to date developed little by way of a general or macrosociological model of long-term or widespread organizational change. (Earlier, crude evolutionary models [e.g., Kerr, Dunlop, Harbison, & Meyers, 1964] have been discredited, and more recent attempts to improve them [e.g., Singh, 1990] are still in their infancy.) Great and systematic changes go on in technically similar organizations, changes across long time periods and many particular societies. They impact organizations on our two dimensions of special interest: (a) the rise of expanded rationalistic complexity or structuration, and (b) the expansion of the rights and perceived capacities of organized individuals. Both processes exhibit world-wide and long-term trajectories. Institutional models, in which such changes are seen to operate at general institutional (or cultural and broadly political) levels, can provide valuable leverage in explaining such changes. Macrosociological ideas of this kind would appear to have special advantages in accounting for changes that involve substantial macrostructural elements.

1

Ontology and Rationalization
in the Western Cultural Account

JOHN W. MEYER

JOHN BOLI

GEORGE M. THOMAS

IN THIS CHAPTER we develop the view that social action in modern societies is highly structured by institutionalized rules. These rules take the form of cultural theories, ideologies, and prescriptions about how society works or should work to attain collective purposes, especially the comprehensive and evolving goals of justice and progress. The collective goods themselves are linked to other institutional elements that define the moral order and the natural world. Following the terminology of the sociology of knowledge, we conceptualize Western society as essentially a cultural project organizing human activity to forge the proper links between the moral and natural worlds.

A central concern of our analysis is the way in which the institutional structure of society creates and legitimates the social entities that are seen as "actors." That is, institutionalized cultural rules define the meaning and identity of the individual and the patterns of appropriate economic, political, and cultural activity engaged in by those individuals. They similarly constitute the purposes and legitimacy of organizations, professions, interest groups, and states, while delineating lines of activity appropriate to these entities. All of this material has general cultural meaning in modern systems and tends to be universal across them, so that all aspects of individual identity, choice, and action (a vote, a consumer purchase, a job decision) are depicted in the institutional system as related to the collective purposes of progress and justice.

It is revealing that the terms *institution* and *institutionalization* have vague and variable meaning in modern sociological discussions. They refer to the broad patterning of social structure and activity around general rules, but with much uncertainty about the nature of such rules: Are they statistical summaries of practice, or are they empirical analyses of the interactions among a given and prior set of units such as individuals, organizations, or some sort of cultural forms? We see *institutions* as cultural rules giving collective meaning and value to particular entities and activities, integrating them into the larger schemes. We see both patterns of activity and the units involved in them (individuals and other social entities) as constructed by such wider rules. *Institutionalization,* in this usage, is the process by which a given set of units and a pattern of activities come to be normatively and cognitively held in place, and practically taken for granted as lawful (whether as a matter of formal law, custom, or knowledge).

Most social theory takes actors (from individuals to states) and their actions as real, *a priori,* elements of modern social processes and institutional forms. We see the "existence" and characteristics of actors as socially constructed and highly problematic, and action as the enactment of broad institutional scripts rather than a matter of internally generated and autonomous choice, motivation, and purpose.

It is important to note that in taking an institutionalist view, we do not postulate a society without people in it. It is rather that we find it problematic—as requiring explanation and analysis—that people invoke and rely on cultural accounts in defining themselves as individuals (persons, human beings, world citizens) with rights, dignity, and value. It is problematic when they invoke and rely on cultural accounts to define their actions as matters of individual choice and decision, filled with individual motives and perceptions and involving such legitimated resources as individual property. The social psychology involved is that of Goffman (1974) and Swanson (1971), and its linkage to institutional structures is that of Mills (1940). But we add the important point that the ontological status of the individual is a social construction, which can be a social resource that actors can draw on to support their actions or can also be a liability, as in Berger, Berger, and Kellner's (1973) conception of the homeless mind.

In this introductory chapter, we consider the problems of actor-centered social theories, discussing first models that are based on individuals and then those based on collective actors such as interest groups, organizations, and states. Such models, we argue, ultimately fall back on soft conceptions of culture as the backdrop of action. Culture is allowed too little content and too much reified inevitability. In the next section, we develop a model of modern cultural systems as institutionalized accounts that map out the entities and processes of modern society and integrate them together within general frameworks.

In the third section of this chapter, we use this institutionalist model to argue that the rationalization of activity and its incorporation in legitimated models of collective life are interdependent with the construction of the entities given status as purposeful actors. This line of thought is pursued by describing the religious and cultural aspects of Western history that led to the prevalent institutional models of actors, organizational forms, and rationalized action.

Actors, Action, and Their Reification

Most explanatory models produced by social theorists in recent decades take for granted much of the organizational and ideological individualism of modern society. Two foundation stones underlie these models: Society consists essentially of individual actors, and social activity ordinarily involves the purposive behavior of individuals. There is an intellectual naturalness about these models that derives from modern society itself—many ideological currents of the social system reinforce and reflect purposive, individualistic conceptions of reality far more than any alternative conceptions. Thus the economy is modeled as the dynamic of individual investment, consumption, and labor market "decisions." The polity is modeled as being built up through individual electoral choices and organizational commitments; and religion and culture are modeled as resulting from individual beliefs, values, and knowledge.

In such models, social structure is relevant as a way of analyzing the processes by which individual choice and consequent action influence the choices and actions of others. Economists tend to allow social structure into their models only insofar as it involves exchange processes that can be expressed in terms of costs and benefits. Psychologists allow for more complex effects, bringing in individual attachments, interaction, and communication. Sociologists are somewhat more reckless. Their analyses of exchange, attachment, and interaction typically uncover highly structured arrangements of individuals—in groups, organizations, networks, and the like—that have strong independent effects on such matters as job choices, electoral preferences, and cultural tastes and values.

For some purposes, such models can be highly fruitful, but they tend to understate the institutional underpinnings of the individual effects that are found; furthermore, with respect to the study of structural change and variation, they are severely limiting. Their naturalness in analyzing contemporary social processes and outcomes is accompanied by strained awkwardness when they attempt to account for the emergence and stability of such recurring social forms as the complex and stable job market, the democratic election, or the highly structured system of education and educational allocation. That such phenomena could be sustained solely or even primarily by the choices and actions of individuals is immediately problematic. One obvious problem is that these forms are so widespread. Is it reasonable to believe that the values and technical knowledge of masses of highly disparate individuals really are so uniform?

This problem leads individualistic social models to conceptualize culture as a general value system for society, and socialization as a mechanism for instilling culture into individuals, as exemplified in the work of Parsons (1951). Socialization is the glue that keeps society together, instilling a cultural set of universalistic, rational norms and values into the character of all (or at least most) individuals. Culture is both a set of values that leads to individual preferences and a system of technical knowledge that informs individuals about which means to choose in order to achieve specified ends.

This heavy reliance on individual socialization and internalized cultural values has met sharp criticism from a number of viewpoints (consider, for example, the critique by Wrong, 1961). For one thing, attempts to establish the existence and strength of cultural values and the ability of diffuse socialization to implant those values appear to be largely unsuccessful. Second, the presupposition that cultural values are largely universal and consensual is contradicted by glaring inconsistencies within the cultural system itself and the obvious centrality of conflicts and competing interests in modern society. Third, and most important for our purpose, the claim that such powerful institutions as the market economy, the bureaucratic state, or the citizen-based polity derive from abstract values internalized by individuals through socialization simply leaves out too much. With this claim, the central features of modern society are "explained" by a residual approach that lumps a number of powerful social forces under the vague concept of culture but does not analyze them further.

One reaction to these problems was a return to a more intensified sociological individualism—the painstaking construction of more elaborate reductionist models of individuals. In Homans's (1964) phrase, theorists had "to bring men back in." Throughout the social sciences—in economics and psychology, of course, but also in political science and sociology—there have been attempts to develop an account of society based on rigid models of individual action. For example, under the general rubric of network analysis, many attempts have been made to squeeze more explanatory value out of theories focused on patterns of human interaction (see the papers in Burt & Minor, 1983; Marsden & Lin, 1982).

These attempts still run into the roadblock erected by the focus on individual dispositions generated by socialization and interaction patterns structured around individuals. In explaining elections and electoral behavior, for example, one can go only so far with an individualistic approach. At some point, one must come to terms with the massive institutional features of the social system itself. People are likely to vote only if there are elections. Education is pursued (and is more likely to affect electoral choices) if there is a universal educational system linked to the system of status allocation. Occupational careers are constituted (and are more likely to determine party affiliation) if there are organized occupations linked to the stratification system. Religious commitments are made (and are more likely to affect political participation) if religious practices are organized, legitimated, and culturally linked to the political sphere. In all these areas, an institutionalist approach suggests the importance of wider cultural issues and the culturally constructed character of microsociological effects.

The main route taken by research in recent years to get around this roadblock has been to abandon the fascination with the individual and turn instead to other "actors" in the social system such as interest groups, organizations, and associations. Social processes and social change thus result at least in part from the actions and interactions among large-scale actors. The modern polity, for example, is seen as a network of interorganizational relations (Scott, 1983; Warren, 1967). At center stage, we find the state, which is also conceived as a coherent organizational actor engaged in purposive behavior on both the domestic and international scene (Evans, Rueschemeyer, & Skocpol, 1985). These lines of analysis retain the *realism* of sociological individualism, where the actors are engaged in purposive behavior through the more or less rational selection of means, but the analysis is much more complex and can involve several levels at once.

Taking collectivities seriously as actors resolves some of the difficulties of individualistic models. Much of what was earlier relegated to the grab bag of culture and propagated in the social system by socialization is now located explicitly in the structure and policies of organized actors. These organizations may channel interests in ways far removed from their starting points, as when the concerns of the handicapped come to be organizationally structured in terms of civil rights laws. Individuals and their free-floating networks of interaction become dependent variables, while causal analysis concentrates on the formally structured rules generated by organized groups. Much of the substantive stuff of society is described in this way: Welfare systems, job markets, and cultural structures become products of organizations or sets of organizations engaged in action and interaction (see Baron, 1984; Baron & Bielby, 1980; DiMaggio & Stenberg, 1985; Wilensky, 1976; Wuthnow, 1980a, 1985). Accordingly, the political participation of individuals receives less attention than the organized systems of participation, which determine electoral choices through class or interest group processes that are more situational than socializing. The educational attainments of individuals receive less attention than the education system itself, which induces individual educational participation through a combination of incentives and coercion.

Accompanying this shift to collectivities as reified actors is widespread concern for the broader environment in which these actors operate. Just as individualistic models ultimately invoke a surrounding web of interaction and relationships, so also do organizational models embed the actors in a wider system—a world economy (Wallerstein, 1974), a system of militarily competitive states (Skocpol, 1979; Tilly, 1975), or a road map of international cultural diffusion (Inkeles & Sirowy, 1983). But the neorealism of the thinking involved imposes a reluctance to see the wider system as having autonomous cultural content that might construct and legitimate as well as channel the collective actors. Content is postulated to lie in the purposes, properties, resources, and sovereignty of the organizational actors, while the encompassing environment is largely culturally vacuous—a set of raw resources, opportunities, or constraints. There is a preference for ecological or resource dependency models that limit the outside environment to little more than the patterns of interactions and competition among states, corporations, social movements, and the like.

These interactions usually are depicted as exchange relations within a competitive order. A given organization or interest group faces an environment providing resources and imposing costs. It acts by engaging in economic, political, military, or communication exchange, often very one-sided, in competition with other organizations. If the wider environment is given any content, that content is tamed as a commodity called *legitimacy,* which actors can exchange with each other (see McCarthy & Zald, 1977; Pfeffer & Salancik, 1978; Tilly, 1975). The content, purposes, technical structure, and integration attributed to a given actor are thus viewed as properties of the actor, quite independent of the wider setting. The open-system assumptions of some such models (see Scott, 1981, on the literature on organizations) imply that the organized actors are involved in complex interaction with the environment at many different boundaries, but the boundaries remain—the actor as an entity is clearly distinct from the environment in which action occurs.

The shift to collective actors as the muscle of the social system alleviates some of the problems of individualistic models, but it tends to exacerbate others. Even if many levels of collectivities are postulated (from the individual to the nation-state) and rational-choice assumptions are loosened to allow for political and symbolic depictions of action, reducing social life to the interaction of organized collectivities meets with considerable difficulties.

There is, first, the crucial problem of explaining the existence of the collectivities themselves—where they come from, how they grow, why they persist. The usual tendency in this theoretical line is to treat them as aggregations of the interests and capacities of lower-level units (perhaps under certain vaguely described ecological or resource conditions). For example: The nation-state is the product of the accumulated interests and conflicts of classes, military factions, or other social groups. Successful collectivities are those that function most efficiently in the competitive environment, and the latter's influence on the outcome is restricted to the general pressures imposed by resource limitations and niche opportunities (Skocpol, 1979; Tilly, 1975).

This line of thought greatly understates the extent to which organizational structures are not only influenced but also internally *constituted by the wider environment*. The wider setting contains prescriptions regarding the types of organizational actors that are socially possible and how they conceivably can be structured. Collectivities are thus as much the embodiment of the prescriptions of the available cultural forms as they are the aggregation of lower-level units and interests (DiMaggio & Powell, 1983; Meyer & Rowan, 1977; Zucker, 1983). In other words, the boundary between the environment and the actor is not only highly fluid but also highly problematic.

A second problem in the reification of collective actors and the focus on their distinctive properties and behavior is that the extraordinary uniformity of their fundamental character is ignored: state bureaucracies, policies, and budgets as well as elections and citizenship; occupational and interest groups and the claims that they make within the polity; the formal organization of schools as well as enrollments, teacher certification, and learning technologies. If such institutions were simply the products of competing interests and political negotiation, there should be much less uniformity in these dimensions across national societies. The source of that uniformity lies in an institutional environment common to organizations in national societies throughout the world system. Common definitions and theories of social organization generate structural similarities in highly disparate societies.

Third, the realist view of collective actors assumes that organizational structure is tightly linked to internal components and activities. There is massive empirical evidence that such is not the case. Research on organizations repeatedly finds very loose coupling at every level—between formal and informal structure, among different structural elements, between structure and action, and between policy and actuality (e.g., March & Olsen, 1976; Weick, 1976). Studies of the behavior of the state find that the implementation of policy is a highly problematic process (Bardach, 1977; Berman & McLaughlin, 1975-1978; Pressman & Wildavsky, 1973). The assumption that collectivities are produced by internal forces is thus empirically countered by the weak relationship between the policy structures of these collectivities and the putative forces that were supposed to control them. This parallels similar findings at the individual level: Action often works obliquely to stated goals and norms; the knowledge and technical competence attributed to individuals by political and economic theory are conspicuous by their absence; the theoretically postulated minimal requirements of consistency in personality and action at a given time or over the life cycle are not met (e.g., Brim & Kagan, 1983; Mischel, 1971).

The common response to this sort of criticism is the charge that the discontinuities between structure and action, or principles and behavior, are themselves largely deliberate. States express commitment to broad-based economic development as a smoke screen to deal with "problems of legitimacy" with respect to their impoverished citizens. School systems are employed to maintain false consciousness on the part of the masses so they will not understand the true nature of the social system. Individuals hide their true intentions and values in order to bluff their way to social power and position.

Such responses provide some reasonable answers but beg the larger question: Where do these legitimacy problems come from? More forcefully, what powerful exogenous factors make possible and necessary the sweeping but unrealistic claims of modern institutions? What forces empower the educational system or the open election to serve as legitimating structures and thus support the disparate and inconsistent activities going on within them? What is gained, and from what source, when individuals or organizations dress their motives and questionable competence in acceptable guises? When questions like these do get attention, the notion of culture is again brought in through the back door as an unanalyzed residual force of such plasticity that it can be stretched to fill the holes in the argument.

Culture as Institutional Rules

Theories that reify social actors, whether individual or collective, thus sweep the big problems under the rug of "culture" without dealing with the debris lying under this idea. Their rather primitive usage limits the concept of culture to a cluster of consensual general values (e.g., religious morality) and a body of consensual knowledge or technique (e.g., scientific rules). Culture becomes important only inasmuch as it surfaces in the conscious structure or policy of actors—in individuals' values and information, or in collective values and technologies (if collectivities are reified as actors). Culture thus enters in only as an influence on the condition of the actors involved.

We employ a broader conception in which culture is more than vague ideas about the moral or natural environment of society. Culture includes the institutional models of society itself. The cultural structure of these models defines and integrates the framework of society, as well as the actors that have legitimate status and the patterns of activity leading to collective goods. Lines of thought treating culture as only rules of value and technique at the moral and natural boundaries of society ignore the fact that the central cultural myths of modern society are those giving meaning and value to society and its components. Beyond a sociology of religion or of science, a proper analysis must focus on institutions—the cultural rules of society itself.

Culture has both an ontological aspect, assigning reality to actors and action, to means and ends; and it has a significatory aspect, endowing actor and action, means and ends, with meaning and legitimacy. In a narrower view, for instance, American culture contains "values" that influence individuals to be assertive and achievement-oriented in all sorts of exchange relations. In the broader view, American culture comprises a set of well-established theories giving reality and meaning, "value," to individual action organized in patterns of exchange as the surest path to progress and justice. At the same time, these rules deny (usually implicitly) the reality and meaning of alternative means, ends, actors, and actions; in the United States, for instance, undercutting the possibilities for immersing individuality in community. The individual may be conscious of these theories in only limited cognitive and normative ways that situationally range in inclusiveness (Douglas, 1966). Yet these theories are the heart of the social system—such rule structures as political and legal definitions concerning property, contracts, association, and the like; economic definitions of the meaning of labor, production, and consumption; and more purely social definitions of such constructs as childhood and the self.

In the narrow view, culture is a set of ideas and values, sharply distinguished from material interests and action. Is the law of property economic (i.e., materialist) or political and religious (i.e., idealist)? Are the rules legitimating the formation of such associations as business corporations materialist or idealist? What about the Reformation doctrines Weber called the *Protestant Ethic*? This idealism-materialism distinction makes sense only if the underlying social theory gives actors (especially individuals) and their motives prior social reality. From a narrow actor-centered posture, such matters all concern ideas that are more or less reducible to material factors.

At the institutional level, this polemical distinction breaks down. Western economic and political forces operate at a high level of generality as rule structures that create, among other things, a peculiar emphasis on the legitimacy of the individual and individual purposes. This emphasis is cultural, not natural. In our view Western culture is a system of rules that make the production and consumption of something like the electric toothbrush a matter of universal value (like groceries or gasoline, it contributes to GNP) and propagate convincing reasons (of health, child hygiene, aesthetics, or social relations) for individuals to choose to produce and consume such a device, thus enhancing the meaning and significance of the individual at the same time. Culture involves far more than *general values* and knowledge that influence tastes and decisions, it defines the *ontological value* of actor and action.

Both social actors and the patterns of action they engage in are institutionally anchored. The particular types of actors perceived by self and others and the specific forms their activity takes reflect institutionalized rules of great generality and scope. It is in this sense that social reality— including both social units and socially patterned action—is "socially constructed" (Berger & Luckmann, 1966). Institutionalized rules, located in the legal, social scientific, customary, linguistic, epistemological, and other "cultural" foundations of society, render the relation between actors and action more socially tautological than causal. Actors enact as much as they act: What they do is inherent in the social definition of the actor itself. Consequently, rules constituting actors legitimate types of action, and legitimated action constitutes and shapes the social actors. For example, changes in Western notions of labor result in changes in the rules and organization governing work. On the other hand, political and economic rules of wage labor as a self-interested class devolve from rules about the collective value of work; the working class changes as legitimate rules of labor value change. As another example, expansion of the types of commodities people may properly consume increases the complexity of the individual, adding new motives and sometimes rights; conversely, adding new aspects to the personality expands the possible commodities one can legitimately consume. For instance, the elaboration of theories of self-esteem lead to personal projects and rights to self-actualization and fulfillment resulting in both organizational programs and commodities that promise these outcomes. Conversely, commodities from the automobile, television, and personalized personal computers to a shampoo that meets the "ever-changing needs" of one's hair or a tennis racket that is made of material and strung so as to correct one's particular weaknesses all greatly expand the legitimate domain of the self and highly articulate subtle nuances of fulfilled selfhood. At other organizational levels, the same reciprocal, tautological processes occur. The definition and standing of the modern organization are constitutively linked to what is legitimate and necessary. In this way, environmental concerns, a broadened conception of worker rights, or more organized conceptions of the economy and its function must be incorporated in the structure and action of the organization. For instance, the new right to pure air produces organizational expansion to manage this right.

Hence the common notion that the actor performs the action is only a half-truth—at the institutional level, action also creates the actor. Not only does the institutionalization of certain forms of organization, such as the corporation, generate rationalized goals and goal-oriented action, but also the institutionalization of rationalized goals and action creates highly general models from which organizations draw their identity and structure. The same can be said of individuals, states, and other social units.

This is not to say, however, that society is a matter of continuous negotiation, communication, and exchange of meaning. Symbolic interactionism and social-psychological variants of phenomenology employ an institutional view of social behavior, but they depict the meanings and rules constructing actors and action as operating at the same level of analysis as the actors affected by them. The local interplay between interaction and its meaning, whereby actors (usually people, in these formulations) continually discover and construct who they are through looking-glass feedback processes, allows for no level of reality external to the phenomenological situation itself. This tradition of research ignores the extraordinary power of exogenous institutionalized definitions of reality. The individual may work out identity details (e.g., an aggressive style to counterbalance a putative socialization defect in assertiveness) and nuances of meaning in the way described by this tradition, but little negotiation at all is required for the individual to know that individuals exist, that they are organized into groups, that rational action is required in the workplace, or that a proper pilot does not snort cocaine in the cockpit.

A fully institutional analysis, then, calls attention to the extent to which, both in the modern world polity and throughout much of Western history, the cognitive and moral frames of activity at all levels are anchored in the broadest institutional (societal and world) levels. Actors and action are illuminated by universalistic lights. The interaction of people buying and selling in a supermarket occurs under the aegis of highly general historical rules legitimating and constructing the economy and its participants: There are rules of property, the collective good in exchange, the principles of autonomous consumption and impersonal exchange, and so on and on. These rules cannot easily be observed and may be completely transparent in the ordinary course of events, but something as concrete and material as the supermarket is an impossible flight of fancy in their absence.

Rationalization and the Construction of Entities

A key task of institutional analysis is to describe the content and coherence of the Western, now worldwide, institutional order and to develop a theory of its origin and evolutionary dynamics. In doing so, our work is informed greatly by the Weberian tradition and in particular by the concept of rationalization. There is a large literature produced by Weberian scholars on the conceptual and historical nuances of types of rationality (e.g., Kalberg, 1980; Roth & Schluchter, 1979; Schluchter, 1981). We do not explore these nuances and typologies. Rather, we use a working definition of rationalization, moving from abstract concept to particular empirical referents or variables that reflect rationalization processes. To summarize concisely, we use the generic term *rationalization* to refer to purposive or instrumental rationalization: The structuring of everyday life within standardized impersonal rules that constitute social organization as a means to collective purpose. Denotatively, through rationalization, authority is structured as a formal legal order increasingly bureaucratized; exchange is governed by rules of rational calculation and bookkeeping, rules constituting a market, and includes such related processes as monetarization, commercialization, and bureaucratic planning; cultural accounts increasingly reduce society to the smallest rational units— the individual, but also beyond to genes and quarks.

The instrumental and purposive nature of Western rationalization results in the constitution of society as a means to collective ends. In this sense Western, and now worldwide society, is a rational project of creating progress and justice—in the traditional West, the millennium. We refer to this character of the world polity as a project, following the lead of the sociology of knowledge. One can also refer to this project as the state, distinguishing the broad referent of state *as project* from its identification with the bureaucratized state (Thomas & Meyer, 1984); for historical reasons, this usage is more common in French or German than in English.

An institutional analysis rests on two central themes. First, the rationalization of social activity stands in a reciprocal relation to the social construction of the actors given ontological status in society. Second, the institutional rules undergoing rationalization and social ontology operate at a very general (now often worldwide) level, not simply at the level of local negotiation.

THE EMERGENCE OF SOCIAL ENTITIES IN THE PROCESS OF RATIONALIZATION

Rationalization involves restructuring action within collective means and ends. In the most general sense, the means are technical development and the expansion of exchange; the ends are the twin pillars of Western thought, progress and justice (most often defined in terms of equality). Rationalization through the elaboration of means-ends chains requires the specification of entities at the end of the causal chain: Equality, for instance, is not attainable without a precise unitary definition of the entities that are to be equal. Rationalization around the goal of equality compels a sharpened conception of the individual and the delineation of the dimensions in which equality is to be sought, yielding notions of human rights and individual personality. The further rationalization is pushed, the more the individual must be enhanced and expanded. In the same way, doctrines and measures of progress and profit require and create bounded entities: individuals, firms, and states.

Thus Weber's argument that the strong ontological status of the individual is one source of Western rationalization tells only part of the story. In our terms, including the more institutional version of Weber's theory (Collins, 1980), the individual is an institutional myth evolving out of the rationalized theories of economic, political, and cultural action.

This myth leads people to posture as individuals, in a loosely coupled way, and they can be fairly convincing about it. The contrast with systems in which people are immersed in corporate identities (e.g., age, gender, familial, communal, or corporate occupational statuses) has often seemed striking to researchers. Modern "individuals" give expression to the institutionalized description of the individual as having authorized political rights, efficacy, and competence; they consider themselves effective choosers of their occupations, investments, and consumption goods; and they willingly give vent to an extraordinary range of cultural judgments, offhandedly responding to questionnaires with their views of the polity, the economy, even the exact properties, including being, of God. Given the possibilities and inducements of the modern system, they also perform a wide range of economic, political, and cultural actions—and *ex post facto* can explain in great detail how their activity was carefully selected as efficient for their particular purposes. This enactment of the institutionalized theory of rational behavior is rarely troubled by the internal inconsistencies and self-contradictions that are so typical of human action. It is precisely that this status of rational actor is a culturally supported posture that explains much specific inconsistency.

Of course, not only the individual but also many other social units are generated by the institutionalized rationalizing project. Rationalization around the goal of progress helps generate several kinds of units. Progress cannot be attained without specifying the boundaries within which progress is to occur; hence the nation-state is reified as the unit within which GNP or life expectancy or book production is measured. The more elaborate the concept of progress, the more reified the nation-state (yielding, among other things, more boundary maintenance activity around the rules defining the national unit). Similarly, rational analysis of the means by which progress is to be achieved leads to a reification of the productive entities that enter into the expansion of technique and exchange—labor, occupational roles, professions, and corporations are all thereby enhanced. The strengthening and elaboration of the cultural rules and definitions of progress support the empowering of the individual and collective actors involved. For instance, groups mobilizing around labor and capital appear in societies that have little to be conceived of practically in either way.

THE GENERALITY OF INSTITUTIONAL RULES

The institutions constructing and giving meaning to modern social entities and their rationalized action have a much wider and more universal character than any particular setting they constitute. This is true in two closely related senses. First, these institutions embody universalized claims linked to rules of nature and moral purpose. Economic, educational, or political action is legitimated in terms of quite general claims about progress, justice, and the natural order. Thus particular conflicts or claims are couched within general cultural elements that are in principle applicable everywhere, across classes and societies. For example, general principles of human rights or economic growth are held to be applicable to any modern or modernizing order. The differences that do arise within local settings are limited and remain within the context of the broader cultural frame. For example, teachers adopt different styles, organizations different management techniques, and state regimes different ideological stances— all within the constitutive order of what it means to be a teacher, a business organization, and a nation-state.

Second, specific institutional claims and definitions tend in practice to be very similar almost everywhere. Differences across particular settings result from the organization of that setting around varying emphases or interpretations of more general institutional rules. For example, socialist notions of justice, progress, and technique are remarkably similar to their capitalist counterparts; albeit specified somewhat more around equality than liberty and organized more corporately by the bureaucratic state. Moreover, beyond the given differences, quite similar goals and means are specified and pursued, even down to the details of particular industries, or welfare and educational progress.

The degree of uniformity of institutional structures points to a strategy for analysis: One must see these institutions in all of the diversity not only as built up out of human experience in particular local settings, but also *as devolving from a dominant universalistic historical culture.* The diverse versions of these general themes are interpretable by the differential penetration and historical syntheses of distinct (sometimes contradictory) elements of this culture.

The institutions of the West devolve from Western religion and the church at least as much as they are built up by the strategies of subunits (Anderson, 1974; Strayer, 1970). The frame derives directly from the Christian church and the invisible conceptual "Kingdom of God" that the earthly church organization was supposed to represent in an imperfect way. Consider this church at an early point (perhaps 1500) in the modern era.

The church was, first, transnational in character. It was a unified symbolic structure encompassing a wide variety of cultures, people—"nations" in the older sense. As such, it provided a common frame of reference for the West—not entirely uniform, to be sure, but in both a literal and a symbolic sense, there was a common language that dominated the cultural arena. Second, the church was universalist, in that it had the duty to bring "the way, the truth, and the life" to all of humanity, recognizing no boundaries to its mission. Its constant proselytizing was remarkably successful, and to an extraordinary degree, it succeeded by the "power of the Word," particularly before the modern era. But for our purposes, the key fact is that the spread of Christianity meant the spread of universalist ideology as such—it became not only common but also natural to develop theories and ideologies of sweeping, all-encompassing scope.

Third, the church as a symbol system provided the fundamental ontological structure of the West. The church consisted, in essence, of a set of institutional definitions—of transcendental reality (God, Christ, Spirit), of humanity (God's creation and children) and human nature (sinful yet creative), of earthly existence and its ultimate purpose (the glory of God). These definitions constituted the ultimate source of authority: *That which is* was an issue that could be addressed only within the context of the church's symbolic structure. The church also provided guidelines for action: It was no distant theological bastion but penetrated every limb of the social body.

This, then, was the overarching cathedral within which the modern cultural system developed: a common, highly legitimated, boundaryless polity where ultimate authority was located at the peak of the vaulted dome (God) and devolved on human entities (popes and priests, kings and nobles) as subordinate beings, with much to say about social ontology, actors, and the relationships among action, nature, and the ultimate.

The content of the overarching framework has changed with the transition of the West from feudal agrarianism to state-directed technical and economic progressivism, but the location of authority and definitions of reality have remained at the highest level, transcending all of the social entities (including the nation-state) that it encompasses. A number of detailed studies show how this structure led to the particular features of the modern institutional framework. For example, Bendix (1978) describes the development of institutional conceptions of the sovereignty of the state from Roman law and the doctrines of the church as a legal and ideological process characterizing Europe as a whole. We should not be misled by the view that modern authority structures are "secular" rather than "religious." Authority structures define the sacred and relate it to the profane. Whether the sacred involves transcendent deities (Jehovah, God, Allah) or transcendental concepts (equality, freedom, rights, livelihood) at its ultimate root is irrelevant, for the sacred in a sociological sense is always religious. Thus the "secular" content of the world polity's ontological structure is no less religious than that of the Christian church (see Ellul, 1973; Wuthnow, 1980b).

Hence in modern social systems, it is fruitful to see social structure not as the assembly of patterns of local interaction but as ideological edifices of institutionalized elements that derive their authority from more universal rules and conceptions. The disjuncture between social structure and observable patterns of activity and interaction, which is the bread and butter of much sociological research, makes sense in this light. The formal structures of society, ranging from the definition and properties of the individual to the form and content of such organizations as schools, firms, social movements, and states, arise from or are adjusted to fit very general rules that often have worldwide meaning and power.

Cultural Accounts

In this usage, *institutions* can be described as *cultural accounts* under whose authority action occurs and social units claim their standing. The term *account* here takes on a double meaning. Institutions are descriptions of reality, explanations of what is and what is not, what can be and what cannot. They are accounts of how the social world works, and they make it possible to find order in a world that is disorderly. At the same time, in the Western rationalizing process, institutions are structured accounting systems that show how social units and their actions accumulate value (in monetary, scientific, moral, historical, and other forms) and generate progress and justice on an ongoing basis. The meaning of the individual, or the corporation, or the state in the cultural account of the West is to a large extent contained in prescriptions for rational action producing increasing amounts of value that are taken as the ultimate goals of the human project. The enormous amount of financial and bureaucratic record-keeping (accounting) that goes on in modern society is one result.

The Western cultural account is distinctive and has generated a transformation of society of extraordinary thoroughness and depth. What general features of this account are most central?

First, the cosmos outside of human society is distinctively simplified and abstracted (Bellah, 1964). Moral authority is integrated in a single high god whose authority is unitary and universalistic. The properties of the single god are elaborated over time, becoming increasingly universal, abstract, and separated from human activity. The god is pervasive and inactive (i.e., in a sense, dead). Other spiritual entities, with their potential for direct intervention in society and nature, are excluded (Weber's "disenchantment of the world"). The natural world is similarly unitary and universalistic, in the sense that nature is objective, lawful, and structured according to discoverable invariant principles. Nature too is removed from human society, something separate and exploitable. The cosmos is radically dualistic. Moral authority and the laws of nature are not linked directly to each other, either through webs of spiritual intervention in nature or the subjection of the spiritual world to natural processes. Contrast the situation described by Geertz (1980) in his description of the Balinese theater-state: There, much political activity is linked to a complex and active cosmos; much natural activity is linked to a complex and lively physical world; and the two are integrated more outside human agency than through it.

Second, the links between moral authority and nature are provided by society. Humans and human society have value and responsibility as moral projects in nature. People and society can achieve progress through activity in the natural world, and they can fail to progress. Hence much purposive rational organization is possible, necessary, and highly legitimate as evidenced by the movement from early monasticism to the universal church and from the nascent medieval state to the modern welfare state and corporation (Coleman, 1982). Individuals too can be organized as rational, purposive actors. All of this progress-oriented activity occurs in a universalistic cultural frame and the degree of success achieved can be evaluated by means of general value measures (which are increasingly expressed in monetary terms as with the GNP).

Third, individual humans have distinctive moral standing. The human soul or personality is tied directly to ultimate moral authority. The links between the individual and the moral and natural cosmos may be mediated by social structure, but any such structure must contain cultural accounts explaining how individual action generates moral value. Thus in Western terms, human society can and should be assessed in terms of justice—a concept that, when reduced to the notion of equality, is difficult to define or operationalize in systems that do not reify the individual. Thus justice, like progress, is linked to both moral authority and nature. Justice is a culturally available perspective with respect to both individual participation in society (work, voting, consuming popular culture) and the distribution of the benefits of nature (income, standard of living, possession of things).

These cultural properties have long been discussed as distinctive features of the West, although there has often been a tendency to adopt a teleological view of them, describing Western history as some kind of necessary unfolding of these features. The teleology should be seen as a property of the Western system and not the perspective of the analyst: Western institutional models are functional ones and for research purposes must be analyzed rather than adopted. Much can be gained by analyzing the role these features have played in the evolution of modern social organization—the rise of the state system, the institutions of private and public property, the shift from absolutism to parliamentarianism, or the changing nature of long-distance exchange. All embody cultural purpose.

By the same token, the social organization generated by the early Western cultural account has amplified and altered the original themes. For example, both the intensive development of the state as a rational project and the expansion of exchange and rationalized production have greatly amplified and secularized the cultural account: An amazing array of activities and commodities, up to and including sociological research and meetings, now enter into the cultural account of progress (GNP) almost everywhere in the world. Notions of justice likewise now cover a range of human rights that is very broad, from the traditional civil and political domains to very comprehensive claims regarding material consumption, cultural participation, and protection from discrimination (Bendix, 1964; Marshall, 1948).

Summary

The themes of this chapter can be summed up as follows. First, rationalization in the context of the radical dualism of the West leads to the formation of an extraordinary array of legitimated actors reified as purposive and rational—individuals, associations, classes, organizations, ethnic groups, nation-states. The chronic tendency of social theory to depict action as the choices and decisions of purposive rational actors has strong cultural roots in the conception of humans as agents of sovereign moral authority or as morally sovereign themselves. We have to step outside this taken-for-granted view in order to analyze Western cultural functionalism or we are all too likely to let our theories be dominated by it. Second, collective actors command greater legitimacy and authority if they are founded on a theory of individual membership and activity, such as the nation-state or the rationalized firm. Other types of actors that reflect more communal structures and submerge the individual within the collective command less authority. Third, organizational entities that are tied into the theories of justice and progress gain special standing above all others—the individual and the nation-state are the most real of all (the only certainties are death and taxes), with the balance between the two varying from one society to another.

Fourth, because they derive from universalistic cultural ideology, dominant organizational forms, including the structure and boundaries of collective action, are relatively standardized across societies. There is only a loose relationship between organizational forms and practical needs and goals operating in local situations. In this sense Western organizational structures are to be seen as ritual enactments of broad-based cultural prescriptions rather than the rational responses to concrete problems that the cultural theories purport them to be. In any complex society, there is bound to be considerable disjunction between ritual forms and practical affairs, but the universalization and high degree of abstraction of the cosmos—both ultimate moral authority and nature—makes this disjunction seem more inconsistent in the modern West than elsewhere and hence more of a pressure for further elaboration and change.

2

Rationalized Environments

JOHN W. MEYER

CONTEMPORARY INSTITUTIONAL IDEAS fall within a broader category of organizational theories that stress the importance of wider environments. In institutional theories, these not only affect organizations and their activities, but constitute and reconstitute them over time. There is now great sensitivity in the field to the extent to which organizations are embedded in broader environments and created and changed by environmental change. Every aspect of organizational life—the existence and identity of organizational populations of various types, the formal structures of organizations in these populations, and the activity routines within them—is now understood to be dramatically affected by environmental forces, many operating through broad changes in legitimacy and the cognitive patterning of rationalized culture (see Chapter 1; Meyer & Scott, 1992; Thomas, Meyer, Ramirez, & Boli, 1987).

Most research on these issues is tilted severely toward the organizational end of the causal chain; that is, researchers look at populations of organizations or at the structures of these organizations as they change in one or another immediate context. They look at variation in specific and local organizational populations—within a particular sector, within a particular country, or within a particular (often, but not always, fairly short) time period. Studies of the rise of personnel departments within firms, for example, look within a particular time period, country, and often region or industry (see

Work on this chapter was carried out at the Stockholm Center for Organizational Research, and was aided by many discussions with colleagues in the F-Section of the Stockholm School of Economics (see in particular, Brunsson, 1989). Specific comments from Ron Jepperson, David Frank, John Boli, and Francisco Ramirez were most helpful.

Chapter 13). This approach is natural to researchers focused on visible and intellectually interesting variations in an immediate set of organizations.

The standard approach, as with any research model that limits dependent variation, tends to select out particular aspects of the environment as especially important. Very often, short-term changes or variations in national or state regulation, in state or local administrative organization, in judicial decisions, or in competitive local market situations, turn out to be most important. Such changes are prominent in the chapters of this book, which emphasize immediate and specific variations among organizational environments. Changed regulatory arrangements, and funding and control patterns (Chapters 7, 8, 9, 11, 12, and 13) or changes in both regulation and professional development (Chapters 10 through 13), are at issue. Most of these chapters—and most of the literature—consider variations only within the parameters of the American political, legal, and cultural context. Even studies outside this context normally consider events in only one country (for exceptions, see Cole, 1989; Dobbin, in press; Hamilton & Biggart, 1988). Population ecology analyses sometimes consider institutional changes (ordinarily within one country) over longer periods of time, although still with a limited focus on aspects of the wider environment (e.g., measures of the density of legitimating and competing organizations: Hannan & Carroll, 1992).

Two closely related and important problems, arising from this research situation, characterize current research developments. First, the focus on locally varying organizational-level outcomes leads to something of an overemphasis on independent variables that vary locally—the regulatory environment and its changes within particular localities or national states, immediate and relatively short-term local changes in professionalization. Consider the two main types of organizational outcomes on which the studies in this book focus. In the arena of expanding individualism and human rights, researchers may be interested in changes in the mix of men and women in administration in various organizations, and they may find differences in immediate environments that help account for this (Baron, Mittman, & Newman, 1991). The researchers tend not to look at bigger environments, such as world society as a whole, because these often do not vary much in the local sample and such variation over time as they do have can be proximately captured (it is imagined) by local or national variables. Thus there is a tendency to ignore the fact that great changes in the gender mix to be found in organizations and administration have characterized the whole world in recent decades.

Changes or variations in organizational complexity, on which we also focus, provide the same situation. Researchers look for, and find, immediate local or national regulation as involved, for instance, in the expansion of personnel administration (see Chapter 13) or the rise of elaborated accounting systems (Miller & O'Leary, 1993). They do not much look at bigger environments: Again, these may not vary much in local samples, and their variation over time can (researchers tend to imagine) be measured locally.

By bigger environments, in this context, we mean several things. One meaning refers literally to a larger unit of analysis—world society and its dominant rules and ideologies, as well as the organizations and professions that structure these. For example, the rise of world-level structures emphasizing ideologies of human rights has important implications for all sorts of organizing: A new set of norms about the status of women, for instance, although unlikely to be directly enforced, becomes available and provides potential grounding for a whole set of new potential criticisms. A second meaning refers to cultural changes or variations of a sweeping, but general, character—universalistic ideologies and scientific doctrines that may also be worldwide in fact but certainly involve general or universal claims to authority. The prevalence of expanded universalistic doctrines about the rights of women expands the range of issues that particular organizations probably must consider. A third meaning refers to arrangements that in fact aggregate to the world level because of common causes or diffusion processes (e.g., through the interrelations among nation-states), which make changes widespread. Thus expanded ideas, policies, and practices about the potential organizational contributions of individuals (women, among others) flow around the world as a matter of international diffusion. The effects of all three of these processes show up in data, usually, as unanalyzed general trends—researchers either lack good measures of them, or they vary in such an undifferentiated way in the data sets that they take on an unexplained residual status.

A second main problem characterizes the organizations field in general, including the more environmentalist and even institutionalist models within it. Researchers often do not seem to notice, or have surprisingly little to say about, the most important and sweeping changes that characterize organizational life almost everywhere. In the individualism and human rights area, for instance, it is clear that a dramatic and worldwide change has been the enormous expansion almost everywhere in the involvement of women in organizational life (e.g., Charles, 1992; Ramirez, 1987; Ramirez & Weiss, 1979): in administrative and professional systems, in the labor force in general, in political organization, and in the secondary and higher educational systems. There are analyses of this in some particular situations, but our research designs and thus explanations do not reach to a level general enough to explain the overall phenomenon (indeed, sometimes theorists and researchers seem not to notice it).

The same situation describes variation related to organizational complexity and differentiation—the rise of many new dimensions or components of organizations, such as rationalized management, accounting, and personnel administration. With obvious variables such as size held constant, there seem to have been dramatic and worldwide changes in this area: All sorts of organizations have incorporated and differentiated dimensions that once were rare. New and elaborated models of management, accounting, consulting, or personnel administration pop up almost everywhere, in trends or waves of a very general character. By and large, the field lacks explanations for such trends and often seems not to notice them. (There is, apparently, still a tacit belief in the older functionalist arguments of the right and the left that economies and political systems evolve toward more and more differentiated states, reflecting the increasing levels of technical specialization. This kind of explanation does not stand inspection, for example, in explaining why Third World countries with the most modest levels of development show the stigmata of modern public or private organizations in the core. Dependency theories tend to fail similarly, even those that imagine that everything is diffused in an organizationally direct way by multinational firms, because organizational diffusion reaches much further than these structures.)

Thus despite much evidence that the most important organizational phenomena show dramatic worldwide trends, there is a studied tendency to ignore them. Few organization theorists could give a reasonable depiction, let alone explanation, of world trends in organizing, though it would seem to be our business.

To change this situation, it is necessary to step back from a focus on the organizational change that results from locally varying environments. There is a need to contemplate the independent variable side: On what interesting changes in wider rationalized environments should we focus? The general thesis here is that environmental rationalization produces organizational effects. In this chapter, we give little attention to the effects and contemplate the nature of the rationalized modern environment and how it has changed over time. We argue that it has become a world environment and has elaborated rapidly at the world level. We argue that this tends to produce worldwide isomorphism in organizing for several direct and indirect reasons. And we argue that the distinctive structure of the rationalized environment at the world level—it lacks a collective actor at the center and is instead made up of fragmented organizational and professional systems that function as rationalizing agents or others rather than actors—has produced rapid organizational expansion and change in national states and other organizations.

Background

In the social research community, formal organizations were once taken at face value as rather autonomously bounded and purposive actors. The formal pattern of organizational structure was taken to be the operative social arrangement. Such conceptions broke down in the 1970s under the weight of evidence of internal decoupling, highly ritualized structures, great isomorphism and isomorphic change among organizations, and deeply embedded transactions with internal and external environments. The rise of institutional theories was a response to this breakdown (DiMaggio & Powell, 1983; Meyer & Rowan, 1977; M. Meyer, 1978; see the review in Scott, 1992).

Thus a series of studies of educational organizations showed great disjunction between policies and practice and between different structural components. Structures themselves (e.g., formal curricula) seemed important as ritual elements and highly isomorphic across the country and even world: Waves of environmentally induced change in these were common (March & Olsen, 1976; Meyer & Rowan, 1978; Meyer & Scott, 1983b; Weick, 1976). Similar analyses of many other types of organizations—including nation-state organizations and organizations in the supposedly more rational market system—showed similar qualities (for a review, see Orton & Weick, 1990).

Thus organizations are now seen as immersed in environments, rather than just interacting with these environments as bounded actors in marketplaces. Organizations are interpenetrated with their environments, which may constitute (rather than affect) organizational identities, structures, and activity routines.

In limiting cases, this shift in intellectual perspective does not really much reconstruct the organization-environment relation. First, in some realist environmental perspectives, the environment becomes simply a bigger rationalized actor, who controls organizations directly through bureaucratic rules or enforced market incentives (e.g., Lindblom, 1977; Williamson, 1991). Instead of seeing typical organizations as independent actors, in other words, they are seen as subunits of a bigger actor—a state or market enforcing some kinds of rules. As an example, the arrangements of institutionalized schooling are seen as controlled by the social control interests of the capitalist system or the credentialing requirements of the bureaucratic state. These, rather than particular schooling organizations, are the (usually rational) actors involved.

Second, sometimes the institutionalized "environment" is seen as almost entirely internal to the organization itself as a social system—as in contemporary views of organizations as embedded in their own distinctive cultural

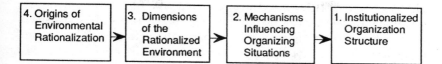

Figure 2.1 Elements of a General Institutional Model

meaning systems. In such views, both organizational structure and activity pattern are matters of constant internal interpretation and reinterpretation (see the reviews by Smircich, 1983; Zucker, 1987). Both meaning and action are simultaneously matters of negotiation and interpretation.

Institutional theories have generally called attention to a third case—in which organizations are dependent on a wider environment, but this environment functions less as a coherent rational superactor (e.g., a tightly integrated state or a highly coordinated invisible hand) than as an evolving set of rationalized patterns, models, or cultural schemes (Meyer & Rowan, 1977; Meyer & Scott, 1983b). These may be built into the public polity, in the laws, or into modernized society through professional and scientific analyses or the models set by exemplary organizations. Such institutionalized patterns affect the rise and evolution of organizations through their dominance as cognitive models; a variety of additional incentives (from prestige to coercive control) also are attached to them (DiMaggio & Powell, 1983). These dimensions of institutionalization presumably feed on one another, as when cultural prestige (e.g., a new organizational device such as a personnel system is generally admired as more rational) leads to cognitive dominance (e.g., ordinary participants and scientists believe that it works better or, indeed, is the only model that really works) and coercive controls (e.g., managers who do not institutionalize it are deemed backward or negligent). Of course, in a monetarized society, all of these dimensions of institutionalization are likely to be definable in terms of monetary value, which is a general index of virtue, effectiveness, and propriety.

THE INSTITUTIONAL MODEL

A general institutional model, as depicted in Figure 2.1, can be seen to have four elements, working back from its outcome.

1. There is the extant set of organizations, with their identities, structures, and activity patterns. All three can importantly result from patterns institutionalized in the rationalized environment, which may certify the

validity of a given type of organization (e.g., drug treatment centers), the structural form appropriate for this type (e.g., properly certified counselors or a standard accounting system), and particular activities that may constitute treatment (group therapy). In some types of organizations and rationalized environments, activity may be defined in terms of environmentally defined outcomes, as when a market is developed for one or another commodity.

Because identity, structure, and activity all tend to depend on wider environments, these contexts are likely to have strong effects. Further, while identity, structure, and activity are likely to be loosely coupled (precisely because of their environmental dependence), each type of dependence on the environment has a tendency to reinforce the others: Organizations of a given identity type come under pressure for standardized structures and activity. Structural conformity with the environment (e.g., incorporating representatives of the appropriate profession) increases pressure for activity conformity (see Chapter 5), as well as probably for identity conformity. And conformity in activity routines leads to demands for proper structures.

Overall, the institutional image of modern organizational life suggests organizations that are (a) somewhat ritualized; (b) internally decoupled; (c) isomorphic with environmental patterns and rules in their identities, structures, and activities; and (d) showing broadly isomorphic patterns of change over time following very general environmental rules. By and large, contemporary research and organizational experience provides much material encouraging this view.

2. Clear causal connections can be found linking organizational identities, structures, and activity routines to institutionalized elements in the environment. Organizational rules built up in the environment change organizational identities (through birth, death, and adaptive identity change), structures (the incorporation of preferred or required professional groups), and activity routines (reporting requirements). But similar processes have a more cultural character, as when changed scientific or public ideologies undercut one sort of organizational form (the large public mental hospital with the associated model of psychiatry and its activity routines) and legitimates another form (the community model).

The two elements above are the heart of contemporary research on institutional processes: Many studies show that general environmental changes in state and society seem to account for shifts in the forms of organizational life, that these shifts have a highly ritualized or rhetorical character, and that they characterize organizations of many sorts at once in a broadly isomorphic way.

The two remaining elements of the institutional model are less developed in current research. We focus on them in this chapter.

3. The rationalized environment provides the source for the effects discussed above; that is, development or change in the rules or ideologies describing or prescribing proper organizational practice lead organizations to develop or change isomorphically—or to arise, in a given domain, in the first place. It is clear that rationalistic formal organization is mainly affected by rationalized aspects of the environment.

The research literature tends to focus on particular aspects of the environment, perhaps especially regimes of public regulation by aspects of nation-states (see Chapters 8, 9, 10, and 13) or their subunits (see Chapters 3, 4, 7, 8, and 13). Some attention is also given to evolving scientific or professional doctrines as having general influence (Chapters 3 through 6, 10 through 13). DiMaggio and Powell (1983) see the state and the professions as the two classical loci of rationalization in contemporary political environments, and the empirical research literature follows this line of reasoning.

Overall, there is no general conception of the boundaries of the domain of the rationalized environment, though there seems to be a good deal of practical agreement about the sorts of dimensions that are involved. The absence of a more general idea may have limited the development of research in the area. So in the subsequent sections of this chapter, we review some of the dimensions that have been discussed, and we consider their implications.

4. Macrosociological processes prominently affect or control the development of the rationalized environment of organizing. If the rationalized environment simply reflects, in a rather short-term way, variations in organizational practices, only a little advantage is conferred by the whole institutional line of thought. Institutional thinking simply becomes the idea that the social processes depicted by the realists may be a bit delayed by social conventionalization.

On the other hand, rationalized public culture can be seen to reflect an array of forces quite apart from the structure and practices of formal organizations within it. There is the logic of the nation-state and its own environment; the logics of the cultures of the various professions and sciences, each with their own environments; and the communication and environments that select out models of organizing for more direct emulation. For example, the evolution of models of social modernity, and in particular the proper role of schooling organizations as intrinsic to it, has a long and highly collective or cultural history (Boli, 1989; Meyer, Kamens, Benavot, Cha, & Wong, 1992; Meyer, Ramirez, & Soysal, 1992).

Research on institutional theories—in the general field and in our own work—has tended to focus on the organizations at the end of this overall causal chain and on the factors (e.g., state policy) immediately affecting them. A good deal of useful work has resulted, and the importance of institutional factors in determining organizational structure and change is now little contested.

On the other hand, the absence of clearer ideas about the nature and trajectory of the rationalized environmental cultures that so affect organizational life has limited the development of the field.

Aspects of the Rationalized Environment

In the wider environment, where do impulses to and models for organizing exist? A brief review of the conventionally discussed loci of rationalization may suggest useful extensions.

STRATIFICATION AND THE STRUCTURING
OF ORGANIZATIONAL SYSTEMS

The world of organizations itself, seen as a stratification system, provides many models for organizing. Elite and successful organizations, within and across domains and societies, may become targets of imitation. This sort of diffusion is likely to depend on interpretive work by such intermediaries as professionals and consultants, who play several useful roles. First, they identify the model and prospective copier as having underlying similarities of identity that make diffusion sensible; that is, an organization or organizing situation is presented with putatively similar success accounts. These may be immediate competitors, organizations in the same sector, organizations in other sectors in the same country, or perhaps virtuous organizations on a worldwide scale (currently, Japanese firms). Second, they isolate and define—often in a way at some remove from reality—properties of the model. A description (e.g., of the Japanese firm) is assembled. Third, they theorize the particular elements to be copied as central to the virtues of the model (e.g., the success of the Japanese firm is traced to the training or management of its employees).

How the diffusion of organizational forms works is determined by the structure and conceptualization of the stratification system of extant organizations. We consider below how this may change over time.

It is important to note here, however, that organizational stratification is by no means unidimensional. Dominant organizations (and there are several dimensions even here) may not be reputed as the most modern, itself a strikingly multidimensional term. Simply looking at nation-states that seem to have attracted attention as some sort of models over the last two centuries, we would find admired cases that were in no sense competitively dominant: a rural and relatively weak early 19th-century United States; quite impoverished Cuba, Nicaragua, and Maoist China; and a rather peripheral Soviet Union. Of course, we would also find an empowered 20th-century United States, together with relatively strong or wealthy countries such as Sweden, Germany, France, and, until recently, Britain. The dimensions of stratification that lead to emulation certainly include dominance, but they may also include various forms of virtue.

The extremely ideological or rhetorical character of the modern rationalized system is indicated by the fact that so many marginal organizations, if they follow the most highly approved lines of expansion, can be seen as models—as instances where one can believe one sees the valid future working. Rationalized virtue, as well as success, becomes important in such a stratification system in determining the loci of proper models. Of course, the dimensions of the proper rationalization may change over time and with them the set of models most discussed: Until recently, models of expanded state activity and control were often noted—currently, market and technical efficiency standards select appropriate models for emulation, with Japan and other East Asian countries receiving much attention.

The organizational stratification system is likely to be an especially powerful influence on organizations under certain conditions. First, it may be especially influential in the absence of strong central regulation (e.g., by a state or by well-established professional or scientific models). Organizations in markets, for instance, may be especially likely to copy each other directly. Second, the stratification influence is likely to be greatest when the organizations in it are understood to have similar identities (see Chapter 5): If nation-states or other organizations possess common identities (e.g., as states or as production organizations of a common type), they are more likely to copy one another. Third, when organizations are seen as instances of common models, operating in terms of highly articulated rationalized schemes, they are more likely to copy other, similarly rationalized, organizations.

THE NATION-STATE

Organizations, nominally public or nominally private, are commonly licensed as operating in the public good. They are both endowed with, and constrained by, this status. The nation-state, in the contemporary world system, has been given something of a monopoly over the public good (i.e., sovereignty) and is thus a principal source of rules of organizing in terms of this good (Jepperson & Meyer, 1991). The church plays a much weaker role, although as we note below, some supranational replacements for it are developing.

DiMaggio and Powell (1983) use the term *state* to describe this source of rationalized organization, but this may be a bit narrow and may overly interpret the entity involved mainly as an organized and purposive actor (Skocpol, 1985 [compare pp. 3-20 with pp. 20-27]; Thomas & Meyer, 1984). Certainly, organizations and their properties can derive directly from the decisions of state bureaucrats. They can also derive from the more loosely integrated activities of regulators, legislators, and judges: And these may be found at any of several governmental levels that may not be tightly integrated in a single state apparatus. The American case is famous for its deliberate fragmentation across and within levels; although this is extreme, something like it characterizes many states. Effects on organizations are discussed throughout the studies presented here.

Even this broadening of the term *state,* however, is not enough to capture the rationalizing impact of the contemporary nation-state polity. Adjacent to the state organization itself is a whole system of collective actors—typically nonprofit organizations and interest groups—who also may act as sources of organizing. Environmental groups, or human rights ones, may intimidate organizations into adaptations and may even provide useful suggestions for ways to organize to avoid trouble with the state (or with themselves). Although not part of the state, such groups are clearly important parts of the nation-state, speak for its collective goods, and may affect particular organizations both through legal processes and their status in less formalized hierarchies of prestige and centrality.

But legitimate capacity to speak to the collective good in modern liberal society reaches a good deal farther than the state, the nonprofit sector, and some interest groups. The nation-state includes civil society or the nation: The component parts of this structure have interests that are simultaneously public and private, which is the special charm of liberal theory. Organizations are everywhere surrounded by actors whose private interests have public standing that may be enforced by courts, by public opinion, by interest groups with standing, and so on. A good deal of organizational formalization may result. For instance, an organization dealing with a modern worker, supplier, customer, lender, or engineering innovator is likely to be much more elaborately formalized than the same organization might have been a century ago in dealing with people who were legally and socially peasants. Propriety, and often the law, may demand this, and much organizing can result.

Another way to emphasize this is to note that in modern individualism, now a worldwide institution (Chapter 1; Thomas et al., 1987), the legitimate interests of the individual have standing as a collective—not just an individual—good. Maintaining individual, or citizen, or even human rights, it is clearly put forward, is in all of our interests or responsibility or both.

The rationalizing environment associated with the modern nation-state thus is quite broad and includes much more than simple bureaucratic dominance. This is particularly true of those classically liberal nation-states that combine high nation building and the limited extension of the integrated bureaucratic state: In these cases, the incorporation of much private authority in the public good produces a great expansion of the domain of public or collective rationalization. Systems such as the American one set records, as is well known, for organizing in domain after domain (see the summary in Jepperson & Meyer, 1991).

The importance of the state, defined broadly as above, in driving organizational structure and change increases rapidly in recent decades with the expansion of the state and its penetration of more and more aspects of social life (from human reproduction to intrafamilial relations to every aspect of economic and social development, and now to the whole natural environment).

SCIENCES AND PROFESSIONS

The knowledge system provides another important part of the rationalizing environment (DiMaggio & Powell, 1983; Meyer & Rowan, 1977). The modern society, built overall as an account of a rational project in a demystified nature, develops scores of occupational groups with authority to speak to the collective good in the name of truths about nature: the nature of the physical world, of human individuals and their psyches, and of the natural workings of the social system itself. The testimony of the sciences, represented by professional consultants of all stripes, is a powerful sort of rationalization (claiming a kind of universal scope) and impulse to organizing.

In recent decades, the expansions in numbers of scientized professions and professionals have been remarkable. Any given organization is now surrounded by a much denser system of organized people and groups of this sort, and they claim much more extensive cultural content with more intensive authority.

Their impact on organizing has obviously increased in importance, and the expansion of professionalized consultancy directly increases the amount and complexity of organizing in many domains.

INTERACTION EFFECTS

Rationalized organizations and organizing densities are obviously affected additively by expanded sets of professions, rationalized polities, and available elite models. But there are interaction effects here, too. The rationalization of public life (e.g., the creation of new rules requiring organizational expansion to deal with the environment, more human rights, or more aspects of recognized production functions) gains force from the existence of hordes of scientific and professional consultants who inform organizing situations about both problems and solutions. It also gains force from known or reputed models of expanded rationality. Similarly, the professional and scientific analyses have more impact if there are elite models of the proper or reputedly proper implementation of their doctrines. The construction of modern rationality becomes more complete with political and normative support, cognitive and professional validity, and the existence of models of its enactment.

Levels at Which the
Rationalized Environment Is Constructed

Rationalization can go on in any or all of a number of environmental levels, from the immediate network around a given organization or organizing situation to world society as a whole. It has been conventional to distinguish industrial sectors, or immediate organizational fields, from national societies and to distinguish both from historical time period (often conceived implicitly as a national or even world-level property).

Consider the two distinct areas of organizational expansion discussed in the chapters of this book: (a) the elaboration of the rights and status of individual members of the organization, and (b) the expansion of organizational complexity. Although we may suppose that individualism makes more progress in some industries (e.g., the public sector—Chapter 13) than in others, most lines of argument might emphasize nationwide effects and might suppose that these dramatically change over time.

There undoubtedly are large national effects, but many of the most dramatic changes in recent decades seem to have been worldwide (see Thomas et al., 1987). Pressures for the greater rights of women in all sorts of organizations have been worldwide, as have their organizational effects (Charles, 1992; Ramirez, 1987). The human rights movement in general has had a worldwide character, and changes may well have gone on in all sorts of organizations in the widest set of countries as a consequence.

To examine our other main variable—organizational complexity—it seems likely that particular industry or sector variables might have more effect here. But there would undoubtedly be some national variation too—national trends in the incorporation of new organizing strategies (Fligstein, 1990), in the development of new organizational technologies (e.g., accounting, financial planning, personnel administration), and so on.

A good many such changes have probably had a worldwide character, going on in all sorts of countries during roughly similar time periods (Barley & Kunda, 1992; Guillen, 1993). One can think of lateral diffusion processes that would spread new forms of organizational complexity—the networks of multinational firms, of consultants, of business schools, of exchange and domination. There are also direct world processes that might play a role, as when world associations of the appropriate professionals put forward new standards or when world bodies of some authority do so (e.g., the Montreal treaty about the world's ozone layer).

The research literature, attending to small variations over short time periods in a limited array of cases, has probably considerably understated the importance of the world as the locus of the rationalized environment and of much organizational formation and change as having a worldwide character. Research designs, rarely comparative and infrequently covering long periods of time, may have made the global character of modern organizational structure a bit invisible.

THE IMPORTANCE OF WORLD SOCIETY
AS A LOCUS OF RATIONALIZATION

Several considerations suggest that among the most common loci of environmental rationalization is world society itself and that the importance of this level increases considerably over time.

The term *world society* here has several different meanings, each of which may invoke distinct mechanisms by which organizations are affected. First, there are many respects in which the world has come to be a meaningfully collective system: a collective order of self-consciously world-level organizations, associations, and cultural doctrines. In this sense, we refer to such phenomena as the organizations of the United Nations system, associations with clear collective goals having to do with the environment or human rights, and the scientific or normative ideologies associated with such structures. In these terms, we refer to the world as a social collectivity, in the conventional sociological sense.

Second, by *world society* we mean the increasing prevalence of regional, national, and subnational associations and organizations that in fact link up across the world and have isomorphic properties across the world; and we mean cultural or ideological claims to universal scientific or normative validity. Here, in other words, we refer to the elements of what is ordinarily called a *social system* (though not a self-conscious collectivity) with shared and universalistic doctrines (e.g., scientific principles about the environment) and organizational linkages (e.g., networks of communication among national environmental organizations). Part of the power of world society in this sense lies in the fact that so many subunit actors—from individuals to organizations to nation-states—legitimate themselves in terms of universalistic rationalized ideas (e.g., about the laws of national development, of scientific technology, of human rights, and so on). This produces a buildup of world ideology in such areas, which tends to be widely shared (see Chapter 1, and Thomas et al., 1987, for extended discussions of this).

Third, *world society* refers to an increasingly dense network of relations (both organizational and in terms of communication) among subunits. Even in the absence of collectivity or social system interdependence, it is clear that dense interactions and communication in the modern world aggregate to something like a society within which the rules and practices of rational organizing may diffuse rapidly.

In all three ways, a world that is indeed more of a "society" has been under rapid construction. There are more collective social entities, there are more homogenizing social links and universalistic ideological claims, and there is more lateral interaction. In all these ways, a more intensely rationalized and rationalizing environment is being constructed at the world level. We may note both organizational and cultural aspects of this.

Content

First, consider the content of modern rationalization.

1. Much of it is rooted, as we have discussed above, in very general ideologies about nature—ideologies that claim universal applicability. There is scientific law about the natural environment (analyzed in terms of universal principles), about human society considered abstractly and universally, and about human persons also considered in universal terms (Frank, 1992; Thomas et al., 1987). All this science is conceived to be applicable everywhere: If scientific truths about effective materials techniques, organizational techniques, and psychological techniques arise in one location of the world and produce a bit of scientific consensus, then they should obviously be applied everywhere. The universalism involved in modern scientific rationalization leads to not only a good deal of expansionism and all-out conflict

(e.g., between scientific Marxism and neoclassical doctrines), but also to a great deal of standardization. Inasmuch as this sort of rationalization fuels organizational construction and change, it should produce similar changes and constructions practically everywhere.

2. Inasmuch as the rationalized environment is constructed in specific modern polities and states, however, one might expect more variation around the world. Nation-states vary a good deal in their structure and thus may make up varying environments of rationalization. This makes a good deal of sense, and it does seem that much stable crossnational variation is to be found in both the collective product of rationalization and resultant organizational structure (e.g., Hamilton & Biggart, 1988; Hofstede, 1980).

On the other hand, it is easy to overstate the case. The nation-state itself takes highly rationalistic forms as a putative bounded and rational organized actor. This means that it, like any other organization, is deeply dependent on a legitimating environment—one that is now worldwide (Thomas et al., 1987). Nation-states thus have surprisingly similar structures (given their diversity in resources and the background cultures of their populations). They have very similar goals (progress, measured in very standardized ways, and also human welfare or equality, also measured in very standardized ways) (Boli, 1987a; Fiala & Gordon-Lanford, 1987). They claim the same sort of sovereignty and from the same international bodies (McNeely, 1989). They adopt very similar technologies, such as very standardized education, to pursue their progressive ends (Meyer et al., 1992; Meyer, Ramirez, & Soysal, 1992). And while they adopt somewhat variant structures of political control (Jepperson & Meyer, 1991), these are sampled from a rather narrow range.

If the nation-state polity, in other words, is an immediate locus of the worldwide rationalized environment, we may expect much of the transmitted effect to have a global character. Throughout its entire history, the Western nation-state has been eyeing its peers and competitors, employing professional consultants from the wider environment, and so on. In fields such as education, from primary school to the university, the homogenizing results are remarkable, given an otherwise diverse world (Meyer et al., 1992; Meyer, Ramirez, & Soysal, 1992; Riddle, 1989).

3. Finally, the models lionized by the organizational stratification system have gone increasingly worldwide, as have the consultants who mediate information about them. There has been an expansion and standardization, in other words, of the content of organization theory as a world ideology, with similar intellectual and cultural movements everywhere.

Some special processes lend force to this and should be noted. And of importance is that there has been a considerable rise in a standardized organization theory. Organizations are now prominently discussed as organizations, rather than only in sectoral terms as schools and factories and government bureaus and hospitals, or rather than as instances of a distinct national polity. This inclination to a disembodied organization theory built up out of all sorts of myths entirely independent of particular countries or sectors has been a dramatic change over time: One can now discuss—and consultants routinely do discuss—management as an abstraction, or accounting, or personnel, or any of a hundred other aspects of organizational structure. As organizations everywhere come to consider themselves in the first instance organizations, their stratification system with its models for emulation comes increasingly to be worldwide rather than mainly structured by country or sector. Thus schools and hospitals are now routinely discussed as lying prominently in the abstract category organizations, a situation that obviously broadens and changes the network of possible models from which copying would seem reasonable.

Organization

If rationalized cultural content has a worldwide character, carried by sciences, polities, and stratification models all supported in a world frame, the expansion of rationalized world-level organizational structure has been extreme.

The number of international governmental organizations (e.g., the UN system, the World Bank, and a variety of others) has grown exponentially since World War II (Union of International Associations, various years, including 1992). One source records 81 of them by 1950 and 242 by 1970 (Feld, 1972): Increases since then have been even more rapid. In sector after sector, from education to welfare policy to health to economic development policies, these organizations promote expanded and homogenized social rationalization. An even more rapid exponential growth pattern describes international nongovernmental nonprofit associations and organizations. One source describes 795 of these by 1950 and 2,296 only 20 years later (Feld, 1972; see also Thomas, Boli, & Kim, 1993; overall data are in the Yearbooks of the Union of International Associations, 1992, and various other years). Finally, a dense network of profit-oriented firms, as is well known, now spans the globe.

Many of the organizations and associations involved here—along with some of the important multinational profit-oriented firms—are in the professional and scientific domains. International organization and communication in these areas has proceeded rapidly, creating stronger and more consensual world cultural pressures for standardized rationalization in many domains.

This expansion of international organization and professional structure, of course, intensifies the rise of organizational stratification systems across the whole world. It becomes increasingly feasible, for instance, to argue that American schools should copy structural forms from Japanese businesses, or that British firms should copy the labor-relations strategies of the Swedish state. The one best system for organizing, once structured mostly at the national level or across a few developed countries, now is argued out worldwide (Tyack, 1974).

Thus as a public polity, as a set of sciences and professions, and as a system of extant organizations, the world has become dramatically more structured. The modern system throughout its history had a kind of cultural unity in all its competition (with some common legitimation in public sovereignty, private rights, and a knowledge system). This has created isomorphic organization in state and society for centuries. The explosion of this systemic culture into all sorts of organizational structure at the world level represents both an expansion and an increase in penetrating power of this rationalistic world culture.

THE STRUCTURE OF WORLD SOCIETY AS A RATIONALIZED ENVIRONMENT

The modern and modernizing world society has a distinctive structure that helps account for its expansion and some of its penetrating power; it also leads to some special effects on nation-states and organizations within it.

The world society, to put it simply, has almost nothing by way of a sovereign and organized collective actor in it (Wallerstein, 1974, makes this a defining characteristic of the system throughout its history, and a similar logic runs through the work of Tilly; e.g., 1984). Its organizations and professions have little power and little responsibility to act or organize action. The system is built of organized subunit actors—several hundred nation-states, a great many firms, and billions of legitimated persons with their representative groups—but has only very weak collective actors in it.

There are, of course, many collectives in the world, as discussed in the previous section. The point is that they are not collective *actors* in the sense that they can legitimately mobilize massive forces in pursuit of their own distinctive ends. The world community of economists is probably important, but it is not much of an actor. Nor is, bluntly, the UN system. Nor probably are the institutions now making up Europe.

We need a term that describes rationalized and rationalizing social structure but does not assume actorhood in the elaborate sense now commonly used in the field: implying sovereignty, internal control, autonomous or self-interested purposes, rational means-ends technologies, independent resources, and clear boundaries. Such concepts do not describe the social units of the supranational world. The world association or community of economists does not have unified sovereignty, clear boundaries, tight control over internal activity, many or clearly definable independent resources, or rationalized technologies as an overall organization. Nor does it principally have its own goals, in the sense that self-interested actors are suppose to have goals. Lesser goals might include the advancement of the status, number, power, and prestige of economists—and modern muckraking social scientists and historians of science try to emphasize the self-interested machinations of professionals. But this is not why the world economists are given so much power to speak with such authority. The major collective goals of the economists seem to be the disinterested pursuit of truths about nature—a matter of general virtue in terms of highly collective goods and the use of the knowledge discovered to advance highly collective goods having to do with human social progress and equality. Their goals are not the progress and equality of particular national states, for which ancient economists might have served as agents: The modern world economist appears to be at the disposal of the general human good anywhere and for all time. It is hard to call this either actorhood or conventional agency, given modern narrow conceptions of the agent as at the service of only one or another actor.

Many of the elements of the structure of modern world society, in other words, have the properties of agency, not actorhood. Except that (a) they are not exactly agents of any definable set of extant principal actors; that is, they speak for things such as general human rights, scientific laws of socioeconomic development, or the environment—in short, moral and natural truth; and (b) they tend not to be agents in the sense of producing complete action on behalf of principals; that is, they tend to produce talk, advice, generalized norms, and scientific principles (Brunsson, 1989, and elsewhere). Whether or not they represent principal actors, they tend to speak to them as regulators and consultants.

Agent nevertheless may be a good enough term to describe the posture of the collective world-level entities now appearing in world society, so long as one bears in mind that they are commonly agents for entities (such as world society, humanity, the truth, or moral authority) that are not social actors, and so long as we recognize that the behavior they produce stretches the limits of what is nowadays considered proper social action (especially in more realist or rationalist models).

But clearly agency does not adequately describe the role these entities play vis-à-vis the nation-states and other legitimated and organized subunit actors (including human individuals) that populate the world. The associations and professions making up this collective world are not by and large mainly agents of actors—but they seem to tell actors what they should do to be proper, rational, effective, and so on.

We need a term for this sort of thing. Terms such as *actor* and *agent* are hopelessly contaminated.

Perhaps we can bring back Mead's (1934) *other*. The contemporary world is filled with rationalized agents who function vis-à-vis organizing as others. They do not much engage in, control, produce, or direct their agents to produce their own decision-based action (or by some definitions, much action at all—see Brunsson, 1989, for a discussion of entities that produce what he calls "talk" as opposed to action). They are not actors, but they instruct and guide putatively self-interested actors in the widest variety of matters: how to organize the good society, how to live safely and effectively in the natural world, how to respect the human members of society, and on and on. In particular, they play Mead's role of the "generalized other," providing national, organizational, and individual actors with reflexive depictions of their proper roles. Exactly as, Mead suggests, they provide identities, structures, and recipes for activity routines that make sense in terms of some larger (nowadays universalized and rationalistic) community.

This is the core role of the sciences and professions. They do not principally produce self-interested purposive action; they are highly rationalized roles functioning as others. They tell constituted actors about the true nature of the world (from details of technology and social structure to grand accounts of greenhouse effects and ozone layers) and about how proper actors might achieve their proper ends in this world. They are rather loose (not bounded) communities with little sovereignty. Their proper posture, in terms of action in the real world, is disinterested rather than interested, so that an American economist can be understood to give sound advice to the state of Turkistan on how to structure itself as a rational collective economic actor.

This is also a core role of the international system—of the UN system, the World Bank system, the collection of treaty organizations, the various European organizations, and so on. There is little here of the classic rational self-interested actor: They may be seen as simple agents of their members, but in good part these entities posture as more than that—as regulatory others, managing, but also constructing, the agreements among and long-run interests of true actors such as human beings, national states, and organizations in light of more general natural and moral laws. Sometimes entities in the international system speak to the requirements of an overall collective good of world society in its natural environment, but the structural capacity of this system to take authoritative action in such directions is obviously extremely limited.

The international stratification system, in good part, also works in the same way: National states clearly posture as self-interested actors and attempt measures of direct domination (analogous to the older colonial systems), but they represent themselves to one another and others in good part as cultural models. Through aid and other forms of international communication, they represent claimed universal ideals of proper nation-statehood (as, for example, in the recent Cold War conflicts, or the recent defenses of human rights, the environment, or properly "marketized" approaches to economic and social development).

The world society we describe has dramatically and discontinuously expanded since World War II, for whatever reasons (e.g., American or liberal hegemony, the breakdown of and conflict with alternative or older world orders such as colonialism, fascism, and communism). It is a most distinctively organized order.

A WORLD OF OTHERHOOD

A world society filled with rationalized others contrasts sharply with a world made up with a strong central collective actor or actors. A genuinely centralized world society would create a simpler and more restrictive environment for nation-states and other organizations within it. A strong center, in developing new responsibilities for subunit actors, would have to take action responsibility itself, defining specific controls and types and amounts of funding for new functions and rights (e.g., for managing the world's ozone layer, for regulating intranational human rights, or for implementing necessary new devices such as expanded education to promote national development). It would have to control and coordinate all of these new demands. It would be forced, in other words, to be cautious and controlled in the creation and legitimation of newly theorized functional requirements about the good and developing society, the requirements of the natural environment, or expansions in human rights. If world society were an organized actor, each new claim would be an action responsibility. Thus a world sovereign might not be eager to hear the ideas of some scientists about a putative hole in an ozone layer over Antarctica and about how this hole required the world regulation of the production, use, and disposal of refrigerators everywhere.

The others who make up world society are very different. The international organizations and professions that fill this world have little action responsibility—authority and funding obligations and powers—and are free to engage in extremely rapid constructions of new functions and responsibility for nation-state and other actors. This is their role: to develop expanded rationalistic ideas of the developing rights and powers and action responsibilities of individuals and organizations and nation-states. All of these are developed with respect to one another so that nation-states and organizations are to come to terms with expanded individual rights and capacities. And all are developed with respect to an expanded conception of the natural environment.

All of this expansion goes on with little or no world-level action responsibility. The theorists and legislators of the laws of social development, individual rights, organizational rationality, and environmental requirements do their rationalizing work without having much responsibility to do the actions or bear the costs involved. Their theories of the proper rational actor, whether individual, organization, or national state, thus expand in virtuous but extremely uncontrolled ways. The theories and ideologies have expanded with extraordinary rapidity in the past half-century—a veritable explosion in the worldwide collective creation of ideologies of modernity and progress. There have been such expansions in theories of the functioning of the modern society, of the modern human individual, the modern formal organization, and, of course, the natural environment of all these. All this is an elaboration of the classic Western constituted order, with a sacralized individual in a sacralized (now national) community, both in a God-ordered world, all to be perfected through organizational action (Hall, 1985; Mann, 1984; Meyer, 1989).

This is the fragmented, but rationalized, environment, with uncontrolled dimensions of ideological rationalization coming from many structural and professional sources, little integrated or restricted by consideration of the problems of realistic collective action. In such respects (though not many others), it resembles the classic American political structure with its fragmented central state (e.g., the separation of powers and the disorganized legal and administrative structure) and its multilevel federalism and localism (Meyer & Scott, 1992). This American political system is renowned for the rapidity with which, in a Tocquevillean way, collective rationalized claims expanded very rapidly in a blizzard of individual, professional, scientific, and organizational and associational participatory structures. The contemporary world society looks a great deal like this for similar structural reasons.

SOURCES OF THE FRAGMENTED
RATIONALIZED WORLD ENVIRONMENT

It is an interesting question why the contemporary world society, after many centuries as a failed world empire of highly competitive (although in some respects culturally isomorphic; see Chapter 1 and Thomas et al., 1987) warring states, has in recent decades generated so much collective organization and institutionalized culture (e.g., scientific and professional doctrine). The empowered nation-state actors in the system have clearly managed to block the formation of much actorhood capacity at the collective level. But they have obviously played central parts in building the dense contemporary environment of rationalized otherhood (Krasner, 1983). The following factors are involved:

First, as conventionally discussed, nation-state competition has generated some collective security protective structures (the League of Nations and later the United Nations) that provided an organizational (and to some extent cultural) framework on which further rationalizing ventures could be promulgated by all sorts of interests. Thus the world agenda could be expanded to include institutions of national development (such as education or scientific concerns, or even population policy; see Barrett, 1992; Finnemore, 1990; Huefner, Naumann, & Meyer, 1987), human rights (Berkovitch, 1993), or the environment (Frank, 1992).

Second, with the expansion and intensification of the nation-state in world competition over recent centuries, states have increasingly built themselves as elaborate rationalized actors. As Marshall (1948) noted, they came to incorporate an elaborate national polity in the 19th century and an economy and ultimately complete model of society in the 20th. As the state has become more "real," it has also become more of an elaborated and rationalized ideology—one whose scientific and normative doctrines were increasingly projected on the world scene as natural and moral truth and as universalistic and rationalized models. This made it easier for professions and organizations, institutionalizing such models, to develop in world society; for example, for the UN system, the World Bank organizations, and the international economics profession to develop models thought to be universally applicable. As another example, the increasingly universalistic and elaborated nation-state models of citizenship made it easier for general principles of human rights to be formulated and expanded.

Third, as conventionally noted, denser systems of communication and interaction in many domains (e.g., economic, scientific, and cultural) made it increasingly easy to organize on a world scale.

Fourth, increasing codification of nation-states around general principles produced increasing competition around such principles (as opposed to simple competitions involving national interests). Recent world conflicts (e.g., World War II, the Cold War) were conflicts among competing rationalized modern ideologies. Successful parties have tended to write aggressive versions of these ideologies into world rules (e.g., the UN system's principles of nation-state integrity formulated against imperialism; the Universal Declaration of Human Rights formulated against fascism; or more recent human rights standards maintained against communism) rather than simply institutionalizing their national interests.

The Impact on Organizations of the Fragmented Rationalized World Environment

THE NATIONAL STATE

One main effect of the world environment of expanded and rationalized otherhood has been to create many new tasks for proper national states, who are instructed by the organizations and professions of the world in greatly expanded action responsibilities (Finnemore, 1990; McNeely, 1989). This creates much new national organization in many areas—all aspects of social, individual, and natural environmental functioning come under the states' world-assigned responsibilities. And states have expanded, in both rich and poor countries, with great rapidity, at least symbolically covering many of these expanded functions. The contemporary state is a long way from an integrated bureaucratic state of a former period, with its monopoly of violence, internal order, and international relations. The contemporary state must have policies and organizations dealing with multiple aspects of social development (e.g., economic responsibilities for growth and employment), of individual rights (e.g., minorities, women, and individuals in general), and of the natural environment and its requirements and resources.

States have expanded extraordinarily, but the contemporary nation-state, immersed in a highly fragmented legitimating environment, is itself a fragmented (but, of course, rationalized) enterprise. It comprises great numbers of uncoordinated policies, organizations, and profit and nonprofit groups. An enormous amount of public organization appears, held together less by any unified imperative authority or genuine technical interdependence than by a web of rationalized ideologies (of human rights and equality, of social development and modernization, of the environment and the larger world). All of these ideologies, of course, are likely to have world and supranational roots in organizations and professions and stratification models from the larger system. That is why and how they are in place.

We live in a period of the expanded national state, but one that is so penetrated by exogenous and multidimensional rationalization that it is no longer a coherent autonomous actor (if it ever was). It retains formal sovereignty, but this is just another name for its multiform responsibilities, mostly derived from world society.

RATIONALIZED FRAGMENTED WORLD SOCIETY AND NATIONAL STATE AND THE EXPANSION OF CONTEMPORARY ORGANIZATION

Surrounded by elaborated but unintegrated demands and supplies for rationalization, modern organizing situations turn into actual organizations at very high rates. New types of organizations spring up and appear in many places almost at once. And extant organizations evolve new structures at the same high rates in response to national and world environments filled with authoritative but nonresponsible rationalized others rapidly at work creating new domains of necessary rationalization.

Thus there seems to have been a worldwide explosion of organizing and in rather standard forms.

1. Considerable organizational structure has arisen from the world and national construction of an expanded individual and human person, infused with more rights and capacities, to manage and use this expanded construction (Berkovitch, 1993). Personnel structures of all sorts rise along with labor relations and training specialists and programs.

2. The modern environmental analysis transcends and incorporates an older one built around conceptions of nature as some resources or commodities (Frank, 1992). Many new organizations and components of extant organizations appear.

3. The official models of the good society—a society meeting expanded standards and analyses of progress and justice, with enlarged national accounting systems, for instance—expand greatly. This makes possible and necessary organizations in many more areas of social life—it floods the world, for instance, with schools (Meyer et al., 1992; Meyer, Ramirez, & Soysal, 1992) and expanded ministries of education. Extant organizations expand to give a more complete account in terms of the new values, with new professionals in many areas and new components to the organizational production function (e.g., new and more subtle legal and financial accounting systems, financial and strategic planning systems rationalizing their way far into the future).

4. Finally, both world and national societies now contain greatly expanded general models of organization itself. With the rise of business

schools, consulting firms, and a great deal of professional and scientific development, the world is now blessed with general theories of organization in the abstract; that is, one can discuss proper organization without much mentioning the actual substantive activities the organization will do (contingency theories suggest taking into account a few properties of these activities, but very few). An older world in which schools were managed by educators, hospitals by doctors, railroads by railroad men now recedes into quaintness. All these things are now seen as organizations, and a worldwide discourse instructs on the conduct of organization. This produces a great expansion, almost everywhere, of management. It also standardizes this management across sectors and countries so that theories of proper leadership or organizational culture or financial accounting can be discussed increasingly consensually between a Korean manufacturer and a British educational administrator.

The modern rationalized but fragmented world society and nation-state, in other words, produce an explosion of diverse values all to be incorporated in formal organization: They also produce elaborate theories of organization that will integrate—often in a very abstract way—these disparate values. We see the expansion of disembodied management, which can be applied in any time and place and activity setting as a proper rationalized form. Its existence and rise produce a great expansion and standardization in the possibilities for organizing.

The effect is that organizational structure tends to be less predictable in sectoral and national environmental factors and more predictable in worldwide trends. These trends may hit with special force on transnational organizations themselves, but they strike all sorts of organizations, increasingly in every country and sector. More frequently, the modern MBA can function everywhere and is increasingly necessary everywhere.

Conclusion

Formal organizations are creatures of rationalized environments: They operate under norms of rationality (Thompson, 1967). In giving broad analyses of their spread, it makes sense to consider where these norms of rationality are spreading and how they are organized.

It is an obvious truth that the norms of rationality are increasingly organized in worldwide discourse and structures—worldwide organizational models, world-level associations themselves, and world-level sciences and professions.

A further obvious truth is that the expansion of norms of rationality in world society has been dramatic in recent decades—peculiarly little controlled by any responsible central actors in the world. World associations, the force of lateral communication about virtuous models, and extraordinarily authoritative sciences and professions are all organized to tell actors what they should do rather than to take action themselves. A world of such rationalized others, all second-guessers and advisors with little action responsibility, is obviously susceptible to rapidly expanding demands of rationality.

Two effects of this highly fragmented but rationalized environment have been to both expand and undercut the tight organizational coherence of the nation-state, which is given many new and unintegrated responsibilities. All the world authorities agree that national states are sovereign actors— indeed, it is precisely on this basis that all the advice and instruction occurs—and they agree so completely that it is no longer clear what *sovereignty* means. It has become, in other words, another term for allocated responsibility.

A fragmented and rationalistic world environment, and a set of similarly structured national states, generates an enormous wave of organizing. The newly created functions must be organized, and extant organizations must come to terms with them. Thus we have worldwide waves of expansionistic organizational change.

Also worldwide we have expansion of pure organization theories about how all of this will be held together. Abstract ideas of accounting, personnel functioning, organizational cultures, leadership, and so on, reinforced structurally by the worldwide professionalization of management (in business schools, consulting firms, and the scientific and professional literatures), make it possible and necessary for everything to be organized. The organization that results may not describe or predict very much, because it is a maze of abstractions. And our model here is far from any vision of an iron cage. We are really discussing the fact that in the contemporary situation, abstractions about organization become metaphors for the widest variety of situations. Another world produced, perhaps, too many preachers: This one seems to generate professional consultants and managers.

3

Institutions and Organizations

Toward a Theoretical Synthesis

W. RICHARD SCOTT

THE STUDY OF INSTITUTIONS is one of the most enduring interests in the social sciences. Like all human interests, there has been ebb and flow—but for the past two decades, we have witnessed flow of a very high volume. All the major disciplines—anthropology, economics, political science, psychology, and sociology—have become engaged and, as we would expect, each has given its particular thrust and contour to the current. Indeed, recent work has displayed almost as much diversity of definitions and interests within as among disciplines.

Although elaboration and variety have their uses, they also pose problems. Students encountering the "new institutionalism" may perceive the diversity as cacophony and decide to dismiss recent work as much ado about too many things. One reason why contemporary work on institutions is so broad and diverse—and so lively—is that it is connected to and enriched by a broader set of intellectual developments in the social sciences variously described as "the new culturalism" (Wuthnow, Hunter, Bergesen, & Kurzwell, 1984), "the interpretive turn" (Rabinow & Sullivan, 1987), and the "cognitive revolution" (Powell & DiMaggio, 1991).

This chapter draws on the work and insights of many scholars, many of whom I know personally, and to all of whom I am indebted. I have also benefited from specific comments and suggestions on earlier drafts by Peter Bogason, Soren Christensen, Peter A. Hall, Christian Knudsen, James G. March, John W. Meyer, and Oliver Williamson, as well as comments received from numerous seminar audiences and several anonymous reviewers.

Although it may be premature, this chapter attempts to draw together some—not all—of the strands of recent work on institutions. I review, using extensive excerpts, the work of several prominent contributors to institutional theory, including Berger, Geertz, Krasner, March, Meyer, North, and Williamson. I argue that while important areas of disagreement remain, more consensus exists than is at first apparent and that, as with the overused but still useful fable of the blind men and the elephant, much of the disagreement among contemporary analysts occurs because they are focusing on different aspects of this complex phenomenon.

Although it is clearly the case that institutions are central and potent social systems of relevance for all sorts of social structures and processes, I restrict attention here to their implications for organizations and organization theory. The modern appeal of institutions is that it provides a much needed counterbalance to a set of earlier theoretical approaches that gave primacy to materialist forces shaping organizations. Contingency theorists stress technical constraints, resource-dependence theorists, the effects of resource and information flows, Marxists, the play of power, and transactions costs economists, the force of cost-minimizing concerns. The new institutionalists attempt to redress this imbalance by stressing the importance of idealist concerns—symbolic systems, cognitive scripts, and normative codes.

In the course of defining and discussing a synthetic model of institutions, I consider some of the principal issues and controversies currently at large in this busy and crowded arena. Where I am unable to resolve them (at least to my own satisfaction), I attempt to clarify what the fuss is about.

Institutions: A Layered Model

I propose a "layered model" of institutions as a means of capturing and taming some of the disparate conceptions. Institutions are viewed as made up of three component elements:

1. meaning systems and related behavior patterns, which contain
2. symbolic elements, including representational, constitutive and normative components, that are
3. enforced by regulatory processes.

The importance of these institutional elements for organizations is that they provide alternative models for constructing organizational fields and organizational forms (see Figure 3.1). I consider each institutional element in turn.

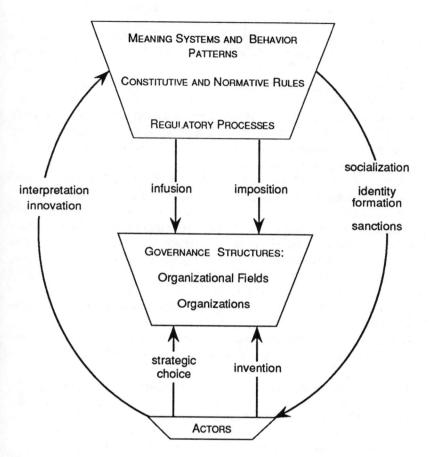

Figure 3.1 Institutions: A Layered Model

Meaning Systems and Behavior Patterns

MEANING SYSTEMS

More than other classical theorists, Max Weber emphasized the importance of attending to meaning in studying social systems. Weber regards "action" as occurring "insofar as the acting individual attaches a subjective meaning to his behavior"; "Action is 'social' insofar as its subjective meaning takes account of the behavior of others and is thereby oriented in its course" (Weber, 1968, p. 4). Shared meanings are indispensable to collective activity. "The stability, or organization, of any group activity depends upon the existence of common modes of interpretation and shared understanding of experience. These shared understandings allow day to day activities to become routinized and taken for granted" (Smircich, 1983, p. 55).

Because meaning is central to social life, Weber (1968, p. 4) insisted that social science must involve its "interpretive understanding"—must take into account the meanings that participants attribute to actions. He argued that any given action could be understood and explained only by examining both the objective conditions and the actor's subjective interpretation of them (see Alexander, 1983, pp. 20-57).

More than any other contemporary theorist, Clifford Geertz has recovered and revitalized this emphasis on the importance of shared meanings.[1] Geertz redefines culture—which earlier had been broadly treated as encompassing the entire way of life of a people—so as to place primary emphasis on its semiotic functions: "Believing, with Max Weber, that man is a social animal suspended in webs of significance he himself has spun, I take culture to be these webs . . . culture consists of socially established structures of meaning" (Geertz, 1973, pp. 5, 12).

Geertz does not himself connect his arguments to the concept of institution, but many recent institutional analysts have appropriated this conception of culture as a fundamental element of institution. Thus Berger and Kellner (1981) emphasize the central role of meanings within institutions:

> [E]very human institution is, as it were, a sedimentation of meanings, or, to vary the image, a crystallization of meanings in objective forms. As meanings become objectivated, institutionalized, in this manner, they become common reference points for the meaningful actions of countless individuals, even from one generation to another. (p. 31)

Meyer and colleagues embrace a similar definition: "We see institutions as cultural rules giving collective meaning and value to particular entities and activities, integrating them into the larger schemes" (Meyer, Boli, & Thomas, 1987, p. 13; see Chapter 1 in this volume).

And Friedland and Alford emphasize, as one of their defining features, that institutions "are symbolic systems, ways of ordering reality, and thereby rendering experience of time and space meaningful" (Friedland & Alford, 1991, p. 243).

There are, of course, many varieties of cultural rules or meaning systems, and only a subset are relevant to organizations. Weber was among the first to examine the emergence of distinctive types of rules—which he referred to as rational-legal rules—likely to support the development of organizations. More recently, Berger and colleagues (Berger, Berger, &

Kellner, 1973) have described the characteristics of two types of belief systems—those underlying technological production and bureaucratization—that are strongly associated with the emergence of modern society with its manifold forms of organizations. Meyer and Rowan (1977) in their seminal article have emphasized the contribution made by rationalized belief systems, independently of technical interdependencies or complex relational networks, to the development and stabilization of formal organizations. And Friedland and Alford (1991) draw together the threads of decades of work on social institutions to remind us that broad institutional forms such as capitalism or the state rest on a set of meanings or "logics" emphasizing accumulation and the commodification of human activity in the former case and in the latter case rationalization and the regulation of human activity by legal and bureaucratic hierarchies, which are quite distinctive from belief systems that underpin other societal arenas such as kinship or religious systems.

As I will emphasize below, institutional theorists need to attend more carefully to the substance or content of meaning systems giving rise to organizations generally as well as to distinctive fields of organizations. Not all types of belief systems support the creation of formal organizations, but a great many do; and taking note of the specifics of these systems can help us to explain how and why formal organizations appear and assume different forms and guises.

BEHAVIOR PATTERNS

It would be a mistake to focus exclusively on meaning systems without attending also to related actions and patterns of behavior. Meanings arise in interaction, and they are preserved and modified by human behavior. To separate meaning systems from behavior is, as Geertz (1973) cautions, to court the danger

> of locking cultural analysis away from its proper object, the informal logic of actual life. . . .
> Behavior must be attended to, and with some exactness, because it is through the flow of behavior—or, more precisely, social action—that cultural forms find articulation. . . . Whatever, or wherever, symbol systems "in their own terms" may be, we gain empirical access to them by inspecting events, not by arranging abstracted entities into unified patterns. (p. 17)

Friedland and Alford sound the same note in defining their conception of institutions: "We conceive of institutions as both supraorganizational *patterns of activity* through which humans conduct their material life in time and space, and symbolic systems through which they categorize that activity and infuse it with meaning" (Friedland & Alford, 1991, p. 232; emphasis added).

Although the focus of institutional theory is on symbols and meanings and rules, I believe that it is essential that we not lose sight of the human agents that are creating and applying these symbols, interpreting these meanings, and formulating, conforming to, disobeying, and modifying these rules. (Note the arrows linking institutional elements with actors in Figure 3.1.)

Symbolic Elements: Representational, Constitutive, and Normative Rules

Institutions are meaning systems, but not all meaning systems are institutions. A poem is a cultural form or product but not itself an institution; neither is a mathematical equation. To qualify as institutions, the meaning systems must incorporate representational, constitutive, and normative rules.[2]

REPRESENTATIONAL RULES

The most commonly observed function of symbols is that they stand in for—signify—other things. Many symbols are used to convey our understandings of the world and how it works. Such symbols, usually linguistic, are connected by broadly shared conventions to the observable world. Our knowledge systems—our beliefs about the objects and events we observe or about which we are informed—are governed by a complex set of representational rules of the form: this is an "X" object; and "X's" exhibit properties of type "A" or behave in specific ways "B"; e.g., water flows downhill, foxes chase rabbits.

Any institutional complex incorporates a collection of knowledge claims. These include not only empirically based observations about specific phenomena, as well as claims or beliefs that have little or no empirical support, but also more fundamental assumptions about how such claims are constructed and validated: what Friedland and Alford (1991) term *institutional logics*. These logics establish the framework within which knowledge claims are situated and provide the rules by which the claims are validated and challenged. The logics employed vary over time, across societies, and organizational fields.

CONSTITUTIVE RULES

Constitutive rules define the nature of actors and their capacity for action. Because these rules are so basic, they are often overlooked by social analysts. In contemporary society, we take for granted that individuals are to be regarded as having interests (e.g., in the acquisition of resources, self-improvement), are endowed with certain rights (e.g., to own property, to vote), and are able to take specified actions (e.g., enter into association with others, express opinions). Such interests, rights, and capacities are not, however, inherent or "natural" characteristics; rather, they are constructed by institutional rules. Economists are prone to treat the instrumental pursuit of self-interest as a universal characteristic of individuals, but such behavior is defined as normal only to the extent that it is constituted and supported by institutional rules such as those defining economic markets. The fact that these interests and behaviors are not "natural" and universal is graphically illustrated by the difficulty faced by current reformers attempting to build a market system in the republics of the former Soviet Union.

An early, but cryptic, statement of the constitutive functions of institutions is provided by Berger and Luckmann: "Institutionalization occurs whenever there is a reciprocal typification of habitualized actions by types of actors. . . . The institution posits that actions of type X will be performed by actors of type X" (Berger & Luckmann, 1967, p. 54). This densely packed definition has been usefully elaborated by Searle:

> Any newspaper records facts of the following sorts: Mr. Smith married Miss Jones; the Dodgers beat the Giants 3 to 2 in eleven innings; Green was convicted of larceny; and Congress passed the Appropriations Bill. . . . There is no simple set of statements about physical or psychological properties of states of affairs to which the statements of facts such as these are reducible. A marriage ceremony, a baseball game, a trial, and a legislative action involve a variety of physical movements, states, and raw feels, but . . . the physical events and raw feels only count as parts of such events given certain other conditions and against a background of certain kinds of institutions. . . . It is only given the institution of marriage that certain forms of behavior constitute Mr. Smith's marrying Miss Jones. Similarly, it is only given the institution of baseball that certain movements by certain men constitute the Dodgers' beating the Cubs [sic] 3 to 2 in eleven innings.
>
> These "institutions" are systems of constitutive rules. Every institutional fact is underlain by a rule of the form "X counts as Y in context C." (Searle, 1969, pp. 51-52)

Meyer and colleagues stress the importance of constitutive rules, especially in linking actors and actions:

> Most social theory takes actors (from individuals to states) and their actions as real, a priori, elements. . . . [In contrast] we see the "existence" and characteristics of actors as socially constructed and highly problematic, and action as the enactment of broad institutional scripts rather than a matter of internally generated and autonomous choice, motivation and purpose.
>
> A central concern of our analysis is the way in which the institutional structure of society creates and legitimates the social entities that are seen as "actors." (Meyer, Boli, & Thomas, 1987, pp. 12, 13; Chapter 1 in this volume)

Krasner (1988, p. 74) specifies four component elements entailed in the social construction of an actor: (a) endowments (e.g., property rights), (b) utilities (preferences), (c) capabilities (capacity to act, resources), and (d) self-identities (internalized definitions of social location or role).

Just as individual persons can be constructed as social actors, so can collectivities. As an important example of the construction of a collective actor, Coleman (1974, 1990) has described the process by which, in various times and places beginning in the 13th century, the notion of the limited liability corporation arose and took on a distinctive profile of rights and capabilities. Changes in legal theory both reflected and supported these developments (see also, Creighton, 1990; Seavoy, 1982). Similarly, Krasner (1988) has examined the circumstances under which nation states came to be endowed with sovereignty; and Wendt (1992) describes the processes by which such states developed an ideology of competition and self-help. All of these analysts assess the manner in which social actors possessing particular capacities and identities—limited liability, sovereignty, self-help—were socially constructed and reconstructed through actions, interactions, and their interpretation.

We need more such studies detailing the construction of social actors. In particular, we need to examine factors that account for the varying characteristics and capacities attributed to individual and organizational actors. One of the few efforts to develop arguments of this type is an essay by Jepperson and Meyer (1991, pp. 220-223), who propose that political regimes vary in how they organize and locate rationality: Liberal societies, for example, "license individual persons as legitimate and rational social actors"; corporatist societies "construct not actors and interests, but people and groups as agents performing legitimated social functions"; and statist societies constitute "pregiven, state-defined, function-specific actors." These differences are argued to influence both organizational structures and the relations between organizations and polities.

Jepperson (1991, p. 146) provides an apt summary of the constitutive aspects of institutions: "All institutions are frameworks of programs or rules establishing identities and activity scripts for such identities."

NORMATIVE RULES

The preceding discussion of constitutive elements has anticipated the third, normative, element of institutional meaning systems. Associated with actors and identities are conceptions of appropriate actions: roles, routines, scripts. These conceptions are not simply anticipations or predictions, but prescriptions (or proscriptions) of behavior. They are conceptions not only of how actors will act but also of how they should act. Some norms are quite general and apply to all members of the collectivity; others are quite specific and apply only to designated positions or actors. Normative rules exist in the expectations that others have for our behavior; and they also often become internalized through socialization processes so that they exist in the expectations that we hold for our own behavior, in our self-identity. Parsons (1951), in particular, emphasized the evaluative dimension of these expectations, which he termed "value-orientations"— expectations that, in the fully socialized case, are held both for and by actors. He viewed this evaluative element as central to the conception of institutionalization (see DiMaggio & Powell, 1991, pp. 15-19).

Some normative rules are implicit, widely shared beliefs—for example, our view in this country that citizens should vote and are entitled to express their opinions. Other norms are quite explicit and may apply to limited occasions—for example, the rules governing the playing of bridge or football.

Regulatory Processes

Institutional rules are backed by enforcement mechanisms, whether formally designated and centralized or informally administered and decentralized. Among institutional theorists, it is economic historian Douglass North who has given greater primacy to this aspect of institutions.

North begins his analysis of institutions with a quite general conception: "Institutions include any form of constraint that human beings devise to shape human interaction" (North, 1990, p. 4). "Institutions provide the basic structures by which human beings create order and attempt to reduce uncertainty in exchange" (North, 1989, p. 238). In developing his conception of institutions, however, North views their core function as stipulating the "rules of the game," whether formal or informal, and emphasizes the crucial importance of enforcement mechanisms as central to a viable institution.

> [Institutions] are perfectly analogous to the rules of the game in a competitive team sport. That is, they consist of formal written rules as well as typically unwritten codes of conduct that underlie and supplement formal rules . . . the rules and informal codes are sometimes violated and punishment is enacted. Therefore, an essential part of the functioning of institutions is the costliness of ascertaining violations and the severity of punishment.
>   Continuing the sports analogy, taken together, the formal and informal rules and the type and effectiveness of enforcement shape the whole character of the game.[3] (North, 1990, p. 4)

One of the major strengths of North's perspective is that it emphasizes the importance of the role played by political structures in relation to other specialized subsystems of society, such as economic systems.[4]

> [Institutions] entail enforcement either of the self-enforcing variety, through codes of behavior, or by a third party policing and monitoring. Because ultimately a third party must always involve the state as the source of coercion, a theory of institutions also inevitably involves an analysis of the political structure of a society and the degree to which that political structure provides a framework of effective enforcement. (North, 1986, p. 231)

North is not alone in focusing on the regulative processes at work in enforcing institutional rules. Thus DiMaggio and Powell's (1983) well-known typology emphasizes this aspect of institutions when it distinguishes among coercive, mimetic, and normative controls that induce organizations to conform to institutional pressures.

Similarly, the typology that Meyer and I developed (Scott, 1992; Scott & Meyer, 1983), in which organizational environments are classified according to the strength of the technical and "institutional" forces to which they are subject, can be viewed as an attempt to focus on the nature of the regulatory processes at work: Whether organizations are controlled primarily by process ("institutional") controls, by output ("technical") controls, or by some combination of these.[5]

Early Summary and Commentary

Three "layers" or components of the concept of institution have been identified. An alternative conceptualization would be to identify just two rather than three components: (a) cognitive elements, including both meaning systems and the representational and constitutive rules; and (b) normative elements, including both normative rules and enforcement processes. Most institutionalists incorporate both elements in their view of institutions, but we observe great variation in the relative emphasis placed on one or the other cluster. Theorists such as Berger, Douglas, and Meyer stress the former; Parsons and North the latter.

COGNITIVE ELEMENTS

Some argue that the defining feature of the new institutionalism is the ascendant role played by cognitive processes. DiMaggio and Powell (1991) stress this theme in their recent thoughtful commentary on institutional theory. They describe the crucial role played by Talcott Parsons in deflecting attention from the cognitive to the normative and evaluative aspects of social action. Parsons (1951) emphasized how the institutionalization of roles is dependent on the internalization of others' expectations motivated by affective ties and social sanctions. By contrast, theorists such as Berger and Luckmann (1967) have detailed the critical importance for social order of a shared conception of the situation and a determination of one's identity within it. These shared conceptions are viewed as controlling "human conduct by setting up predefined patterns of conduct" that exert their effects "prior to or apart from any mechanisms of sanctions specifically set up to support an institution" (p. 55). Cognitive framing exercises control apart from and in the absence of normative constraints.

Similarly, Mary Douglas (1986) emphasizes the cognitive aspects of institutional controls. In her treatise *How Institutions Think,* she argues that "the entrenching of an institution is essentially an intellectual process as much as an economic and political one" (p. 45). Institutions are seen as effecting and shaping social action by creating classification systems, specifying what is taken as similar and what different; by conferring identities on actors, by determining what is remembered and forgotten. These and similar controls do not depend primarily on explicit rules and enforcement machinery, but on subtle, shared beliefs: "The high triumph of institutional thinking is to make the institutions completely invisible" (p. 98) (see also, Zucker, 1977).

Meyer and associates (1987) also assert the primacy of cognitive controls:

Both social actors and the patterns of action they engage in are institutionally anchored. . . . Institutionalized rules, located in the legal, social scientific, customary, linguistic, epistemological, and other "cultural" foundations of society, render the relation between actors and action more socially tautological than causal. Actors enact as much as they act: What they do is inherent in the social definition of the actor itself. (p. 22)

For these theorists, institutions control actors by providing definitions of situations and identities. We are not surprised to hear that the quarterback of the football game handled the pass from center; we are prepared to believe that Ann, the bride, will participate in a wedding ceremony. Social life is predictable and orderly because of shared role definitions and expectations, the authority of which rests in a shared conception of social reality—a complex of taken-for-granted assumptions—rather than [only] in the promise of rewards or the fear of sanctions.[6]

NORMATIVE ELEMENTS

Other theorists from Parsons to North stress the role of the more explicit control mechanisms, ranging from evaluative signals of mild disapproval to the development of specialized surveillance and enforcement machinery and powerful sanctions lodged in regulatory agencies. North emphasizes the importance of rules but insists that for them to be binding, they must be backed by meaningful sanctions. Cognitive controls alone might be sufficient given consensus and complete information; but information is always incomplete and often asymmetric. Much important exchange in the modern world takes place among strangers—among individuals who do not necessarily share the same values or cognitive frames. Specialized regulatory systems are more likely to be necessary as exchange processes widen to incorporate larger numbers of diverse participants spread over time and space.

COGNITIVE AND NORMATIVE ELEMENTS

March and colleagues (March & Olsen, 1989; March & Simon, 1958) take a relatively balanced view, insisting on the importance of both cognitive and normative elements. Their emphasis on rules as the basis of order in organizations would seem at first to put them in the camp giving priority to normative controls and explicit regulative processes:

> Institutions have a repertoire of procedures, and they use rules to select among them. The rules may be imposed and enforced by direct coercion and political or organizational authority, or they may be part of a code of appropriate behavior that is learned and internalized through socialization or education. (March & Olsen, 1989, pp. 21-22)

However, they proceed to extend the definition of rules to encompass a broad range of both normative and cognitive controls:

> By "rules" we mean the routines, procedures, conventions, roles, strategies, organizational forms, and technologies around which political activity is structured. We also mean the beliefs, paradigms, codes, cultures, and knowledge that surround, support, elaborate, and contradict those roles and routines. It is a commonplace observation in empirical social science that behavior is constrained or dictated by such cultural dicta and social norms. Action is often based more on identifying the normatively appropriate behavior than on calculating the return expected from alternative choices. (p. 22)

Sociologists tend to emphasize the importance of shared values and common understandings as the basis for social order, in part because they focus more on institutional complexes such as kinship and religious systems. Economists are more likely to stress divergent interests and hence the need for referees and regulatory frameworks, in part because they focus on situations in which actors compete for scarce resources. Each can learn from the other. Sociologists need to attend more to value differences and divergent assumptions among actors, and economists need to recognize the common assumptions and shared conceptions that underlie the operation of markets.

In short, it is useful, I believe, to recognize the presence and importance of both cognitive and normative elements in all institutional complexes. The strength and staying power of institutions can be attributed to their multiple sources of support. They are, as D'Andrade observes, "overdetermined" systems: "Overdetermined in the sense that social sanctions, plus pressure for conformity, plus intrinsic direct reward, plus values, are all likely to act together to give a particular meaning system its directive force" (D'Andrade, 1984, p. 98).

More particularly in terms of the components I have identified, institutions shape behavior by means of:

- Representational rules that involve shared logics or modes of reasoning that help to create shared understandings of reality that are "taken for granted"
- Constitutive rules that create social actors—that is, identities linked to specified behaviors and action routines
- Normative rules that stipulate expectations for behavior that are both internalized by actors and reinforced by the beliefs and actions of those with whom they interact
- Enforcement mechanisms, both formal and informal, involving surveillance, assessment, and the application of sanctions rewarding conformity and punishing deviance

At the same time it is also useful to recognize that the relative emphasis placed on cognitive or normative controls can vary from one institution to another. Jepperson (1991, pp. 150-151) suggests that the extent to which one or another dominates can be viewed as one dimension along which institutions vary. He distinguishes between alternative "carriers" of institutionalization— between regimes that embody institutional authority in some type of explicitly codified rules and sanctions (see also Krasner, 1983) and cultures that rely on widely held beliefs and understandings without "monitoring and sanctioning by some 'central' authority." (A third carrier, formal organization, is discussed below.) These modes of control can be expected to operate differently, and Jepperson suggests that it may be useful to distinguish sectors or historical periods by the dominance of one or another type of carrier.

We arrive then at the following definition: *Institutions are symbolic and behavioral systems containing representational, constitutive, and normative rules together with regulatory mechanisms that define a common meaning system and give rise to distinctive actors and action routines.*

Alternative Governance Mechanisms: Organizational Forms

My attempt at synthesis has to this point emphasized the contributions of anthropologists, sociologists, and economic historians while neglecting those of a different collection of theorists engaged in developing the "new institutional economics" and the "positive theory of institutions" in political science. These labels cover a range of diverse work, as Langlois (1986a) has pointed out.[7] I emphasize here the transaction costs perspective in economics, which has had a major impact on organization theory, and the related work on political institutions.

Most of this work addresses the origins of institutions, asserting that they are social arrangements devised in order to deal with collective action problems (positive theory) or in order to economize on costs arising in connection with the negotiation and enforcement of contracts to manage economic exchanges (transactions costs) (see Moe, 1990a; Williamson, 1975, 1985). I will focus later on the varying arguments concerning why institutions arise; the issue now is to determine what these theorists mean by the concept of institution. In general, these theories view institutions as "governance structures," to use Williamson's term: They are frameworks of norms, rules, and enforcement mechanisms that help to account for the regularities of individual behavior, increasing predictability and providing continuity in social situations (see Langlois, 1986a). Examples of institutions examined in this literature include markets, specific organization structures such as unitary and multidivisional companies, and legislative and regulatory bodies such as the Food and Drug Administration.

Note that while this conception of institution shares much in common with that developed in the previous discussion, two principal differences are apparent: (a) the neoinstitutional political science and economic literatures place more emphasis on the normative, regulative aspects of institutions than on their cognitive dimensions;[8] and (b) the formulations tend to point to different levels of analysis. Most of the anthropological and sociological work is at the supraorganizational level: The reference is to wider societal (or even world-system) cognitive and normative frameworks, to systems existing in the environments of organizations. By contrast, most of the economic and political science work attends to the organizational level, focusing on specific agencies of the state or particular forms of economic enterprise.[9]

Friedland and Alford (1991) strongly embrace the sociological stance, insisting that institutional systems should be conceived as operating at the societal rather than the organizational or individual level. They suggest that all three levels should be viewed as operating autonomously, albeit interdependently with one another:

> An adequate social theory must work at three levels of analysis—individuals competing and negotiating, organizations in conflict and coordination, and institutions in contradiction and interdependency. . . . We conceive of these levels of analysis as "nested," where organization and institution specify progressively higher levels of constraint and opportunity for individual action. (pp. 240, 242)

The other theorist who forcefully argues the importance of distinguishing organizations from institutions is North. Recall that for North, institutions are, fundamentally, rule systems. Although North recognizes that both organizations and institutions provide "a structure to human interaction," he sees institutions as providing the "rules of the game" in which organizations act and compete as players (1990, p. 4). He argues that economists such as Williamson focus principally on how organizations are constrained by rules. North (1989) comments:

> Valuable as this work has been, it leaves out the most important contribution which institutional analysis can make to economics; and that is to go deeper than simply looking at forms of exchange, accepting the rules of the game. Instead, what we need to do as economic historians is to explore the way the rules of the game change. (p. 240)

Earlier economic theorists also recognized differences in the levels or types of institutions, as Langlois (1986a) has noted. Thus Menger (1963) attempted to differentiate between "organic" institutions, such as law and money, and "pragmatic" institutions, such as a corporate structure. And Hayek (1973) distinguished more "abstract" from more "concrete" institutions.

I agree with arguments about the value of distinguishing wider rule frameworks from narrower governance systems, although I also agree with those who recognize that governance structures within organizations are made up of institutional elements: meaning systems, symbolic elements, and regulatory processes. It seems helpful to recognize that organizational structures incorporate, perhaps even better, instantiate institutional elements. One possibility, following Williamson (1992), is simply to distinguish between two levels of institutional phenomena: institutional "environments" and institutional "arrangements." Another is to follow Jepperson's lead and to identify a third "carrier" of institutional forces: To cultures and regimes, we simply add formal organization. In either case, we can thus incorporate the work of sociological analysts such as Selznick (1957) and Zucker (1988a), who have concentrated attention on the development of institutionalized systems within organizations. These analysts emphasize that institutional processes go on at both the macro (environmental) and micro (organization and interpersonal) levels—the latter processes being examined by both ethnomethodologists and students of corporate culture. Individuals create and sustain new meanings in interaction; and normative and regulative processes are developed and operate in these situations.

My own framework calls attention to the effects of wider institutional systems on organizational forms. Organizations participate in, and incorporate, transorganizational institutional frameworks. It is this more macro level to which the new institutionalism in organizational analysis—particularly that in sociology—has primarily been addressed (see DiMaggio & Powell, 1991, especially pp. 11-15). Nevertheless, we can incorporate the recent work of the neoinstitutionalists in both economics and political science by adding the following addendum to our earlier definition of institution: *Institutions operate at a variety of levels, and their elements can be embodied in and carried by cultures, by regimes, and by formal organizations.*

Organizational Fields

The application of institutional arguments to organizations occurs, in my view, most appropriately and powerfully neither at the level of the entire society nor at the level of the individual organization but at the level of the organizational field. Indeed, DiMaggio and Powell (1983, p. 143) define the concept of field as referring to "those organizations that, in the aggregate, constitute *a recognized area of institutional life:* key suppliers, resource and product consumers, regulatory agencies, and other organizations that produce similar services or products [emphasis added]." I subscribe to DiMaggio's assertion (1986, p. 337) that "the organizational field has emerged as a critical unit bridging the organizational and societal levels in the study of social and community change." Fields identify communities of organizations that participate in the same meaning systems, are defined by similar symbolic processes, and are subject to common regulatory processes. The rationalizing frameworks giving rise to and shaping organizational fields are, in the modern world, constructed primarily by the professions and agents of the state. Their degree of coherence and structuration—and institutionalization—vary over time and across societies (DiMaggio & Powell, 1983; Scott & Meyer, 1983, 1991).

Like individual organizations, organizational fields develop governance mechanisms ranging from market-like, competitive controls to self-regulating mechanisms to the development of hierarchical, centralized control centers—in short, institutional elements at the field level may be carried by cultural beliefs, regimes, or formal organizations. Some of the most important recent work attempts to characterize these governance structures, the forces that have brought them about, and the ways in which they affect individual organizations. (See Campbell, Hollingsworth, & Lindberg, 1991; Cawson, 1985; Fligstein, 1990; Streeck & Schmitter, 1985; Whitley, 1992; for a review, see Scott, in press.)

Explaining Institutions and Governance Systems

To account for the development and the transformation of institutional frameworks and governance systems is a task of obvious importance to which economists, economic historians, political theorists, and sociologists have devoted attention. Organization theorists are latecomers to this ongoing discussion. Accounting for institutional change is of special significance to economists because their conventional arguments posit a condition of equilibrium, and it can be argued that changes in institutional rules create new and different equilibrium conditions affecting the survival of organizations. Therefore a sizable body of economic literature has developed around this topic in recent decades. (For reviews, see Hodgson, 1988; Knudsen, 1992; Langlois, 1986a.)

Organization theorists are naturally most concerned with institutional arguments insofar as they help to account for the characteristics of organizational structures. Only a few analysts, including Meyer and colleagues (Jepperson & Meyer, 1991; Meyer, Boli, & Thomas, 1987; Meyer & Scott, 1992; Meyer, Chapter 2 in this volume), DiMaggio (1991), and Fligstein (1990, 1991) have dealt extensively with processes affecting the development of institutional frameworks at wider levels with emphasis on their organizational implications. Here I focus primary attention on debates regarding the design of governance structures at lower levels, in particular, organizational structures. I emphasize two distinctions: (a) what assumptions are made regarding the role of rationality and intentional action in organization design; and (b) does the analyst take primarily a "bottom-up" or "top-down" approach to the development of organizational structures?

RATIONAL DESIGN VERSUS PROCESS MODELS

Whether the interest is in explaining institutions as cultural rule systems or as organizational governance structures, recent work by social scientists tends to diverge into two camps: those emphasizing rational design versus those advocating a path-dependent process. Rational design theorists, exemplified by Demsetz (1967), Williamson (1985), Moe (1990a), and Coleman (1990) embrace a bounded rationality model but treat the design of organizational forms as simply a special case of the economic choices confronting actors. Individual actors are viewed as making choices of both activities and of structural forms so as to efficiently pursue their interests. As Masten (1986, pp. 445-446) notes in describing Williamson's perspective:

> The approach that Williamson advocates begins with the insight that decisions regarding organizational form require choices among variously faulty alternatives. The task is therefore to assess the costs and limitations of these alternatives and evaluate their relative merits. . . . [Thus] the choice among institutions may be viewed as part of an economic actor's overall optimization problem.

In a similar vein, Moe (1990a, p. 215) asserts that "[i]nstitutions arise from the choices of individuals, but individuals choose among structures in light of their known or presumed effects." These types of arguments assume that choices are being made under an equilibrium condition such that surviving organizational forms reflect "implicit solutions to an optimization problem" (March & Olsen, 1989, p. 54). The logic employed is often functionalist: Analysts point to the consequences of forms in order to account for their existence (see Elster, 1983; Granovetter, 1985).

These assumptions are challenged by the second camp of theorists, including political scientists such as March and Olsen and Krasner, by economic historians including North and David, and by sociologists such as Fligstein and Powell. They insist that "history is not efficient"; existing arrangements cannot be assumed to be optimal in their adaptation for many reasons, including the recognition that current choices are not perfectly free but are constrained by existing structures; information is imperfect, and outcomes are often unanticipated; environments may change more rapidly than attempts to adapt to them; change may not be smooth and gradual but episodic or "punctuated," disrupting existing organizational adaptations and giving rise to quite different organizational forms; and because organizations achieving dominance under one set of circumstances can use their power to subvert the development of more efficient forms (David, 1985; Fligstein, 1990; Krasner, 1988; March & Olsen, 1984, 1989; North, 1990; Powell, 1991).[10]

BOTTOM-UP VERSUS TOP-DOWN EXPLANATIONS OF GOVERNANCE STRUCTURES

A second point of divergence is apparent in explanations offered to account for governance structures. The new institutional economists and political scientists employ primarily a bottom-up explanation of organizational forms. Executives or administrators are viewed as designing these structures: Taking into account the characteristics of the transactions involved, these actors are alleged to devise appropriate governance arrangements, deciding perhaps between a market structure or a hierarchy or between one type of hierarchy and another (e.g., a unified or multidivisional form). Williamson argues that participants in exchange systems subject to efficiency pressures will develop—whether by adaptation or environmental selection—governance structures that economize on transactions costs (Williamson, 1975, 1985).

While Williamson has concentrated his efforts on economic organizations, in related work, a number of economists and political scientists have applied similar kinds of arguments to explain the development of political structures such as legislative bodies, committees, and administrative structures. (For example, see Moe, 1990a; Shepsle & Weingast, 1987; Weingast & Marshall, 1988.)[11]

By contrast, sociological institutionalists such as Meyer and Rowan (1977), DiMaggio and Powell (1983), and Tolbert and Zucker (1983) take a top-down perspective, emphasizing the extent to which existing institutional models are infused throughout an organizational field: Frameworks external to organizations provide models of organizational arrangements from which organizational participants choose or to which they are subjected. Organizational participants are viewed as being subject to normative pressures and cognitive constraints to embrace forms regarded as appropriate or legitimate for organizations of the type to which they belong. From this perspective, executives may not be designing their governance structures in the light of the particular problems confronted but rather choosing a structure from a menu providing a set of options. Indeed, under many circumstances, participants may not be allowed to select a structure: rather, one is imposed on them. As Meyer and colleagues (1987) argue:

> The wider setting contains prescriptions regarding the type of organizational actors that are socially possible and how they conceivably can be structured. Collectives are thus as much the embodiment of the prescriptions of the available cultural forms as they are the aggregation of lower-level units and interests. (p. 19 & Chapter 1 in this volume)

And DiMaggio and Powell argue that as organizational fields become more highly structured, "powerful forces emerge that lead [organizations operating within] them to become more similar to one another." Certain types of structural forms become "normatively sanctioned" and, over time, are widely adopted, reducing the "extent of diversity within the field" (DiMaggio & Powell, 1983, pp. 148-149).

These top-down arguments gain support from their ability to account for two important features of organizational forms: first, why, given the great variety in specific settings, participants and tasks, we observe so much uniformity in the structural arrangements adopted by organizations. Second, these same arguments help to explain the ubiquitous observation—dating at least from the earliest research on "informal" patterns of behavior within formal organizations—of the loose connections between rules or formal structures in organizations and the behavior they are designed to channel and control (see Meyer & Rowan, 1977; Meyer, Boli, & Thomas, 1987). If governance systems arose out of specific interaction settings and in response to particular problems, one would expect to see both more variety in governance structures and a closer correspondence between rules and activities than is observed.

These controversies—whether actors, on the one hand, are making choices rationally and without restriction or are doing so subject only to informational and attention constraints or, on the other hand, are unable to make choices (because options are imposed on them) or are selecting alternatives under severe constraints—are characteristic of many battles that are waged between economists and sociologists.[12] Underlying the controversy are fundamental differences in both theoretical and methodological assumptions made about the "nature of social order"—whether individualist or collectivist assumptions are being made (see Alexander, 1987, pp. 10-11).

RECONCILING THE APPROACHES

Although it is possible to let the matter remain unresolved—attributing the impasse to incommensurable paradigms—I believe that there is evidence of progress in reconciling the two perspectives. Moreover, efforts toward rapproachment are underway in both camps.

Model Versus Models

Beginning with the top-down camp, sociological theorists increasingly recognize the multiplicity and complexity of belief and rule systems. Early arguments stressed the coherence and consistency of institutional rules, but more recent work has pointed out that such systems vary in the range of models they promote and in the extent to which conflicting belief systems are present (see Brunsson, 1989; D'Aunno, Sutton, & Price, 1991). Complexity and conflict in any situation open up possibilities for discretion and strategic behavior by actors, both individuals and organizations. This view is elaborated by Swidler in her discussion of the relation between culture and action: "A culture is not a unified system that pushes action in a consistent direction. Rather, it is more like a 'tool kit' or repertoire from which actors select differing pieces for constructing lines of action"[13] (Swidler, 1986, p. 277).

This imagery is consistent with Meyer and Rowan's (1977) early description of the nature of institutional systems and the ways in which organizations relate to them:

> The growth of rationalized institutional structures in society makes formal organizations more common and more elaborate. . . . After all, the building blocks for organizations come to be littered around the societal landscape; it takes only a little entrepreneurial energy to assemble them into a structure. (p. 345)

These "building blocks" include, for example, rationalized personnel systems, various professional specialists such as economists or accountants, research-and-development units, training and safety programs. Which combination of blocks is required or will be appropriated varies from organization to organization.

The recognition of multiple and, in some instances, competing institutional frameworks curbs the tendency of analysts to embrace deterministic explanations and opens up the opportunity for the development of a more voluntaristic perspective of social action and structure.

Broadening the Conception of Rational Actors

Langlois (1986a) has argued that one of the general themes linking the diverse efforts of the new institutional economists is a broadened conception of rationality. The newer work departs from the traditional definition of rationality as restricted to "the conscious maximization of an explicit objective (such as utility) within the constraints of well-defined alternatives" (p. 6) to "admit of other kinds of reasonable action in certain situations, including satisficing (in the narrow sense), rule-following behavior, entrepreneurship . . . and so on" (Langlois, 1986b, p. 252). The hard line between interest-driven and rule-oriented behavior is beginning to soften.

March and Olsen (1989) embrace and extend this broadened conception:

> To say that behavior is governed by rules is not to say that it is either trivial or unreasoned. Rule-bound behavior is, or can be, carefully considered. Rules can reflect subtle lessons of cumulative experience, and the process by which appropriate rules are determined and applied is a process involving high levels of human intelligence, discourse, and deliberation. . . . [Moreover], the number and variety of alternative rules assure that one of the primary factors affecting behavior is the process by which some of those rules, rather than others, are evoked in a particular situation. (pp. 22, 24)

Recognizing the diversity of institutional systems and broadening the conception of rationality moves us toward resolving the controversy as to whether institutional arguments are necessarily in conflict with rationalistic arguments based on self-interest (see DiMaggio, 1988). Viewing behavior as occurring within institutional frameworks first implies that interests themselves are institutionally determined (see Friedland & Alford, 1991; Scott, 1987); second, emphasizing choice within and among cultural models or rule systems suggests that actors conforming to rules need not be regarded as helpless puppets or as being unaware of or indifferent to their "interests" in the situation. As Swidler (1986, p. 277) notes, this interpretation of "cultural theory should lead us to expect not passive 'cultural dopes,' but rather active, sometimes skilled users of culture whom we actually observe."

This view also implies that organizational actors can be expected to engage in strategic behavior as they relate to institutional complexes. Oliver (1991, p. 149) has noted that early institutionalists "tended to focus on conformity rather than resistance, passivity rather than activeness, and preconscious acceptance rather than political manipulation in response to external pressures and expectations." She correctly insists, however, on the utility of examining the full range of possible reactions—variation in "resistance, awareness, proactiveness, influence, and self-interest" (p. 151)—by organizations to institutional pressures.

All of these arguments are broadly consistent with Giddens's (1984) model of the duality of structure and action. Structure (including cultural systems) is seen to be both the context of action, constraining and supporting individual activities and choices, and the product of action. But structure does not exist apart from the actions that continually produce, reproduce, and transform it minute by minute, day by day. Similarly, as Geertz (1973) emphasizes, cultural meaning systems exist independently of any particular individual actor, but individual actors are continually engaged in transmitting, interpreting, and reinterpreting these meanings.

These arguments further imply that while organizational participants are often better described as choosing rather than designing the governance systems under which they operate, some choices of governance systems and their diverse components will be better suited to managing a given organization's activities than will others. It is not inconsistent with an institutional perspective to ascertain whether one organization's choice of a given structure proves to be more or less effective—by one or another criterion of effectiveness—than that made by a different organization. Organizational participants are constrained to make choices among institutional models, but not all choices are equally felicitous for the organization's agenda. Nor is it inconsistent to suggest that innovative activities by individuals and organizations can, under the right conditions, become the basis for delegitimating old and establishing new institutional models.

In sum, in this conception, a concern for self-interest, issues of effectiveness, the use of strategic behavior, even rational calculation and innovation are not incompatible with an institutional approach.

Bottom-Up and Top-Down

Recent empirical research suggests that there is merit in being open to the possibility that organizational arrangements may result from top-down, bottom-up, or some combination of these processes. For example, DiMaggio (1983) provides a clear instance of top-down processes at work in his discussion of how the creation of the National Endowment for the Arts in the United States led to the building of quite homogeneous public arts councils at the state level and increased structuration of the arts field in general. By contrast, Suchman's (1991) study of the role of lawyers in creating the organizational field known as Silicon Valley suggests that they were operating more from the bottom-up, consulting with individual companies and gradually "compiling" models of appropriate governance structures by inductive processes. And the study by Dobbin and colleagues (1993; Chapter 13 in this volume) of organizational responses to federal affirmative action requirements in the United States posits that both top-down and bottom-up processes are sometimes at work. In this situation, affirmative action requirements were imposed on organizations conducting business with the federal government. However, exactly what procedures were required was under dispute. Personnel officers proposed a variety of approaches to meeting the requirement, to which state agents (primarily federal judges) responded, determining which of several proposed solutions was acceptable. When, over time, a solution was identified and agreed upon, it quickly diffused through the organizational field, being rapidly adopted as a modification to organizational governance systems.

Conclusion

In an earlier review article (Scott, 1987), I suggested that institutional theory in organizations was in its adolescent period—still in its earlier formative stages. Now, somewhat later, but also taking into account not only sociological work but also developments across the social sciences, it seems to me that there has been considerable progress. I see convergent developments among the approaches of many analysts as they recognize the importance of examining meaning systems, symbolic elements, regulatory processes, and governance systems. Divergence occurs along several fault lines: in the relative emphasis on normative versus cognitive dimensions; in whether attention is focused on the environmental rule systems or the organizational governance structures; in regard to what assumptions are made concerning the rationality of the processes by which rule systems or governance structures are created; and in whether organizational governance structures are viewed as constructed from the bottom-up or represent infusions from the wider environment.

Although the various disciplines are focusing on different levels of analysis and sometimes use contrasting assumptions, I believe that the areas in which there is agreement are growing. At the very least, economists are now taking seriously the existence of organization structures and are attempting to examine both their determinants and consequences. Economists, political scientists, and sociologists productively debate the uses and limits of rational choice; and some economists have begun to wonder whether rule-driven behavior may not have its rational aspects.

Anthropologists and sociologists have rediscovered the importance of symbolic systems and their role in framing and forming organizational behavior. And the study of organizations generally has benefited from more attention being paid to the cognitive and normative aspects of these complex social systems.

Notes

1. The most influential precursor of Geertz's cultural perspective was German philosopher Wilhelm Dilthey. For a discussion of the similarities and differences in their views, see Alexander, 1987, Chapter 16.

2. My discussion of these components draws heavily on the work of anthropologist Roy D'Andrade (1984). In addition to the three elements I embrace, D'Andrade discusses a fourth—the "evocative" or "affective" dimension that emphasizes the "emotional side of meaning" (p. 99). While I omit this dimension in this discussion, I acknowledge the importance of affect in creating and maintaining social order and recognize that these processes merit, and are receiving, increasing attention from sociologists (e.g., Thoits, 1989).

3. While the types of rules associated with competitive games provide an important instance of institutional rules, they are not, in my view, "perfectly analogous." Other, different types of institutional rules would be those associated with noncompetitive activities such as more habitual routines or rituals.

4. North's perspective is fruitful in ways just described and in other respects discussed below, but his analysis tends to neglect the important role played by constitutive processes. Like many "social realists," North assumes that the social actors—the players of his games—are given, and he proceeds to examine how they are affected by the various rules and enforcement machinery. He overlooks the important institutional processes by which the endowments and capacities of the players are established.

5. This interpretation helps to overcome a serious limitation of this typology. Crossclassifying the dimensions "technical" and "institutional," as we did, implies that the dimensions are independent and thus that technical or market-like environments are not institutionally structured. I, of course, believe that all social life, including technical aspects, is institutionally defined. (See also Powell, 1991.)

6. Indeed, Berger and Luckmann (1967, p. 55) suggest that regulatory mechanisms may signal the weakness of institutions, arguing that "additional control mechanisms are required only insofar as the processes of institutionalization are less than completely successful."

7. Langlois (1986a) includes among the new institutionalists evolutionary theory, the modern Austrian school, transactions costs economics, and certain aspects of the property rights literature.

8. Formulations such as Williamson's also give some attention to the cognitive dimensions of institutional frameworks. Thus following Simon (1957), Williamson asserts that one of the ways in which organizations reduce transactions costs is to provide framing assumptions and operational routines that help to overcome the limitations imposed by the bounded rationality of participants (see Williamson, 1975, pp. 21-23).

9. Political scientists oriented more to the earlier institutionalist tradition in political science and less to that of positive theory give more attention to the broader assumptions and normative frameworks as central to institutional analysis. For example, Krasner (1988) and

Hall (1992) define institutions more broadly as including constitutional provisions and basic assumptions regarding property rights.

10. Early efforts to develop such path-dependent models tended to be descriptive: efforts described pejoratively by mainstream economists as "storytelling." More recently, game theorists such as Schotter (1981), Axelrod (1984), and Sugden (1986) have attempted to develop formal models of how institutions emerge. They have specified the processes giving rise to differing institutions (rule systems) as solutions to problems in repeated games. (See Knudsen, 1992.)

11. Even though Moe (1990b) argues that the administrative agencies of political systems are crafted by a set of political interests and actors (e.g., elected officials) different from those who will participate in the agency (bureaucratic officials), this does not constitute a top-down structure in my view. Both sets represent actors directly involved (as designers or operators) in a particular governance structure.

12. The oft-quoted aphorism from Duesenberry (1960, p. 233) remains an apt summary: "[E]conomics is all about how people make choices; sociology is all about how they don't have any choices to make."

13. While embracing the general argument developed by Swidler, I shy away from the metaphor of "tool kit" because I subscribe to Geertz's (1973, p. 17) view that "cultural systems must have a minimal degree of coherence, else we would not call them systems."

4

Institutional Analysis

Variance and Process
Theory Approaches

W. RICHARD SCOTT

INSTITUTIONAL THEORY has been revitalized during the past decade, and if it has not come of age it has certainly claimed attention from a large and growing circle of organizational researchers. Although there continues to be disagreement about the scope and domain of this theoretical enterprise, I argue that the essence of an institutional perspective resides in focusing on the cognitive and normative frameworks that provide meaning and stability to social life. The cognitive elements include widely held beliefs and taken-for-granted assumptions that provide a framework for everyday routines, as well as the more specialized and explicit and codified knowledge and belief systems promulgated by various professional and scientific bodies engaged in elaborating our cultural knowledge base. The normative elements incorporate traditional mores and informally sanctioned social obligations of the type found in all societies; they also include the more explicit rulings of legislatures and courts as well as the specialized surveillance and enforcement mechanisms of the regulatory agencies and the police.

I emphasize two points that are implicit in the above definition. First, cognitive and normative frameworks vary in their substance or content,

The first draft of this chapter was prepared while I was a Fellow at the Center for Advanced Study in the Behavioral Sciences. I am grateful for financial support provided by the John D. and Catherine T. MacArthur Foundation. This revised version benefited from helpful comments received from John W. Meyer, Randal S. Franz, and several anonymous reviewers.

with some varieties being more supportive of formalized organizational forms than others. As Weber was the first to argue, more rationalized belief systems give rise to more formal organization. Second, the "carriers" of institutional forms also vary across social systems: In more modern societies, cultural beliefs are more likely to be promulgated by specialized bodies such as professionals and norms, by formalized agencies of the state. (See DiMaggio & Powell, 1983; Meyer & Rowan, 1977.)

The "new" institutionalism places more emphasis on the role of cognitive factors; earlier institutionalists, on normative elements. In my view, however, both deserve attention and are properly included within an institutional framework. An emphasis on cognitive and normative elements serves as a counterbalance to earlier theories formulated to account for organizational structure, such as contingency theory, resource dependence, and population ecology, all of which stressed more materialist factors such as exchange and network interdependencies and competition for scarce resources.

The past decade or so has witnessed a flurry of theoretical and empirical activity exploring institutional factors relevant to organizations. In this chapter, I focus attention on recent empirical research and provide a schema for sorting among the various types of work now underway. I take an admittedly imperialistic stance, arguing that a good deal of work relevant to understanding institutions and organizations is being conducted outside the formal boundaries of our academic specialty. I identify three dimensions along which institutional studies of organizations may be arrayed, cross-classify them to produce a matrix of 12 cells, and then provide examples of each type of study identified by the categories.

In a brief final section of the chapter, I comment on three issues raised by this exercise in classification.

A Typology of Institutional Research

Students first encountering institutional studies of organizations are invariably confused by the great variety of work subsumed under a single label. Some confusion is generated by legitimate disagreements over concept development and application; but much unnecessary mystification is produced by a failure of researchers and commentators to discern the diverse styles of research approaches, appreciate the different objectives being pursued, and recognize the different levels at which the argument is formulated.

Three distinctions are proposed to differentiate among the large number of studies that make up contemporary institutional analysis. The first distinction focuses on the type of theoretical model employed, the second on the study objective, and the third on the level of the unit of study.

THEORETICAL MODEL

Quite early, Zucker (1977, p. 728) noted that "institutionalization is both a process and a property variable." The distinction implied in Zucker's comment has been more fully developed by Mohr (1982), who differentiates between variance theory and process theory approaches.

In variance theories, abstract variables are identified and their causal relations examined. Precursor (independent) variables are seen as a necessary and sufficient condition for variation in the outcome (dependent) variables, emphasis is placed on efficient causes that exert effects on the outcome, and the time ordering among the precursor variables is viewed as immaterial to the outcome. Variance theories attempt to determine what factors influence the outcomes observed: They address the question, why did this happen?

By contrast, process theories deal with a "series of occurrences of events rather than a set of relations among variables." These events are viewed as necessary but not sufficient conditions for the outcome, the emphasis is on final causes, and "time ordering among the contributory events is generally critical for the outcome" (Mohr, 1982, pp. 38-60). Process approaches address the question, how did this happen?

Although these two types of approaches are sometimes combined in the same study, the distinction is useful for broadly differentiating among styles of research on institutionalization.

OBJECTIVE OF INQUIRY

The second distinction focuses on the objective of the inquiry: What type of question is being asked about institutionalization? In the case of variance studies, this query is most easily operationalized by asking simply whether institutional factors are treated as independent or dependent variables. Some analysts seek to explain why institutions develop; others use institutional factors to explain other features of the social world, such as differences among organizations. In the case of process studies, because variables do not play so central a role, it is more helpful to distinguish between whether the study focuses on the processes by which institutional forms are created or generated or on the processes by which they are reproduced or diffused.[1]

TABLE 4.1 Institutional Research: Variance Theory Examples

Institutionalization Treated as	Level of Unit Studied		
	Intraorganizational	Organization Field	Societal
Independent Variable	1 Zucker, 1977	3 Mezias, 1990 Meyer, Scott, & Strang, 1987 Edelman, 1990	5 Hamilton & Biggart, 1988 Hofstede, 1980
Dependent Variable	2 Boeker, 1989	4 Porter, 1980 Schmitter, 1990	6 Gershenkron, 1962 Tilly, 1978 Thomas, Meyer, Ramirez, & Boli, 1987

LEVEL OF UNIT

The third distinction focuses on the locus of the unit of analysis: Are the institutional factors of interest located at the organization (micro) level or at broader, environmental levels? Rather than simply using the organization-environment distinction, as Zucker (1987) did in her review of this literature, I believe it is helpful to distinguish between narrower and broader levels of environments. An important development during the recent decade has been the recognition and widening use of an intermediate unit—variously called *industry system* (Hirsch, 1985), *societal sector* (Scott & Meyer, 1983), and *organizational field* (DiMaggio & Powell, 1983). I endorse DiMaggio's (1986, p. 337) enthusiastic assertion that "the organizational field has emerged as a critical unit bridging the organizational and societal levels in the study of social and community change." Thus three levels are differentiated: the intraorganizational or microlevel, the organizational field or mesolevel, and the societal or macrolevel. It must be recognized, however, that any attempt to characterize varying levels of social units is arbitrary because there exists a diverse array of social forms ranging from small groups to world systems. For present purposes, however, a three-category schema will suffice.

CROSS-CLASSIFYING THE DIMENSIONS

The three sets of distinctions are independent and so usefully cross-classified. Doing so generates 12 categories of institutional research, and I will identify and discuss prototypical studies of each type. Beginning with the variance theory approach, Table 4.1 identifies prototypical studies of research for each of these six categories. Each category is described in turn. However, this review will not be evenhanded because some of the categories merit more attention than others.

Studies Employing Variance Theories

Studies in category 1 of Table 4.1 treat institutional factors as independent variables and examine their consequences within organizations. Zucker has emphasized the importance of intraorganizational institutionalization processes in her work (Zucker, 1977, 1988a). In experimental studies, she investigated the effect of different degrees of institutionalization on various aspects of cultural persistence: transmission across generations, cultural maintenance, and resistance to change. She shows that the greater the institutionalization of role differentiation among participants—the identification of formal roles that increase the impersonal quality of relations and increase the sense of exteriority—the more likely that subjects were to adopt and maintain conforming responses (Zucker, 1977).

Category 2 incorporates studies that emphasize factors within organizations giving rise to institutionalization. An instance of this type of study is Boeker's (1989) research on subunit power within a sample of semiconductor organizations. His analysis shows that power differences existing among organizational subunits at the time of their founding were more likely to persist (become institutionalized) in organizations that were performing well and in which the founding entrepreneur had remained longer.

Although my primary intent is simply to illustrate various types of institutional studies, not to provide a comprehensive categorization of existing research, I do want to note the paucity of studies relating to categories 1 and 2. Systematic research probing the intraorganizational determinants or consequences of varying amounts of institutionalization within organizations is, according to my cursory review of the literature, rather rare. Most of the studies that have examined institutionalization occurring within organizations have adopted a process rather than a variance perspective. I give examples of such studies in the next section of this chapter.

A substantial number of studies have examined institutional factors in intermediate environments that influence the structure or activities of organizations (category 3). An example of a study examining the effect of changes in institutional frameworks on organizations at the sector or field level is provided by Mezias's (1990) study of how changes in the interorganizational field of federal agencies and professional bodies responsible for setting policy for accounting requirements resulted in changes in the financial reporting practices of corporate organizations under their jurisdiction. Other examples of this type of study are the research by Meyer, Scott, and Strang (1987; see Chapter 8 in this volume) on the effects of differences in funding and regulatory environments on the structure of school districts, and research by Dobbin, Edelman, Meyer, Scott, and Swidler (1988) and Edelman (1990) on effects of changes in the legal environment on the adoption of due process protections for employees within firms and agencies.

Category 4 encompasses studies that attempt to explain the characteristics of institutional frameworks at the meso or organizational field level. If attention is restricted to the efforts of organizational analysts, it appears that little work has focused on this problem: Few organizational researchers have dealt with factors affecting the nature of institutional frameworks at the field level, and those that have typically adopt a process approach (see below). The neglect of these issues by organizational researchers should not come as a surprise, because most of us have only recently begun to focus on systems operating above the level of individual organizations. Fortunately, others—largely economists and more recently political scientists and political sociologists—have conducted studies examining the determinants of institutional structures at the field level.

Economists have long been interested in what they term "the structure of an industry": the extent to which firms engaged in producing a given product or service confront more or less competitive conditions. These conditions are defined by a number of factors, including barriers to entry, degree of concentration, product differentiation, and governmental policies including regulatory systems. Industry structures vary from highly competitive through oligopolistic and monopolistic to state-managed forms (see Porter, 1980; Sherman, 1974). Although the language used emphasizes the economic consequences of such structures, it is apparent that they can also be regarded as different types of governance structures—embodying differing cognitive, normative, and regulative mechanisms—at the field level. Explanations for variation in these structural arrangements include variables such as technology (e.g., rate of innovation, state of technological maturity), importance of economies of scale, transactions costs arguments, and the level of problems posed by externalities (see Scherer, 1970; Williamson, 1975).

Political scientists, for their part, have long pondered the ways in which the interests of various groups are articulated, aggregated, and adjudicated in modern societies. Most of this interest has focused on the organization of national political structures, for example, contrasting pluralist and corporatist systems of representation (see Berger, 1981; Lowi, 1969;

Schmitter, 1974). Recently, however, many of these analysts have come to recognize that the ways in which interests are organized varies greatly within as well as between societies; that different sectors or fields (or industries) exhibit different kinds of governance systems or regimes for coordinating interests and managing conflict. Thus Cawson (1985, p. 1) acknowledges "the importance of the meso-level of interest articulation"; Kitschelt (1991, p. 453) suggests that "the success of industrial strategies may depend more on sectoral governance structures than on national ones"; and Schmitter (1990, p. 12) agrees that the sector has emerged as "the key unit for comparative analysis. . . . [A] number of changes in technology, market structure and public policy are converging to make this meso-level—that is to say the intermediate location between the micro-level of the firm and the macro-level of the whole economy—particularly salient."

These analysts have begun to develop typologies of governance systems at the meso or field levels (see, e.g., Lindberg, Campbell, & Hollingsworth, 1991; Schmitter, 1990), and they are developing and testing arguments regarding the factors accounting for these differences in governance systems. Schmitter, for example, identifies a complex set of variables, including changes in technology, changes in competitiveness, and national policy style to explain differences in sectoral governance. Lindberg and colleagues use a more process-oriented model (see Campbell & Lindberg, 1991).

Organizational theorists need not reinvent this and related literatures, but we do need to recognize that our politically and economically oriented colleagues have discovered the existence of organizational fields and are developing and testing interesting arguments to account for the differences in institutional forms that operate at this level. Our own work can benefit from these efforts.

Category 5 contains studies emphasizing that all organizations are subject to the effects of broader, macroenvironmental forces. Three subtypes of societal-level units have been used in institutional studies. First, for many analysts, the individual society is the appropriate unit of study, and investigations have examined the influence of varying societal-institutional contexts on organizational forms and practices. A recent example is provided by the research of Hamilton and colleagues (Hamilton & Biggart, 1988; Orru, Biggart, & Hamilton, 1991), who compared and contrasted societal authority styles governing organizational practice within Korea, Taiwan, and Japan and noted their effects on the structure of industry groups and firms. And a study by Carrol, Goodstein, and Gyenes (1988) examined the effects of Hungary's fragmented socialist regime on the organization of agriculture cooperatives, both at the level of field structure (e.g., the elaboration of interorganizational ties) and individual firm structure (e.g., the size of the administrative component).

A second tier of studies within this category examines broader clusters of societies sharing similar institutional features. Thus Lammers and Hickson (1979) have identified three general cultural models—Anglo-Saxon, Latin, and traditional—that they assert are associated with fostering and supporting different organizational forms. Hofstede (1980) has devised several scales to assess variation among societies in four value dimensions: power distance, uncertainty avoidance, individualism, and masculinity. A society's value profile, as measured by these dimensions, is shown to relate in a predictable manner to differences in its organizational forms and activities. And Carroll, Delacroix, and Goodstein (1988) have identified several types of nation-state structure (e.g., centralized, corporatist, distributive, socialist) and proposed hypotheses regarding their effects on organizational forms.

Finally, at the most general level, we have those theorists who identify even more encompassing societal patterns—patterns that are thought to be worldwide. Variance is found among individual societies in the extent to which such world-system features are exhibited because of differences in their location (e.g., core versus periphery) or differences associated with the time when a nation entered the world system. Working at this general macrolevel, Thomas and Meyer (1984) describe the rationalization processes that characterize the growth of nation-states. Following Bendix (1964) and Rokkan (1975), Thomas and Meyer assert that a fundamental distinction among societies experiencing modernization is whether the rationalization is primarily seated in the state apparatus itself or resides in the broader society. This distinction, Meyer (1983b) argues, has important consequences for the number and types of organizations that develop: In state-centered systems, organizations are predicted to be more rare, more highly rationalized, and linked more directly to the state than in societal-centered nations. These hypotheses have yet to be empirically tested.

Category 6 contains studies that attempt to account for differences among societies in institutional patterns supporting organizations. Here again, as with category 4, we have a corpus of work that lies outside the normal boundaries of organizational research—work that moves us into the realm of political science and political sociology. Research and theory development in this area, which has been termed "comparative political economy" (Evans & Stephens, 1988), has been unusually vigorous and productive during the most recent decades; and much of this work can be viewed as attempting to account for variations among nation-states in institutional regimes. Modes of political and economic organization have been variously shown to be affected by the timing of industrialization (e.g.,

Dore, 1973; Gershenkron, 1962); the structure of the state (e.g., Mann, 1984; Skocpol, 1979); the level and type of organization of peasants, workers, and other affected participants (e.g., Thompson, 1963; Tilly, 1978); as well as the position of the state and society within the changing world system (e.g., Wallerstein, 1974, 1980). These and related historical and comparative studies are directed toward explaining similarities and differences in the institutional structure of societies.

Bergesen, Meyer, Thomas, and colleagues (e.g., Bergesen, 1980; Thomas, Meyer, Ramirez, & Boli, 1987) have focused attention more particularly on the development of global cultural models that are embraced by societies as they enter the world system. Empirical work has examined the cultural patterning common to modern educational institutions the world over and has charted their effect on the organization of schooling within a large number of societies (e.g., Meyer, Ramirez, Rubinson, & Boli-Bennett, 1977; Ramirez & Boli, 1987); and their studies document that the expansion of state authority and administrative organization is more closely associated with being incorporated in the world order than with internal national power or societal economic development (e.g., Boli, 1987b).

Studies Using Process Theory

The initial discussion of theory modes identified the general features that distinguish process from variance theory perspectives. Process theory approaches, however, vary considerably in the extent of their formalization and specification. In more informally developed and less specified process theories, the analyst constructs a narrative—a history—that "accounts" for the particular end point observed. Such accounts consist of "stage-naming" concepts and descriptions of events that identify necessary conditions but fail to "supply the external forces and probabilistic processes constituting the means by which that sequence of events is understood to unfold" (Mohr, 1982, p. 53). Specific institutional structures are "explained" by recounting historical occurrences or sequences of events. Most studies of institutional processes are of this less formalized type.

By contrast, in more formally specified process theories, the analyst attempts to make explicit the nature of the probabilistic process that connects events with outcomes (see Lave & March, 1975). Chance or random processes may enter into the explanation, but their nature is specified—e.g., as "random draws from simple or joint probability distributions of various shapes that are either explicit or implied" (Mohr, 1982, p. 46). To date, two kinds of work have attempted to construct more formalized and explicit models of institutional processes: game theoretic approaches in economics and rational choice theories developed by a range of investigators, including economists, political scientists, and sociologists.

In addition to there being more and less formally developed process models of institutionalization, there are, as I have noted elsewhere (Scott, 1987a), two somewhat competing conceptions of what sort of process is entailed in institutionalization. Selznick (1957, p. 17), following Michels and Barnard, views institutionalization as the process by which social entities are "infuse[d] with value beyond the technical requirements of the task as hand." He thus emphasizes the motivational or affective aspects of the process. The second conception stems from the work of Berger and Luckmann (1967), followers of Dilthey and Schutz, who view institutionalization as the social process by which social reality is constructed. In this view, institutionalization is primarily a cognitive process giving rise to distinctive conceptions of social reality. Both conceptions stress the historical nature of the process. Selznick emphasizes the "natural history" of the evolution of organizations that are viewed as products of interaction and adaptation, becoming receptacles of commitment and shared values. And, for Berger and Luckmann (1967):

> Institutionalization occurs whenever there is a reciprocal typification of habitualized actions by types of actors. . . . Reciprocal typifications are built up in the course of a shared history. They cannot be created instantaneously. Institutions always have a history, of which they are the products. It is impossible to understand an institution adequately without an understanding of the historical process in which it was produced. (pp. 54-55)

Keeping in mind these differing conceptions (of both process models generally and of institutionalization processes specifically), we will proceed to classify process approaches to institutionalization using the same types of dimensions used for variance approaches. As discussed above, one of the dimensions—that distinguishing micro, meso, and macro units—remains unchanged whereas the second, rather than identifying study objectives in terms of independent versus dependent variables, distinguishes between studies focusing on how new institutional forms are created versus those that examine how they are diffused. Table 4.2 depicts this typology with illustrative studies.

Some of the earliest and most influential treatments of institutionalization view this phenomenon as a process. At the intraorganizational level, most analysts do not make a sharp distinction between institutional generation and diffusion; it is primarily a matter of emphasis. Category 7 contains intraorganizational process studies that emphasize the diffusion of new institutional structures. An example is provided by Barley's (1986)

TABLE 4.2 Institutional Research: Process Theory Examples

Process	*Level of Unit Studied*		
Emphasized	*Intraorganizational*	*Organization Field*	*Societal*
Diffusion	7	9	11
	Barley, 1986	Tolbert & Zucker,	Cole, 1989
	Bartunek, 1984	1983	
Creation	8	10	12
	Selznick, 1949	DiMaggio, 1991	Skowronek, 1982
	Garfinkel, 1967	Fligstein, 1990	Baron, Dobbin, &
	Schotter, 1981	Westney, 1987	Jennings, 1986
	Shepsle & Weingast,		
	1987		

case studies of the changes associated with the introduction of CT scanners into two hospitals. His account primarily addresses the process by which one institutionalized regime of professional dominance involving radiologists and technologists was overturned and then replaced by alternative institutionalized power structures. Attention is given to subunit differences within hospitals as well as to differences between hospitals in the change processes occurring over time. Barley's emphasis in on the shaping and diffusion of new models of social reality. An example of a study focusing on the diffusion of a new belief system that entailed changes in the emotional commitments of members is provided by Bartunek (1984), who studied the transformation of the mission of a Catholic order as it occurred over time and across several levels of the organization.

Category 8 includes studies that describe the processes by which institutional forms are generated within organizations. Selznick's study of the TVA provides a classic illustration of the value-infusion model as he depicts in detail the process by which social commitments were generated among participants to "the goals and needs of the organization and at the same time to the special demands of the tools or means at hand" (Selznick, 1949, p. 258). A series of studies carried out by ethnomethodologists detail the process by which individuals create and sustain meaning and social reality in interaction. Several of the most influential studies in this tradition were conducted in organizational settings and deal with the joint production by participants of meaningful behavior through the formulation of what Garfinkel (1967) characterizes as "a recognizably coherent, standard, typical, cogent, uniform, planful, i.e., a professionally defensible, and thereby, for members, a recognizably rational account" (p. 17) of activities in the work setting. (In addition to Garfinkel's research, see also Cicourel, 1968; Zimmerman, 1969.) More recently, students of corporate culture have provided descriptions of organizational participants creating common interpretative frameworks and shared values (see Deal & Kennedy, 1982; Frost, Moore, Louis, Lundberg, & Martin, 1991). Although both enthnomethodologists and analysts of corporate culture concern themselves with the generation of common cognitive and normative frameworks, they typically do not connect their arguments explicitly to institutional theory (but see Van Maanen & Barley, 1985).

Several formalized models of the processes by which minimal institutions—social conventions that constrain individual behavior—can emerge in interaction between individuals have been developed by game theorists such as Schotter (1981, 1986), Axelrod (1984), and Sugden (1986). These models are based on a set of players engaged in iterative or repeated games, with explicit rules specifying payoffs, such as the prisoner's dilemma, or posing problems of coordination of behavior. The players sometimes consist of experimental subjects or other types of volunteers, or their activities can be simulated by computer. The object of these efforts is to determine what sorts of conventions develop that will yield stable rule sets for the players. Although these types of efforts produce highly formalized and predictive models, they rest on quite narrow assumptions concerning the interests and characteristics of actors, and they focus attention on the normative features of institutional frameworks.

Related work based on rational choice theory by sociologists and political scientists attempts to account for the emergence of more complex institutional forms (see Coleman, 1990; Hecter, Opp, & Wippler, 1990). Hecter (1990, p. 15) differentiates between "conventions" such as the rule that we all drive on the right side of the road, compliance with which provides its own reward, and "cooperative institutions" in which incentives are such that individuals will be motivated to violate rules unless specific regulatory mechanisms are established. To date, the development of these arguments tends to proceed by logical proofs accompanied by historical accounts of the emergence of specific institutional forms.

Similarly, political scientists have used rational choice models to account for the characteristics of specific governance arrangements, such as the rules that define legislative procedures and committee jurisdictions (for example, see Moe, 1990a; Shepsle & Weingast, 1987). This work, however, is typically less highly formalized; instead it develops an account of how particular institutions could have emerged as a specific solution to a problem of collective action, assuming rational self-interest on the part of actors. Critics of this work point to the narrow and sometimes unrealistic assumptions that underlie the arguments; in addition, the arguments are often functionalist in character, explaining a set of institutional structures by referring to their consequences.

Tolbert and Zucker's (1983) study of the adoption by municipalities of civil service reforms is a good illustration of a study of the diffusion of an institutional form at the organizational field level (category 9). Although these analysts do identify some specific variables—characteristics of municipalities—that they argue affect the adoption of reforms, their major story concerns the way in which the effects of variables are modified by the changing state of the organizational field. Specifically, their analysis argues that in its early stages reform adoption was determined by municipal characteristics related to need or demand whereas later, as the reforms became more widely institutionalized, cities adopted civil service mechanisms irrespective of need. Questions remain, however, concerning whether the argument is supported, because it is possible that a different set of city characteristics may have determined adoption in later stages.

Although, as already noted, organizational analysts have not been centrally involved in developing variance theory approaches to explain the origins of new institutional forms at the field level, they have recently begun to address this topic using process approaches (category 10). DiMaggio (1988) relishes the question of institutional origins because, in his view, it offers the hope of bringing "agency" (actors intentionally pursuing interests) back into institutional analysis:

> New institutions arise when organized actors with sufficient resources *(institutional entrepreneurs)* see in them an opportunity to realize interests that they value highly. The creation of new legitimate organizational forms—such as the corporation, savings and loan associations, advertising agencies, universities, hospitals, or art museums—requires an *institutionalization project.* (p. 14)

DiMaggio has been engaged in a study of one such project. He is examining the forces that have shaped the institutional infrastructure created to support an organizational base for high culture in 19th-century Boston (see DiMaggio, 1982, 1991). He argues that a coalition of upperclass individuals created a cognitive framework by which they could distinguish vulgar from high art and established a set of nonprofit enterprises under their control by which they could exhibit and conserve their cultural capital.

Fligstein (1990) adopts a broadly similar perspective in his recent study of the changing structure of industrial corporations in the United States during the past century. He argues that managers and entrepreneurs in the most powerful firms together with agents of the state establish the rules governing behavior within an organizational field. The state plays a key role in defining the legal context within which powerful economic interests must be played out. A stable set of interorganizational relations and associated firm strategies under one regime can be quickly undermined by the promulgation of new rules. As an important instance of such a change in rules, Fligstein (1990, chap. 6) provides a detailed analysis of the political factors giving rise to the Celler-Kefauver Act, enacted in 1950, and then traces its effects on subsequent merger and acquisition strategies.

A rather different scenario of institutional generation by macro agents is described by Westney (1987), who examined events leading to the introduction into Japan during the Meiji period of three new organizational models—for the police, the postal system, and newspapers. As an important vehicle of their modernization project, Japanese officials during the 1860s undertook a careful survey of existing Western practices, explicitly searching out and adopting the "best" organizational models for each population of organizations. Westney describes the basis on which each model was selected as well as the process by which it was adapted to fit distinctive features of the Japanese scene. Her analysis uncovers a subtle combination of institutional "imitation and innovation" processes. Also, her arguments give much less emphasis to interests and power processes and more to the role played by status value and prestige in motivating the adoption of new models. (For an elaboration of this type of argument, see Meyer & Scott, 1992, and Chapter 5 of this volume.)

As a final example of studies of the creation of new institutions at the sector level, interesting and promising studies have recently been conducted of the emergence of new industries. Such studies trace efforts to establish governance structures and procedures for the overall industry and to secure legitimacy and support from other industry and political systems (see Leblebici, Salancik, Copay, & King, 1991; Van de Ven & Garud, 1989).

The approach of all these analysts, although differing in some respects, is similar in the emphasis placed on detailed historical analysis. The institutional project is seen as working itself out through time and as being shaped by particular interests and events as well as by timing, coincidence, and circumstance. Although I believe that much is to be learned from historical inquiry, it is important to recognize that all of these studies are examples of less formalized process theories: They remain at the stage-naming and event-recounting stage and provide descriptions rather than explanations of the generation of new forms.

Category 11 contains studies dealing with process studies of the diffusion of institutional forms at the societal level. An example of research of this type is provided by Cole's (1985, 1989) study comparing differences in the nature and prevalence of small group activities, such as quality circles, within organizations in Japan, Sweden, and the United States. Cole argues that such activities diffused much more widely in Japan than in Sweden, and in Sweden than in the United States because of differences in governmental posture, managerial mobilization activities, and union orientation. Varying national infrastructures representing differing macropolitical alignments are argued to affect the adoption and persistence of new forms of work-group structure.

The final category (category 12) contains process studies of the creation of new institutional forms at the societal level. Of course, in one sense, almost every conventional history focusing on developments in the institutional structure of one or more societies is eligible for inclusion in this category. However, I restrict attention to examples where analysts have examined such developments in order to draw explicit implications for the structuring of organizational populations. An excellent example is provided by Skowronek's (1982) history of the development of the administrative capacities of the American nation-state at the turn of the century. Skowronek describes changes in the domestic economy and foreign challenges that gave rise to the civil service system, the professionalization of the army, and the emergence of regulatory agencies. His analysis is keenly sensitive to the constraints on new institutional arrangements imposed by existing structures. Crises and challenges generate demands, but these demands are expressed through existing channels and must be interpreted by incumbent officials, so that the new state institutions are conditioned by the old: "In the final analysis, the new American state was extorted from institutional struggles rooted in the peculiar structure of the old regime and mediated by shifts in electoral politics" (Skowronek, 1982, p. 13).

An analysis of more recent changes in the institutional structure of the U.S. state is provided by Baron, Dobbin, and Jennings (1986) in their study of the evolution of personnel administration in industry. They examine the role of three key constituencies in shaping modern systems of work force control—labor unions, personnel professionals, and the nation-state—concluding that it was the efforts of the latter that had the greatest impact at midcentury. They argue that

> government agencies fostered a widespread diffusion of personnel innovations during World War II by mandating specific models of employment, by providing incentives for organizations to create or expand personnel departments and bureaucratic controls, and by providing a set of overarching interests that prompted labor-management accommodation. (p. 378)

As with Skowronek's argument, Baron and colleagues emphasize "the role of crises in institutional change" (1986, p. 378) but equally insist on what

March and Olsen (1984, p. 741) term "the causal complexity of political history." Crises may shake or topple the old institutional order, but the shape of the new is neither easy to predict nor entirely free of the subsoil in which the old order was rooted.

CONCLUDING COMMENTS ON THE CATEGORY SCHEMA

The foregoing typology is, I believe, useful in several respects. First, as emphasized, it employs rather commonplace distinctions to illuminate the considerable diversity that exists in institutional arguments relevant to organizations. Studies that seek to explain why institutionalized features emerge are quite different from those that seek to understand what effects these features have or how they are reproduced over space and time. Also, I think it is helpful to be reminded about the increasingly wide scope of "organizational" research, which encompasses research ranging from the examination of intraorganizational processes through studies of the emergence and structuring of organizational fields to those that attend to the development of institutional structures at the societal level on to analyses of the evolving structure of the world system.

Second, the typology emphasizes that all of the theory and research relevant to institutional studies of organizations have not been and need not be carried out by organizational researchers. We can and should accept with gratitude the assistance rendered by our colleagues as they attempt to explain differences in the political economies of societies and their industry or sector structures across space and over time.

But, third, to be rendered profitable for organization theory, we do need to appropriate and adapt the work of these macro social scientists, linking them with theoretical arguments to organizational variables. This work is just underway; much remains to be done, and if the typology encourages efforts in these areas, it will have served its purpose.

Although the proposed typology may resolve some disputes and clarify some issues, it also distorts some central ideas associated with institutional analysis and raises new issues. I conclude by recording—not resolving— three such issues.

Persisting Issues in Institutional Analysis

CONCERNS WITH THE LEVELS DISTINCTION

The notion of social units existing at varying "levels" of the social structure is a familiar one common to many types of social analysis. It has been used here to demonstrate the wide range of social phenomena encompassed by contemporary institutional researchers. However, a serious drawback to the levels metaphor is that it obscures a central insight associated with the institutional persuasion.

An institutional perspective encourages us to take the symbolic world seriously. According to some thoughtful theorists, such as D'Andrade (1986, p. 22), this penchant can have profound implications, shifting our scientific ground from a "hard" or natural science to a semiotic science base. The semiotic sciences consist of "those fields that study 'imposed' order based on 'meaning' rather than on natural or physical order." In particular, although a more physical model of the world emphasizes a set of elements, with their measurable properties, that can interact with one another and develop various types of relations, the

semiotic-social science world view, on the other hand, sees a complex generation of meanings and symbols that serve to structure social action. *The causes operate primarily, not across institutions, but within the human mind.* (D'Andrade, 1986, p. 25; emphasis added)

This conception challenges the assumption of independent and distinct levels of social phenomena. The cultural environment is not "out there" but, in D'Andrade's phrase, within the human mind of the organizational participant. Thus it is oversimplifying, if not misleading, to describe organizations or their participants as if they were independent of institutional systems operating in the wider environment. Cultural rules define— they create—social entities, whose existence is not as unassailable and whose boundaries are not as solid as they appear to the naive observer.

To be sure, rules can be more or less encompassing—they differ in their jurisdiction—and, in this sense, exist at different levels. But the levels thus created are more like Chinese boxes—the smaller being contained within the larger—than they are like children's blocks. Moreover, the Chinese boxes are porous so that it is frequently impossible to say that a given element—whether actor or idea—is in one system rather than another, because it is in both. The mechanical metaphor of levels is misleading. Institutional environments are in organizations and inside individuals. How can our causal arguments and our statistical methods accommodate this more complex version of interdependence?

ISSUES OF CAUSATION

Because of its emphasis on the centrality of symbolic systems, the institutional perspective also challenges the natural-science conception of causation. Natural science views the socioeconomic world as an object, a thing with interrelated parts (D'Andrade, 1986). Social entities are seen as interacting and as engaged in exchanges. If norms or rule systems are evoked, the emphasis is on what Searle has termed *regulative* rules. Regulative rules specify relations between antecedently or independently existing forms of behavior; for example, rules of etiquette regulate interpersonal relationships that exist independently of the rules (Searle, 1969, p. 33).

The regulative view of rules assumes the existence and capacities of the units to which they apply and then focuses on exchanges among those units: exchanges of demands, resources, sanctions. Much of the theoretical and empirical research on institutions correctly focuses on regulative agencies, such as professional associations or components of the state, which exercise legitimate powers to formulate and enforce rule systems: laws, regulations, practice standards (see Parts II and III of this volume). Most analyses examine their functions from a regulative vantage point, emphasizing the flow of rewards and sanctions. Such a conception fits easily into the natural science mold.

But, as I have attempted to underscore (see Chapter 3), institutionalists need to give at least equal attention to the effects of *constitutive* rules. "Constitutive rules do not merely regulate, they create or define new forms of behavior" (Searle, 1969, p. 33) and, indeed, new types of social actors (Meyer, Boli, & Thomas, 1987; Chapter 1 in this volume). To cite a striking example: The early church and political bodies and the more recent state legislators and courts that fashioned out of their "rule kit" a new social entity—the limited liability corporation—fundamentally altered the course of social development (see Coleman, 1974; Seavoy, 1982).

To focus on constitutive rules is to emphasize the cognitive aspects of symbolic systems. And cognitive effects are not easily assimilated into our conventional models of causation. Cognitive effects occur "within the human mind": They change how actors see the world and themselves and in so doing change the possibilities of social action. Meyer, Boli, and Thomas (1987, p. 22; Chapter 1 in this volume) spell out the implications of this view for causation:

> Institutionalized roles, located in the legal, social scientific, customary,
> linguistic, epistemological, and other "cultural" foundations of society, render
> the relation between actors and action more socially tautological than causal.
> Actors enact as much as they act: What they do is inherent in the social
> definition of the actor itself. Consequently, rules constituting actors legitimate
> types of action, and legitimated action constitutes and shapes the social actors.

That "teachers engage in instruction" or that "venture capitalists are more likely to enter into risky financial transactions" does not seem to be proper causal assertions, although it is clearly the case that knowing what an actor is helps us greatly to understand and predict what that actor will do. The use of such arguments, however, is inconsistent with the more conventional models of scientific causation and requires us to reexamine the assumptions that underlie our attempts to provide explanations for how and why things happen.

RELATING VARIANCE AND PROCESS APPROACHES

A third and final issue raised by the typologies presented concerns the relation between variance and process conceptions of institutionalization. At least under some circumstances, we observe that the operation of institutionalization processes acts to undermine variance-based predictions. In cases where belief systems are increasingly institutionalized and diffused through the organizational population, factors originally predicting such beliefs lose their power. The research by Tolbert and Zucker (1983) of municipal characteristics predicting the adoption of civil service reforms and by Fligstein (1985) of corporate characteristics associated with the adoption of multidivisional structures illustrates this effect. The power of organization-specific variables to predict differences in the adoption of new structures was diminished over time. This suggests that the appropriateness and efficacy of variance theory studies vary, depending on the state of the system, the stage of development of the institutionalization processes (see Scott & Meyer, 1991; Chapter 11 in this volume). There is another important sense in which variance and process models interact. A primary insight associated with process theory is the recognition that how a sequence of actions develops can profoundly influence what transpires: the result or outcome observed. Recent work exploring the utility of path-dependent models provides one approach to analyzing the effects of process on end states (see David, 1988; Tushman & Anderson, 1986).

Note

1. Zucker (1987) proposes a similar distinction in her review article on institutionalization. However, she equates—mistakenly, in my view—organization-level studies with a focus on the question of institutional generation and environment-level studies with a focus on "reproduction"; that is, she does not differentiate between the organization-environment distinction and the generation-reproduction distinction. This confusion is a source of much mischief in institutional analysis.

5

Institutional Conditions for Diffusion

DAVID STRANG

JOHN W. MEYER

MUCH SOCIAL SCIENTIFIC INQUIRY seeks to specify the conditions and mechanisms underpinning the flow of social practices among actors within some larger system. Sociology, anthropology, geography, economics, advertising and market research, and communication studies all have rich traditions of diffusion research (see Rogers, 1983, for a general review). Virtually everything seems to diffuse: rumors, prescription practices, boiling drinking water, totems, hybrid corn, job classification systems, organizational structures, church attendance, national sovereignty. Whether viewed as a ubiquitous hindrance to functional analysis (Naroll, 1965), the deposited trace of social structure (Burt, 1987), or a fundamental source of social control and change (Skog, 1986), diffusion seems critical to social analysis.

Most sociological analysis treats diffusion as a primarily, or even exclusively, relational phenomenon. When diffusing practices are rich in social and cultural meaning, however, simple connectedness seems an insufficient explanatory principle. Our aim is to suggest how institutional conditions operating in wider social systems affect the rate and form of diffusion. We argue that diffusion may be importantly shaped and accelerated by culturally theorized understandings of the nature of social actors and of diffusing practices. The institutional conditions promoting diffusion

---

The authors have made equal contributions to this chapter. We would like to thank Ronald Jepperson and Marc Ventresca for their helpful comments.

may be especially rife in "modern" social systems, and may account for the intimate connections between social scientific interest in diffusion and its empirical prevalence.

PREVAILING THEORY AND ITS WEAKNESSES

Sociologists tend to be committed to a perspective of sociological realism, within which social units (often seen as purposive, rational "actors") and their relationships are reified as ontological givens, and as exhausting the meaning of the social.[1] This has produced lines of explanation and empirical research focusing on the relational aspects of diffusion.

Flows are expected to vary with rates of interaction within a population. When the diffusion process is socially meaningless, as in the spread of measles, physical contact may be all that is required for transmission to occur. When adoptions are socially meaningful acts, it is common to think of actors as making different choices cognitively available to each other, developing shared understandings, and exploring the consequences of innovation through each other's experience.

Exchange dependence is thought to further increase flows of elements. Narrowly, common conventions or protocols seem needed at the boundaries where exchange occurs. Handshaking arrangements aid in interpersonal (and electronic) exchange, and common accounting systems in interorganizational exchange. More broadly, similarities in internal structure may arise from transactions. The fact that graduates flow from secondary to tertiary educational organizations promotes common definitions of students, subjects, and grading, and the values arising from the exchange may homogenize internal structures too.

Theories of diffusion often emphasize the rationalities involved. DiMaggio and Powell (1983) argue that imitation becomes a reasonable decision-making strategy when uncertainty about means-ends relationships prevents actors from calculating optimal arrangements. Inkenberry (1989) suggests that diffusion is especially likely in the wake of crisis or dramatic failure. And economists note the powerful advantages of isomorphism under increasing returns to scale (Arthur, 1983). Businesses benefit when they buy the kinds of typewriters that secretaries have been trained with, and typewriting schools benefit when they train secretaries to use the kinds of keyboards that businesses own (David, 1985).

Sociological realism, with its focus on actors and relationships, has generated much useful diffusion research. Coleman, Katz, and Menzel's (1966) work on the prescription of tetracycline is the classic study in this tradition. Coleman et al. demonstrated the relational basis of diffusion by noting differences in the temporal dynamics of diffusion of socially integrated and socially isolated doctors. An S-shaped curve of adoptions among socially integrated doctors suggested a contagion process, where physicians learned about and adopted the drug through interaction with other adopters. By contrast, socially isolated physicians adopted the drug at a constant rate, suggesting dependence on sources of information outside the population.

Continuing work on diffusion processes has sought to further specify the relational underpinnings of diffusion. A number of theoretical and empirical analyses treat diffusion as a spatial process, where the probability of transmission is a function of geographical distance (Hagerstrand, 1967; Knoke, 1982; Land, Deane, & Blau, 1991). Others have used diffusion processes to examine social structure, generally conceived as a network of social relations (Burt, 1987; Carley, 1990; Marsden & Podolny, 1990; Strang, 1990, 1991).

Despite the vigor of these lines of research, problems remain. Empirically, many systems witness rapid and unstructured diffusion unpredicted by the above considerations. For example, the modern world system has been observed to exhibit remarkable homogeneity in organizational structures and ideologies. Inkenberry (1989) notes a few of the policies that have diffused internationally—19th-century free trade policy, social Darwinism, Keynesian economic planning, liberal multilateralism, and privatization. Institutions like mass education and social security have spread rapidly among states (Collier & Messick, 1975; Meyer & Hannan, 1979), and even national sovereignty appears to have diffused among colonial dependencies (Strang, 1990). Yet levels of international interaction and interdependence are not self-evidently high, relative to national or local settings.

Similar patterns obtain in the American polity. Flows in educational practices among American states are high, despite a weak federal role and little obvious interdependence. Most prominently, despite the diversity, size, and lack of centralization of American society, commentators have for two centuries noted the homogeneity in character of American individuals and organization. Tocqueville, as we will note, had useful ideas to add to sociological realism.

The theoretical problem is that diffusion processes often look more like complex exercises in the social construction of identity than like the mechanical spread of information. Granted, interaction can increase solidarity and similarity; it can also increase conflict and boundary formation. And while exchange can create some small boundary isomorphisms (e.g., trading roles and languages), it can also generate cultural divisions of labor of great stability (Barth, 1969; Cohen, 1969). Purely relational considerations seem inadequate to determine the effects of interaction and interdependence.

We need, at minimum, to formulate the wider conditions under which expanded social relationships lead to rapid diffusion. In doing so, we call attention to a class of quite distinct factors that may act to increase the flow of social material.

Factors Affecting Diffusion

PERCEIVED SIMILARITY

We begin with the observation that flows are increased where the actors involved are perceived as similar (by themselves, and others, and within social institutions more generally). Most obviously, perceptions of similarity provide a rationale for diffusion. They make it sensible for an actor to use another's choices and the consequences of those choices as a guide. Perceived similarity may also enhance rates of diffusion in less rational ways, as actors find themselves enmeshed in the effort of "keeping up with the Joneses."

Rapid diffusion within the world system thus seems grounded in the way contemporary nation-states are culturally constructed as formally equivalent. States subscribe to remarkably similar purposes—economic growth, social equality, political and social rights. States are also understood as possessing identical legal and political rights—doctrines of internal jurisdiction and external freedom of action apply equally to microstates and superpowers. And while these cultural definitions are frequently violated, they provide fertile ground for the rapid diffusion of public policies and institutional structures. Consider how much diffusion would be slowed if states were seen as wholly primordial, or occupied differentiated positions within a hierarchical structure, or inhabited entirely different moral and political universes.

In the same way, the construction of formal organizations under schemes defining them as similar produces rapid diffusion (DiMaggio & Powell, 1983; Meyer & Rowan, 1977). Small software firms become likely to emulate IBM, Hewlett-Packard, or Apple in management forms and organizational culture. It becomes insightful for organizational analysts and consultants to provide recipes for successful management based upon the experiences of a few innovators, with little concern for differences across industry, market position, or historical background. Consider how wrongheaded such recipes would seem in the absence of generalized notions of "organization."

Social scientific researchers are of course part of the cultural system in question, and share in common understandings about the nature of the actors they study. Assumptions of similarity are thus built into almost all diffusion research. Where researchers study diffusion—that is, where they assume actors are not only connected but also ultimately similar—flows between actors are in fact more likely to occur.

Similarity and connectedness are not perfectly correlated, however. The pervasiveness of perceived similarity in modern systems means that diffusion is often less structured by interaction and interdependence than expected. Practices diffuse along the lines of social relations, but also to other actors broadly considered similar. American educational researchers, for instance, are often quite depressed about the prospects for authoritative implementation of virtue, but at the same time overwhelmed by the overall faddishness of the system.

More sophisticated relational models may capture at least some of these effects. Burt (1987) and Galaskiewicz and Burt (1991) examine diffusion between actors in structurally equivalent positions—that is, between actors who have similar relations to other population members. They find that diffusion between such actors is more rapid than diffusion among directly connected actors. Here, interaction and exchange are replaced as conduits of diffusion by a rather abstract and subtle form of perceived similarity.

THE THEORIZATION OF ADOPTERS

A process of cultural theorization underlies perceived similarity and its impact on diffusion. By theorization we mean both the development and specification of abstract categories, and the formulation of patterned relationships such as chains of cause and effect. Without such general models, the question of similarity is unlikely to arise and gain force. And without such models, the real diversity of social life is likely to seem as meaningful as are parallelisms. Both points are central to the work of Mead (e.g., 1934).

In part, theorization increases perceived similarity by simplifying the phenomena. Even complex theoretical constructs like Weber's ideal-typical bureaucracy are extreme simplifications when compared to the richness of the real world. Armed with the notion of bureaucracy, observers and participants are in a strong position to identify many 'apparently' distinctive organizations as having much in common. And as organizational practices and structures are simplified and generalized, they can be more easily appropriated.

Theorization also expands diffusion by providing causal accounts. Many theoretical models are effectively functional, providing explanations of why all sorts of components are necessary to each other and to actor and collective goals. This adds to available rationales for flows. Modern education, for instance, is not only prestigious in its own right, but also modeled as crucial to all sorts of other virtuous features of society (e.g., economic development, the realization of human potential, and political integration).

To some extent, it is possible to imagine theorization emerging directly out of local interaction. As noted above, contact and discussion between socially engaged individuals can produce shared cognitions that spur joint adoption. They presumably also produce cognitions about the similarity of the interacting parties, facilitating diffusion between them.

But perceptions of similarity generally rest on broader understandings imported into local situations. Interaction gives rise to expanded perceptions of similarity when such perceptions make sense within the larger social context. For example, the fact that laymen generally fail to influence the prescription patterns of physicians is not due to low levels of interaction between laymen and doctors. Instead, the knowledge that only doctors can usefully and legitimately influence other doctors is built into the legal and occupational structure of medicine.

The sciences and the professions promote diffusion by expanding the opportunities for perceiving similarity. Our usage of the term *theorization* is broader than social scientific theories as social scientists themselves understand them (including, for example, the social and legal construction of an occupation like medicine). But the sciences and professions are highly legitimated, well funded, massive activities devoted to the theorization of human activity in terms of standard categories.

The importance of theorization in diffusion processes has a dramatic empirical consequence. Where prevailing theories are firmly grounded, perceived similarities may be constructed despite substantial differences in actual social conditions. In such cases, social rules and practices are likely to flow in ways often judged to be unrealistic or maladaptive. In American society, even individuals of extremely marginal status often acquire the standard stances and aspirations of citizenship. And organizations such as schools adopt standard forms despite wide variation in resources and constituencies (Meyer & Rowan, 1977, 1978). A striking feature of many social systems penetrated by theorization is ritualized isomorphism.

THE THEORIZATION OF DIFFUSING PRACTICES

If flows are more rapid when units are theorized as similar, so also the actual social elements that flow are creatures of theorization. A theory of a social form emphasizes certain features as central and relevant, while treating others as variable, or unnecessary, or derivative. The social elements marked as theoretically relevant are then privileged candidates for diffusion.

To illustrate, consider the interplay of organizations and theories about organizations. A tradition of research (March & Simon, 1958; Simon, 1957) and professional practice (in accounting and managerial science) conceptualizes organizations as information-processing and decision-making systems. Many proposals for organizational structure and practice are inspired by this theorization. Strategic planning schemes, information-gathering and processing technologies, and organizational structures designed to combat bounded rationality flow rapidly.

On the other hand, theories conceptualizing organizations as collections of individuals engaged in cooperative interdependent action privilege alternative kinds of flows. Small armies of human relations and resources consultants, industrial psychologists, and personnel specialists suggest organizational reforms. Job enlargement, job rotation, suggestion boxes, and quality circles diffuse.

THEORIZATION AS A DIFFUSION MECHANISM

Finally, theorization enters not only as a property of the diffusing practice, but also as a property of the diffusion process itself. Theorists are often the central conduits of diffusion, moving practices from one location to another. For example, Keynesian fiscal policy may be described as having flowed from London to Washington via the Harvard economics department. More abstractly, we can describe theorization itself as the diffusion mechanism, and see Keynes's general economic theory as the vehicle through which particular fiscal policies were able to move from Britain to the United States.[2]

Under these conditions, we suppose that what flows is rarely an exact copy of some practice existing elsewhere. When theorists are the carriers of the practice or theorization itself is the diffusion mechanism, it is the theoretical model that is likely to flow. Such models are neither complete nor unbiased depictions of existing practices. Instead, theoretical models systematically capture some features of existing practices and not others, or even fundamentally revise the practice altogether.

For example, the peculiar organization of American education (the absence of unified national authority, considerable local autonomy, and the PTA) is less copied around the world than are abstract models of an expanded, unified curriculum and mission. Individuals in liberal societies take on abstracted models of the theorized individual (in forming standard opinions and ideas about political efficacy) as much as concrete properties individually observed (Jepperson, 1991). New nation-states adopt organizational forms built up and legitimated as models in the world society and organizational system (McNeely, 1989). They embellish upon existing models rather than mimic extant forms, so over time more and more individual rights and state powers are written into constitutions (Boli, 1987a).

In extreme circumstances, innovation masquerades as diffusion. It is a common theoretical gambit to claim that the elements proposed for diffusion are actually found somewhere. Modern organizational innovators often present their ideal models as devolved from Japanese practices, while in previous decades American locales were often the supposed sources of organizational innovations in the Third World. Yet the source may be better identified as the theorist.

MODERNITY AND DIFFUSION

By the above logic, flows should be most rapid where theorization is central to the construction of both units and specific elements, where partial theorizations articulate with each other, and where a network of congruent theories forms a hegemonic cultural frame. The outstanding instance of this in the contemporary world is modernity itself. A core substantive point in our argument is thus that the more social units are constructed and legitimated as modern entities, the more social materials flow among them.

At the level of the world system, the more that societies are organized as nation-states (and not as "primordial" religious or ethnic groups), the more social structures diffuse among them. Within nation-states, the more social organizations are constructed as rationalized formal organizations, the more they become isomorphic with each other and with the rules of both nation-states and world society. And at the individual level, the rise of expanded and unified notions of citizenship, capacity, and moral worth (in a word, the construction of personal "actorhood") leads individuals to rapidly adopt attitudes and practices from each other, and from national and world centers (Jepperson, 1991).

A specification of the conventional meanings of "modernity" makes the logic of this situation clearer. *Modernity* generally refers to the rise of standard models of society and the nation-state as rationally organized around notions of progress and justice, as built up of rationalized organizations and associations, and as composed of autonomous, rational, and purposive individual citizens. And it refers to the rise of these models as integrated systems, so that collective goods are enhanced by individual and organizational progress and contribute to such progress.

Analyses from a modern point of view can call attention to dissimilarities across local contexts, and hence to differing strategies appropriate to each. But in a more basic sense such analyses are a powerful force for homogenization. Modern theories advocate a more universalistic moral order, a more scientific and standardized analysis of nature and means-ends relationships, and a more ahistorical view of human nature and human society. The construction of actors around these notions makes them more similar, and in easily perceived and communicated ways.

From this point of view, the rapidity of flows among contemporary social actors becomes comprehensible. After all, they have the same legitimate purposes, so they are susceptible to the same social demands. They depend on the same technologies legitimated on the same grounds, so flows of improved techniques can be rapid and little constrained by traditional loyalties. And they have the same relatively scientific conceptions of basic resources, remarkably similar definitions of human nature, collective authority, and social control, permitting "innovations" in these areas to flow rapidly (Boli, 1987a).

But the impact of modern ways of organizing the social world seems to go beyond the standardizing effects that any dominant theoretical framework might provide. Modern perspectives locate much value and responsibility in social "actors," both individual human beings and purposive rationalized organizations. The sovereignty and the competence of these actors is celebrated. Social structures (the market economy and liberal polity) are shown to be optimal, given the self-interested action of autonomous actors.

The cultural construction of empowered actors carrying ultimate values seems especially favorable for diffusion. Such actors are assumed to have the capacity to innovate and reform; they also have the moral duty to do so. And as highly valued entities, actors can sensibly look to one another as models for their action. In the more liberal, more egalitarian, and more reductionist versions of modernity, actors are powerfully "motivated" to copy each other and identify with collective standards. This, in fact, was Tocqueville's argument about the homogeneity of individuals and groups within the American polity.

The core idea here also suggests a basic proposition about the kinds of rules and practices that are most likely to flow rapidly. Rules and practices most tightly integrated with prevailing theories of the modern are most likely to diffuse. Thus a mechanism to enhance the equality or the productivity of the handicapped will flow more readily than one justified by less modern standards of charity. A scientifically legitimated technology will flow more than a customary or traditional one. And a practice requiring standardized resources (e.g., public funds) will flow more than one relying on less modern commitments of individuals or groups.

The sciences and the professions are of the greatest importance. They are devices for turning social rules and practices from local and parochial ones into universally applicable principles that can "rationally" be adopted by all sorts of superordinate authorities, implemented by subordinate ones, and copied by modern (and thus intrinsically "similar") units everywhere. As social rules and practices come under scientific and professional analysis, they become potential candidates for rapid diffusion in the modern system.

For instance, it is clear that modern arrangements of mass education have flowed very rapidly around the modern world system. These flows have been more rapid in the post-World War II period, in which both the political and economic benefits have been scientifically defined and elaborated (Meyer, Ramirez, & Soysal, 1992). Education is prestigious, is thought functional for all sorts of goods, and is seen as both individually and collectively beneficial. Everyone, now, has highly legitimate reasons to pursue educational expansion.

Diffusion research is built fundamentally around assumptions of modernity. It nearly always investigates the spread of "innovations": boiled drinking water, more productive agricultural inputs, new prescription drugs. In the anthropological tradition, those accepting modern practices are often distinctively nonmodern. But in sociology, not only the diffusing practice but also the adopters are modern.

The modernity of both practices and adopters is so pervasive in sociological diffusion research that its consequences are generally ignored. But the cultural match between practice and adopter may have substantial effects on the pattern of diffusion. For example, Marsh and Coleman (1956) found that centrally placed farmers within progress-oriented communities are early adopters of new practices, while they are not particularly quick adopters where community values are opposed to innovation. Becker (1970) showed that items with "high adoption potential" (defined in terms of the attractiveness and communicability of the innovation for professionals) were adopted early by centrally placed actors, while items with "low adoption potential" were adopted early by social isolates.

In both cases, the researchers connected their findings to the social meaning of the diffusing items and the adopters. Where adoption is highly prestigious, because the practice is obviously modern and the community values modernity highly, relationally central actors initiate adoption. Where the practice is less obviously modern or the community disvalues modernity, it will be the "marginal men," those relatively unconstrained by community norms, that adopt early. Clearly, the predictions of simple relational models will go astray if they are not made conditional on the larger cultural context.[3]

Analytic Strategies

Several research strategies seem useful in empirically examining the ideas discussed above.

Specify Relational Models

Conventional interpretations of diffusion depend on notions of communication opportunities, solidarity, and interdependence. Standard approaches in diffusion research do not take advantage of such concrete linkages to specify "diffusion channels." Instead, the aggregate time path of adoption is modeled assuming homogeneous mixing, where transmission probabilities are equal for each pair within a population (see Bartholomew, 1982, for an extended review).

Recent sociological analyses examine hypotheses about the social structures relevant to diffusion. In particular, Strang and Tuma (1990), Strang (1991), and Marsden and Podolny (1990) develop diffusion models within an event history framework, where adoption rates are a function of previous adoptions by connected actors and exogenous covariates.

These analytic advances can be employed to test how well network relations structure the timing of adoption. We may then wish to ascribe some portion of the residual variation to the impact of the sorts of cultural processes discussed in this chapter. For instance, notions of a larger "world polity" gain plausibility when it can be shown that the crossnational expansion of mass education seems unrelated to exogenous factors like level of economic development and unmediated by linkages such as those connecting metropoles and former colonies (Meyer, Ramirez, & Soysal, 1992).

This research strategy is fairly weak, because residual variation is employed as evidence for an argument of central interest. It is always possible that structures of interaction or interdependence are poorly specified. Positive evidence would be more persuasive.

Specify Theorized Similarity

A second strategy, which is methodologically a variant of the first, provides such evidence. Theorized similarities can be measured explicitly, and treated as a particular kind of channel of diffusion, methodologically playing the same role as interaction or interdependence in the models above. For example, in seeking to understand the diffusion of educational systems, we could distinguish between societies organized as recognized nation-states and societies regarded as outside state society.[4] It would then be possible to examine the impact of social definitions on diffusion in a more positive vein.

Examine Variation Among Populations

A third strategy takes a somewhat different tack. One can compare diffusion across different populations, where the population as an aggregate is measured in terms of interaction, interdependence, and socially constituted or theorized similarity. Marsh and Coleman's (1956) analysis of diffusion in progressive and traditional farming communities is one example of this sort of study. In general, it becomes possible to examine the degree to which the rate of diffusion, or other aggregate characteristics of the diffusion process, are functions of both relational and cultural characteristics of the population.

Examine Variation Among Diffusing Practices

A fourth strategy follows Becker (1970) by comparing the diffusion of different kinds of practices across the same population, contrasting more and less "modern" practices, or more and less theoretically privileged practices. One could also study practices before and after they became understood as "modern" (see Tolbert & Zucker, 1983).

Examine the Content of Diffusion

An alternative approach is to examine the content of adopted practices, rather then the timing of adoption. Content analyses of diffusing policies would permit insight into who is copying whom within the population.[5] They can also provide evidence for theoretically mediated diffusion, if adopted practices closely resemble theoretical models. In such cases, the overall level of variability in adoptions should be relatively low, and "transmission errors" should not cumulate over time. Along the lines suggested above, such analyses could draw comparisons between different populations or different diffusing practices.

Conclusion

We have argued that the flows of social elements among units in a wider system are enhanced by their perceived and theorized similarity, by the rise of theorized models of social elements which make them more relevant for diffusion, and thus by the rise of universalized and integrated models of the "modern." We see such cultural factors as adding to purely relational understandings of diffusion, and as suggesting a range of empirical analyses among individuals, organizations, and nation-states.

These arguments give importance to legal, and especially professional and scientific, cultural materials. These forms of theorization, and their rise to dominance in the modern world, greatly speed diffusion of rules and practices. They define or construct social units as comparable, and theorize the universal and beneficial relevance of new and otherwise alien social materials. Both by reconstituting units and by redefining social elements, modern theorization greatly expands the motives and rationales for society-wide and worldwide standardization. As these forms of theorizing penetrate more and more aspects of society (from agricultural extension services to educational innovations to the rights of wives and children), standardizing flows increase.

We moderns tend to treat homogeneity as natural. But in many previous social worlds, distinct social and organizational arrangements were retained over long periods despite considerable rates of interaction and interdependence. The change involved is not simply in interaction and interdependence rates, but also in culture.

Notes

1. In this chapter we too adopt the terminology of social "actors" (which may be individuals, organizations, or other collective entities). This is a metaphorical device, and is not meant to minimize the aspects of the process that do not seem well described as choice. For example, much of our argument can be fruitfully applied to implementation (flows among hierarchically placed units) as well as diffusion (flows among formally autonomous units).

2. We refer to this particular historical case for purely illustrative purposes. There is considerable scholarly debate over the relationship between academic theorizing, state structures, and policy initiatives in the case of Keynesian fiscal policy. For a pointed discussion somewhat at odds with our general perspective, see Weir and Skocpol (1985).

3. Relational models can be repaired by arguing that centrally placed actors in modern communities typically have extensive relations to the outside world, while in nonmodern communities it is the marginal men who have outward-looking relations (Menzel, 1960). But this argument also serves to further demonstrate the distinctiveness of modernity (i.e., why are these network structures different?).

4. Historically, most non-Western societies were seen as outside "international" society. Taiwan, South Africa, and Palestine occupy something of the same status today.

5. In exploring diffusion patterns among the states, Jack Walker (1969) quotes the observation that the California Fair Trade law was "followed either verbatim or with minor variations by twenty states; in fact, ten states copied two serious typographical errors in the original California law."

II. INSTITUTIONAL ENVIRONMENTS AND ORGANIZATIONAL COMPLEXITY

From the earliest thinking about organizations as somewhat distinctive aspects of social structure, analysts have attempted to account for the existence and elaboration of organizational structure. For most, the emergence of a formal structure—codified rules; designated positions or offices—has been either the defining feature of or a prominent characteristic of these systems. Organization theorists have spent much time and energy attempting to account for the increasing prevalence of formal organization.

Organizations also exhibit considerable diversity in their structural features. Some are tall and highly centralized, others flat and decentralized. Some develop disproportionately large and top-heavy administrative components; others appear relatively lean with modest resources devoted to management.

Accounting for the increased amount and for the existing diversity of organizational structures is an ongoing activity to which institutional theorists are making contributions.

More Organizations

A part—a very significant part—of the transformation that social structures have undergone in the last few centuries has to do with the increased prevalence, spread, and scale of formal organizations. There are more formally organized collectivities at every level—at the local and community level; the regional and state level; and the national, transnational, and international level. Interests that once were represented only informally and episodically are likely to give rise to more enduring, special-purpose organizations. A wider range of purposes and activities becomes legitimate grounds for organizing: child care; leisure activities and recreation; even finding a compatible marriage partner. And organizational forms have increased in scale. Branch offices, franchises, multidivisional and multinational firms, joint ventures, alliances—these are familiar forms supporting and advancing changes in scale.

There have been many efforts to explain the advance of organizations. Early students—from Adam Smith (1957) to Frederick Winslow Taylor (1911)—stressed the centrality of the work being performed: the advantages of dividing tasks in specified ways among participants (creating horizontal differentiation) which then results in creating new kinds of tasks—for example, coordinating, evaluating, hiring, training, and, of course, inventing new and better ways to divide up the original work—or creating vertical differentiation. These themes continue to be stressed in the arguments of contingency theorists, who point to the varying complexity of the work to be done and of the need—in the interests of efficiency—to match differentiation demands with coordination responses (see Galbraith, 1973; Thompson, 1967). Organization grows because it provides a superior basis for designing and coordinating complex tasks.

Related arguments have been developed by agency theorists (Alchian & Demsetz, 1972) and transactions costs economists (Williamson, 1975), who substitute the costs of managing and monitoring exchanges for those of managing the various factors of production.

Blau and colleagues (Blau, 1970; Blau & Schoenherr, 1971) stress the importance of increases in scale itself as a source of differentiation and formalization. Organizations may grow for various reasons, but their growth produces increasing complexity and formalization of structure.

Still other theorists have stressed the importance of power processes and political context. Marxists argue that much differentiation of work is not in the service of efficiency but exploitation: Work is simplified to reduce worker control, to foster artificial divisions among the interests of workers, and to create (make) work for managers. More formalized structures are adopted because they serve to depersonalize hierarchical power and to legitimate inequalities of power and monetary returns (Braverman, 1974; Edwards, 1979). Resource dependency theorists use related arguments—but shift attention from power processes within organizations to external power processes—to emphasize the importance of information and resource flows between organizations. Organizations devise more elaborate coordination and control structures—wider and more encompassing organizational structures—to contain and make more predicable critical resource flows (Pfeffer & Salancik, 1978).

All of these arguments have their uses, and each can be used fruitfully to explain some features and facets of organizational expansion. We, however, emphasize a different set of forces and processes. Institutional theory calls attention to the role of wider cultural rules—cognitive and normative frameworks—in stimulating and supporting the growth of formal organizations. Independent of the effects of technological complexity, scale, or interests in increasing dominance or reducing uncertainty, the existence and elaboration of cultural rule systems embodying rational templates acts to advance the spread of organizational forms. Activities—the same activities—conducted under the canopy of a formalized structure conforming to a rational framework will be taken more seriously, will be regarded as more legitimate by both internal and external participants than those carried out using a more traditional or informal structure. And existing organizations that incorporate available rationalized components—accountants, personnel systems, legal representatives—will be more likely to reap the rewards of good opinion and increased confidence from a variety of internal and external constituents. Formal structure signals rationality and thereby increases legitimacy in the views of many different internal and external parties in contemporary society.

In addition to helping to account for the expansion of organizational forms that is so characteristic of modern societal structures, institutional theorists are also attempting to examine how organizational structures are distinctly shaped by institutional forces. How are we to account for the diversity of existing structures? The following chapters propose and evaluate several arguments regarding institutional factors affecting the nature of organizational forms.

Diverse Organizations

AXES OF RATIONALIZATION

We distinguish (in Chapter 6) between two dimensions along which rationalization processes may proceed: (a) causal process, which emphasizes the construction of means-ends chains linking activities; and (b) control systems, which emphasize the construction of systems of status and property relations linking social actors. Although the two processes often proceed hand-in-hand, their relative importance can vary. Systems relying more on the rationalization of causal processes are argued to produce more accountants, and similar types of expertise (engineers, systems designers, operations researchers)—and less formal organizational structure. Rationality is stored in procedural and professional rules rather than in codified control systems linking social actors. At the extreme, procedural controls focusing on activities allow for the construction of "virtual" organizations: organizations lacking formal boundaries, memberships, or other trappings of administrative structure.

An emphasis on rationalization based on the building of control systems linking actors and specifying status and property rights, by contrast, produces more formal organization. Here rationality resides in and is defined and promoted by such specialists as lawyers, managers, and personnel professionals. These and similar actors define and refine organizing recipes and preside over the creation and elaboration of formal organizational structure.

UNIFIED VERSUS FRAGMENTED SOVEREIGNS

Whereas most theories regarding environmental effects on organizations focus on the local or proximate environment, our own emphasis has been on the effects of wider and more distant structures. We have argued (see Meyer & Scott, 1983b; also Chapter 2 in this volume) that the existence of more independent sources of authority or sovereigns promulgating rules or exercising control over an organization—higher levels of fragmentation—will create more complex and elaborated administrative structures in subject organizations than will be the case for organizations operating under unified sovereigns (see Chapters 6, 7, 8, 10). These isomorphic tendencies, in which complex environments become mapped into complex formal organization components, may result from many specific mechanisms, including coercive pressures from the sovereigns, resources provided by them to create linking positions in subject organizations, and mimetic processes (see DiMaggio & Powell, 1983; Scott, 1987a). Administrative structures are particularly likely to be affected, as opposed to core technologies, because these are the boundary-spanning parts of the organization designed to deal with environmental forces.

To the extent that the sovereigns operate somewhat independently and can require different and even conflicting responses, the resulting administrative units of organizations operating in such contexts are likely to be loosely coupled in relation to one another and in relation to other parts of the organization (Meyer & Rowan, 1977; Meyer & Scott, 1983b; Chapters 6 and 7 in this volume). Although such structures depart significantly from textbook models of rational structure, these "bloated," convoluted structures indicate that modern organizations must respond not to one but to many, sometimes conflicting, rationalities; and that these systems are sometimes better viewed as loosely related collections of roles and units whose purposes and procedures come from a variety of external sources, not a unitary internal superior.

FORMAL VERSUS INFORMAL CONSTITUENTS

Whether environmental actors are more local or more distant from an organization, we argue (see Chapter 8) that the more formally organized such actors are, the more likely they are to induce increased formalization in the focal organization. Organizations surrounded by and relating to informal groups and interests are less likely to create new rules and formalized roles than organizations that must deal with formally organized constituencies. Hence formal structure breeds formal structure.

THE LOCI OF FORMAL STRUCTURE

Although we have not developed specific predictions, we are interested in exploring factors accounting for the loci of formal structure: Where in a nested collection of organizations will structural elaboration occur? We explore this question among others in Chapter 7, where we contrast public and private school systems. We observe that in the more complex environments faced by public schools, the principal locus of administrative expansion occurs at the intermediate layers—at the district and state levels rather than at the level of the local school. Because such expansion occurs there, we argue, public schools show lower levels of administrative complexity than private schools of a comparable size. Public schools can be less administratively developed because district offices are more highly developed. In a world in which formal structures are increasingly layered—where federal and state offices oversee local agencies and national and multinational corporations operate regional offices and local establishments—we need, in our thinking and our empirical research, to give more attention to the factors shaping the vertical architecture of organizational structure.

A Concluding Note

Three of the four chapters in this section deal with schools as their empirical base, and the first chapter discusses the role of accounting in organizations. Some would see schools as the "soft underbelly" of organizational life, and even accountants may be viewed as somewhat marginal functionaries in contrast to "real" line managers. It is possible that some will view the processes we discuss as only operating in limited sectors (public, nonmarket) of the economy or restricted sections (staff components) of the organization. Such is not our intent.

We acknowledge that by concentrating much of our empirical work on schools and professional service organizations, we have contributed to the misconception that institutional arguments pertain only or primarily to certain (limited kinds of) organizations. We no doubt inadvertently reinforced this error by distinguishing in our work between "institutional" and "technical" organizations and environments (Meyer & Rowan, 1977; Meyer & Scott, 1983b). Our intent was to differentiate between different bases of regulating organizations—by attention to process versus outcome controls, not to suggest that some organizations operate outside the framework of institutional forces (see Chapter 3).

Fortunately, this misconception is slowly being corrected, as we along with many others (e.g., Fligstein, 1991; Mezias, 1990; Orru, Biggart, & Hamilton, 1991) expand the range of institutional analysis to incorporate the full range of organizations (see Chapters 11, 12, and 13).

6

Social Environments
and Organizational Accounting

JOHN W. MEYER

THIS CHAPTER DEVELOPS HYPOTHESES about the factors affecting the incidence of accountants and accounting work in organizations. Clearly there is much variation. Organizations vary in the amount of accounting work they contain. So, probably, do general types of organizations—at least by reputation, some kinds of organizations are overrun by accountants, while others have relatively few. Such distinctions also characterize whole social sectors or domains, with some industries taking the lead, and others reputed to be backward. National societies differ substantially in the degree to which activities fall into the hands of accountants, or occur under their blessings: The United States is obviously on the high side here. And finally, there is much variation over time: Activities done now may generally require the participation of more accountants than the same activities done decades or centuries ago.

Whether one sees the expansion of accounting activity as progress in rationality or as the expansion of bureaucratic restrictions on life and choice, the phenomenon calls for research. There are a number of ways in which this research could usefully go on. One can envision historical case

This chapter was first presented at the Symposium on the Roles of Accounting in Organizations and Society, University of Wisconsin, 12-14, July, 1984. Work on the chapter was supported by Stanford's Institute for Research on Educational Finance and Governance, with funds from the National Institute of Education. Neither Institute is responsible for the views presented here. I am indebted to my continuing collaboration with W. R. Scott. Some of the ideas here are taken from Meyer and Scott (1983b).

studies and qualitative ones. In the present chapter, we consider lines of thought that could be investigated with rather formal multivariate analyses of the factors affecting the presence of accountants and accounting work, taking advantage for explanatory purposes of the variations in prevalence that exist among organizations, kinds of organizations, institutional sectors, national societies, and time.

Intellectually, such an investigation could start from the classic premises of organizations theory, looking closely at the technical activities of organizations as the central predictors of such organizational phenomena as accounting (see Perrow, 1979, or Scott, 1981, for a review). One would arrive quickly at the argument that the expansion of accounting work reflects the expanded size and differentiation of modern organizations (Blau & Schoenherr, 1971), as a matter of technical necessity. In a version of the same idea more suited to the political language of the left, accounting work arises to maintain a central control in a situation of increasing complexity or differentiation.

More recently, arguments about the origins of organizational structure have stressed the importance of the wider environment as a determinant (Scott, 1981; M. Meyer, 1978). In these lines of work, the amount of accounting done in an organization is less likely to reflect intrinsically necessary technical work processes than environmental constraints, resources, or opportunities. There are two main lines of relevant theorizing about the relation of environments to organizations. One line sees the environment as a structure of power, posing problems with which organizations must deal (e.g., Pfeffer & Salancik, 1978; Zald, 1970, 1984). Accountings and accountants are thus likely to arise in response to the demands made by powerful elements in the environment on which organizations are dependent: Their strength and prevalence vary with environmental variations in the strength of these external elements. In such an explanation, the expansion of accounting in the United States might be taken to reflect the early expansion of capital markets and the dependence of firms on them.

A second line of thinking about the impact of the environment stresses less the power of environmental demands for particular products or exchanges than the power of the environment as a supplier of the cultural materials for organizing. The key notion in this tradition is legitimacy (DiMaggio & Powell, 1983; Meyer & Rowan, 1977; Zucker, 1983). Environments create organizational elements such as accounting and accountants, make it easy and necessary for organizations to use them, and treat organizations that have them as by definition more legitimate than others. In thinking about the emergence of accounting, this tradition might emphasize less the impact of powerful constituencies of organizations than of the state that charters them.

In this chapter, we work mainly from the point of view of this last line of thought on organizational environments. Under what environmental conditions would the accounting profession and its technologies arise and become routine elements of all sorts of organizations? We begin by considering the broadest sort of cultural factors that are involved, and then go on to discuss the conditions under which general cultural rationalization would be channeled into patterns encouraging the development of accounting rather than other potential forms.

Finally, we consider a closely related issue that arises from thinking about environmental determination of organizational structure: The rules of wider environments determine not only what organizations do, but also which organizations can exist at all. In considering accounting, we should consider not only which kinds of organizations have more or less of it, but also what kinds of organizations are made possible (and even necessary) once accounting technologies and professions are institutionalized (Hannan & Freeman, 1977). An environment that creates general rules, an ecological argument might have it, greatly expands the scale of possible organizing. It also lowers the degree of direct hierarchical authority necessary to build up an organization. It may also lower the capacity of small-scale organizations to survive competitively.

A Note on Definition

We proceed from general theoretical discussion on environments and organizations rather than a more specific sociological literature because the latter is little developed. This may be especially true in the United States. In any event, the term *accounts* in the sociological literature refers not to the work of accounting and accountants, but to the verbal explanations actors give of the events going on around them—most especially, of deviant or anomalous events (Scott & Lyman, 1968). The social constructions participants give to such events are called accounts. There seems less awareness that the main stories told—also ones that are highly socially constructed—about organizational life are the tales of accountants (and lawyers). Perhaps the sociologists are too timid to see these too as ideology rather than as a reality to be taken for granted. For whatever reason, the sociology of accounting is little developed. As a result, a sociological definition of accounting work is also undeveloped. For our purposes here, we rely on a commonsense notion of accounting as the set of specialized systems for abstracting the monetary value of stocks and exchanges. By such a definition, aspects of record keeping that become routine parts of social life, practiced by all sorts of actors and in no way tied to a differentiated role, are a distinct phenomenon from specialized accounting.

Cultural Rationalization

A starting point is the classic argument that the rationalization of activity in a cultural setting leads to, and is historically affected by, the spread of countings and accountings (e.g., Weber, 1927). For our purposes here, the important point is to see cultural rationalization in a specific area, an institutional sector, or a society generally as affecting the expansion of accounting work. A number of processes are involved. First, cultural rationalization involves standardization. It thus makes things much easier to count: Data require measures, and measures require some notion of the homogeneity of the units in which they focus. Once rationalization has standardized and tamed the social meaning of the components of activity—actors, objects, and actions—accounting becomes easier. Actors, in the rational system, come in secure categories of varying specificity, but all standardized: persons, workers, assemblers, labor per hour. Objects also become standardized in the rationalized culture, often through scientific activity: One can count shoe production across a whole society, or reserves of iron (in various measured quantities and grades), or reconceptualize unique trees and forests as standing board feet of lumber. Similarly, actions come to be standardized in very detailed notions of work, as when household goods become so many pounds moved so many miles, and carted up so many steps to a third-floor apartment.

A second aspect of rationalization that furthers accounting is the reduction of standardized elements to a common yardstick. Most often, in modern societies, this means monetarization, as when human actors and actions and objects are all reduced to monetary prices. Obviously, the possibilities for accounting are greatly enhanced by such reductions. Aside from money, modern systems create parallel generalized commodities, all of which promote various forms of accounting. In the United States, for instance, all legitimate university instruction can be reduced to credit units (in two variant, but intertranslatable, currencies), which means that all university instruction can be accounted on the same yardstick—thus physics and sociology are integrated in a common value and measurement scheme: The potential of this for furthering accounting work has only partly been realized.

A third aspect of rationalization—related to monetarization—is causal integration, around notions of exchange or production. Once one conceives of a production process integrated around a goal, much accounting becomes possible. One can track activity from initial costs through ultimate gross and net profit. If cultural faith in rationality is strong enough one can do this even when market monetarized value is not available (e.g., through shadow prices of various sorts).

All of this can proceed in very specific social contexts, as particular organizations rationalize activities in their own schemas. Organizations that do this, one can hypothesize, have more accounting work. But the process really goes on at a more general social level than that of the specific organizations. Large-scale social changes institutionalize new patterns of rationalization, which then increase the likelihood that all sorts of parties count and account. Thus the social changes that create the free labor market over several centuries create impulses (and pressures and opportunities) for organizations to count workers, various types of workers, and later labor costs calculated in more and more refined ways. Now even a small and relatively unrationalized specific organization can quickly acquire accountings of labor cost that include the Christmas ham and even pension and sickness and disability costs. Even a very rationalized organization a century or two ago would not have had such possibilities.

Thus beyond rationalization at the level of specific organizations as a causal factor in increasing accounting work, the really important effects result from the rationalization of whole institutional sectors and societies. For instance, recent arenas of rationalization that increase accountings and their prospects include medical care, the psychology of job satisfaction, and air quality. And note that these changes go on at a very general, often worldwide, level (Meyer, 1980). Measures of health care and its costs are growing worldwide, as are assessments of the quality of the environment and various benefits and costs. The general point here is thus that the presence of accounting work in a particular setting is heavily dependent on the much wider environment, not primarily on the local situation itself. Regardless of the interests and tastes of the modern organizer, much rationalization and much accounting is likely to be necessary. The community insists on measures of environmental impact (air quality, water quality, traffic congestion, noise). The national state has rules making necessary the most detailed accounting of workers, and wages, and all sorts of benefits, of safety, and sometimes of production: Much accounting work derives from this source (Baron, Dobbin, & Jennings, 1986; Dobbin, Edelman, Meyer, Scott, & Swidler, 1988). Similarly there are the accounting results of institutional rationalization in the practices of banks and investors (often aided by the modernizing state), of labor unions, and so on. The evolution of accounting goes on at a more macrosociological level than is commonly assumed.

The point deserves special emphasis, because accounting is often discussed as if it were the creation of "real" people facing "real" problems. Invention of this sort goes on, though much aided by cultural encouragement. But even invention often seems to have a somewhat theological character—as much the elaboration of interpretations as the practical steps of the problem solver. This helps to explain why so much of the "best" accounting is rarely put into practice.

We have stressed the impact of cultural rationalization on the expansion of accounting. The causal processes obviously run the other way too—one of Weber's (1930) main themes. Accountings provide impetus to rationalized organizational and cultural settings. A new accounting development tends to liberate all the apparatus of rational organizing: policies, plans, rules, controls, differentiation, professions, and so on. One can see this whole flood of expanded organizational rationality following main changes in countings of the modern period. The creation of the GNP, for instance, has had much impact on the fashionable structure of the state (e.g., economic planning agencies). Similarly, with the rise of unemployment measures, or health cost indices, or environment quality measures. Each makes possible much more rationalized organization.

Counting and Accounting

General processes of rationalization are not coterminous with the rise of an accounting profession. Many forms of rationalized counting are not likely to lead to the institutionalization of such a profession, but are located in other ways. We need to make a distinction between two forms of rationalization—one organized around monetarization and notions of causal process, which are more likely to lead toward accounting expansion; and the other organized around social control or authority, which may generate other sorts of countings.

CONTROL STRUCTURE VERSUS CAUSAL PROCESS

Western rationalization generates (and may result from) the organization of value around two sharply distinct poles, or noncommensurable dimensions. The first is the dimension of causal process, or technology, or means-ends relationships. Rationalization, generalization, and integration on this axis commonly take the form of monetarization, though scientific standardization plays a role too. Thus everything in a local setting, or now a whole society and most of the world, can be conceived to be property with a certain monetary value. It enters into social life as resources and costs. Much human action enters in, analyzed as productive, with a definite value. The products have value too, and now the concept of a GNP or even a world product is given meaning. All together it makes up wealth, and a conception of the total monetarized value of the world is not too difficult to work out. Thus the world can be seen as a web of means-ends relations— a conception now common in the newspapers as well as the social sciences.

But all this is predicated on, and reinforces, a second dimension of rationalized value. Causal analysis requires a theory of existence. The building and institutionalization of the Western rationalization of means-ends relations is accompanied by the construction of a rationalized mapping of the entities that enter into these relations (Berger & Luckmann, 1967). Here we have the scientific reconstruction of the natural world (resources, in the technical scheme) and the legal organization of things as property. We also have the legal and later scientific development of social entities: human individuals, associations, corporations, and the state (MacPherson, 1962). These entities are created, given standardized and countable form, and linked to each other with rules of property and membership. Later, the controls over social entities extend to the construction of detailed occupational and educational categories, and their regulation, so that persons come in many standard types (Ramirez & Boli, 1987; Ramirez & Meyer, 1980). It all amounts to the social construction of reality in a grand control structure.

Both aspects of Western rationalization—the construction of processes and the construction of entities—lead to orgies of counting. On the one side, there is much counting of persons, workers, occupational members, organizations, products, and resources. On the other side, there is the counting of the flows of value from costs and investments to productive value and profits. But the two systems of value are necessarily kept bounded and distinct from each other. Attempts to integrate them seem dangerous and likely to raise ethical questions. Thus one can discuss the worth of a person's estate, but the worth of the person is established in a different frame, and it seems dangerous to talk about whether a person should be born or aborted, live or be terminated, in monetary terms. So also the right of a corporate group to exist is kept somewhat separate from an assessment of its monetary value, and so also with property relations between social and natural objects. Similarly, individual memberships in certified occupational and educational categories are regulated by credentialing social rituals quite apart from productive value (Collins, 1979; Meyer, 1977). And the boundary between social equality (a standardization of the value of persons as entities) and unequal achievements and productive rights is a matter of great social and political tension throughout the modern period.

One side of this dual structure of rationalization seems much more likely to generate and sustain the distinctive forms of counting called *accounting*. This is the monetarized organization of means-ends flow. Despite many efforts, to think the unthinkable and to talk "reasonably" about the value of human life, of a society or ethnic group, or even of mankind, the rationalization of entities in the modern system tends to fall into other hands: the hands of scientists and statisticians and demographers, and beyond these, the hands of lawyers who manage the certification of existence and relation. Even so simple a question as to the relation between one's wealth and one's entitlement to medical life support raises too many questions for comfort.

This point becomes important because Western societies seem to differ in their reliance on the distinct dimensions of rationalization. Thus they differ in their relative reliance on accountants versus lawyers. In general the two forms of modernization go together, but there is variation in the way complexity is introduced. Some institutional systems elaborate more the rationalized theory of existence, with very complex status systems and property rules, in a form of rationalization of a system of control. Others leave this structure simpler, and build more complexity into institutionalized theories of process. American society elaborates both, and generates much work for both accountants and lawyers. One gets the impression that British society generates much more accounting than legal work, while German society generates the opposite. Following this line of reasoning, one could develop a good many testable hypotheses about the prevalence of accounting work.

Over time, rationalization has expanded, worldwide, on both dimensions. In the arena of technical process and monetarization, rationalization has expanded to include health, education, leisure, and some aspects of family life. One interesting change has been the extension of productive reasoning into aspects of human status previously handled by the other value system: the detailed invention associated with the human capital revolution in economics, by which such aspects of persons as education can be assigned productive (rather than status) value (Blaug, 1968, 1969). This has provided a fertile field for accounting work, though the ultimate establishment of a new boundary has not yet been accomplished. The present outlines are fairly clear. Work dissatisfaction, despite many efforts, is not to be counted as a cost, but is to be managed by the market choices of free persons. Education, but not sexual competence or satisfaction, is to be accounted. The key issue, of course, is monetarization, with its two aspects: the secure integration of an element into definite myths of means-ends relations, and the attachment of the element to one or another entity given reality in the value system defining existence.

ORGANIZATION AND ACCOUNTING

As elements of the rationalized system, the rise of large-scale modern organization and accounting work are naturally associated. But within this general frame, there are some interesting negative trade-offs. Not all

countings require accounting, or the intervention of specialized professionals acting as third-party guardians of a wider reality.

When does organization, with its routine bookkeeping accounting structures, do without specialized accounting functions and accountants? And
when does organization incorporate accountants and a professionalized mys-
tique of counting? We have put forward one part of an answer above: Aspects
of rationalization that spell out the status and function of particular entities in
an explicit and lawful way lower the likelihood of accounting expansion. For
instance, German modernization tended to evolve, as its ideology of the
entities making up society, not in liberal ideas of free individuals and firms
engaging in contractual relations (and requiring accounting), but substantive
notions of the modern community as made up of fixed and definite occupational parts (for educational implications of this, see Benavot, 1983). This
approach was sometimes indicted as feudal, but in fact permitted great
modernization, as long as the spelled out occupational rules defining the rights
and obligations of a given occupational group were organized according to
modern aims. In such a system, attention goes to the formulation of the rules
that constitute the relations among occupational groups, not to the accounting
of abstract exchange value.

This is clearly one situation in which a form of social organization preempts
the role of accounting in more liberal systems. But one can generalize beyond
this to argue that any form of organization that spells out its rationalized
structure in formal rules is likely to lower the involvement of accounting and
accountants. We have here the idea of the "complete organization," or the
bureaucracy. Its division of labor is completely, explicitly, and authoritatively
spelled out. So is its hierarchical control structure. Whatever cultural rationalization is available in the domain in question is completely monopolized by
the organization itself, and located in its formal role structure. In such a closed
system, why would accounting, beyond the most limited record keeping, be
useful? One might find some inspection systems monitoring control, and some
simple counting systems keeping track of flows among units in the division
of labor. But accounting, with a perspective on reality independent of the
legitimate bureaucratic rules, would seem a bit redundant, or even potentially
disruptive, because the accounting story and the official one would almost
certainly diverge.

By this argument, accounting arises in partially rationalized (or partially
bureaucratized) settings. When organization is relatively complete, controlling its own definition of reality, accounting becomes less necessary,
and sometimes intrusive. Thus one expects fewer accountants per dollar
processed in a university or a government bureau than in an organization
in the private economy. Institutionalized, or decoupled, organizations
(March & Olsen, 1976; Meyer & Rowan, 1977; Weick, 1976) that consti-

tute their own reality should be found to rely less on accountants. A typical school, for instance, organizes its production around the course or credit unit. The value of this (toward, for instance, a degree) is fixed by rule, and thus organizationally determinate. There is no procedure by which a bad course gives the students less credit toward their degree. Having subtle accountants around to point out that one course (with few students, a differently credentialed teacher, or one with more seniority) is worth more or less than another in cost terms may not be very useful, and may even be destructive in calling attention to what is best concealed (Boland & Pondy, 1983; Meyer & Rowan, 1978). In such a situation, organizational rules (defining, for instance, costs) take precedence over accounting abstractions (Covaleski & Dirsmith, 1983). Contrast the school with a defense contractor producing a real product for a national state: The price is obviously likely to be in dispute, and perhaps there is no market. Here accounting is everything—success in linking the organization's interests, through accounting rules, to a tale of production in the real world is absolutely necessary.

We thus expect to find accountants in greater numbers where organization is not self-sufficient, or tightly linked to institutional definitions that insulate it from reality (Meyer, Scott, & Deal, 1983). Thus accountants should be more common in economic organizations, in market organizations, or in private organizations. Highly institutionalized organizations like the state may no longer need to "keep score" with a complex reality, and indeed many have interests in avoiding doing so, and thus many avoid elaborate accounting.

TECHNOLOGY

We argue above that accounting work arises to link organization to some sort of technical reality, when this cannot be avoided or rendered tautological. But how about those instances, as in classic materials processing, in which clear, consensual, and definitive technologies are established (Perrow, 1979)? Here there may be fairly clear agreement on the causal processes, on the countability or objective status of each step of the process, and on the value of all the necessary elements from initial costs to ultimate price. It seems likely that such situations, also, generate relatively little specialized accounting work. Accounting is more likely when organizations must confront a reality, but a reality that is uncertain or opaque: Accounting arises to count, not the visible, but the invisible. By this reasoning, accounting work should be most common under such technical conditions as the following: (a) when there are long time lags involved in reaching the ultimate goal (i.e., the effort to get to the moon), or in acquiring resources (e.g., waiting for seedlings to become lumber);

(b) when the value of elements of the production process is uncertain or highly variable; or (c) when the technology contains elements of low visibility (such as professional services of various kinds) or great uncertainty. Thus we expect to find accounting work not simply paralleling the general flows of monetarized value in society, but clustered in nodes around the problematic yet rationalized activities and domains (Boland, 1982). The past and the future are problematic: Accountants may be especially required to deal with the capital market as it arises, the abstractions of the tax systems, situations requiring future planning, and aspects of the organization related to products only in a very long-term way (like research and development, or personnel activities, or safety).

We have everyday accounting functions internal to organizations, but obviously they arise with special frequency in what are called organization-environment relations (Warren, 1967). Thus market relations should involve fewer accountants than exchanges of invisible products or services. And organizational relationships involving incomplete authority should create more accounting work, as with holding companies, decentralized firms or other organizations, or partially dependent organizations.

The Organized Environment

One can see societal environments as themselves rationalized structures with some organizational form. Depending on political structure, societies clearly differ quite systematically (Meyer & Scott, 1983b). American society is in this respect rather loosely structured in terms of an organizationally imposed hierarchical structure and lateral organizational division of labor. It generates many organizations with much overlapping, interpenetration, and systems of partial or fragmented dominance. An American school or hospital, for instance, might on the vertical axis have partial authority relationships with 20 or 30 inarticulated political governing bodies, and quite complex lateral relationships too. So also with an American firm. French society seems more sharply organized in a formal sense, with clearer interorganizational division of labor and hierarchies: The sprawling set of relations of partial dominance characteristic of American society would seem in the French context impossible and unreasonable. Many other societal variations seem likely.

Similar variations also characterize various particular social sectors or domains within societies. They may be organized in markets, mixed or overlapping systems, or coordinated bureaucracies.

Following the general arguments above, one can see these variations in societal or sectoral organizational structure as generating variations in the amount of accounting work. Simple hierarchically and laterally differentiated bureaucratic systems ought, by our arguments, to generate relatively little accounting work. Direct organizational systems of counting and inspection may be expected. Mixed or fragmented systems, we suppose, would generate much accounting activity. Partial authority relationships or partially differentiated lateral ones lead the parties involved to utilize third-party counters. Pure market systems should generate little accounting requirement, but here a cautionary note is in order. What are, in the literature, *considered* pure market systems of organizations are often in this situation at only one or two of their many boundaries. An organization of this sort may in fact be linked in the most complex and overlapping or partially dependent way at other boundaries. An American "market" organization, for instance, organized in clear and visible exchange relations in the sale of its product, may be involved in the most complex relations at other boundaries: paying taxes to many different and unintegrated political jurisdictions; dealing in uneasy marriage with several unions; subject to a host of zoning, environmental, safety, and professional partially governing bodies; exposed to a capital "market" that is very far from a market involving simple visible exchange; and so on. A system of this kind, by our arguments above, should generate much accounting work, quite apart from the many relations of uncertain meaning internal to the organization.

Overall, we suggest an ambiguous answer to the question of the relation between general expansions of organizational scale in a given rationalized environment and the expansion of accounting work. The expansion of organizational structures with complete and rationalized specifications of vertical authority and lateral differentiation may lower the total amount of necessary accounting work, substituting organizational rules (and organizational construction of entities) for accounting analysis. But much expansion of organizational scale does not take this form of complete rationalization—it rather creates systems of partial and overlapping controls. These seem to be fertile soil for accounting work.

INSTITUTIONALIZATION AND DEACCOUNTING

So far, our arguments suppose that as the modern system expands, and especially as it expands into disordered domains and activities, accounting work expands very rapidly. This is partly true, but overstates the case. There are a good many mechanisms that reduce the complexity involved and lower the need for accounting work. That basic point is that the specialized roles and activities associated with accounting become institutionalized, routinized, and absorbed by changing organizational structure. Many of them disappear as specialized activities (becoming routine work of ordinary actors), and others may disappear entirely (replaced by other social processes).

First and most important, there is a drift from specialized accounting work toward ordinary organizational process. Much counting and record keeping becomes so routine as to be shunted off into routine bookkeeping, into secretarial work, or into the work of ordinary members. Obviously there has been a great expansion, over the decades, in the accounting competence of ordinary members: beyond this, routinized data systems built up by computerization also function to absorb specialized accounting roles and work.

Second, in some measure expanded *organization* replaces accounting work. Spelled out organizational rules of vertical and horizontal differentiation, as discussed above, lower requirements for accounting. If accounting characterizes fragmented or partial relations among organizations and organizational elements, the inclination to expand bureaucratization lowers it. Less accounting is required in situations of definitive hierarchy or organizationally specified lateral differentiation. The organization chart is, partly, an alternative to accounting. If a production process, for instance, is managed by explicit organizational rules (each likely to be dependent on such institutional considerations as the law, or national union agreements), accounting of complex kinds may be redundant. Thus the general expansion of organizational structure, with the rationalization of modern society, may lower the rate of accounting expansion.

Third, and more general, the process of entity construction lowers the pressures for accounting. For instance, the creation of educational and occupational categories for labor, and the fixing of the differential meaning and rights going along with these categories, turns what might previously have been an accounting problem into an organizational one. So may the creation of more and more organizational units and subunits—as authoritative vertical and lateral differentiation in society replaces accounting fictions with legal or organizational ones. As a concrete example, the increasing use of educational certification as a substitute for methods of assessing value that rely on measures of performance and exchange greatly reduces potential accounting problems (Collins, 1979). We are conscious of the accounting costs of modern medical care: Imagine how much more difficult these would be if each patient's account had to be billed in proportion to the actual medical care, or improvement, produced. At present, the billing may simply reflect the attention of a certified person. Similarly with educational accounting: It quickly becomes an impossible problem if society is to pay each teacher in terms of accomplished instruction and learning (Meyer & Rowan, 1978).

Context and Types of Accounting Work

Arguments similar to those above may be useful, not only in accounting for variations in amount of work, but also in considering variations in kinds of accounting work that go on. Some of this has already been considered through our somewhat casual distinctions between counting, bookkeeping, and accounting. A comparative study might usefully treat all three as dependent variables, considering variations in each as to be affected by different independent factors. We have, roughly, treated accounting as reflecting the organizationally uncontrolled monetarization of socially invisible value, bookkeeping as reflecting more organizationally controlled and visible value, and other forms of counting as likely to reflect the complexity of entity construction.

Going further, the specific sorts of work that call for professionalized accountants and their legitimation should vary depending on the points in the organization's internal and external relations at which invisible or only partly visible value assignments must be made because of more general social rationalization. Thus the accounting work created in an environment with much dependence on capital markets without clear organizational hierarchy should have a quite different character than similar dependencies on a system of taxation, or accounting efforts to deal with monopoly customers like the state. Theories about how accounting work should generally evolve in different directions in different national societies and thus different organizational frames should be fairly easy to formulate. Of special interest here might be the examination of the ways accounting styles vary as one moves to Third World situations in which organizations often operate under rather direct state controls, but in which these controls are somewhat disconnected from technical daily reality. The associated activities, which provincial Westerners might consider to constitute a high level of corruption, must generate interesting kinds of accounting work.

The Impact of Accounting Evolution on the Organizational Environment

We have emphasized the contextual factors affecting the expansion of accounting work, but effects in the opposite direction seem important. This becomes especially the case when one considers accounting rules, not as features of particular organizations, but as properties of institutional domains, national societies, or now the evolving world (some developments in accounting seem to have a worldwide character). It is now common to see organizations as isomorphic with such available institutional rules as accounting systems (DiMaggio & Powell, 1983). Certain kinds of organizations become easier to construct and legitimate, given a set of such rules, and others become harder to justify and fund. But one can go further than this and argue that whole systems of organizations are dependent on accounting systems that may tie them together in different ways (Meyer & Scott, 1983b). In one society or at one time, it is easy and profitable to construct giant holding company organizations, held together not by clear authority or technology, but by accounting rules. In another system, less flexible accounting rules mean that expansion in scale takes the form of bureaucratization, with the substantive specification of vertical and lateral differentiation: or in the extreme, the direct expansion of the state organization. Some hypotheses can be put forward here:

Expanded and complex accounting systems expand the scale of organizing that is possible, both in terms of organizational size and in terms of the domains that can be covered in a single structure.

Such accounting systems, however, lower the extent to which expanding organization takes a bureaucratic form, or is linked directly to the authority of the state.

Thus expanded accounting systems facilitate organization, but lower the substantively rational organization that results—that is, the degree to which interdependence is spelled out in explicit rules of authority and specialized role. This is true both within particular organizations and in interorganizational systems. Elaborate accounting systems permit expansion in scale, without the elimination of overlapping rules, unclarity, and interpenetration that would be necessary for bureaucratic specification. Accounting rules, that is, consist of sets of treaty frameworks that make possible much organization whose rationality is not spelled out organizationally (Meyer & Scott, 1983b).

One of the striking features of modern organized society is that, contrary to much earlier speculation, real bureaucratization of the kind envisaged by writers from Weber (1946) to Crozier (1964) has made such a weak advance. The world is filled with formal organization, now, but the research literature discusses this organization mainly in terms of how little real rationalization there is, in the sense of spelled out authority relations and organizationally explicit, authoritative, and binding divisions of labor. Main theses in the modern literature run against these emphases, which were supposed for better or worse to make up the future. Now, the literature stresses not the substantive rationality of organization, but very different aspects: loose coupling both vertically and laterally, interpenetration both among organizational units and between organizations, matrix structures, coordination rather than authority, exchange rather than specialization, and so on. Perhaps the enormous expansion of accounting in the modern period has made this possible—the expanded and flexible logics of assumed rationality make the bureaucratic formulation of substantive rationality unnecessary (Meyer & Scott, 1983b).

Research Designs

The arguments above are intended to be of use in formulating broad comparative research on the prevalence of accounting work. Such research would be a useful adjunct to present efforts that take a more detailed case study character. In the practical sense, broad statistical comparative work requires simple and primitive dependent variables, with a certain inattention to variations in meaning. Obviously, any scholar in this area can put forward a hundred reasons why a broader statistical study would make no sense: Accounting after all has different meanings and boundaries in every different context. There is always some truth to such arguments. But there is often a good deal of information to be obtained by trying out the other strategy—starting with the assumption of primitive statistical homogeneity and letting the variation in meaning from context to context show up in analysis. In the present instance, the scarcity of comparative statistical approaches would make a few attempts especially valuable.

Once one suggests this strategy, the independent variables that come to mind, considering the collective character of accounting, are features of national political contexts that set conditions of organizing. In one usage, the term *state* is used to describe the web of rules that generate and sustain the modern ideology of collective action. In the arguments above, I have simply been suggesting some conditions under which accounting would be a more or less important aspect of the state in this larger sense: a more or less important mechanism in the expansion of integrated myths of value.

7

Environmental Linkages
and Organizational Complexity

Public and Private Schools

W. RICHARD SCOTT

JOHN W. MEYER

WE CAN NOW DISCERN A GRADUAL SHIFT in the direction of studies pursued by organizational researchers generally and studies of educational systems more specifically. The shift involves increasing attention to the external context as a basis for explaining internal features of organizations. Early signs of this development may be found in the emergence of general systems theory in the 1950s, but clear and strong efforts to revise organizational models did not appear until well into the 1960s. These contributions, most notably by Katz and Kahn (1966) and by Thompson (1967),

The research for this chapter was supported by funds from the National Institute of Education (Grant No. NIE-G-83-0003). The analyses and conclusions do not necessarily reflect the views or policies of this agency. The private and public survey was designed and conducted in collaboration with other researchers at IFG, principally Jay Chambers, Dennis J. Encarnation, and Joan Talbert. Mary Bankston, Lauren Edelman, and Douglas Roeder participated in designing the survey instruments for the school and district study. Mary Bankston played a key role in coordinating the collection of the data. Data files were created primarily by Edward M. Gilliland and Janice Radle with the assistance of Kendyll Stansbury. And Edward M. Gilliland and Janice Radle implemented most of the analysis on which this chapter is based. Our project officer at NIE, Dr. Gail MacColl, provided continuing support and helpful feedback throughout the performance of this project.

served to effect a change in the dominant perspectives from closed- to open-systems models stressing the interdependence of organizations and environments. (For a detailed review of these changes, see Scott, 1987.)

A second change, a more modest adjustment in course, is currently underway as attention is shifting from technical aspects or views of organization-environment interdependence to more institutional views of this relation. Earlier emphases on the distribution of requisite resources or information in the environment and the strategies employed by organizations to secure them (Dill, 1958; Lawrence & Lorsch, 1967; Pfeffer & Salancik, 1978) have begun to be supplemented by approaches that stress that environments are more than stocks of resources and technical knowhow. Environments as contexts supplying legitimacy and meaning coded in cultural symbols; environments as political systems comprising more and less dominant contending interests; environments as storehouses containing the remnants and survivors of earlier times and processes; environments as stratified and differentiated labor markets; environments as increasingly structured systems of organizations—these are among the new images that are shaping the current agenda of organizational research. (See, for example, Baron & Bielby, 1980; DiMaggio & Powell, 1983; Karpik, 1978; Meyer, Scott, Cole, & Intili, 1978; Meyer & Scott, 1983b; Rogers & Whetten, 1981.)

This chapter continues and extends this more recent emphasis by focusing on the environment of schools, noting the extent to which that environment is itself organized, and attempting to discern what effects these more general organizational frameworks have on the structure and operation of particular organizations within them, for example, individual schools and school district offices. The organizational environment of schools may be expected to vary by place (for example, across national systems or among the several states within a society), by time, by type of school (for example, elementary, secondary), and by auspices (for example, private and public). We focus here on differences between private and public school systems.

Private and public organizations differ in a number of respects. We emphasize the extent to which these labels are associated with distinctive administrative contexts or organized environments. We argue that some of the differences in the internal organization between public and private schools can be attributed to differences in the structure of their environment. Although the potential range of environmental variables to be examined is substantial, we limit attention here to selected properties of administrative systems and funding arrangements. *Our general prediction is that organizations operating in more complex and conflicted environments will exhibit greater administrative complexity.* The evidence regarding environmental arrangements and their organizational consequences comes from two sources: a review of the existing literature on school organizations and their environments, and data gathered through a small-scale survey of public and private schools in one area of California.

All of our own data and the other studies reviewed pertain to the United States. Important changes have occurred within this country in recent years in the organizational environments of schools—particularly schools in the public sector. We briefly review these changes in the next section, first for public schools and then for private, and attempt to conceptualize the environments of schools in terms that highlight their organizational significance. Then we examine associated characteristics of educational organizations, in particular, their administrative components at varying system levels: districts, schools, and the nature of administrative work.

The Environments of Public and Private Schools

PUBLIC SCHOOL ENVIRONMENTS

The environment of public schools in the United States has become increasingly complex and disorganized over the past few decades. A series of reforming and centralizing forces have created many new sets of legitimate authorities over the public schools without integrating them with one another or with previous authorities. At the same time, a growing number of varied stakeholders and claimants whose rights are explicitly defined in law are entitled to representation and due process. Attempting to characterize the particular shape and form of the evolving order, we argue that the environments of schools are increasingly centralized, federalized, and fragmented.

Centralization

There is little doubt that the public school system has become more centralized over the past few decades. Historically, decision making in the educational sector has been highly decentralized in this country. It has traditionally been the case that local educational authorities—school districts and individual schools—have dominated educational decision making. Most state departments of education have, until quite recently, been small, weak, and ineffectual. And, until the 1960s, the federal government took virtually no role in elementary and secondary education, recognizing the rights of state and local agencies in educational governance.

This situation changed dramatically in 1965 with the passage of the Elementary and Secondary Education Act. Aimed primarily at achieving greater equity for disadvantaged groups, this legislation introduced a strong federal voice into educational affairs. Subsequent legislation extended services to additional groups—e.g., educationally handicapped and bilingual students—or attempted to stimulate educational reform and innovation—for example, creation of the Teacher Corps and grants to improve state and local planning. Although at its peak level in the late 1970s, federal aid accounted for only 9.2% of total educational revenues, most observers agree that the use of categorical funding targeted to the support of particular groups and programs allowed the federal government to exercise a disproportionate influence on education (see Berke & Kirst, 1975; Levin, 1977).

Moreover, it appears that the federal presence has stimulated and strengthened state educational authorities both directly and indirectly. Directly, states not only were delegated power to supervise the implementation of the federal programs but also were allocated federal funds to augment their staffs to perform these functions. As a consequence, state education departments have grown dramatically: "They have doubled and tripled in size since the mid-1960s and the amount they receive from the federal government for their administrative budgets has grown to an average of 40% of the total" (Murphy, 1981, p. 127). In recent years they have declined somewhat as federal appropriations have been reduced under the Education Consolidation Improvement Act of 1981, but the long-term growth has been sustained relative to the 1960s and 1970s. Indirectly, the increased size and power have attracted more competent and aggressive personnel at the state levels who have been able to both encourage and benefit from the political efforts of the 1980s to use block grants and other revenue-sharing proposals to return more power and discretion to the state level.

Although the federal role in financing education did not change appreciably during the decade of the 1970s, the states' contributions have increased relative to local funding. Funds controlled by states increased from about 39% of the total expenditures for schooling in the early 1970s to about 45% by the end of the decade, bringing them to a par with local revenues (Sergiovanni, Burlingame, Coombs, & Thurston, 1980). These trends accelerated during the 1980s as states continued to oversee the distribution of federal funds and to increase their funding and programmatic authority in relation to local education agencies.

Thus beginning at the national level, but continuing now at the level of the states, new administrative units have emerged and grown within the educational sector, shifting some types of decisions formerly made within a local community to the state or national level.

Federalization

To argue that new decision centers have emerged is not necessarily to conclude that former authorities have atrophied. The authority of local educational systems and the influence of local interests have not been displaced but only supplemented by the growth of power at the state and national levels. One set of authorities has been layered over another, with each claiming legitimacy to make some types of educational decisions— the federal agencies basing their claims on overriding "national interests," the states standing on their constitutional grounds, and the communities affirming continuing faith in the "religion of localism," a dogma with many adherents in the realm of education. Thus increasing centralization of educational authority at the state and federal levels has been associated with federalization: "the explicit establishment of independent authorities with both separate responsibilities and overlapping jurisdictions" (Scott & Meyer, 1983, p. 131). This doctrine within education receives legitimacy and support from its congruence with wider political beliefs prevalent in the United States regarding the need to divide and juxtapose powers in order to prevent their abuse (see Grodzins, 1966; Scott, 1983, p. 171).

The practice of pitting educational authorities against each other at various levels is characteristic not only of administrative agencies but also of the system of courts, an institution that has played an increasingly active role in education since the early 1950s. Beginning with the landmark *Brown* decision of 1954, both the federal and the state courts have become involved in every major area of education policy (see Kirp & Jensen, 1986; Levin, 1977).

FRAGMENTATION

In addition to the complexity generated by the existence of multiple uncoordinated layers of educational authorities, additional complexity is associated with the fragmented nature of educational authority. Fragmentation refers to the extent to which authority is "integrated or coordinated at any given level" of the educational sector (Scott & Meyer, 1983, p. 145). The independent operation of courts and agencies is a prime example of fragmentation at each level—national, state, and local—as well as of federalization—the lack of integration across levels.

Numerous observers have called attention to the extent of fragmentation that characterized educational administration at all levels in the early 1980s. Sergiovanni and his colleagues (1980) have described fragmentation at the federal level:

One could, in fact, question whether it is even accurate to speak of "federal policy" in education. Certainly there is no single center of planning and coordination within our nation's capital. Programs which bear upon education emerge, rather, from literally dozens of agencies and congressional committees. (p. 162)

They note that in addition to the Office of Education, located at that time within the Department of Health, Education and Welfare, and the independent National Institute of Education,

There are countless pockets within other agencies and departments that exercise control over highly significant programs. The Office of Civil Rights has been instrumental in enforcing desegregation guidelines. Head Start, Follow Through, and Upward Bound programs make their home in the Office of Economic Opportunity. Dependents' schools on overseas military bases are administered by the Department of Defense, and many Indian children attend schools administered by the Bureau of Indian Affairs within the Department of Interior. (p. 164)

As might be suspected, the fractured character of state education agencies is not unrelated to fragmentation at the federal level. Consistent with predictions that organizational structures tend to reflect the characteristics of the environments to which they relate. McDonnell and McLaughlin (1982) report, "During their time of greatest growth, most state departments developed organizational structures that matched that of ED/USOE (Department of Education, formerly the U.S. Office of Education) and faithfully replicated, unit for unit, federal program categories" (p. 24).

Moreover, linkages among governmental levels take a variety of forms that add to the complexity and fragmentation confronting any particular layer (Berke & Kirst, 1975, p. 224). In addition, in the period under consideration, different officials associated with distinct offices were engaged in monitoring compliance. The interpretations of the rules and regulations by U.S. Office of Education officials were found to sometimes vary from that of HEW auditors working out of 10 HEW regional offices (see Goettel, 1976).

Summary

Some societies have developed highly centralized and unified ministries of education in which the chain of command is clearly defined from the top down with the local school systems functioning as "branch offices" (Meyer, 1983a). Public education in the United States has not followed this model, and although centralizing processes have been evident in recent decades, they have not replaced local powers nor have they succeeded in overcoming the divisions among authorities competing with one another at each level. The resulting system is one of considerable complexity and disorder.

PRIVATE SCHOOL ENVIRONMENTS

Discussion of the environment of private schools is rendered difficult by three conditions. First, much less information is available about private schooling in this country than about public education. There are questions about the accuracy of existing data on the number of private school students and schools—rather fundamental facts—and private schools have been surprisingly neglected by organizational researchers up to the present time (see Erickson, 1983). Part of the responsibility for the present lack of accurate information lies with the schools themselves, some of which are small and short-lived while others wish to avoid surveys.

A second barrier to understanding is posed by the great variety of private schools. Although Catholic schools—which themselves vary in type from parish and diocesan to those of specific religious orders—make up about half of the population (and account for about 65% of the students), a large variety of other types of religious schools comprise an additional 30%, while the remaining 20% are independent or secular in orientation. Moreover, the composition of the population of private schools has been changing, with Catholic schools declining precipitously since the mid-1960s, while high-tuition independent schools have experienced steady growth, and fundamentalist schools have grown rapidly during the past decade (Erickson, 1983).

Third, private schools receive varying levels of public support and are subject to varying degrees of public regulation. Thus it is incorrect to distinguish too sharply between the environments of public and private schools. Estimates are that, on the average, nonpublic schools receive approximately 26% of their total income from government, about half of which is derived from indirect tax deductions or exemptions and the other half from direct program expenditures (Sullivan, 1974, p. 93). The latter programs include transportation, textbooks, and health and welfare services available in many of the states and compensatory education, child nutrition, instructional materials, and aid to handicapped students from the federal government. Although most private schools take advantage of the tax benefits, a smaller number receive direct categorical aid, virtually all of which is designed to serve targeted student populations (Encarnation, 1983).

The same dimensions used to characterize the environments of public schools can be employed to describe those of private schools. The blurring of boundaries between public and private systems is ignored in this discussion, but will be considered later. Also, it is important to note that environmental variation for private schools is related strongly to school type.

Centralization

Private schools vary in the extent to which decision making has been centralized. Some, like Catholic and Lutheran schools, belong to hierarchical systems, while others belong only to loosely organized federations, such as the National Association of Independent Schools, and still others operate as completely independent units. Little research has been done on governance in private school systems (see Bridges, 1982).

Federalization

Private schools may experience federalization because they are subject to control exercised by both local and state authorities. Although there is great variation across the 50 states, private schools are subject to state regulation in such areas as minimum educational standards, attendance reporting, licensure, and teacher certification (O'Malley, 1981). Other agencies regulate private schools as a business subject to "state and local building, fire, health, sanitation, child welfare, and zoning codes" (Encarnation, 1983, p. 188). Private schools applying and qualifying for more direct forms of public aid, such as textbook or compensatory educational programs, are subject to review by public authorities. Because the programs are defined as benefiting targeted student populations, the great majority of them are not administered by the private schools but by public school districts.

Private schools vary by type in the degree to which they participate in larger private educational systems and hence are subject to additional controls at more than one authority level. Catholic schools no doubt represent the most highly developed system of private education with the possibility of control exercised at the parish and diocesan levels. Most other private school systems are much less complex. In general, it appears that the extent of federalization experienced by private schools is relatively low, because although multiple authorities exist, they do not overlap greatly in jurisdiction.

Fragmentation

Similarly, private schools appear to be confronted by less fragmented environments than their public counterparts. Sources of funds are fewer and programmatic authority is more likely to be located at the school level.

What variation exists is likely to be associated with the receipt of public funds, as discussed below.

Environments and Educational Organizations: Predicted Relations

The pattern of fragmented and federalized centralization that characterizes the educational sector in the United States provides the environment within which individual educational organizations must function. What are the consequences of this type of environment for educational organizations? We have argued that several organizational effects are expected (Meyer, 1983c; Scott & Meyer, 1983). Here we emphasize their effects on administrative complexity.

A widely accepted proposition in open-systems theory is that organizations located in more complex and uncertain organizational fields will exhibit more complex internal structures. When the environmental units take the form of funding and regulatory bodies, organizational complexity is likely to develop particularly at the administrative level, where boundary-spanning activities are centered. Even more particularly, when the external pattern exhibits centralization of funding flows combined with fragmentation and competition among regulatory bodies, we expect to see environmental controls exercised through accounting and statistical mechanisms. The result within organizational units will be an expansion of the numbers of accountants, bookkeepers, and clerks hired. We would also expect general administrators to report spending more time in tracking and overseeing the functioning of those programs linked to special funds and reporting requirements. Specific hypotheses to be tested are:

1. School organizations exposed to an increased variety of funding and programmatic authorities are expected to have larger administrative components than those relating to less complex environments.
2. School organizations exposed to an increased variety of funding and programmatic authorities are expected to have a higher proportion of business, accounting, and financial personnel in their administrative staff than those relating to less complex environments.
3. General administrators in school organizations exposed to an increased variety of funding and programmatic authorities are expected to spend a greater proportion of their time overseeing such programs than general administrators in school organizations relating to less complex environments.
4. Federal funds and programs, because they are more likely to be fragmented and federalized than comparable state funds and programs, are expected to

generate larger administrative components in school organizations than state programs.

5. Public school organizations are expected to exhibit larger administrative components than private schools because of the relatively greater complexity of the fiscal and regulatory environments they confront.

Environments and Educational Organizations: Evidence

PRELIMINARY CONCERNS

Before reviewing evidence relating to these predictions three preliminary issues require brief attention: the issue of organizational levels, alternative explanations for our dependent variables, and the nature of our sample of public and private schools.

Organizational Levels

School organizations vary in the extent to which they are components of hierarchical structures with different organizational units located at higher or lower levels of the system. When a multiple level system exists, an important question to be addressed is where, at what level, are the predicted organizational effects likely to be manifested? If complex and conflicted environments are expected to be associated with administrative complexity of the component organizational units, which units are most likely to be affected? It is possible to argue either that *all* organizations will be affected or that only some levels will be affected, forms at one level serving to manage or absorb complexity in the environment. We can offer no theoretical basis for selecting among these competing possibilities and so will simply observe and report on the empirical situation in the U.S. educational sector.

Alternative Explanations

Our perspective focuses attention on environmental sources of administrative complexity and educational coherence. More conventional organizational arguments view administrative complexity as primarily the product of *internal* characteristics, either size (see Blau, 1970) or technical complexity and interdependence (see Galbraith, 1973; Thompson, 1967). We control for the effects of organizational size on administration in assessing our own propositions. We assess technical or instructional complexity and interdependence only through the distinction between elementary and secondary schools or the number of grades included within the school organization.

Public and Private School Study

Data on a sample of public and private schools, public school districts, and Catholic school dioceses in the six-county San Francisco Bay Area were collected in the spring of 1981 by an interdisciplinary team of researchers at the Institute for Research on Educational Finance and Governance, Stanford University. Because the study was expected to serve multiple objectives, its design was complex. Chambers and Lajoie (1983) provide a description of the study objectives and general design (see also Gilliland & Radle, 1984). Table 7.1 reports sample size and return rates for public schools and districts and for the various categories of private schools surveyed. Return rates for the entire sample averaged only about 30%, with significantly lower rates characterizing public middle and elementary schools, independent schools (not associated with a parish or diocese), and other types of private religious schools.

For purposes of our analyses, respondent schools were divided into three categories by auspices: public, Catholic, and private. Catholic independent schools are being assigned to the private category because their organizational environments are similar to those of private schools. Four categories of schools were identified by grade level: elementary, middle, secondary, and comprehensive. These categories and the numbers of schools in each are reported in Table 7.2. As is clear from Table 7.2, the middle school is primarily a public school form, while the comprehensive school is a private school type. Also, private schools were more likely than either public or Catholic systems to combine junior and senior high programs into a single school type.

Most of the data reported in this chapter are based on questionnaires mailed to schools and district offices. Differentiated but comparable survey instruments were prepared for each type of school included within the study (see Chambers & Lajoie, 1983). A survey form was mailed to principals and superintendents with the request that it be completed by the recipient or a person designated by him or her as knowledgeable in the areas covered. Initial return rates were disappointingly low, but were somewhat improved by telephone follow-ups. Data on Catholic diocesan activities were collected by interview.

ADMINISTRATIVE COMPLEXITY

District Level

The administrative staffs within public school districts have certainly grown. As Rowan (1981) reports, "In 1932, the earliest year for which records on the number of administrators in the public school system are

TABLE 7.1 Sample Size and Return for Schools and Districts

Type	Sample Size	Number Returned	Percentage Returned
Public Schools			
High school	153	49	32
Junior high/middle	82	20	24
Elementary	299	61	20
Public School Districts			
District offices	110	49	45
Private Schools			
Secondary			
Catholic parochial	16	6	38
Catholic independent	20	4	20
Other religious	8	2	25
Nonreligious	17	9	53
Elementary			
Catholic parochial	151	69	48
Catholic independent	5	1	20
Other religious	62	15	24
Nonreligious	56	15	28

SOURCE: Gilliland & Radle (1984), Tables 8 and 9.

TABLE 7.2 Number of Responding Schools and Grades by School Categories

Categories	Number of Schools	Mean Number Grades
Elementary		
Public	61	6.5
Catholic	69	8.4
Private	31	8.2
Middle		
Public	20	2.7
Catholic	1	2.0
Private	1	2.0
Secondary		
Public	49	4.0
Senior high	(48)	(3.9)
Combined senior and middle	(1)	(6.0)
Catholic	7	4.3
Senior high	(6)	(4.0)
Combined senior and middle	(1)	(6.0)
Private	16	4.7
Senior high	(11)	(4.0)
Combined senior and middle	(5)	(6.2)
Comprehensive		
Private	9	12.8

SOURCE: Gilliland & Radle (1984), Table 14.

available, there were only .23 local administrators per district. By 1970 that number had increased to 6.8 administrators per public school district" (p. 47). By 1982, in our six-county sample of school districts in the San Francisco Bay Area, the average number of administrators was 12.80. What factors are associated with this increase?

Of course, the consolidation movement has contributed to district size: As larger territories with more schools are created, the number of administrators per district is likely to increase. It is also possible that the work performed within schools—the "technology" of schooling—has become more complex, requiring more administrative input. Although this is possible, there is little evidence to suggest that district administrators are closely connected with the instructional work of schools. Indeed, what evidence we have suggests the opposite (see Hannaway & Sproull, 1978-1979). Another possibility is that the work confronting school districts is not so much how to manage students as how to manage schools themselves, and that schools as organizations have become more complex over time, and perhaps also more interdependent, requiring more administrative attention and coordination. It is clear that considerable administrative growth at the district level is related to such internal organizational changes. In virtually all districts, the budgeting process has become more highly centralized; and in most districts, critical personnel decisions are made at this level. Note, however, that these types of changes are largely a result of change in school environments, not of internal processes. Thus budget decisions are more centralized largely because a greater proportion of school funds come from outside the district, and districts are held accountable according to standards set and enforced by these external authorities. And personnel decisions are more centralized partly in response to the pressure of professional associations and unions and to state licensure requirements that are external to any specific district.

To focus attention on effects of environmental changes on the administrative structure of school districts, we and our colleagues at Stanford have carried out several empirical studies. The first, based on data collected in a survey of 20 elementary school districts in the San Francisco Bay Area in 1975 (see Cohen, Deal, Meyer, & Scott, 1979, for details of sampling procedures), was conducted by Rowan (1981). After controlling for district size, measured by average daily attendance, Rowan found a strong positive association between the amount of special federal and state funds received per student and size of district administration, measured as the number of full-time equivalent (FTE) administrators per student. These effects were much greater than those associated with measures of internal district complexity (whether the district was administering only elementary schools or was unified, managing both secondary and elementary schools) and of interdependence (whether there existed a district-wide reading program).

A second study, conducted by Bankston (1982), examined in depth a single large school district in an urbanized location within the San Francisco Bay Area. For the fiscal year 1979-1980, the district received 8% of its funding from the federal government, 69% from the state, and the remainder from local sources. Combining both state and federal special programs, 20% of the district's funding came from categorical programs while 80% was received as general aid. Although only one fifth of the district's income was associated with categorical programs, one third, 17 of 53 central district officers, were funded by these programs. And although only 8% of the funding was derived from the U.S. Department of Education, Bankston estimated that about 30% of the required annual reports were directed to this source. Finally, not only the activities of the administrative staff but also their titles and the structural differentiation of the district office reflected the patterning of external funding packages and reporting requirements. Thus Bankston's descriptive study, although based on a single case, provides strong evidence in support of the view that school district organization is shaped by the structure of its administrative environment.

A third study, also conducted by Rowan (1982), utilized data from a random sample of 30 city school districts that existed in California in 1930. Using published data at 5-year time intervals, Rowan analyzed changes over time in the composition of district staff. He observed that

> The most pronounced tendency of districts in the sample was to differentiate positions with business and personnel functions. The proportion of districts with these specialties rose from 0% in 1930 to 83% with business positions and 67% with personnel positions in 1970. Such a marked pattern of growth reflects not merely the growth in scale of operations within school districts, but also an increased concern with financial accountability and with credentialing and labor management contingencies. (p. 49)

These results are consistent with our arguments that changes in the organizational environments of schools are associated not simply with larger administrative components within educational organizations but also with the addition of certain types of administrative personnel, in particular, business and accounting specialists.

Turning now to the data from our private and public study, we examine first the results based on survey responses from 49 public school districts. Questionnaires were mailed to superintendents who were asked to respond personally or to locate a knowledgeable associate who could do so. As the principal measure of environmental complexity, respondents were asked to indicate from a list of 22 federal and state programs all those in which the district currently participated. The number of external programs in which the district was involved was regarded as an indicator of environmental fragmentation. The locus of the programs—whether federal or state—was taken as an indicator of environmental centralization. The average Bay Area district reported participating in 11.1 programs (for a description see Gilliland & Radle, 1984, pp. 41-44).

Throughout these analyses, our primary measure of administrative complexity is simply the number of FTE administrators in the district. Administrators reported as "part-time" were considered as 0.5 administrators. We avoid administrative ratios to eliminate the problems of definitional dependency (see Freeman & Kronenfeld, 1974).

Multiple regression was used to determine which factors were associated with size of the district's administrative staff and to assess the relative impact of each factor. Table 7.3 reports, in both standardized and unstandardized regression coefficients, representative results for three equations (columns 1-3). We note that size, whether measured in total district enrollment or in number of schools within the district, was highly associated with size of district administration, as expected. The greater effect of number of schools is consistent with the expectation that district size is more a function of complexity in managing schools than students.

Two more direct measures of complexity within the district are whether the district was unified or restricted to either elementary or high schools. Like Rowan (1981) we found no effect on number of district administrators of whether the district was unified, but districts administering high schools— known to be larger and more complex systems than elementary or middle schools—were observed to have larger administrative staffs. In sum, internal complexity as represented by number of schools and by the complexity of the individual schools themselves, was found to increase district administration over and above that associated with numbers of students enrolled.

With respect to our central concern, we found that environmental fragmentation, as measured by the number of public programs in which districts participated, was consistently and significantly associated with larger district administrative staffs. Related results (not reported in Table 7.3) showed no differences between the effect of participation in special state programs or federal programs, an index of centralization. The combined effects of size, internal complexity, and environmental complexity accounted for approximately 90% in the observed variance in number of administrators among public school districts (see Table 7.3).

Administrators are not the only types of personnel within district offices. Two other general categories of staff include nonadministrative professionals

TABLE 7.3 Factors Affecting Size of Public District Administration

	1	2	3
Constant	−5.614	−5.672	−5.801
Size			
Enrollment	.875**		
	.0011		
	(.000071)		
Number of schools		.8866**	.907**
		.658	.674
		(.042)	(.039)
Internal complexity			
Unified district	−.019	−.059	
	−.606	−1.868	
	(1.759)	(1.762)	
High school district			.129**
			5.684
			(1.859)
External complexity			
Fragmentation (number	.146*	.161**	.124*
of public programs)	.631	.698	.536
	(.263)	(.259)	(.220)
$R^2 =$	.91	.92	.93

NOTE: First listing in table for each variable is standardized regression coefficient (beta).
Second listing is unstandardized coefficient.
Third listing, in parentheses, is standard error of the estimate.
*$p = <.05$
**$p = <.001$

and classified personnel. The first category includes various types of personnel providing support services to schools including counselors, social workers, librarians, psychologists, and resource specialists. These personnel are located at the district level because they provide only "staff" services to teachers and students or because they serve more than one school. Classified staff includes secretaries, bookkeepers, clerks, and similar administrative support personnel. The only significant predictor of numbers of classified staff at the district level was size, whether measured by district enrollment or number of schools. The measures of internal and environmental complexity were not significantly associated with the size of the classified staff. To our surprise, the number of professional staff at the district level was significantly associated not only with the district size measures but also with the number of publicly funded local, private-school programs—but not the number of public programs—administered by the district.

In summary, it appears that school districts are strongly influenced in their size and composition by involvement in public programs. After taking into account the size and internal complexity of the district, the larger the number of public programs managed, the larger the number of administrators.

County Level

In addition to district administrative development, other public administrative staff are located within the office of the county superintendent of schools. We did not attempt to examine developments at this level systematically but call attention to it as another important locus of administrative services for schools. In order to obtain some sense of the scale of operations at this level and the types of services provided, we conducted interviews with officials in two Bay Area county offices, one in a smaller county encompassing 16 school districts, and the other in a larger county encompassing 19 districts. The smaller county office contained a staff of 65 professionals and 191 clerical workers. The types of functions reported included the administration of development centers for handicapped students and court schools; the provision of in-service classes for teachers and other professionals, such as training in computers; and the performance by contract of specific functions for schools, such as training workshops and payroll services. In addition, the larger of the county offices reported that they provided liaison with private schools, the county serving as the "representative of the SEA," collecting private affidavits every fall and occasionally serving as an intermediary between private and public schools for joint programs.

Diocesan Level

Turning now to the private sector, only one type within our sample, the Catholic parochial schools, was organized into a larger system at the "district" level—the diocese. (One other nonreligious private school in our sample reported that it belonged to a statewide regional system.) All of the parochial schools in our sample were incorporated within one of three systems—two diocesan and one archdiocesan. Interviews with school administrators located in each of these offices revealed the presence of very small administrative staffs. In the smaller diocese, only two full-time administrators and one part-time clerical person exercised oversight for a system containing 32 schools—28 elementary and 2 secondary. In the second diocese, 4 full-time administrators, 4 secretaries, a bookkeeper, and an accountant managed 57 elementary schools and 4 secondary schools. And in the larger dioceses, 7 administrators and 2 clerical persons administered a system containing 94 schools—75 elementary and 19 secondary.

Given the size of these central offices, it is not surprising that diocesan administrators reported carrying out primarily staff functions—collecting system-wide data on academic performance and teacher qualifications and credentials, conducting training workshops, and consulting on curricula. All these offices reported having at least informal contact with the independent private Catholic schools within their areas. The diocese takes almost no fiscal responsibility for parish schools that are funded from fees, collections, and fund-raising activities. No state funds were received, and any federal funds were administered by public districts and routed directly to qualified schools. Parochial schools were reported to be receiving ESEA Title I (now Chapter I) funds, ESEA Title IV-B (now part of Chapter II) library and learning resource funding, ESEA Title VII (also part of Chapter II) bilingual education funds, and National School Lunch Program funds. Although not involved in the administration of these programs, two of the three diocesan officers reported conducting regular on-site inspections of those schools participating in publicly funded programs.

In sum, by comparison with the public system, private schools are much less likely to be organized at a regional or district level, and those that are exhibit only relatively small and rudimentary administrative staff functioning at this level.

School Level

Another of our colleagues, Ann Stackhouse (1982) utilized data from a survey of a 10% sample of U.S. secondary schools conducted in 1977 by NIE (see Abramowitz & Tenenbaum, 1978) to test hypotheses similar to those we have advanced. Stackhouse expected fragmentation within the environment of secondary schools to increase the size of the administrative component of the school. The primary measure of fragmentation was similar to our own: the number of types of special categorical funds from which a school was receiving funds. The two primary measures of administration were the number of general administrators and the number of specialists (for example, special education teachers, resource teachers, media specialists) on the staff of the school. After controlling for school size, region, and urban location, her findings were that fragmentation (but not centralization) in the funding environment of secondary schools was significantly and positively related to the number of specialist personnel but not to the number of regular administrators.

Turning to our own study of public and private schools, we first categorized the sample into seven relatively homogeneous classes, by level and type: three classes of elementary schools—public, Catholic, and private; public middle schools; and three classes of secondary schools—public,

TABLE 7.4 Average Number of Students and Number of Students per Administrative and Professional Staff, by School Type and Level

Level and Type	N	Average Enrollment	Students/ Administrator	Students/ Professional
Elementary				
Public	60	386	358	23
Catholic	66	296	204	31
Private	27	185	129	16
Middle				
Public	19	784	320	19
Secondary				
Public	46	1446	326	24
Catholic	7	715	194	21
Private	16	325	92	12

SOURCE: Based on Gilliland & Radle (1984), Table 21.

Catholic, and private. Recall that the category of Catholic school refers only to those schools with direct ties to the local Catholic hierarchy, that is, to parochial and diocesan schools. Independent Catholic schools were assigned to the private school category.

As Table 7.4 demonstrates, enrollment varied greatly by both level and school type. Secondary schools were, on the average, from two to three times larger than elementary schools; and public schools were, on the average, from two to three times larger than private schools. Catholic schools were intermediate in size between public and private schools: And middle schools were sized between elementary and secondary schools.

Table 7.4 also contains information on staffing ratios. The category of administrator was defined to include principals or heads, assistant administrators or vice-principals, instructional or program administrators, and general or business administrators. The category of professional included teachers, counselors and psychologists, social workers, librarians, nurses, chaplains, resource specialists, and other types of student support services professionals. Size of both types of staff was calculated as the number of full-time staff members plus half the number of part-time members.

There was a slight tendency for staffing ratios to be higher in the more complex types of schools: Secondary and middle schools had more administrators per student than did elementary schools, and Catholic and private (but not public) secondary schools had more teachers per student than did elementary schools. But these differences by level were overwhelmed by the staffing differences by type of school. The private schools in our sample had, on average, almost three times as many administrators per student as did the public schools, and the Catholic schools, nearly twice the number of the public schools. Similarly, private schools contained a significantly higher number of professional staff per student than public schools, with Catholic schools being intermediate. The only exception to these general patterns was that Catholic elementary schools in our sample contained fewer professional staff members per student than did public elementary schools.

Although the relative differences in staffing ratios by school type were substantial, the absolute numbers of administrators at the school level were small. The typical elementary school in our sample contained between one and one-and-a-half administrators: 1.07 for public schools, 1.45 for Catholic schools, and 1.43 for private schools. The average middle school contained only 2.4 administrators. And the average high school contained between three-and-a-half and four-and-a-half administrators: 4.43 for the public secondary school, 3.68 for the Catholic schools, and 3.53 for the private high schools in our sample.

Parallel to our examination of the factors affecting size of administration at the district level, we examined similar regression equations at the school level. As expected given the staffing patterns just described, dummy variables used to indicate a Catholic or a private school were significantly associated with a larger administrative component. Similarly, a dummy variable to indicate secondary versus elementary school—an indicator, among other things, of internal organizational complexity—was significantly associated with size of administration, with secondary schools having more administrators. Given these differences, we sought to determine, for a given type and level of school, whether school size and complexity of the school's external environment were associated with size of administrative staff. Two measures of size were employed: number of students enrolled and number of grades within the school. No attempt was made to directly measure internal school complexity (although number of grades can be regarded as an indicator of complexity as well as of size). Rather, we attempted to control for this variable by distinguishing between and conducting separate analyses for elementary, middle, and secondary schools. Two measures of external environment were employed, both indicators of fragmentation. First, as with districts, we determined for each school the number of public programs in which it was currently participating. Second, we asked an informant in each school to rate the degree of integration or coordination of federal and state programs and reporting requirements.

Table 7.5 is similar in form to Table 7.3 in that each column represents a regression equation including the variables listed in the rows. In order to control for school type and level, separate equations were estimated for each type of school examined. Catholic secondary schools are omitted

TABLE 7.5 Factors Affecting Size of School Administration

| | Elementary Schools | | | Public Middle Schools | Secondary Schools | |
	Public	Catholic	Private		Public	Private
Constant	.014	.869	−.169	3.751	1.856	1.347
Size						
Enrollment	.644***	.260	.919***	−.239	.464**	.369
	.003	.003	.013	−.002	.002	.001
	(.0005)	(.0016)	(.0015)	(.0022)	(.0005)	(.002)
External complexity						
Fragmentation						
number of	.100	.290*	.029	.676*	.278*	.572
public	.027	.272	.039	.516	.221	.887
programs)	(.035)	(.149)	(.168)	(.284)	(.111)	(.769)
Perceived						
integration	−.009	−.287*	−.149	−.492	−.382**	.310
	−.003	−.105	−.103	−.484	−.533	.252
	(.035)	(.055)	(.086)	(.360)	(.196)	(.423)
$R^2 =$	.47	.24	.90	.27	.43	.53

NOTE: First listing in table for each variable is standardized regression coefficient (beta).
Second listing is unstandardized coefficient.
Third listing, in parentheses, is standard error of the estimate.
*$p = <.1$
**$p = <.05$
***$p = <.001$

because of the small number of these schools in our sample. Given the exploratory nature of this analysis and the small numbers involved for some of the school types, we identify associations significant at the .10 level as well as the .05 and .001 levels.

Size of school as measured by enrollment was generally associated positively and significantly with size of school administration although there are exceptions. Turning to the measures of environmental complexity, number of public programs was positively associated with size of administrative staff across all the types of schools studied, but this association was statistically significant only for public middle and secondary schools and for Catholic elementary schools. Further, as expected, perceived integration in the administrative and reporting requirements imposed by participation in state and federal programs was negatively associated with size of the school's administrative staff. Five of the six coefficients were in the expected direction but only two—those for public secondary and Catholic elementary schools—were statistically significant.

Other data pertaining to the composition of the support staff for administrators indicated that public and Catholic but not private schools that participated in a larger number of public programs employed higher proportions of accountants and bookkeepers to other types of supporting staff members. Moreover these results held just for all public and for federal programs not for state or local programs.

Overall our results on increasing demands by the external environment on the time of school administrators are consistent with a number of recent studies based on detailed observations of the principal's work profile. Thus based on his in-depth study of the work activities of a single elementary school principal Wolcott (1973) noted that in his "representational role" the principal performed an important interface function mediating between the demands of the school system bureaucracy and the regulatory environment on the one hand and the school's client community on the other (see also Morris, Crowson, Hurwitz, & Porter-Gehrie, 1981).

Summary

To summarize the school level findings, we found substantial differences in size of the administrative component by type and level of school, with private and then Catholic having larger ratios of administrators to students than public schools and secondary and middle schools having slightly larger ratios of administrators than elementary schools. The differences associated with type appear to reflect both the smaller average size of the Catholic and private systems and the absence of any substantial intermediate buffering structure such as the district office represents for the public system. Participation in public programs was observed to be associated with more elaborate administrative components for Catholic elementary and for public middle and secondary schools. And the perception that state and federal program requirements were well integrated was associated with reduced administrative components in both Catholic elementary and public secondary schools.

Complexity and Organizational Level

It appears that we have an empirical answer to the question: at what level does organizational structure become more elaborate and complex to deal with environmental pressures? For the case of the public school system, we found that administrative complexity is generated at both the district and school level (not to mention the state level where, as noted, educational agencies have expanded enormously in recent years). Although school district offices do expand and function to manage and, partially, to mediate between individual schools and state and federal program requirements, they do not completely absorb these demands. That individual school administrators both expand in number and devote increasing amounts of time to managing such external demands is not surprising when one reviews the extensive descriptive literature detailing the processes by which specific federal or state programs are implemented at local levels within individual schools (see, for example, Hargrove, Scarlett, Ward, Abernethy, Cunningham, & Vaughn, 1981; Weatherley, 1979). The view of individual schools directly confronting and responding to a fragmented regulatory and funding environment in addition to responding to these pressures more indirectly as mediated by superordinate structures reinforces an image of educational organizations as loosely coupled systems (see Davis et al., 1977; Weick, 1976).

Conclusion

We have compared public and private schooling organizations with the argument that their differing organizational environments should produce quite different organizational arrangements even though in many respects their internal tasks are similar. We find substantial differences in two areas. Public schooling has a much more elaborate organizational structure than does private schooling. It is not necessarily a larger organizational structure in terms of ratios of administrators to students but it is certainly much more complex. Catholic and private schooling systems have high ratios of building level administrators to students but above this level very little administrative structure. This reflects their funding and controlling environment. Public schooling has complex and expanding structures running above the school level. And it is exactly these organizational levels that expanding environmental controls from state and national levels have acted to foster in recent decades: the complex fundings, programs, and requirements in which public schooling is immersed create pressures that generate much administrative expansion. Public schools are in a sense collections of organizational structure from a very complex and increasingly organized environment rather than highly bounded and internally coherent organizations in their own right. They are immersed in, and interpenetrated by an organized environment, not simply affected by it.

8

Centralization, Fragmentation, and School District Complexity

JOHN W. MEYER

W. RICHARD SCOTT

DAVID STRANG

IN THIS CHAPTER, we examine the effects of the institutional environment on the administrative component of American public school districts. These units function in the complex and many-layered structure of American education, with pressures coming from parents and community groups, states, the national government, and a wide variety of professional and interest groups organized at all these levels. Districts differ radically from similar schooling organizations in highly centralized national educational systems, where districts and schools often function as simple subordinate units in a sovereign national bureaucracy.

The study examines the effects of the changing American institutional context on the administrative complexity of school districts. We use a unique data set on school districts to explore three main ideas. First, the

The research reported here was conducted with funds from the Institute for Research on Educational Finance and Governance (now the Stanford Education Policy Institute) under a grant from the National Institute of Education (Grant NIE-G-83-0003). The analyses and conclusions do not necessarily reflect the views or policies of either institute. We are pleased to acknowledge the contributions of Young Hwan Lee, Kyoung-Ryung Seong, and Zueguang Zhou, who assisted us in compiling, organizing, and analyzing the data on school districts and federal programs.

expanding federal involvement in education, given its fragmented organizational character, expands administrative burdens at the school district level. Second, the expansion of state involvement, given the legitimated sovereignty and more integrated bureaucracies operating at the state level, lowers administrative complexity in school districts. And third, dependence on local funding, where interests and pressures are diverse and complex but less formally organized, produces an intermediate level of administrative complexity.

The environment of U.S. school districts has changed dramatically over the course of this century. From a situation in which virtually all funding and control resided exclusively in the local community, the role of both state and national governments has gradually increased:

> Prior to 1930, localities provided more than 80 percent of school revenues, the states less than 20 percent. Though the state share reached 30 percent just before World War II, it did not edge above 40 percent until 1973, by which time there was also a visible—though always small—federal contribution. The local share, which in 1973 was down to 50 cents of the school dollar, continued to erode during the past decade until in 1979, for the first time ever, the state share slightly exceeded the local contribution. (Doyle & Finn, 1984)

Because there is great variation among states in school funding and control arrangements and among districts in the amount of support received from federal sources, it is possible to examine the impact on district organization of cross-sectional variations in their funding environments. To do this, we employ data compiled from several national educational surveys of school districts in the United States as of 1977.

Theoretical and Research Background

Earlier organizational theories viewed organizational structure—in particular, the complexity of the administrative component—as derived from the nature of technical tasks performed by organizations (see Galbraith, 1973; Perrow, 1967; Thompson, 1967; Woodward, 1965). This line of argument provides little leverage in explaining public school organizations, which tend to carry out similar tasks but exhibit wide variation in size and complexity (Meyer & Rowan, 1978). Failures to account for the characteristics of school organizations, as well as inadequacies in accounting for much structural variation among other types of organizations, have led theorists to shift from a focus on technology as the primary determinant of structure to emphasize the role played by the environment (Meyer &

Scott, 1983b). Organizational environments vary in complexity of re-source and power arrangements (Pfeffer & Salancik, 1978) as well as in the configuration of their wider structures and legitimating rules (DiMaggio & Powell, 1983; Meyer & Rowan, 1977). In this chapter, we build on these conceptions, seeing the organizational structures of American school districts as created and shaped by the resource flows and control structures in their environment.

We start with the general notion that administrative expansion in organizations reflects complexity in the wider environment. But in order to spell out what environmental complexity means, and the conditions under which it produces formalized complexity within organizations, it is useful to distinguish several dimensions of environmental structure. Here we distinguish the *fragmentation* of the environment from the *formal structuring* of environmental actors. We touch briefly on the effects of environmental centralization, in the sense of shifts upward in the social structural locations of environmental actors.

Fragmentation reflects the number and distribution of organizations or social actors a focal organization is dependent upon. A unified or unfragmented environment exists when the resources relevant to a focal organization stem from the same source and are integrated in some clear way. This is the position of an organizational subunit, when the larger organization effectively buffers it from direct external forces, provided the larger organization itself does not present a highly fragmented structure. At the other extreme, a focal organization is dependent upon and penetrated by multiple, quasi-independent organizations and social actors, each presenting possibly conflicting, and at best uncoordinated, sets of demands and pressures. By many lines of argument, administrative structures within the focal organization should expand as the environment fragments in this way. If administration arises to deal with environments (as much or more than internal technologies), then environmental complexity should expand administrative work.

Formal structuring refers to the extent to which an organization is surrounded by formally organized interests, sovereigns, and constituency groups, as opposed to environments made up of less formally organized groups, communities, or associations. The core idea here is that over and above the degree of complexity of an environment, formalization in the environment is especially likely to generate formal administrative structure within organizations. A highly formalized environment, containing many varieties of organized professions, associations, regulatory bodies, or interest groups, is expected to generate administrative expansion in focal organizations such as school districts. When the complexity of the environment is more loosely structured or diffuse, taking the form of multiple, interpenetrated, and shifting political interests and informal pressures, local units may be highly penetrated, but their response is less likely to be reflected in increased formal complexity, or bureaucratic expansion. In school districts, the multiple demands of less rationalized environments are met less by formalized administrative expansion and differentiation than by the informal behavioral adjustments of participants, whether administrators or teachers, as they attempt to accommodate and fend off pressures and demands. Many current lines of organizational theory—institutional arguments, along with resource dependency and ecological ones—can produce the argument that formalized administration reflects not only environmental complexity but environmental formalization. This argument can explain why traditional local school systems in the United States have evinced less administrative formalization than their quite complex social and political environments would be expected to generate.

The dimensions of formalization and unification are quite distinct. One can imagine organizations whose environments are high on both—as with a subunit of a big bureaucracy or a firm dominated by a single large supplier or customer. But a consensual community—a technical profession, for instance—may unify an environment without formalizing it. Obviously, many organizations such as small firms or traditional one-room schools may function in an environment neither formalized nor unified. And environments with many formalized but inconsistent groups are common—perhaps especially in the American federal context. A local hospital now faces, for instance, all sorts of regulatory pressures from local, state, national, and professional governors, as well as a highly formalized system of third-party payers.

We use the dimension of environmental unification versus fragmentation to better specify what is sometimes, in the literature, meant by centralization. It is often assumed that an environment in which control is shifted upward in level (and thus centralized) is thereby unified and simplified: complexity is absorbed at the central level, and a given local organization therefore faces a simpler environment. This is not necessarily so. Authority may be shifted upward in level in an environment, without becoming more integrated in a unified sovereign body and, thus, without consolidating the environment of a given local organization. This is often strikingly true in American society, given a federalist structure, and is certainly often the case in American education, in which upward shifts of authority often build up a highly fragmented political control system. We have elsewhere used the term *fragmented centralization* to describe this process (Meyer & Scott, 1983b).

In the section below, we consider how these general distinctions and expectations are applicable to American school districts and their environments.

Evolution of Educational Environments
and School Organizations

Nineteenth- and early twentieth-century American schooling operated mainly within a local context. State statutes provided a general framework supporting education with rules specifying attendance requirements for pupils, the length of the school year, and minimum qualifications for teachers. But most educational decisions were made within local communities, first at the school and then increasingly at the district level. Funding provisions were also predominantly local, based on property taxes.

The relevant environment was local, but not necessarily simple. Education affects a wide range of individuals and groups, including many specialized interests—from economic and class groups to familial and religious ones—so that schools are often a prime focus of public attention and political pressure. The multiple functions and meanings attributed to education tend to give rise to complex and active environmental pressures, often reflected in boisterous school board or school bond elections and prolonged disputes over the selection of library books or sites for new schools.

The local environment of schools often entails complexity but not of the sort that is highly structured. Multiple, urgent, and shifting pressures are placed on school systems, making demands on board members, principals, and teachers, but not of a type to foster much administrative expansion. In the small school district, much of the administrative burden is not codified in the elaboration of formal structure but in the broad and nuanced definitions of citizen, parent, school board member, principal, and teacher.

Beginning late in the 19th century and proceeding up to the present, there has been continuing consolidation of schools. Early in this period, urban school reformers sought to integrate the many schools into a few districts, each with a single sovereign board representing the entire community and managing the schools through a more efficient, bureaucratic district office. Tyack (1974) has chronicled the history of this movement and has characterized its driving ideology as an intent to create and impose on all schools "the one best system." This movement has made steady progress, although its development has been slower and has continued longer than is generally recognized. Data we have compiled and reported elsewhere (Meyer, Scott, Strang, & Creighton, 1988; reprinted as Chapter 9 in this volume) reveal that the consolidation of schools and districts continued steadily well into the 1970s. Mean school enrollment increased from 142 to 440 over the 1940 to 1980 period, while the mean number of school districts per state declined eightfold, from 2437 to 330, during the same period (Meyer et al., 1988). This type of centralization has been associated with some bureaucratization of the system: Superintendents and their administrative staffs expand over time, and there is increased formalization of administrative roles both at school and district levels. But much of the complexity of the local environment continues to be managed informally.

The 20th century has witnessed a great expansion of the role of the states in education. In recent decades, state funding has risen to match and surpass levels of local funding, and state authority has expanded in all the domains of education (e.g., curriculum, accreditation, setting minimum standards, personnel certification, and meeting the needs of special groups). There has been considerable conflict and much variability in this process, although state authority is constitutionally grounded. In the earlier period, and up to the present, there has been much genuine and legitimated local authority in education—indeed, a religion of localism. But always, in the background, there has been the authority of the states. Thus, even in the 19th century, states defined the basic framework of schooling, imposing such requirements as compulsory attendance laws, teacher certification requirements, and all sorts of other specifications. In the early period, these control attempts were weak, in an organizational sense—for example, the median American state department of education contained a staff of two in 1890 (National Education Center, 1931, p. 5)—but the political, legal, and cultural principles of state sovereignty were well established. And as centralization and consolidation have proceeded throughout the 20th century, they have conformed to well-established organizational control principles.

Thus the expansion of state funding and decision making could take the form of direct organizational authority. The impact on local organization, following the lines of theory discussed above, is clear. The gradual evolution of a strong node of authority in the environment in one sense adds complexity to the situation of the local school district but, in a more important sense, simplifies it. The environment becomes more centralized but also more unified; the organizational rules constituting schooling become more clear, better specified, more uniform and integrated than before. The result is bigger and more standardized school districts, each having a common and highly authorized form, with relatively small administrative components. Much complexity is absorbed thus by state-level integration.

Although the general trend toward increased state authority over education is clear, states vary enormously in the extent to which funding has become centralized, in the development of the administrative and professional capacity of the state educational office, and the political culture supporting a more centralized and integrated view of educational decision making (see Burlingame & Geske, 1979; Fuhrman & Rosenthal, 1981;

Kirst, 1978; McDonnell & McLaughlin, 1982). This variability among states is exploited in our design to test the effects of increased state centralization and unification on local district administration.

Since the early 1960s, as a part of the Great Society reforms initiated under Presidents Kennedy and Johnson and continuing through the 1970s, the federal government has become involved in the funding and management of education. Prior to this time, federal efforts in education had been highly restricted and conducted with relatively low levels of direct authority. The most prominent federal programs had been in the area of vocational education, developing in the 1920s, but this effort was limited in funding and largely marginal to mainstream educational programs and institutions. This was due largely to the lack of constitutional provision for a federal role in education (Timpane, 1976).

The U.S. constitutional pattern—differing greatly from that obtained in many other modern states—has also heavily influenced the evolution of federal funding and authority in education in recent decades. Rather than expanding direct national controls in the management of education, reform efforts during the 1960s and 1970s took the form of categorical or special-purpose programs. No programs were created for the general support and management of education, and none defined or attempted to assist its primary goals or core processes. Rather, special purposes were defined and furthered with specially organized fundings in a highly fragmented system. The high point of this expansion came in about 1977. There were special fundings to deal with specific types of students (rural, urban, migrant, needy, physically handicapped, academically handicapped, neglected, or adult); with a few types of special educational topics (consumer education, work-study programs, vocational training, or cooperative educational programs); and with special resource problems (state administrative costs, local administrative costs, innovation, community services, research dissemination, and especially libraries—public libraries, school libraries, cooperation among libraries—and library facilities for special groups such as the handicapped or the disadvantaged). The funding impact of these programs on local school organizations is suggested by Table 8.1, which reports the level of funding received from each of the main programs by the average school district as of 1977.

Complexity in the environment of schools has been greatly enhanced by these developments. Although more decisions are made at higher levels, not only have decisions become more highly centralized, but also the actors involved are both more structured and more fragmented. The various programs establish their own rules of eligibility, of operation, of accounting. Although the bulk of these funds as routed through the state educational agencies, "by 1979, 25% of all federal grants-in-aid funding

TABLE 8.1 Numbers of School Districts and Revenue Amounts From Federal Programs*

Program Name	Number of School Districts Receiving Funds (N = 894)	Average Amount of Money per District
Adult education	194	14,043
Handicapped children	55	34,908
Migrant children	46	81,343
Local education agencies	824	138,214
Special incentive	35	35,156
Library resources	40	1,925
Education centers	41	39,656
Handicapped in public school	96	36,270
Strengthening instruction	32	1,023
Basic grants	585	18,367
Special needs	98	9,092
Research	13	4,224
Innovation	19	17,857
Consumer and homemaking	600	3,143
Cooperative education	103	14,931
Work study	199	2,232
Library resources	783	10,097
Educational innovation and support	79	30,536

*Taken from detailed federal data on a subsample of districts

bypassed state governments and was allocated directly to local jurisdictions" (McDonnell & McLaughlin, 1982, p. 7). Even though the amount of federal funding never accounted for more than a small fraction of total educational funding—the upper limit reached in 1977 was less than 10%—the organizational impact on school districts appears to have been considerable. According to our line of argument, the combination of increased structuring and increased fragmentation should greatly expand the administrative burden imposed on the local level. In a longitudinal analysis within five states, Freeman, Hannan, and Hannaway (1978) showed substantial increases in district administrative staff associated with higher levels of federal funding.

Federal fragmentation imposes administrative burdens on school districts through a number of mechanisms, illustrated in great detail in qualitative research (e.g., Bankston, 1982; McDonnell & McLaughlin, 1982). From the side of the agencies in the federal environment, the lack of integrated sovereignty over schooling leads to control efforts that take specialized and very directive forms: The impulse is to require that funds from each federal program be kept separate organizationally and, in accounting, that specialized reports be made on the needs, programmatic structures, and effects associated with each program's purposes, and even that distinct administrative positions carry responsibility for the federal program aims and funds. Sometimes special funding directly supports these mandated administrative activities. Given the number of federal agencies involved, Bankston (1982) showed that the required proposals, reports, and accountings for a medium-size school district could easily add up, during the high period of the 1970s, to hundreds of documents per year.

From the perspective of the school district, there is obvious interest in conforming to these federal legal requirements. But the interest may go beyond passive conformity: maintaining an administrative system isomorphic to the complex federal system carries advantages for obtaining funding preferment. Such an administrative system can develop the competence to search out funding prospects and adapt to changed funding potentials, can learn to conform to program and reporting requirement more readily, and can develop relationships that smooth over the whole process.

The mechanisms that link federal fragmented complexity with district administrative elaboration thus serve both federal and local interests and take the form of legal, financial, and organizational pressures for isomorphism (DiMaggio & Powell, 1983).

Study Design and Hypotheses

A direct examination of the arguments presented above would investigate the effects that reporting requirements and program fragmentation have on administrative complexity at the district level. We do not have direct measures of environmental complexity and rely on the results of much past research, cited above, to assume that federal programs embody the most complex, and state programs the least complex, sets of demands on the local district. And, as discussed, local funds are assumed to be associated with intermediate levels of demands on the administration of local districts, involving diverse but less formally structured interests. We thus take the sources of revenue to embody distinctive degrees of complexity and examine the relation between the district's sources of revenue and its organizational structure.

The structure of district organization is measured in two distinct areas: administration and instruction. We argue that environmental complexity is mirrored in the complexity of administrative roles, enabling the organization to buffer from external demands the actual work done. The corollary is that instruction, the technical work of the district, should not be much affected by environmental complexity.

As a baseline, we expect that more revenue of any sort tends to expand the district organization along any dimension. We thus focus on the relative effects of the sources of revenue and not on their absolute effects. Our hypotheses are:

Hypothesis 1: Federal funding involves especially large increases in district administrative structure compared to those of state or local funding.

Hypothesis 2: State funding involves lower increases in district administrative structure than do either federal or local funding. Because the local environment is less organizationally structured, we expect the impact of its complexity on formal administration to be less than federal funding but greater than that of state-administered funds.

As an extension of this line of reasoning, we take advantage of a measure of state programmatic centralization developed by Wirt (1978) to argue:

Hypothesis 3: The centralization of a state's educational system lowers the degree of administrative complexity of school district organizations, independent of any funding effects.

Hypothesis 4: There are few significant differences among federal, state, or local funding effects on the complexity of district instructional roles and expenditure levels.

Our main interest is to explore the federal effect suggested by Hypothesis 1, because the federal system is highly unusual in its degree of bureaucratic fragmentation, providing the best test of our central theme. We can go further than a simple aggregated federal effect by examining the effects of specific federal programs. Over time, older federal programs have been captured by the state departments of education; the funding channels have become less differentiated and the reporting requirements less extensive.[1] Federal programs initiated in the 1960s and 1970s should thus have larger effects on district administration than earlier ones: the federal effort has been bigger, and time has not yet routinized it. In our data, this involves a comparison between the Elementary and Secondary Education Act (ESEA) programs and the older federal education programs, such as the National Defense Education (NDEA) and vocational education programs. Our final hypothesis is thus:

Hypothesis 5: Funding from newer (ESEA) federal programs leads to more expansion of district administration than does funding from older federal programs.

DATA

Data for this study are taken from four independent governmental surveys done in 1976-1977. These are the Bureau of the Census's *Survey of Local Government Finances,* the *Elementary and Secondary Staff Information Survey* of the Equal Employment Opportunity Commission (EEOC), the *Elementary and Secondary School Civil Rights Survey* of the Office of Civil Rights, and the *Tabulations of Census Data by School District* done by the National Institute of Education. These surveys can be used in conjunction because of the important work of the National Center for Education Statistics in merging and editing the files. Because each survey has its own unique history, this combination of data from different sources is only available for 1975-1976 and 1976-1977.

Most of the surveys in the data set attempted to reach all of the 16,853 school districts in the country. Our analyses of administrative expenditure variables in fact included 15,013 (or 89%) of this population: The missing cases lacked information on one or another of our independent variables or sometimes enrolled no students.

Our analyses of school district administrative positions took their measures of this dependent variable from the EEOC survey noted above. This survey sampled 6,889 cases from the population of American school districts. The sample was a weighted random one—somewhat oversampling urban cases with minority populations. Our analysis was based on 6,718 cases, or 97% of this sample. Again, a few cases were missing because of missing data on one or another independent variable.

The variables in the analyses are described below. Table 8.2 gives their means and standard deviations. It shows that the sample with data on personnel variables is quite similar to the overall population of school districts. The overrepresentation of urban, minority, and Southern districts was not for our purposes problematic, because these variables were controlled in the analyses.

DEPENDENT VARIABLES

Administrative positions includes the total number of district and school administrators. School administrators include principals and assistant principals. District administrators include superintendents, assistant superintendents, and special services administrators. Collected by the EEOC, Fall 1976.

Teaching positions includes the total number of teachers in the district, including elementary and secondary school teachers and teacher aides. Collected by the EEOC, Fall 1976.

Administrative expenditures: total administrative expenditures as measured by the Bureau of the Census, 1976-1977, *Survey of Local Government Finances.*

Teaching expenditures: total instructional expenditures, also measured by the Bureau of the Census, 1976-1977, *Survey of Local Government Finances.*

TABLE 8.2 Means and Standard Deviations of Variables in Regression Analyses

Variables	Overall District Data Set (N = 15,013) Mean	S.D.	Data Set with Personnel Information (N = 6,717) Mean	S.D.
Administrative positions students	—	—	.004	.002
Teaching positions students	—	—	.053	.023
Administrative expenditure students	82.35	90.08	—	—
Teaching expenditure students	914.00	339.54	—	—
ESEA funds students	41.95	51.46	41.13	40.58
Other federal students	73.90	140.84	71.52	93.36
State funds students	625.95	422.29	651.51	269.99
Local funds students	905.46	744.86	748.31	518.45
State centralization index	3.58	.52	3.61	.46
Suburban	.24	.43	.39	.48
Urban	.02	.15	.05	.22
1 Enrollment	.008	.030	.001	.001
Percent black	.056	.14	.08	.16
Percent poverty	—	—	.15	.13
South	.11	.32	.18	.38

INDEPENDENT AND CONTROL VARIABLES

State funds: total revenue received by the district directly from the state. All revenue variables were collected by the Bureau of the Census, 1976-1977, *Survey of Local Government Finances.*

Local funds: school district revenue derived from local sources. These include the property tax, the parent government funding (local city or county), and revenue from other school districts.

Federal funds: school district revenue from the ESEA, the NDEA, Federal Vocational Programs, School Lunch monies, and direct federal aid through Public Laws 815 and 874.

State centralization index: Wirt's (1978) measure of the programmatic authority of the state department of education. Wirt did content analyses of state law, involving items such as accreditation, textbook, and attendance requirements, and combined these into an index varying between 0 and 6.

Enrollment: total enrollment in the district, measured by the Bureau of the Census, 1976-1977, *Survey of Local Government Finances,* and edited by the National Center for Education Statistics. We include enrollment as a control variable, given the much discussed effects of organizational scale on administrative intensity (see Freeman & Kronenfeld, 1974). (Other analyses not reported here also tested for curvilinear size effects.)

Number of schools: total elementary and secondary schools in the district; measured by the National Institute of Education's Special Tabulations of Census Data by School District. The number of organizational units has clear implications for administrative complexity, following Blau's (1970) arguments.

Urban, suburban location: two dichotomous variables (*rural* is the omitted category), developed from a Bureau of the Census code based on population count. Urban districts are often thought to be more administratively complex, sometimes because greater diversity of students leads to higher technical complexity.

Black students: the total number of black pupils in the district, collected by the Office for Civil Rights, Elementary and Secondary School Survey, Fall 1976. We controlled for the enrollment of blacks and poor students because such students are sometimes thought to create administrative burdens— among other reasons, because they increase technical variability.

Poor students: the total number of children between 6 and 17 in the district who were classified as poor by the National Institute for Education, Special Tabulations of Census Data by School District.[2]

South: a dummy variable, coded 1 if the district was in a Southern state. The comparative literature suggests that Southern public administration is more centralized, so this factor was held constant in the analysis.

ANALYSES

The models reported here are multivariate regression analyses of the effects of levels of funding from local, state, and federal sources on school district administrative staff size and expenditures. The control variables described above are included in the models. For comparative purposes, effects of the same independent variables on district instructional staff size and expenditures are also estimated.

Because the dependent variables are raw staff size and expenditure figures, rather than ratios of these figures to, for instance, enrollments, they are naturally scaled to district size. This poses no problems for examining the effects of the main independent variables—funding dollars from various sources—because these are also naturally scaled to size; that is, it is reasonable to suppose that a given raw number of dollars (or students) would produce a given raw number of administrators or dollars of administrative expenditure. This is also true of a number of the control variables, such as the raw number of black students or students from families below the poverty line or district enrollment itself. The other control variables do not have this built-in property. It makes sense to hypothesize that the effects of state educational centralization, the urban or suburban character of the district, and location in the South affect administrative staff size or expenditure *in proportion to the size of the district.* For instance, location in a centralized state might lower the number of administrators in a small district by less than one full position, while the same effect in a large district might amount to a half-dozen positions. Thus in the analyses the effects of state centralization, urban and suburban location, and Southern location are estimated with the interaction of these variables with the enrollment of the district.

In estimating the equations, ordinary-least-squares techniques are not really appropriate. All the variables, both independent and dependent, are very highly skewed in distribution, because they all reflect size variations. Thus the residuals in ordinary-least-squares analyses are far from normally distributed. Bigger districts have much bigger staffs, more funds of all sorts, and will tend to have larger residual errors in absolute terms. Our solution was to weight all terms in the equations by the reciprocal of district enrollment, for estimating purposes—i.e., to use weighted-least-squares estimation. This produces analyses with better distributed residuals, as well as less skewed variables.

Results

Table 8.3 reports multivariate analyses of the size of district administrative staff (equation 1) and of administrative expenditures (equation 3). For comparative purposes, effects on instructional staff size and expenditures are also presented (equations 2 and 4). To simplify presentation, the staff size estimates are made in terms of 1/1000 of a position. The issues relevant to the hypotheses have to do with the relative effects of local, state, and federal funds. The latter are broken down into (a) those funds linked to the recent reforms of the ESEA and (b) all other federal funds to permit a test of the idea that ESEA funding produces especially large effects on administrative expansion.

The overall findings are very clear. State funding, as expected, generates the lowest levels of administrative expenditure and staffing. Local funding generates higher levels of both. Non-ESEA federal funding generates still higher levels of both. And ESEA federal funding generates very high levels of administrative expenditure and staffing.[3]

These differences are generally not paralleled by effects on instructional staffing and expenditure. Local, state, and non-ESEA federal effects here differ little. Federal ESEA funding, on the other hand, does generate distinctly larger effects on instructional funding and staffing than do the other funding sources. But this differential is still much less than the differential ESEA effect on administrative staffing and expenditure.

TABLE 8.3 Effects of Various Types of Federal, State, and Local Funding on School District Administration and Instructional Expenditures and Personnel (All terms weighted by 1/Enrollment)

Equations*	Federal ESEA	Other Funds	State Funds	Local Funds	State Central-ization	Suburban (= 1)	Urban (= 1)	Percent Black	Percent Poverty	No. of Schools	South (= 1)	Enroll-ment	Constant
1. Administrative positions/1000	.0060*	.0012*	.0003*	.0009*	.09	.011	.17	.06	.44	.002	.17	1.16*	1.399*
2. Teaching positions/1000	.078*	.009*	.012*	.016*	-2.6*	-1.76*	1.66*	9.76*	7.01*	.008	4.91*	30.0*	11.971*
3. Administrative expenditures ($)	.22*	.07*	.037*	.059*	-3.77*	-12.59*	-13.21*	.60	—	-.26*	-9.59*	10.91	-.217
4. Teaching expenditures ($)	.69*	.26*	.26*	.30*	9.16*	87.4*	65.0*	138.4*	—	.78*	-114.2*	349	2.210

*p ≤ .01
Number of cases: for equations 1 and 2, 6,718; for equations 3 and 4, 15,013.

174

For administrative expenditures, the differences between each pair of the four effects are statistically significant. For administrative personnel, all differences are statistically significant except for that between non-ESEA federal funding and local funding. And substantively, the effects are quite large. A local dollar generates about three times the administrative staffing of a state dollar, non-ESEA federal dollars about four and one-half times as much, and ESEA federal dollars about 19 times as much. On administrative expenditures, local dollars produce about one and one-half times the effect of state dollars, non-ESEA federal dollars about twice the effect, and ESEA dollars six times the effect. And most of these effects are larger than the differential effects of the fundings on instructional expenditure and staffing. The extraordinary ESEA effect on administration, however, is diminished by this comparison: It still remains higher than any other effect on administrative expenditure but is no longer higher (relative to the instructional effect) than the non-ESEA effect on administrative staffing.

These data provide substantial support for our main hypotheses. State funding, as expected, has the smallest effects on administrative funding and staffing, with local funding having greater effects and federal funding much greater yet. The differences are large. Further, the recent-ESEA-funding variable has, as expected, greater administrative effects than older federal fundings: Our confidence in this result on the staffing side is diminished because ESEA funding also seems to substantially increase instructional staffing (which we did not predict).

We also hypothesized that state centralization would tend to lower administrative expenditures and staffing. The results do not support this idea: An effect of this sort occurs in the expenditure analysis, but an insignificant positive effect appears in the staffing analysis.

With funding structure held constant, the effects of the control variables tend to be small. Enrollment still has some additional positive effects. Urban and suburban districts have lower administrative and higher teaching expenditures than rural ones but do not differ much on staffing. Southern districts have slightly lower expenditure levels. Districts with more black students appear to have slightly more teachers and teaching expenditures. Districts with more students below the poverty line have slightly more teachers, too. The reported expenditures analysis does not include this variable (in order to reduce missing cases, as noted above).[4]

We conclude that the data provide support for the argument that the more fragmented local and federal environments are associated with higher levels of administrative complexity of school districts than the more integrated—state—environments. And, given environmental complexity, the more formally structured federal environment is associated with higher levels of administrative complexity than the less formally structured—local—environments. That these effects are not simply a matter of centralization but of fragmentation of funding is supported by the finding that earlier federal programs that are less fragmented in form of administration are associated with lower administrative complexity of districts than are the more recent and more highly fragmented federal programs. Over time, federal programs have been captured and integrated by state and local organizations. Finally, the data do not support the expectation that greater programmatic authority over education at the state level, by providing a simpler environment, would be associated with lower administrative complexity at the district level.

Discussion

We have described the funding environments of American public school districts to see whether the organized complexity of these environments predicts administrative elaboration in both positions and funding. The results show that federal funding—especially in the newer federal educational programs—generates unusually high levels of administrative expenditures and staffing size, in comparison to state and local funding. There is some further evidence that state funding and centralization reduce relative levels of administrative expenditures in comparison to the effects of local funding.

The results of the district-level analyses in some respects contrast with those we found in another analysis, using data aggregated to the state level (Meyer, Scott, Strang & Creighton, 1988). There we found dramatic changes over time, apparently reflecting the general expansion of state and federal funding and authority, but few differences among states in aggregated administrative expenditures or positions dependent on particular patterns of (aggregated) state and federal funding. It seems clear that the present analysis—conducted at the appropriate level of analysis—is to be taken much more seriously. The fact that state expansion produces much larger districts, with corresponding changes in administrative structure (Strang, 1987), was apparently inadequately controlled in the earlier analyses. Our central result on the special administrative burden created by federal funding is consistent with the results of an earlier analysis of district structures within several states (Freeman, Hannan, & Hannaway, 1978), though in that study, state funding was also associated with expanded administrative structures (perhaps reflecting effects of particular states).

These results lend considerable support to the idea that a complex or fragmented organization environment is likely to expand the administrative burdens of an organization. In the case of education, such burdens take on clear and palpable meaning—specialized outside agencies (recently, especially agencies at the federal level) provide funds in exchange for detailed administrative controls and reports. Sometimes, there have even been external rules in effect *requiring* local schooling organizations to differentiate their programs administratively in terms of the external funding and requirements involved. These results suggest that over time, with routinization, such effects may decrease—for example, the older vocational education supports are no longer accompanied by much special administrative pressure.

The results of this study come from the late 1970s—the period of high and recent reformist federal intervention into many aspects of education. It seems likely that the administrative effects of the recent programs—designed, as they were, to penetrate and reconstruct aspects of local education—have attenuated over time. Federal funding has shifted away from special-purpose grants toward block grants and has shifted from programs attempting direct controls over local educational organizations toward more general support filtered through state education departments. The long-run effects of these changes has undoubtedly been to reduce the local administrative burden and probably to reduce the special effects of federal funding that we have reported here. Further research covering longer time periods would be useful in examining this question.

It would also be useful, in further work, to see if the earlier periods of expansion in state organizational control and funding were accompanied by similar administrative pressures on local districts. In the short term, the addition of a new organizational layer would ordinarily add complexity. But the state's role in education has typically been rather simple and direct—the expansion of that role is closely tied to the consolidation and standardization of schools and school districts. From early on the state departments of education may have had the net effect of undercutting the complexities of local political pressures on schooling and providing for a simpler environment for local administration.[5] From this point of view, then, the distinctive aspect of federal involvement lies in its special lack of authority to provide direct and integrated educational control over the whole educational system—and thus in its intrinsically special-purpose and fragmented character. Unlike the rise of state authority, federal involvement has not lowered the legitimate pressures impinging on local organization from existing loci of authority and control. It thus added complexity, in an overall sense, to the system.

Overall, our analyses lend support to the general ideas with which we began. Environmental fragmentation does seem to increase the formal administrative burden in organizations, as does the formal organization of the environment. Centralization by itself, independent of these other factors, may have little effect on administrative complexity. In the case of the American federal system—especially pronounced, perhaps, in the instance of education—centralization to the national level may increase fragmentation, thus increasing the administrative complexity or demands faced by local organizational structure. This line of thought may help explain why, in a period in which many issues are raised to national attention, the great increases in complexity in American organization seem to have been at the local or intermediate (e.g., district) level.

Notes

1. A similar process is occurring at the present time, as the more recent federal programs of the 1970s have increasingly been "block granted," coming more under state control during the 1980s. However, our data set does not include these developments.

2. This variable was not included in the analyses of administrative and instructional expenditures because its inclusion reduced the sample size by more than 2,000 cases.

3. Data were also available for district-level "professional staff," a heterogeneous category including such titles as counselors, librarians, and instructional specialists. We examined the effects of federal, state, and local funding on this category but found inconsistent and unconvincing results largely due, we would argue, to the variable types of personnel included in this category. We have omitted these analyses to simplify the presentation of results.

4. Parallel analyses including the poverty variable give very similar results to those reported here.

5. Of course, we would expect important variation among states in their interest in and capacity for consolidating controls over local districts. Assuming the development of an adequate measure of state centralization, this variance could be exploited to provide a more sensitive test of the arguments advanced.

9

Bureaucratization Without Centralization

Changes in the Organizational System of U.S. Public Education, 1940-1980

JOHN W. MEYER

W. RICHARD SCOTT

DAVID STRANG

ANDREW L. CREIGHTON

PUBLIC SCHOOL CLASSROOMS IN THE UNITED STATES have changed greatly over their history. So has the organizational structure that holds these classrooms together in a national system. There have been great changes in the U.S. system of schools, districts, county offices, state departments, and national bureaus. One aim of this chapter is to describe some of these organizational changes over recent decades, using available data. Many important changes can be summarized with a very traditional word—*bureaucratization*. The framework of rules, pressures, and interests that hold a given classroom in place within the national educational system has

The research reported here was conducted with funds from the Institute for Research on Educational Finance and Governance under a grant from the National Institute of Education (Grant NIE-G-83-0003). The analyses and conclusions do not necessarily reflect the views or policies of either institute. We would like to thank JoEllen Shively for providing research assistance and comments. We are indebted to our IFG colleagues for their comments and suggestions.

become more explicit and formalized. The classrooms are connected by organizational rules and roles, by formulas and functionaries, by lawyers and accountants. Once held in place by the pressures in *society* that make much of U.S. life seem homogeneous, the classrooms are increasingly organized by the administration of the *state*.

Beyond tracing the bureaucratization of U.S. public education, a second main task of this chapter is to examine hypotheses about why this bureaucratization occurs. One common theme of most discussions is to see bureaucratization as a consequence of the centralization of power, authority, and funding. Patriotic scholarship has often seen the decentralized and associational (rather than bureaucratic) character of U.S. public education as celebrating populist democracy. But accounts of the oppressive conformism and homogeneity within U.S. educational institutions raise questions about what the term *decentralization* might mean. In any event, we test below the hypothesis that the source of the bureaucratization of U.S. educational structure in recent decades reflects the expanded power of the federal government in the system.

Bureaucratization

In most countries, the rise of central educational bureaucracies precedes expanded mass public education. There is a national minister, compulsory attendance principle, curriculum, teacher certification system, and centralized structures of funding long before most children are enrolled (Ramirez & Boli, 1987; Ramirez & Rubinson, 1979). The U.S. experience has been quite different. A full century after this country developed the largest mass public education system in the world, a central educational bureaucracy of much substantive authority has yet to emerge. As of the last few years, there is a cabinet officer, but there is no national attendance rule, or curriculum, or teacher certification rule. And federal funding makes up less than 10% of public educational expenditures. The central body of functionaries has expanded but with fragmented authority over special programs rather than over the main structure itself (Meyer & Scott, 1983b).

We can move one level down from the national center and find earlier bureaucratic expansion. Education is, constitutionally, more a creature of the 50 states, and there has been some real bureaucratization at this level, which compels pupils to attend, defines teachers, specifies some features of curricula, and provides more than 40% of the funds. But historically, these developments at the state level postdate mass educational enrollment in the great northern and western bulk of the country. A system of mass education was already in place by the last third of the 19th century—the time during which most states developed rules of compulsory education, built up small state departments of education, elaborated curricula, and certified teachers.

To carry the point further, even the modern school district—a structure with a bureaucratic staff commonly controlling a number of schools in an area—postdates the creation of mass education (Kaestle & Vinovskis, 1976; Tyack, 1974). And so does the modern school—a large enterprise of many classrooms integrated by at least a small bureaucratic unit. Even in the cities, earlier 19th-century schools were small neighborhood structures.

The data we are about to review provide evidence of substantial organizational development. The average U.S. high school now has a larger administrative staff than that of the average state department of education in 1890 (Tyack, 1974). Yet it would be a mistake to conclude from the history of bureaucratic elaboration that the term *centralization,* with all its connotations, applies. After all, the school was built up around universalistic rather than local rules and around general institutional beliefs rather than around formal organizations. After independence, religious ideals became secular ones, and pressures for schooling were built into both national (the Northwest Ordinance) and state law. These were not bureaucratic forms—both national and local states were "states of courts and parties" (Skowronek, 1982) rather than bureaucracies—but in both law and culture they embodied sweeping universalistic and national goals, not local ones (Meyer, Tyack, Nagel, & Gordon, 1979). In education as in other areas, it is a mistake to infer from the weakness of the 19th-century national state as a bureaucracy to fragmentation as a purposive national society.

DIMENSIONS OF BUREAUCRATIZATION

The discussion above raises the issue of different aspects of the general phenomenon called *bureaucratization.* In the literature, much of the discussion of different aspects or defining characteristics of bureaucratization—including Weber's (1946)—conceals in its typologies arguments that should be causal and explicit. For purposes of our discussion, the following distinctions should be made:

1. Most generally, bureaucracy involves *formalization* of rules and roles. Activities, rights, and obligations are removed from the web of interactions in society, located in an organization, and thus bounded off.

2. But not just any sort of formalization is involved. In most definitions, *rationalization* is another aspect of bureaucratization; that is, the formalized roles and rules must be integrated around unified sovereignty and purpose.

3. It is generally understood that bureaucratization in a domain is greater when the formalized rationalization involved extends over a wider domain; increased scale of units is another feature of bureaucratization.
4. Seen as the lateral extension of bureaucracy, this expansion clearly involves a measure of *homogenization* or standardization of subunits.
5. Seen as the vertical extension of integrative capability, it involves the expansion in number of *levels of authority*.

We provide below evidence on changes in all these aspects of bureaucratization in U.S. education and show that there is not much question but that great changes have taken place in recent decades.

The central question concerns the causal role of centralization in the whole process. In most usages, bureaucratization implies centralization or includes it as a dimension. It is assumed that bureaucracy reflects the expansion of the scale of administrative power. Such an assumption is involved not only in colloquial talk about bureaucracy but also in Weber's original discussions, which focused on Prussian models. In these models, and this historical experience, it was difficult not to see bureaucracy and centralization as intertwined and the latter as anything else but a cause of the former.

In our analyses below, we present evidence on this main question: Does the expansion of central power in U.S. education account for the increased formalization and scale and standardization in the system? The data suggest a negative answer to this question. In a concluding section we speculate on the meaning and implications of this point.

BUREAUCRATIZATION IN THE CURRENT PERIOD

The research discussion of the history of bureaucratization in U.S. education is weakened by two common mistakes. One, alluded to above, is to mistake the rules or bureaucratic structure of the system as either similar to or a cause of public educational expansion. Thus histories focus on the educational reforms of a Horace Mann as if they *created* the schooling system. It then requires revisionists to note that these reforms may have played no role in the actual creation and expansion of the schools (Kaestle & Vinovskis, 1976). So also with the state-after-state crusade for compulsory education after the Civil War: The revisionists' statistics have it that these great organizational reforms show no effects on enrollment expansion (Fishlow, 1966; Solmon, 1970). Similarly with the whole bureaucratization process of the turn of the century—there is no evidence of its association with expansion (Meyer, Tyack, Nagel, & Gordon, 1979). Not only are educational expansion and bureaucratization distinct and decoupled processes, but one can argue that some negative relationships connect them (Boli, Ramirez, & Meyer, 1985).

A second mistake is to assume that bureaucratization is all of a piece—that the creation of general rules, laws, or principles means enactment in organizational reality. The awareness in the modern literature on innovation that adopted policies are often not implemented (see Berman & McLaughlin, 1975-1978; Hargrove et al., 1981; Weatherley, 1979) is often underemphasized in more historical discussions. There is much decoupling here too.

Thus the literature on the creation of the large graded school and the modern district and superintendency focuses on the late 19th century. So does that on the bureaucratization of the state departments of education. And discussions of the general construction of the larger consolidated bureaucratic district and the standardized state educational system focus on the interwar period. Too much attention is directed to the period of legal and rhetorical excitement associated with a new phase of bureaucratization and too little on the longer organizational process.

Our own venture into historical description below considers post-World War II bureaucratization. We looked for organizational changes associated with the federalization of educational issues (and to a lesser extent funding) since the 1950s—such as the waves of federal reforms concerned with racial and other inequalities and with educational quality after 1957 and Sputnik and again in the late 1970s. What we found, however, looks more like the continuation of changes resulting from earlier reforms and longer trends. We found the construction of long-term bureaucratization rather than a shift in character or direction.

DATA SOURCES

A main function of the national Office of Education since its creation in the 1860s was the reporting of data on education in the United States. This is a function now carried out by the National Center for Education Statistics, which surveys U.S. mass education every 2 years. NCES simply requests the states to provide summary data on basic educational matters; all the data presented in this chapter are thus state totals calculated by the states themselves. In itself, this process says much about the weakness of federal controls over education.

Although the surveys of state educational systems sometimes change in topic and method, there is enough continuity to make tentative inferences from comparisons plausible. We assembled reports from the period 1940 to 1980 to see what rough evidence we could get on changes in the bureaucratic shape of the national public education system during the period. Reports from 1940, 1946, 1950, 1956, 1960, 1966, 1970, 1974, and 1980 were used to approximate 5-year intervals (Statistics of State School Systems, 1940-1980). Because statistics on Alaska and Hawaii were not collected for the first four periods, those cases are omitted throughout to increase comparability. Other omissions of data for particular states are rare and commented on in the text. On the other hand, for many of the variables, data are missing for particular years. The tables simply leave those entries blank.

FORMALIZATION AND SCALE

The first two rows of Table 9.1 show the changing enrollment base of the system. Because elementary enrollment was practically universal through the period and the great bulk of it was in the public system throughout, the long enrollment increase and the more recent decline reflect demographic changes. Parallel changes affect the secondary enrollments, but to them must be added a strong secular increase in rates of secondary enrollment (and completion).

Numbers of teachers provides an alternative base figure to students, and in Table 9.1 we report mean numbers of teachers and student-teacher ratios during the period. Teacher data parallel student data but also reflect a long secular decline in the student-teacher ratio (Inkeles & Sirowy, 1983). The results below are similar whether we use teacher or student data as their base, so we stay with the latter.

Our central interest is in the bureaucratization of schooling, and we turn now to address this question. The national data report the number of public schools of various types in each state. The size of schools is one indicator of bureaucratization: A system with many little schools is less organizationally developed than one with a few big ones.

Rows 5 and 6 in Table 9.1 report the mean numbers of schools and students per school, averaged across states. The latter is one crucial item for assessing bureaucratization. The curve for mean numbers of schools is graphed in Figure 9.1. The results show a striking change in mean school size during the whole modern period up to the middle 1960s. The mean school size increases from 142 to 440 pupils in the 1940 through 1980 period. An organizational change discussed in the literature as going on in the 1890s and 1920s is a main feature of the contemporary period.

These figures are divided between elementary and secondary schools in Table 9.1. This shows that the bulk of the decline in numbers of schools reflects the closing of elementary schools, while the numbers of secondary schools per state has stayed almost constant. However, the growth rates in mean numbers of pupils for elementary and secondary schools are quite

TABLE 9.1 Selected Indicators of Bureaucratization and Funding, 1940–1980*

Name	1940	1946	1950	1956	1960	1966	1970	1974	1980
1. Enrollment	527,862	483,448	512,792	646,875	719,286	853,840	924,714	905,455	829,870
2. Percentage enrolled of 5-17 cohort		.81	.80	.84	.83	.87	.90	.89	.89
3. Teachers	18,175	17,246	18,965	23,530	28,009	35,340	41,784	44,506	45,046
4. Students/teacher		27	26	27	26	25	23	21	19
5. Schools		3,841	3,179	2,714	2,438	2,065	1,877	1,831	1,794
Elementary		3,336	2,668	2,172	1,904	1,514	1,333	1,296	
Secondary		505	510	541	534	550	496	487	
6. Students/school		142	176	254	309	402	471	469	440
Elementary		130	172	257		406	474	470	
Secondary		229	233	277		429	527	579	
7. Principals	765	696	910	1,104	1,313	1,595	1,868	2,073	2,186
8. Students/principal		1,053	715	653	597	564	500	449	380
9. Principals/school		.224	.332	.452	.549	.738	.943	1,048	1,160
10. School districts	2,437	2,109	1,734	1,141	843	561	398	347	330
11. Students/district		1,619	1,831	2,557	3,041	3,914	4,613	4,661	4,423
12. Superintendents	260			284	277	284	270	267	
13. Superintendents/district	.360			.598	.579	.688	.785	.844	
14. Assistant superintendents				88	118	180	278	478	
15. Assistant supts./district				.544	.750	1.027	1.783	1.950	
16. School board members		7,405	5,850	4,646	3,551	2,621	2,115	1,987	
17. Board members/district		4.349	4.365	5.186	4.779	6.375	5.657	5.865	
18. Intermediate units (cases)				68(34)	66(31)	59(28)	55(25)	53(20)	
19. SEA staff	74	114	161	187	208	318	400	448	
20. Students/SEA staff		4,241	4,022	4,335	4,083	2,848	2,305	1,961	
21. Revenue/student		207	281	353	433	595	786	868	892
Percent federal		.6	2.7	5.79	6.40	10.13	10.13	10.42	9.30
Percent state		35.0	38.1	38.27	39.89	39.85	41.60	42.67	46.69
Percent local		64.4	59.2	55.69	53.70	50.01	48.25	46.89	43.99

*Entries are means of state values for 48 states.

185

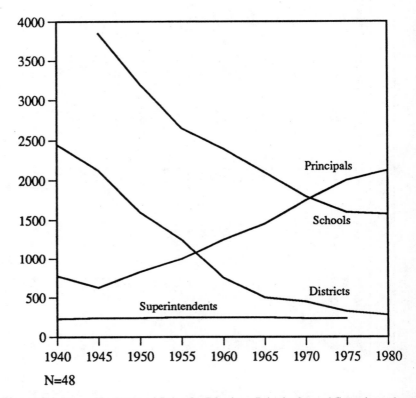

N=48

Figure 9.1. Mean Numbers of Schools, Districts, Principals, and Superintendents per State

comparable. Schools of either kind have expanded sharply between 1946 and 1980.

Note that these data describe state averages of the mean size of *schools* in the system. They do not describe the average experience of students. This is an important distinction: Although massive public attention has been focused on other issues, the educational system has been quietly continuing to clean out the hosts of little schools (often in rural areas) that were once its main organizational feature. Thus the decline is most dramatic in the Midwest, where the educational systems are historically the most decentralized—although it is visible enough in every state. As schools become larger, they acquire other bureaucratic attributes such as specialized administrative functionaries. Our data contain state reports of numbers of school principals. In rows 7 through 9 of Table 9.1 we report state means of principals and also means of the ratios of principals to total

TABLE 9.2 Comparisons of Number of Schools per District, 1940-1980, 48 States

	1946	1950	1956	1960	1966	1970	1974	1980
Schools per district (state means)	10.65	9.76	9.21	8.78	8.47	8.34	8.63	8.83
Schools per district (national total)	1.57	1.50	1.56	2.9	3.69	4.73	5.31	5.45
Schools per district (north, central, and west)	2.24	2.26	3.18	3.48	4.36	5.13	5.63	5.92
Schools per district (east and south)	18.38	16.72	14.75	13.66	12.26	11.29	11.39	11.51

students and schools. Mean number of principals per state is graphed in Figure 9.1. Although in 1940 less than a quarter of the schools have principals, in 1980 there are more principals than schools in the nation. This change from a situation in which few schools had specialized administrators to a situation in which almost all do involves a big step in formalization.

Now we consider the next organizational level. Schools are organized in school districts that have controlling authority over a wide range of issues from teacher employment to building ownership and maintenance. The great changes in education from 1890 to 1930 are commonly thought to have witnessed the consolidation of schools into modern rationalized district structures.

Rows 10 and 11 of Table 9.1 show the mean number of school districts per state and the mean number of students per district. The former is plotted in Figure 9.1. This curve indicates perhaps the most dramatic organizational change in the system. The number of school districts declines eightfold, from around 2,400 to 300 per state. Again, the long process of bureaucratization goes on at a very high rate long after it is assumed to have been accomplished.

It also occurs in very different places. Table 9.2 shows four comparisons of schools per school district over the 1946 through 1980 period. The first (row 1) is comparable to those discussed so far: the mean of the school to district ratio over the 48 states. The second (row 2) shows the changing ratio of total schools in the nation to the total number of districts in the nation. The two trends are very different: Overall the numbers of schools per district has more than trebled, but the mean state ratio has actually declined.

Understanding this discrepancy requires a closer inspection of the patterns of change of schools and districts. The average number of schools has declined rather uniformly across the states. Districts, however, show a great deal of heterogeneity. In many Eastern and Southern states, there were very few districts by 1940—often the county was also the school district—and in these states the number of districts has stayed roughly constant. Thus for these states the ratio of schools to districts declined as the average size of schools grew. Other states had very large numbers of districts in the earlier periods (Illinois had more than 11,000), and here districts were consolidated at a much more rapid rate than schools. Rows 3 and 4 point to these regional differences. District consolidation, unlike the other processes described in this chapter, thus has a marked regional component. (Although schools per district is the only case where the trend reverses, most of the change rates presented here are greater when computed as national totals than as state means.)

At the school district level, the statistics give us rather detailed information on administrative structure. For instance, they report the number of school district superintendents in a state—a rather clear instance of a bureaucratic functionary. Rows 12 and 13 of Table 9.1 report, over time, the mean number of school district superintendents per state (see Figure 9.1 and also the ratio of school superintendents per district). Along with these data, Table 9.1 (rows 14 and 15) shows comparable figures for assistant superintendents—another bureaucratic role recorded in the statistics. The results are striking: The average school district in the average state is *much* more likely to have a superintendent now than in earlier decades and is also much more likely to have assistant superintendents. The numbers of superintendents per pupil has not changed so much, but what has obviously changed is the proportion of districts that are large enough to be bureaucratized. By and large, the little districts have been eliminated and with them some of the prebureaucratic arrangements of U.S. education.

With the enlargement and bureaucratization of school districts, and the drastic decline in their number, there is a great decline in the amount of nonbureaucratic administration of the educational system. The classic U.S. structure of this sort is the local school board made up of laypersons assuming responsibility. Row 16 in Table 9.1, and Figure 9.2, shows that the mean number of school board members per state has declined sharply, from more than 7,000 per state to less than 2,000. The next row shows that, as for superintendents per student, the number of board members per district is quite stable (in fact it increases slightly). Again, the change reflects the decline in numbers of districts. The modern cry for (and special programs to encourage) more community involvement accompanies a sharp decline in what was once the main mechanism for such involvement.

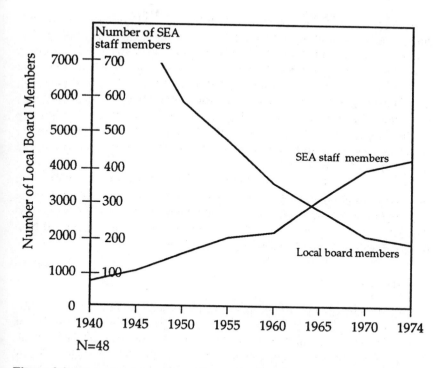

Figure 9.2. Mean Numbers of Local Board Members and State Education Agency Staff per State

Above the organizational level of the school district, in many states, is an additional intermediate structure—most commonly, a county office of education. These offices handle a variety of special programs (such as vocational) or fundings (such as for various special handicaps) or both (such as for televised classes). The national data contain some information on the number of these units and the size of their administrative staffs.

The mean numbers of intermediate units per state are reported in row 18 of Table 9.1, with the number of states reporting intermediate units in parentheses. The means indicate a slow decline in the numbers of these units, implying that they have either expanded or been dissolved. The important datum, however, is the decline in the number of states reporting these units, from 34 to 20. Rather than expansion at this level, a more plausible account might be that a primary function of the intermediate units—to provide services to many small districts—has become unnecessary with the creation of larger, rationalized school districts. The intermediate unit may have been squeezed by expansion at other levels.

At the top of the chain of authority in the U.S. state-controlled system, and the nearest thing to a sovereign in it, is the state education agency (SEA). We have data on the size of the administrative staffs of these units, both absolutely and relative to enrollment. The data are reported in rows 19 and 20 of Table 9.1, and absolute staff size is graphed in Figure 9.2. The data show a steady and large increase in bureaucratic organization of the state educational systems. The authority of these units, typically established in the last half of the 19th century but achieving symbolic sovereignty only in the 20th century, has become more extensive in the modern period.

At every level, then, our data show an enhanced scale and formalization in the educational system: Schools, districts, and states are all more bureaucratically organized in educational matters. Less is left to the informal political arrangements of the community, and more is managed by a highly developed formal organizational system.

STANDARDIZATION

Bureaucratization involves the expansion in scale and formalization that we have shown above. The term also implies, in most usages, the notion of standardization or homogenization in the structure of roles and organizational subunits and a reduction in overall idiosyncracy. Our national data on the organization of schooling in the various states provides some information on the issue of the standardization of educational organization during the modern period.

The basic question is the degree of variability in educational organizational structures across states. Had we more complete data, we could consider the same question across school districts or school organizations, but our present data set is at the state level. So we consider variability across state means in a series of simple analyses below.

The standard deviation is a conventional measure of variability. However, when overall means on variables change a good deal—and it is the message of the data above that they do change and quite systematically—standard deviations are not comparable over time. A simple example will illustrate the point. In 1940 very few school districts were big or formalized enough to have a superintendent. Percentages were small, state mean percentages were small, and standard deviations of state means around the overall mean were numerically small. By 1980 state means were much larger, and it was possible for standard deviations to be larger too—but looking at the data, it is clear that the larger 1980 standard deviations around much higher means nevertheless indicate reduced variability and more standardization among the states.

TABLE 9.3 Coefficients of Variation, Educational Structure, 48 States (Standard Deviation/Mean of State Values)

	1940	1946	1950	1956	1960	1966	1970	1974	1980
State education agency staffs	1.43	1.44	1.54	1.28	1.23	1.03	.92	.80	
Schools/school districts		1.50	1.56	1.35	1.28	1.15	1.07	1.03	1.03
Students/school districts		1.54	1.52	1.46	1.45	1.42	1.37	1.33	1.26
Students/school		.58	.54	.50	.46	.37	.35	.32	.30
Principals/school		.76	.64	.54	.48	.39	.30	.30	.30
Superintendents/ district	1.05			.83	.59	.41	.36	.29	

The conventional way to resolve this statistical problem is to employ the coefficient of variation as an index of variability or standardization. It consists simply of the standard deviation divided by the mean of the variable and essentially relativizes the measure of variability in terms of the scale of a variable.

Coefficients of variation for a number of our indices of bureaucratization are reported over time in Table 9.3. They show strikingly consistent increases in homogeneity among state educational systems in the modern period. The data show increased homogeneity among states in (a) the staff size of the state department of education, (b) the mean number of schools in a district, (c) the mean number of students in a school, (d) the mean number of students per school district, (e) the ratio of principals to schools, and (f) the ratio of superintendents to districts. The changes are quite consistent. Most of them are very large.

Clearly, the bureaucratization of U.S. education has involved a long-term movement, not just to greater scale and formalization but also toward a more homogeneous or standardized set of organizational structures in each of the states.

Centralization and Bureaucratization

Having established the strong trends in increased scale, formalization, and homogenization continuing in educational systems down to the present time, we move to our second concern. How are such changes to be explained? As already noted, a conventional explanation would link the growth of bureaucratization to increased centralization: the shift in power

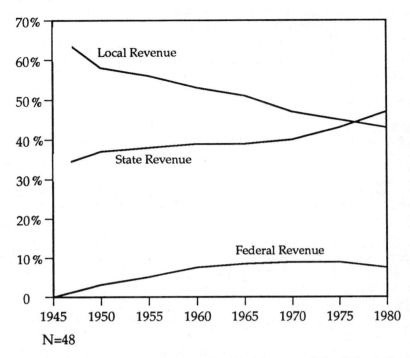

N=48

Figure 9.3. Mean Percentages of Total Education Revenue From Federal, State, and Local Revenue per State

from lower to higher levels of government. Such shifts would be constituted, or at least indicated, by changes in the control of funds for public
education. Certainly, contemporary images of educational change over the
last two decades stress the importance of the expanding federal educational
budget in producing bureaucratization. Some older analyses call attention
to the centralization of funding at the state level as having the same effect.
(These latter are less likely to take a negative view of either the centralization or the bureaucratization involved. They are more likely to emphasize the process as involving efficiency, professionalism, and more recently equity.)

The data contain state reports of public school funding from local,
intermediate, state, and federal sources. We report changes over time in
state means in Table 9.1, row 21. The figures are graphed in Figure 9.3.
First, we report mean state educational revenues per pupil in constant 1967
dollars. The means rise throughout the period. It is important to understand
that in important ways the expenditure expansion involved *itself* indicates

bureaucratization: the shift from amateur to professionally credentialed and paid teachers, administrators, and staff personnel; and the shift from local unpaid school board management to modern formalized structures all the way up to the state and federal levels.

Beyond this basic change in the nature of the educational system, the data show substantial changes over time in the locus of schooling revenue. The proportions of federal and state revenues to total revenue both rise by about 10%, the federal from practically nothing to 10%, the state from 35% to 46%. The big change, then, is in local revenue, which declines from 64% to 43% (being finally topped by state revenue only in the late 1970s).

A caveat: The ultimate sources of revenue are not always the best guide to who controls the money. An original federal expenditure may be distributed by the state and come to be counted as, or have the organizational meaning of, state money. This may be an accounting problem, but it has substantive importance. The great increase in educational expenditures by higher levels of government in recent decades has in part gone to reinforce the power of the units already authorized to manage U.S. education— school districts operating under state authority. Just as, on other levels of analysis, the modern expansion in worldwide economic power has reinforced the authority of the nation-state, or the earlier construction of national stratification systems reinforced the logic of individual citizenship, so the nationalization of U.S. education may be occurring through the funding and authorization of the expansion of state and local bureaucracy. It is a point to which we will return.

CAUSAL MODELS OF BUREAUCRATIZATION

We turn now to examine data on the central hypothesis that flows from the discussion above. Several lines of empirical work on districts within particular states suggest that more centralized funding is associated with the expansion of bureaucratic administration (Bankston, 1982; Freeman, Hannan, & Hannaway, 1978). We have established that both trends occur over time—there is an increase in state and federal financial control, and there is more bureaucratization. Are these trends related? With enough data, one could address such questions with national-level time series data and analyses. But limitations of data and problems of analytic specification restrict the value of such an approach. In the analyses below, we take advantage of the variability among U.S. states and focus on examining how variations in their funding of public education affect the degree of bureaucratization of each state educational system.

Our analyses are a series of cross-sectional and longitudinal multiple regressions. As dependent variables we employ a number of indicators of bureaucratization at various levels of the educational system. We use the staff size of the SEAs, the number of school districts in the state, the number of schools, the amount of administrative expenditures, the number of assistant superintendents, and a measure of the number of district administrators in the state. Following the above discussion, the three explanatory variables of substantive interest are the amounts of federal, state, and local revenue in the state. We also include the number of school districts as an explanatory variable where appropriate because we believe bureaucratization at the district level may increase bureaucratization in schools or administrative structure. Enrollment is used as a control variable for state system size.

We proceed in two steps. First, we consider cross-sectional analyses for 1970, 1974, and 1980: Do states with centralized funding have more bureaucratic educational systems? Then we shift to panel analyses over the same period: Do states with more centralized funding shift over time toward more bureaucratic structures? In a concluding section we discuss possible interpretations of the argument and findings.

MODEL ESTIMATION

The form of the regression equations that we estimate is driven by an artifactual multicollinearity in the data. The units of analysis are U.S. states, which differ greatly in their size and population. Because each variable is a count of local units or activities, there are bound to be large positive correlations between most variables. Big states have more local revenue, more state revenue, more schools, and more school districts than small states. For example, the correlations between the three revenue variables are all greater than .6, high enough to markedly increase the variance of the coefficients. We are thus more likely to reject true hypotheses about the effects of our variables.

Our strategy in dealing with this multicollinearity is to standardize the variables. Enrollment is our best indicator of the size of the state educational system: We divide every term in the equations by the number of pupils in the state to cancel the scale differences among states. (Except in the SEA regressions, where we use the natural logarithm of enrollment as a control variable.) Although the regressions can then be seen in a generalized least-squares framework, we prefer to think of the variables divided by enrollment as having substantive meaning. We can thus speak naturally of the effect of federal revenues per pupil on the numbers of schools per pupil. Dividing the equations by enrollment thus plays a double function; it lessens the problem of multicollinearity and provides a consistent basis for talking about all effects in "per pupil" terms.

A few words about the coefficients will make the tables easier to read. Both the sources of revenue and enrollments are measured in thousands. The coefficient for federal dollars on schools, for example, thus gives the impact of an extra dollar of federal funds per pupil on the number of schools per 1,000 pupils. Because enrollment appears as a reciprocal, a positive effect means that higher enrollments in the state lead to decreases in the dependent variable. Finally, the financial variables are not measured in constant dollars, so comparisons across years must hold constant the changing value of the dollar. This is important in the regressions on administrative expenditures, where increases in the coefficients of the nonfiscal variables reflect inflation.

As in the descriptive statistics, Alaska and Hawaii have been omitted from the analyses. Hawaii has only one school district, making it impossible to calculate separate figures for state and local revenues. Alaska is also a special case because of its very low density of population; it is such an extreme outlier in all the equations that we thought it advisable to omit it entirely.

CROSS-SECTIONAL ANALYSES

Size of the State Department of Education

We begin with analyses of the size of the bureaucracies at the top of the state system—the SEA. We have seen that these have increased greatly in size (see also Murphy, 1981). Our question now is whether they are larger when state and federal funding is high and local funding is low.

Table 9.4 presents relevant cross-sectional analyses. The dependent variable is the natural logarithm (taken because of the distribution of the variable) of the number of employers in the SEA. We hold constant the natural logarithm of public enrollments in the state—states with more students tend to have much larger departments of education. Then we include federal, state, and local educational funds per pupil. Finally, we include a dummy variable for Southern states, which have a history of central activity in fields like education. The analyses are reported with data from 1970, 1974, and 1980.

The data show that SEAs are larger in Southern states and especially in more populous states. But we do not find consistent evidence that more central federal and state funding increases the size of the bureaucratic center. In two of the three analyses, local funding shows, in fact, a positive effect. And the federal effect is significantly positive only in the 1980 analysis.

TABLE 9.4 Cross-Sectional Regressions: Effects of Funding Source on Selected Bureaucratic Structures, for 1970, 1974, and 1980, 48 States

| | | | *Independent Variables* | | | | |
| | | | Federal Education Revenue per Student | State Education Revenue per Student | Local Education Revenue per Student | South (Coded 1) |
Dependent Variable	*Year*	*Constant*	*Log Enrollment*				
1. Log State	1970	1.36^a	$.52^a$	$-.002$	$.001^a$	$.001^a$	$.69^a$
Education	1974	1.02^a	$.60^a$	$.001$	$.0004$	$.0006^a$	$.53^a$
Agency staff	1980	1.37^a	$.51^a$	$.002^a$	$-.0002$	$-.00001$	$.02$

| | | | | Federal Education Revenue | State Education Revenue | Local Education Revenue | |
Dependent Variables	*Year*	*Constant*	*1/ Enrollment*	per Student	per Student	per Student	*Districts per Student*
2. Districts per	1970	$.80$	196^a	$.0009$	$-.003^a$	$.001$	
student	1974	$-.45$	119^a	$.006$	$-.001^a$	$.001^a$	
	1980	$.33$	127^a	$.0008$	$-.0005$	$.0002$	
3. Schools per	1970	1.97^a	105^a	$.004$	$-.002^a$	$-.00005$	$.84^a$
student	1974	2.32^a	126^a	$.001$	$-.001^a$	$-.0003$	$.83^a$
	1980	1.60^a	100^a	$.001$	$-.0002$	$.0001$	$.92^a$
4. Administrative	1970	$-.004$	332	$.03$	$.04^a$	$.04^a$	2.67^a
expenditures	1974	$.003$	697	$.03$	$.02^a$	$.03^a$	3.69
per student	1980	$.01$	1072	$.12$	$-.006$	$.04^a$	6.07
5. Assistant	1970	$-.0004$	4.6	$.002$	$.0009^a$	$.0005^a$	$-.005$
superintendents	1974	$-.0003$	18.89	$.0004$	$.0008$	$.0005$	$.007$
per student							
Total district							
staff per student	1980	$.001$	38	$.002$	$.0003$	$.0006$	2.35^a

a. $p \leq .05$

Districts and Schools

Two other indicators of bureaucratization discussed above are the average size of school districts and schools in a state. Our hypothesis is that more central funding increases the average size of these organizational units.

Table 9.4, row 2, shows the results for the number of school districts in a state, standardized by enrollment size. There turn out to be more school districts per student when a state has low enrollments, reflecting rural conditions. (As mentioned above, the positive coefficients for the reciprocal of enrollment mean that the number of districts decrease as enrollments increase.) For our hypothesis of interest, the results are suggestive. Local funding shows the expected positive effect on the number of school districts, although it is significant in only one of the years. State funding shows the expected negative effect, and it is significant in two of the three years. Federal funding shows neither a consistent nor a significant effect.

Table 9.4, row 3, shows parallel analyses of school size. In this case, we add district size as an additional independent variable because larger and more bureaucratic districts might be expected to generate more consolidated and bureaucratic schools. The results conform to those above. Low state enrollments reduce average school size. And states with fewer (and thus bigger) districts have fewer and bigger schools. Once again, the effects of state revenue are in the hypothesized direction and significant in 1970 and 1974. In this case, however, local and federal funding are generally in the wrong direction and never significant.

Administrative Expansion

We can also analyze data on the expenditures on administration reported for the states—these expenditures occur mainly on the local level. Table 9.4, row 4, shows the relevant analyses. Two findings of interest occur. First, higher levels of revenues of all kinds are associated with more reported administrative expenditures. But there is no evidence that this relationship is stronger for the more central funding sources.

Second, we observe greater administrative expenditures associated with many small school districts in contrast to fewer large ones, although the effect is significant in only one of the equations. This is an important finding. The appearance of bureaucracy is associated with fewer and larger organizations. This finding may be accurate, but bureaucracy may also be associated with reduced administrative expense.

The general conclusion is strengthened by Table 9.4, row 5, which reports similar analyses of district administrative personnel—numbers of assistant superintendents—per state. Again we find the result that higher levels of funding of any sort tend to be associated with more administrative personnel, but our hypothesis that this would be especially true of federal or state funding is not confirmed. The effect of many small school districts expanding administrative personnel is not great until the 1980 analyses, at which point it becomes massive. The explanation for this is revealing. Our 1980 data on administrative personnel comes from a different source than the others—they are not national statistical reports, but the reports of Market Data Retrieval, a private survey firm that collects with impressive skill and much experience the names and addresses of school and district officials around the country (Market Data Retrieval, 1980). These data report any person having a given function as an administrator, unlike the NCES data, which report in full-time equivalents. The differences lie in the huge numbers of part-time or unpaid or multifunction administrative personnel in small districts around the country.

The administrative cost and personnel data in rows 4 and 5 of Table 9.4—especially this last finding of the effect of small districts on administrative personnel—are suggestive of the major social changes involved in bureaucratization. Explicit administrative positions replace the multifunction teachers characteristic of an earlier and highly decentralized system. Visible administration is expanding, but in fact the economies of scale involved may mean the actual amount of administrative work is declining.

Longitudinal Analyses

In order to test more convincingly the causal orderings implied in our cross-sectional models, we can repeat them using our longitudinal panel data on the states. This involves (a) using the same basic analytic structures but examining dependent variables in 1980 as affected by independent variables in 1970 and (b) using the lagged dependent variable as a crucial control. The research question then becomes whether independent variables create *changes* in the dependent variable.

Table 9.5 repeats the cross-sectional analyses reported earlier with panel data from 1970 to 1980. In two cases in which our 1980 data are not comparable to the earlier ones, we use 1966 through 1974 panel data as a substitute. We examine in sequence changes in

1. the staff size of the state department of education,
2. the numbers of districts (per student enrollment),
3. schools and enrollments,
4. administrative expenditures, and
5. administrative personnel.

As before, 2 through 5 are standardized by enrollment (of the base year). In each case, the main hypothesis continues to be that central sources of funds produce bureaucratization.

This hypothesis fails. Overall the analyses show no special inclination for states with higher levels of state or federal funding to become more bureaucratized over our period. The effects of state centralization on numbers of schools and school districts, which were supported in the cross-sectional analyses, do not appear longitudinally. And as in the cross-sections, federal and local funds do not seem to influence any of the indicators of bureaucratization.

TABLE 9.5 Panel Regressions: Effects of Funding Sources on Selected Bureaucratic Structures, 1966-1974 and 1970-1980, 48 States

					Independent Variables			
Dependent Variable	Year	Constant	*Log State Education Agency Staff 1966*	*Log Enroll-ment 1966*	*Federal Education Revenue per Enroll-ment 1966*	*State Education Revenue per Enroll-ment 1966*	*Local Education Revenue per Enroll-ment 1966*	*South (Coded 1)*
1. Log State Education Agency staff	1974	−.40	.32	.35[a]	−.007	.001	.001	.30[a]

					Federal Education Revenue per Enroll-ment	*State Education Revenue per Enroll-ment*	*Local Education Revenue per Enroll-ment*	*Districts per Enroll-ment*
Dependent Variable	Year	Constant	*Lagged Dependent Variable*	*1/ Enroll-ment*				
2. Districts per enrollment	1980	.42	.55[a]	15.9[a]	−.003	−.00005	−.0001	
3. Schools per enrollment	1980	.69	.73[a]	7.24	−.0006	−.0001	.00005	.08
4. Administrative expenditures per enrollment	1980	80[a]	1.85[a]	2574	−.29	−.06	−.07	4.16
5. Assistant superintendents per enrollment	1974	−.18	−.16	29	−.001	.001[a]	.001	−.01

a. $p \leq .05$

Rethinking the Relation
Between Bureaucratization and Centralization

We have seen a strong trend toward expanded formalization and scale in U.S. public education, with schools, districts, and state organizations that are expanded in size and differentiated administratively. Clearly, a particular classroom and school is more *organizationally* connected to other classrooms and schools now than in the past. Funding is also more structured through state and federal governments now than in the past. There are several ways to think about this, the most common of which is to see it as the centralization of power and authority.

In the analyses described above, we examined this line of reasoning. If shifts upward in funding indicate centralization of control, they might be followed by the expansion of educational bureaucracy seen as a centralized system. Such a conception of bureaucratization as an imperative control system fits comfortably with conventional organization theory and its Weberian roots.

But we find less evidence than expected to support the idea of a close linkage between a shift toward state or federal funding and bureaucratic expansion. The chain of reasoning from funding changes (seen as centralization) to bureaucratic expansion as its expression is clearly weak. In fact, it is useful to rethink the whole structure of this causal argument.

Consider the several meanings of the term *centralization*. In some usages, it becomes almost coterminous with *bureaucratization*, reflecting the widening scale or standardization of a given set of rules. Centralization, in this sense, is the opposite of localism. In this kind of language, any sort of integration in a given social domain signifies centralization and domination. Obviously, thinking along these lines conceals a particular theory of history as driven by exploitation and control interests. It would be better to make the theory explicit, rather than to bury it in definitions.

If we try to formulate a definition of *centralization* that is distinct from what we have called *bureaucratization,* notions of power and domination must be involved. There must, in brief, be a center. Whether or not this center's power is legitimated, centralization involves the ideas of (a) some sort of distinct set of central purposes, (b) set against or separate from the rest of society, and (c) dominating it. The first two elements are the crucial ones, and in modern terms distinguish between state formation and nation building, so that only the former entails *organizational* centralization (Bendix, 1964). We thus exclude from a reasonable definition of centralization processes—no matter how coercive—by which standardizing rules evolve *in the larger society* that bring individual subunits into conformity. (Such processes have been seen as central to U.S. homogeneity since de Tocqueville [1947]. They have also been seen as the antithesis of organizational centralization.)

There has indeed been a funding shift toward state and (to a lesser extent) federal revenue. And there are clearly shifts away from organizational localism and toward bureaucracy. Do these shifts constitute centralization? We consider the centralization of funding different from the centralization of substantive authority. The latter would involve the endowment of the state center with some right of power and purpose against society: the right to mobilize collective resources around the *center's* chosen collective goods. Increased centralization of educational funding in the 1960s, 1970s, and 1980s in the United States does not seem to have empowered the agents at the center. At the federal level, there is the ostentatious denial of any distinct federal purpose. There is only the assumption of responsibility for other prior goals of a highly decentralized kind: in the 1950s, areas impacted by federal activity; in the 1960s, minorities and the poor; in the 1970s, the handicapped. In all U.S. educational history, one finds only a shadowy reflection of the *organized nation-state's* autonomous purposes—a few military schools, an eviscerated vocational educational system, and the National Defense Education Act—as opposed to those seen as vested in society as a whole. The implication here is that one should not expect to find the expansion of federal educational funds, which are not allocated toward the reconstruction of education around nation-state aims, to produce bureaucratic centralization. In fact, in our related work (Scott & Meyer, 1988; reprinted as Chapter 7 in this volume) we had seen this "fragmented" character of the federal involvement in education as possibly generating laterally extended bureaucracy *because* it could not generate centralization. We will have occasion below to reconsider even this argument. At present, we simply note that the nature of federal involvement is not to be seen as centralist, given the absence either of legitimate sovereignty over education or distinctive purposes for it.

In the U.S. system, states do have sovereignty over education, and it makes a bit more sense to imagine that the expansion of their funding might lead to centralizing bureaucratization (see Doyle & Finn, 1984). On the other hand, consider here the few distinct collective purposes or missions a U.S. state can have for its public educational system. Can Indiana mobilize its educational system, following the Prussian example, to help wage war—even Kulturkampf—against Illinois? The states play a role akin to that of service organizations as much as dynamic leaders and carry out a mission defined on a wider scale than their boundaries. They attempt, in funding, to equalize resources among communities, classes, and ethnic groups, following norms set by national courts and ideology or to upgrade education along nationally standard lines. One can see an impulse to bureaucratize standardization here but not to centralization around autonomous purposes.

Once we get rid of the image of a central *power* using its funds to drive bureaucratization as a means of enforcing its will, we have also given up one rationale for seeing the whole process as causally driven by changed funding patterns. We have seen a great change in organizational scale in education—funding changes are part of it but not the crucial causal link.

BUREAUCRATIZATION AS
EXPANDED SCALE OF ADMINISTRATION

Suppose we drop the fashionable social scientific language of power to talk about the process we observe and avoid the demonic image of increasingly centralized authorities using resources to dominate U.S. education. We are then left with the more traditional language of U.S. organizational thought, which talks about organization rather than bureaucracy and coordination rather than power. Perhaps such themes capture the reality of expanded scale that we observe better than do ideas that trace these developments to central nodes of power.

Once we see the changes as reflecting standardization, different causal imagery seems reasonable. Instead of thinking of the changes as reflecting nation-*state* power, other aspects of nation building seem more important; that is, society itself—not primarily the state—is being reconstructed along increasingly rationalized lines and on an enlarged scale. And the forces legitimately empowered by the changes, as well as those advocating them, arise in society more than in the state organization. Thus a whole series of changes in U.S. education reflect and emphasize standardization around highly professionalized models. They partly reflect, and most certainly enhance, the authority of the educational profession as part of national society. Similarly, there have been all sorts of pressures toward the involvement and equality of many different groups in national society, from classes to ethnic groups to regions and communities. There have been many different pressures toward general improvement (meaning, in part, conformity with standard national models) and the elimination of diversity and communal authority (backwardness) in various hinterlands. There have been many pressures for expanding educational services demanding larger scale of funding and control (such as vocational specializations, instruction in new subjects and for new groups, services in counseling and health). And there have been continuous pressures for the upgrading of the basic profession involved—teaching—that have led to more emphasis being placed on general certification controls.

We may note some of the specific forces involved in this expansion of collective nationwide control. It is noteworthy how few of them operate only or especially through central nation-state authority, how many of them tend to lead to expansions in scale of organization, and for how many of them changed funding patterns are consequences more than causes. (a) There are all sorts of forces generating and expanding nationally standardized notions of educational quality: professional educators, intellectuals, parent and community groups, occasional national leaders, competitive pressures. (b) There have been many forces pursuing more standardizing notions of equality and operating organizationally at every level of the system: constituent and professional supports for equality for the poor, minorities, the handicapped, females, and so on. (c) Many different forces strengthen the social standardization of the basic units of the whole educational system—the definition of the properly credentialed teacher and of the appropriate classroom and curriculum. The increasingly standardized notion of education, in this sense, makes expanded scale more sensible. If education is a social contract between individuals as teachers and other individuals as parents and members of the community, local bargaining may be necessary. With the increasing social prefabrication of both teacher and community, it becomes easier to organize on a larger scale. And all these changes make large-scale organization necessary. Failure to expand, and retaining too many localistic or particularistic roots, begins to look like backwardness or even corruption. And failure to standardize looks like inequality.

Thus we see the expanded scale, formalization, and homogeneity of U.S. educational organization as reflecting the expansion of general national standards of education and the imposition of these on the particular subunit communities. In every area, general norms about education have expanded and become unified and national. Bureaucracies arise incorporating and reflecting them and maintaining their status in local jurisdictions. What we do not see is the emergence of a dominating organizational center in the system, from which the other changes flow and by which they are integrated and regulated. There is much bureaucratization, but it is dispersed in the several states and their component districts.

In fact, we can usefully see the modern period, and the rise of a more intensely national educational system, as organizationally enhancing the authority of the states and districts rather than any more national organizational center. National interests and concerns create national social movements, often built into piecemeal federal legislation and fragmented funding programs. But the units that derive power from this process are the states and local districts. In the absence of an authoritative nation state center, U.S. nation building—as throughout its history—expands the scale of intermediate units. In this case of a public good, it is the public sector that expands.

Consider the programs resulting from the recent concerns about educational quality, for example. There is much national discussion, a bit of legislative activity, a few national commissions, and a little money. But this has fueled a huge industry at the state and district level, as these more sovereign units employ the general concerns to expand their own domination over the local scene. *They* are the units, acting on the national concerns, that embody the ethic of standardization: They control testing and degree granting, curricula, and teacher quality. Expanded controls unthinkable (as undemocratic) a few decades ago have been advocated by literally hundreds of state commissions and implemented in legislation. Here is where the bureaucracy is located. Like many other instances of bureaucratization, it draws its agenda from wider concerns but not those of a unified organizational sovereign.

Thus, we argue, the increase in national concern and debate about education in this country has ended up expanding even further the organizational power of the units with organizational sovereignty—the state and district organizational structures. Their expanded authority could be seen as a form of centralization, perhaps, but because they seem to follow rather than to generate the educational agenda, it is hard to see their authority as power. It seems unlikely that the expanded state and district organizations will function as autonomous decision-making bodies, capable of going off in their own directions. Rather, they will probably (following the old pattern) be the agents at the disposal of a national culture, serving to bring each subunit into conformity with it.

Overall, then, there has certainly been centralization in the sense of the destruction of local and communal and particularistic control in U.S. education and its replacement by bureaucratic organization in districts and states (and the enlarged schools, too). We find a shift from the informal and political management of schooling to the bureaucratic form. From the local point of view, this is centralization. But at the other end of the scale, we do not find the emergence of a unified organizational center. There is rather the classic pattern of a profusion of professional standards, court decisions, special-purpose legislative interests, and a huge network of interest groups. It is the traditional liberal society, redrawn on a larger and more national scale. The local teachers no longer confront the local school board in quite the same way—both groups are now components of a much wider system of organized relationships, and teacher organizations make demands of taxpayers at district and state and national levels rather than local ones. Similarly, a whole network of organized interests affects the curriculum in much the same way as the past—but it is all done at a higher organizational level. We expect to find states much more involved in the curriculum in the future, reflecting these shifts—but we also expect to find the decisions made through the classic bargaining processes rather than by a single bureaucratic center.

From an organizational point of view, the educational map of U.S. *society* has been redrawn in a much larger scale but has retained something of its earlier form. The organizational changes occur at the bottom, where there is much more bureaucracy reflecting the national discourse about educational matters. This bureaucracy is a standardizing holding company for institutional rules and preferences built up externally. But these institutional rules continue to reflect the associational structure of liberal society—although now at the national level—rather than the organizationally integrated purposes of an emergent bureaucratic state center.

Conclusions

We find much evidence that recent decades have seen a rapid expansion of bureaucracy—formalization, expansion in scale, and standardization—in U.S. educational organization. The changes are national and nationwide and clearly reflect the expanded dominance of a national educational culture.

It is difficult, however, to see the process as driven by the rise of a dominating organizational center in the system and as thus reflecting a move toward centralization in this sense. Direct national funding is too small, and in our data too poorly correlated with organizational expansion at lower levels, to be a plausible candidate for an important causal role.

The modern changes, like earlier instances of U.S. bureaucratization (in education and elsewhere), reflect the expansion and imposition of standard models but not those of a central national organizational structure. It seems more reasonable to see the expanded national concern for (and even investment in) education as leading to a further expansion of the organizational units already endowed with sovereignty in the federal system. It would not be the first time in U.S. history where expanded national integration and coherence generated not an expanded and dominating center but empowered and homogeneous organizational subunits.

All these subunits reflect a complex institutional system that is made up of increasingly national elements (interest groups, professions, a correction system, court and administration rule, and so on). As education becomes a national business, local and state bureaucracy grows. It reflects a growing national institutional structure but not one controlled by the central bureaucratic state.

III. INSTITUTIONAL ENVIRONMENTS AND THE EXPANSION OF INDIVIDUALITY WITHIN ORGANIZATIONS

Organizations and organizing situations are confronted, in their environments, with both demands for and supplies of rationalized structure. The term *demand* here means that some part of the multidimensional uncertainty surrounding any social situation is environmentally recognized as a rationalized problem for which an organization or organizer is responsible. For instance, the quality of the air around many industrial plants has long been noxious and problematic, but not consciously articulated and not formulated as a rationalized problem or uncertainty that must be dealt with. Now, in developed countries, organizations must incorporate elements to deal with this recognized problem.

The same sorts of environments that define such problems commonly supply the proper rationalized solution. For example, air-quality problems may require certain reports to be written, physical measurements to be taken, consultants or professionals employed, or standards to be met.

Fundamental uncertainties that lead to the construction of organizations, of course, have to do with the humans who function in them.

If these people are seen as entirely erratic—as primitives incapable of orderly conduct—there is an obvious uncertainty, but not a rationalized one that can function as both demand for and supply of rationalized organization. Little complex formal organization is likely to result, though some simple and fairly coercive forms may be tried.

Now suppose social changes rationalize all these uncertainties. People are constructed as interpretable and coherent modern actors, and are so seen. They have modern purposes of their own (motives, commitments, and so on). They come in specifiable categories of education and occupational certification, of experience, of personal qualities (e.g., measurable abilities and personality dispositions), along with a good many legal rights.

Thus rationalized forms of uncertainty are created and must be dealt with. Organizations can and must formulate ways in which to extend their rationalized structure to meet these new and professionally sanctioned individual marvels of modernity. If people and their qualities and competences vary in known and officially predictable ways, responsible rationalizers must take this into account. The simple and orderly plantation must come to terms with, in short, (a) greatly expanded and (b) explicitly and formally variable human actors. The rise of formal organization in great part is a response to this situation.

What environments demand, environments (often the same ones, and often at the same time) supply. Contemporary world and national environments provide great expansions in the overall rights and rationalized properties of persons, and also in the complexity of the classification systems of rationalized types of persons. The recognized vita of the typical person around the world—especially, of course, of higher status persons in higher status countries—has greatly expanded.

Some or most of this expansion is implicit in the vita rather than spelled out. Individual vitas do not need to bother to claim the general rights and assumed capacities of persons and citizens and now human beings that have so greatly expanded in recent decades. Nor would they mention that such rights have, in quite sweeping ways, been extended to formerly excluded groups (women, minorities of various sorts, sometimes regional or national peripheral groups): This would be assumed, by and large. Nor would many vitas mention the obvious though not always true "facts"—now built by assumption into most developed country structures—that the person has a basic education, is literate and a bit numerate, and has a measure of general familiarity with a larger society and world that would have been rare two or three generations ago. What would be put forward, of course, would be the intricate rationalized properties of the person—the exotics of education and occupational training and experience along with some materials on skills, interests, and accomplishments.

It is not always recognized how dramatically this whole structure has changed in recent decades—how many more rights and capacities are generally established for individuals, and how many more complex educational, occupational, and psychological properties they possess. Both demand and supply for rationalized organization in this domain have greatly expanded. The expansion is worldwide (Boli, 1987a; Meyer, Ramirez, & Soysal, 1992; Thomas, Meyer, Ramirez, & Boli, 1987).

Formal organizations must deal with these rather forward and much differentiated people. That is the demand side. The supply side, of course, is that the people come equipped with qualities that directly fit into (modified) formal organization. Organizations differentiate and expand to meet the new heroic individuals. New occupations can be defined and recognized, with new educational qualifications. Whole new areas of activity become plausible. Personnel professionals and human resources specialists are required, and the organizational infrastructure for dealing with individual members expands. Organizational culture and organizational culture managers and previously unknown accountings and accountants are created (Miller & O'Leary, 1993).

It is important to stress that the long-term expansion in the rationalization and formal status of persons has many implications for individual welfare. Formal rights may be gained—these may or may not be effectively implemented in organizational life and may or may not be beneficial even if they are implemented. Expanded rights may carry with them expanded and intrusive organizational controls—some would argue that is part of the historic organizational purpose involved. They may also create incentives for organizations to limit and externalize employment. The force of the chapters below is to show the impact of the expansion of individualism on organizational structure, not to argue that this is somehow beneficial for individuals.

Expanded Personhood

Many dimensions are involved in the general expansion of personhood. At the world level, there are a great many treaties and resolutions defining expanded individual rights and status, and making them qualities that inhere in the human being (i.e., are reflections of a general worldwide status) rather than the individual as citizen (which leaves the status at the national level, only indirectly certified by the world) or soul (which defines mainly a transcendental existence). Such world-defined individual rights include quite general rights to education, to all-purpose individual development, to civil, political, and social protection (Bendix, 1964; Boli, 1979; Fiala & Gordon Lanford, 1987; Marshall, 1964). These tend to be backed up by the definitions of international organizations, by world scientific (e.g., psychological) professions, and of course by the prestige standards involved in world society (which define countries as models of virtue or opprobrium in good part on human rights criteria).

All this gets elaborated in national policy too, sometimes in direct response to changed world principles (McNeely, 1989).

Implementation at lower levels is variable and uncertain. But in some core areas, the structures of expanded individualism are well established. Education, for instance, has become worldwide, and in fact more than 90% of the world's children experience enrollment in a school (Meyer, Ramirez, & Soysal, 1992). These schools worldwide tend to emphasize the status of the individual student—very few curricula, for instance, take the older form of celebrating high sacred truths through ritual instruction (Meyer, Kamens, Benavot, Cha, & Wong, 1992). Formalized social welfare systems, too, are very widespread.

The past half-century has seen a very rapid expansion in such arrangements, in both world and national policy talk and organizational form. Presumably this emphasis on the individual as a direct element of the collective good (world good, even) reflects a long period of American and liberal dominance and the spread of the forms of individualism characteristic of these models throughout world society.

Impact on Organization

The demand for and supply of these presumptively expanded rationalized individuals is great. Organizations expand to incorporate, use, respond to, and control these entities. The chapters that follow note some of the effects.

Obviously one effect is the creation of whole new classes of organizations that create and modify individuals. Schools of many sorts, mental health organizations of many types, prisons, elaborate health systems, and a richer variety of religious and others associations result. The rationalization of the individual creates organizational work. Chapter 10 discusses the problematics of organizing repair work on this expanded individual.

Extant organizations, too, can and must enrich their structures with individual processing. Chapters 11 and 12 discuss the great expansion of "organizational citizenship" training in recent decades. The expanded modern individual is understood to possess extraordinary rights and capacities for a measure of organizational sovereignty. This individual is capable of rationally modifying the organization itself, as well as particular positions in it. Such rights and capacities, then, must be built into and managed by the responsible organization. To leave so valuable a resource as the self-activating individual unincorporated would be to irresponsibly neglect to manage a now rationalized uncertainty. Thus organizations need not just a bit of ideology, but also whole cultures, broad training arrangements, and so on: In rationalizing their structures on such dimensions they conform to modern models of effectiveness and the proper control and utilization of crucial resources.

Chapter 13 stresses the "rights" side of this equation. Expanded and rationalized individuals must be dealt with properly in organizational arrangements: Here the modern organization confronts a newly enriched rational environment (each individual now has the quality of organized actorhood, and the old primitive labor contract is superseded by organizational structuration). The connection to the rise of whole new professional components of organization—the personnel sector—is quite direct. One way to manage the expanded individual is to structure a component to deal with this entity: and empirically, the incorporation of this component—a personnel department, for instance—has a direct effect on the rate at which organizations adopt generally elaborated and rationalized personnel systems.

General Consequences

Overall, the expansion of the rationalized individual has a sweeping structural effect on modern organization and helps explain a most important secular trend over many decades. Formal organizations, incorporating expanded and rationalized individuals at many points, lose simple formal rationality in their structures (Meyer, 1983b). They become more structurally complex, they lose a great deal of imperative authority, they take on network (or matrix) forms, they develop "staff" functions and elaborated white-collar and management elements, and they emphasize lateral and coordinative relations. The bureaucratic forms envisioned by the Europeans (e.g., Weber and Fayol) tend to disappear, and the word *bureaucracy* is replaced by the looser term *organization*. But the tight systems of technical control envisioned by the Americans (e.g., Taylor) also tend to disappear as the main frame for overall organizational structure. Barnard, the human relations tradition, and modern management theories become more appropriate models. Scott (1992) describes this evolution in theories and ideologies of organization: The point here is the evolution probably characterizes the "real" world of organizations too, and that it is in substantial part driven by the rise of the modern rationalized individual. This individual is both a resource for, and a source of demands for, contemporary organizational forms. And the socially certified existence of this individual as canonical makes the older forms unfeasible and irrational. Who now gives orders? And who now can construct roles in organizations principally around mechanized assembly-line doctrines and rules? All this, of course, creates a modern organizational structure with some arational properties. But it would be completely unrealistic to imagine that these organizations are in danger of falling apart.

A second main trend over many decades works to create new and more abstract rationalized myths of the organization as rational actor. This is the discovery of management in the abstract—the organization as constructed not of people in authority relations or of specific substantive technical flows and interdependencies but of abstract control systems. For instance, there is much expansion of management information systems, elaborate accounting systems making great new claims, legal regulations, and generalized theories of personnel management. Many conceptions arise of organizations as held together by cultures, by technologies of leadership, by interpersonal communication skills and techniques, by new financial control arrangements, or by economists and lawyers who oversee the nexus of contracts. Organizations are seen and theorized as independent of the people and roles making them up, and of the specific technologies they use and substantive work they do. They are discussed, and present themselves, as organizations built up around generalized models of management.

The Environment

The chapters below note that much of this elaboration has long roots in the rationalized fragmentation of the American polity, which has encouraged rather uncontrolled expansion in theories of the individual as a rationalized entity. Psychology has been given free play (Frank, Miyahara, & Meyer, 1992) in expanding human motives and capacities. Legal processes and ideologies, operating in the absence of a controlling central state, have developed rights and standing for the individual. A network of both professions and organizations develops the appropriate story lines (e.g., about the personhood of women, or even of students or other inmates). The chapters that follow suggest something of the range of this, in the independent variables they consider. They also make clear that the impact on organizations in the United States is a general one—cutting across specific types and sectors and functions.

We may note here that the same processes have gone on at the world level, though this is not studied in the chapters that follow.

The world too—perhaps because of a half-century of American influence—is a massive rationalistic communication system little constrained by central state authority. This world too has rapidly enhanced the status of the individual. We suppose that the findings and ideas reported in the chapters below may—though perhaps in an attenuated way—be describing worldwide trends in typical organizational structuring. One does not need to imagine an entirely homogeneous world in order to suggest that world models of organization—prominently including expanded individuals and the effects of these—have widespread influence on standard organizational patterns in many countries.

A Concluding Caution

The ideas and analyses in the chapters below properly take no position on the value of the effects of expanded individualism in modern organizations. Their central point is that modern organizations formally expand and differentiate to incorporate the enhanced status of the individual, as modern nation-states do. As critics of the modern system have often noted, this expansion can be seen in many ways—as a benign improvement in human (especially working) conditions or as a new set of demands and controls on individual persons (Miller & O'Leary, 1993). In the contemporary economic climate, it can also be seen as providing incentives and justifications for organizations to externalize substantial fractions of their working populations into the raw labor market, or unemployment, or Third World countries with low labor costs. Finally, much of the organizational rationalization involved may simply be decoupled from day-to-day practices and conditions. All of these possibilities suggest caution about any effort to simply see the expanded formal status of the individual in modern organizational life as a step toward progress.

10

Institutional and Organizational Rationalization in the Mental Health System

JOHN W. MEYER

MODERN ORGANIZATIONAL THEORY is highly attentive to the environmental underpinnings of organizations and, in particular, to the institutional legitimations that sustain organizations and organizational systems (Scott, 1981). In one sense, practically all modern organizations are creatures of the modern state, supported by its legal and political arrangements.

In examining the bases of the mental health organizational system we look therefore at the institutional bases of the system: the rules that make it possible (and necessary) to construct rationalized *organizations* in so peculiar a domain. Mental health is the last area in which older-style organizations theory, stressing the technical bases of organization, might take a stand. It is not obvious that there *are* technical considerations in this field of any consensual status that require much organization.

We look therefore at the institutional rules that define the bases of organizational rationalization in mental health systems. The institutional rules involved are very unclear, and for this reason the modern U.S. mental health organizational system is continually perceived as being in some state of disorganization and crisis. In a situation in which perceptions are

This article builds on research conducted at the Institute for Research on Educational Finance and Governance, Stanford University, under the sponsorship of the National Institute of Education. Neither institute is responsible for the views presented here. I am indebted to a continuing collaboration with my colleague W. R. Scott and with other research colleagues in the IFG and Stanford's Training Program on Organizations and Mental Health in the Department of Sociology.

more real than reality is, crises are matters of perception in important ways. We first consider crisis, then the institutional supports of the mental health system, and finally the organizational system that results.

Crisis

It is routine to speak of crises in the mental health system, especially in this country. The perception of crisis is common, although there is no evidence that Americans have high rates of mental disorder. And crisis talk is much more common in recent decades than it was 50 or 75 years ago although again there is no evidence that problems have worsened.

Further, American mental health crises cover many different dimensions of the mental health system rather than recurring at only one or another point. There are the crises of purpose and outcome—as when high proportions of the population have some symptom or disturbance, when in high proportions of the cases the disturbance is untreated, or when the disturbance and its treatment are unequally distributed. There are resource crises, centering on amounts, rates of increase, equality of distribution, or waste. There are crises of organization and technology, dealing with illicit, irresponsible, or inefficient practices or practitioners. And there are crises of sovereignty, with allegations of inattention and unconcern on the part of the authorities or sometimes of perverse attempts to dominate society through insidious controls.

The talk goes on in a society that has what seem to be high levels of mental health and what are certainly high levels of organization and investment in the area. The same pattern characterizes other human service areas in American society: Education, for instance, is much more expanded in the United States than elsewhere and is also accompanied by routine discourse about crisis. Welfare services, although not exceptionally expanded, are certainly arenas for crisis. It would seem that crisis is the American way of organizing in the human service area. And indeed this is our argument: Crisis and inconsistency follow from an emphasis on collective goods in the human services area in the absence of strong state centralization.

Crisis, in this context, refers to collective, normative interpretations of situations. Crises are not collections of individually problematic situations or simple descriptions of problems. They involve a conception of a system—in our case, a national one—for which failure is envisioned or for which vastly better functioning can be envisioned (Habermas, 1975). In societies with more centralized states, crisis construction may involve perceptions of the failure of an ongoing highly organized structure. For obvious reasons this is an uncommon form in the United States; crises involve the perception of an ongoing decentralized structure that fails to meet the real collective problem. An important point is that crises are issues of *legitimacy* and only secondarily problems in organizational functioning: Crisis construction involves the use of immediate functional problems (e.g., funding difficulties, evidence of scandal, or data on unmet purposes) to sustain imagery of systemic failure. A second point is that crisis depiction almost intrinsically involves the normative depiction of an ideal, proper, and successful organizational system.

We turn now to discuss the processes by which the wider environment has built up a system of mental health organizations and the features of this environment that continually generate questions about the legitimacy of the organizations produced.

Environments

The modern research literature sees rationalized organizations as greatly affected by their environment, which both influences and constitutes them (see Scott, 1981, for a review). The constitutive aspect of this relation is now seen as so broad that the term *legitimacy* is widely used to describe the way environments make possible organization in given domains. Thus even in so straightforward a domain as market production, institutional environments both enable and constrain organizing in rationalized forms. (a) They develop, sustain, and legally enforce monetarized markets in the objects produced. They legitimate the definition of objects as commodities. This makes large-scale organization possible and necessary, given the scale and variability of the market that is produced. (b) Environments both provide technologies and define technical constraints (e.g., safety and pollution regulations, transaction costs of modifying common technologies). (c) Environments socially construct labor markets, with appropriate personnel categories, and define appropriate conditions for their use. They also prohibit or impede alternatives to labor markets (e.g., long-term or communal commitments). (d) Environments develop and enforce monetarized markets in the necessary resources and block alternatives. (e) Environments legitimate unified organizational sovereignty over relevant internal activities (e.g., through extensions of rules of property and the legal individual) and at the same time constrain its use (invoking various definitions of rationality and arbitrariness). All this structure is built up and constrained under notions of the collective good that give public legitimacy to delegated private action.

In the case of other commodities that are given more standing because they are considered collective goods, the environmental effects are even more direct (Meyer & Rowan, 1977), and the organizations developed are direct creatures of the wide environment (now, usually, the state). Thus our organizations for the maintenance of military forces or the delivery of pension checks are determined largely by environmental forces.

VISIBILITY

The environmental forces that lead to formal organization are those that rationalize elements of an activity domain: the construction and monetarization of commodities, labor, and resources, and the creation and legitimation of professions and technique. There is an element of simple regulation here, the organization of activity according to fashionable modern values. But there is also a strong element of social construction or invention. When people are led to think not only of forests but also of trees, and to think (and act) in terms of trees as potential board feet of lumber, not only new forms of organization but also new forms of activity are created. So also when produced commodities are given abstract market definition: The modern range of objects one can legally call and sell as shoes would be hard to conceive of in a world of traditional production and exchange. The legal and social definition of working persons as labor has similar effects. All these elements—in one sense social fictions—expand possibilities for organization and activity. They cause aspects of reality that previously had been invisible to become socially visible.

The expansion of institutional rationalization into such domains as the human services—mental health, especially—is an extreme example. Here there are typically no traditional and visible commodities at all. There is no visible and consensual production or technology, and therefore there is no clear definition of the necessary labor or resources. In order for the modern emergence of so much formal organization in this domain to become possible, a great deal of rationalization of the wider institutional environment was necessary.

COLLECTIVE GOODS

The construction of a collectively legitimized private good of mental health is one thing. It led to some institutional rationalization and thus to the formation of limited organizational structure. Shifting this good to the direct status of a public good (beyond the tradition of custodial protection) is another. It involves a great deal of institutional work and the elaboration of much consequent organizational structure.

We may use a historical parallel with education as an example. The 18th-century rise in conceptions of education as a good led to a limited amount of institutional rationalization and very limited organization. There were vague specifications of identified purpose, some development of the professionalized teacher as a technical theory, and a heavy reliance on private or centralized sources of resources. By the late 19th century education had become a major *national* good (Ramirez & Meyer, 1980). This involved a series of changes that made education *visible:* the standardization of degrees and credits, the professional certification of teachers, the construction of curricula and pedagogical theory, and the detailed classification of the pupils in a gradual sequence and sometimes with such personal properties as ability. But education had to also become *collective;* and in most nation-states its theory and regulations were spelled out at the national political level (Boli-Bennett & Meyer, 1978).

Once these two changes occurred—and they went on in wider cultural and political institutions rather than in narrower organizational ones—the massive educational organizations we know today became possible: Big schools that are integrated in large systems tied to the center of the state. Building rational organizations in so internally ambiguous a domain as education requires the creation of such massive social fictions. They are very real in their organizational structure although they sometimes still seem comical. We laugh at, but build our organizations around, the credit unit and degree—both visible and standardized in a way impossible to reconcile with the complex reality we envision as real education. We puzzle at the utterly arbitrary—but necessary—rules of teacher credentialing and school accreditation. We remain chronically disturbed by the gap between the classification of pupils and any assessment of their real achievement. But education has been built and its organization is now worldwide. It is a visible and collective good, and its further organization is easy.

The Institutional Construction of Mental Health

The construction of the legitimated Western self and of mental illness clearly go together (Foucault, 1965). Structures of individualism arose, with theories of political, economic, and cultural society resting on individual action, consciousness, and sometimes sovereignty. The liberal theory and constitutional structure of the 18th and 19th centuries leave this endowed individual a relatively unspecified black box, free to act within some zone called *reason.* This in itself, of course, opens new ground for a legitimated form of interpretable mental illness called unreason and for some possibilities for the social management of this new institution. However, in such theories, the collective authorization that exists is mainly for individuals (and their communal agents, such as families or local authorities) to pursue remedy for disease of the mind. During this period, various technologies and professions dealing with the problem began to emerge, building on older medical or religious authority. It becomes reasonable for individuals and their agents to devote resources to the cure of their unreason.

In this system, the definition of mental illness was vague, as was the social specification of the proper techniques or professions for its management and remedy. Organization arose, but on a very limited scale: Much activity took place in the relationship between particular practitioners and their patients, along the traditional medical model. However, a few larger organizations were created. Many of these asylums dealt custodially with the one aspect of mental illness that even in a liberal period involved the collective good: the care of the dangerous and endangered.

From this overall system arose a limited number of custodial organizations, a very few therapeutic organizations, and a great many socially licensed professional-client relationships justified as reasonable in the wider context but given little standard meaning.

The turn of this century marked a major change in institutional organization in practically all modern societies. Polities, economies, and cultural institutions came to be managed not under the myths of private transactions within society, but by society itself. Large numbers of goods took on a collective dimension and were collectively regulated (among them, aspects of labor, capital, and market transactions). Everywhere, demands for both justice and efficient progress led to the explicit social organization of previously decentralized legitimate activities.

This change involved a considerable alteration in the definition of the Western self. From being a sovereign point in social space, the self took on more and more socially and legally legitimated substantive meaning. Political and economic substantive rights and needs appeared. Psychology developed—with long lists of normal human needs and motives and capacities. In this more corporate individualism, a vastly expanded theory of the individual self was required if political, economic, and cultural goods and opportunities were to be distributed justly and efficiently through the explicit mechanisms of social organization.

The emergence of the legitimated individual can be seen on two dimensions (Meyer, 1987). One is the competent, achieving individual, whose productive action brings rewards to the self and corresponding gains to the collectivity (in such conceptions as the gross national product). This individual is institutionally located and managed primarily in the system of education, although some elements are interpreted as related to mental health. The second aspect of the emergent individual is the legitimated personality in terms of needs and motives and satisfactions. Here the criteria are not competence and productivity but happiness and self-esteem. And on this dimension, the rules of equality rather than those of differential achievement (and social progress which is, in the ideology, its accompaniment and product) are dominant. The modern self, in terms of satisfactions and self-esteem, is a descendant of the medieval soul; and selves, like souls, are ultimately equal. The associated rights and responsibilities of the self seem to be at the core of the expanding 20th-century mental health movement, institutions, and organizational structure. Of course, we are concerned here with institutional sources and legitimation, not necessarily with the actual problems and difficulties confronted in providing services to people. Those often have a broader (and more traditional) character. For instance, for many kinds of mental illnesses, organic problems seem central. Our purpose here is to consider the institutional frame under which the system operates—in the nature of things, institutional frames are inevitably unrealistic. They structure much organizational life, and the kinds of legitimating ideas discussed above are necessary to explain the peculiar character of the mental health organizational system and why it contrasts in a good many ways with the more established medical one.

We thus have expanded the mental health rights of individuals and have assumed more collective responsibility for them. It has been a situation ripe for organizing, and the number and diversity of organizations in the field is striking. The question is, What institutional structures have arisen to structure and stabilize this development? Mental health, like education, is a business of very uncertain consensual visibility. It is now defined as a major human need and collective responsibility. But effective and stable organization requires institutional definitions that construct visibility—of the product, of the techniques that produce it, of the necessary resources, and of the sovereign authority to manage it all.

Problematics of the Social Construction of Mental Health

GOALS

Consider first the product or goal. Without clarity in this area, organization is difficult. What is the institutional history here, comparable to the creation of the credit hour and degree in education (which turns the invisible into the definitively visible)? The striking aspect of the mental health system is that there are no consensual institutional rules defining people as healthy or sick, better or worse, or for differentiating between a clearly successful treatment or a failure. One can find authoritative (professional) opinion on every side of every question—everyone is sick and needs treatment, or almost no one does. Even a patient's suicide can be, in some versions, defined as a sort of therapeutic learning experience. There is nothing quite equivalent to the grade-point average, the SAT score, the credit hour, or the degree, all of which institutionally turn hopeless uncertainty into social certainty. We know exactly who among us has a certain degree and is hence eligible by rule for certain social position. What rules tell us who is mentally healthy?

There is, clearly, much comparative variation here. Some modern societies, turning the definitive decision over to a particular set of licensed practitioners as a closed group, operate with much more clearly institutionalized decision rules. In such societies there is less mental health organization, in our terms, but considerably more stability and uniformity in its structure.

TECHNOLOGY

The conventional way societies rationalize technical definitions in such an invisible and unclear domain is to professionalize them. This holds in education: Education is that which is passed on by a licensed practitioner. What, correspondingly, is mental health treatment? American society has spawned a good many professions in the area, but there are very unclear authority rules. The situation, again, differs comparably: Other modern societies locate such authority more clearly in a given class of professionals, creating greater uniformity. The result for American society is greatly expanded mental health organizations, organized in very complex ways, showing a great deal of variation. But it is all unstable. Each form of treatment, and each profession, raises questions about the legitimacy of the others.

RESOURCES

Consider next the required resources. Given an uncertain production function, deciding on amounts of necessary resources becomes highly problematic. In other societies, location of a technology by fiat in a given occupational group simplifies and stabilizes the problem. The American system generates a sprawling system of radically different prices.

And a second resource question arises: Which collective authority is to pay? This is extremely unclear in American normative principle, and the system is mixed and inconsistent. There is a private sector. There is, left over from older conceptions of injury, some legally enforceable private right against other private bodies. Also, one can sometimes collect from one's employer on grounds of occupation-related tension or grief. There are even attempts to sue parents and other loved ones for mental injury. And there are a variety of principles of insurance.

The real problem is the lack of agreement within the public system about which level of the collectivity is responsible to maintain rights to mental health. There are local authorities, states, and the federal government, and there are leftovers of older religious and charitable associations. Again, the effect is to create a mental health sector filled with a motley assortment of ever-changing organizations, all open to one or another question of legitimacy. It is a massively expanded system and is obviously massively disorganized.

SOVEREIGNTY

Consider finally the question of sovereignty: Who is responsible for running the system? There is no answer—no authority that can provide an unquestioned shelter in which stable bureaucratic organization could grow. The number of different authorities entrusted with responsibility for the mental health of the persons under their jurisdiction is astonishing. There are the religious and charitable groups, multiple levels of government, and multiple licensed professions, not to mention the ancient institutions of community and family life.

Here is the core of the problem in American society. It is exactly such a society—one that celebrates to an extraordinary extent the rights of personhood—in which it is most difficult to define the collectivity that is responsible for repairing breaks in this personhood. The well-known high scores of Americans on personality tests (self-esteem, satisfaction, or locus of control) are related to the fact that American personhood has standing in many collectivities. But it is exactly this property that causes a great many collectivities to be involved when collective authority over broad mental health issues expands. In very traditional societies, no general authority may preside over such a matter as individual mental health. In American society, a great many authorities do.

Note that the collectivities most involved tend to be those in which the individual has very broad standing. Mental health rights are much less securely established in specialized purposive organizations like firms or other work places—perhaps less so than in some European societies. They inhere in the many collectivities in which citizenship inheres.

Effects on Mental Health Organizations

We have thus an institutional system in which mental health is given attention and value, and in which it has increasingly been defined as a collective good. But the social construction of visibility in goals, technologies, required resources, and sovereignty has not proceeded to consensual definitions: A great deal of visibility is promulgated by one or another interest or collectivity, with little standardization. In part, this is because of the diffuse importance of the individual in American society and the number and diversity of different collectivities in which the individual has standing.

The system is thus an increasingly centralized one, but one in which the centralization is highly fragmented (Meyer & Scott, 1983b). Many different collectivities and interests affect it, *not only at its boundaries but also in the very definition of its internal structure and purpose.*

The organizational impact of this institutional system can best be phrased in terms of a series of comparative research propositions about how contemporary mental health organizations in the United States may be distinct from those of the past or those of other modern societies:

1. *A great amount* of mental health organization appears, given the centrality of the substantive individual and its happiness in the American political culture. Many aspects of mental health are recognized in this country (by reputation, especially in California, or, according to Northern Californians, in Southern California). Many different professional groups and techniques receive attention, and there is much legitimation of private and public expenditure. So mental health organization is very extensive. This is especially the case because the good involved has increasingly collective aspects. We live in a society in which it is routine to suggest the pursuit of various therapies to others in both formal and personal relations. One can even legitimately give a blanket recommendation of one's newest therapy to all the random others at a party.

2. Greater *numbers* of mental health organizations and more types of organizations appear because of both the cultural emphasis and the dispersed controlling context (Hannan & Freeman, 1977). The different organizations reflect the different collectivities, professions, ideologies, definitions of the problem, technologies, and funding systems.

3. The system lacks integration or structure. This appears on both classic dimensions of structure in an organizational system: vertical and horizontal. *Vertical* differentiation is unclear, with anarchic networks of partial control or sovereignty—there is nothing like a clearly differentiated hierarchy or organization running up to a national ministry. *Horizontal* differentiation is also unclear—any given organizational unit handles in fact multiple problems, and any given mental health problem is simultaneously dealt with by many different and unintegrated organizations.

4. As a consequence, any given organizational unit must carry more of the burden of external coordination than would be the case elsewhere. The network of vertical and horizontal linkages among mental health organizations is cloudy and requires constant surveillance. We therefore expect American mental health organizations to have more administration, and higher proportions of administrative time, devoted to external relations than would be the case in other societies or periods. This should be true because the maintenance of stable external supports in terms of resources, the legitimation of professions and techniques, and the specifications of legitimate goals is continually problematic. The days in which the collective aspects of the system could be maintained by a simple administrative structure in a custodial mental hospital sheltered by the sovereign control of the state government seem long gone.

5. Organizations are more unstable than elsewhere. Given organizations appear and disappear with greater frequency than in a more structured institutional context. It is easier to form them, and easier for them to die. They are also more likely to change in internal structure, with new goals, new professions or technologies, and new sources of resources and control. A huge population of mental health organizations is maintained, but its composition continually changes.

6. American mental health organizations are more internally decoupled (March & Olsen, 1976; Weick, 1976) than are systems elsewhere. Formal structures must be adapted to a complex and changing environment that demands new goal claims, new technologies (professions, techniques, or programs), new authority acceptance, and new funding arrangements. All this, for survival, must be driven by the urgent political problems posed by the environment. Yet at the same time reasonably coherent systems of internal activity must go on—there are the obvious practical problems of daily activity. The organizational solution in such situations is decoupling: Formal structure becomes in part a masquerade, and detailed control linkages between it and activity are avoided. The report to the government must fit the new governmental categories, but practical reality is likely to fall into quite different categories.

One can see the decoupling system easily in the practical literature it generates. Nothing is ever quite clear. There are glowing or critical accounts of programs and policies, but what actually happens is left very muddy. Therapies, management programs, patient counts, and so on are described, but in ways that do not make clear who is doing what to whom. Rational organizers commonly see such a system as arising from sloth, inefficiency, and a lack of intelligent thought and management. They are wrong: The obfuscation is necessary and reasonable, created by people trying to protect some order in a conflicting and inconsistent environment (see Meyer & Scott, 1983b, for educational examples). It takes very able and thoughtful people to write and formalize descriptions of a mental health organization and treatments that cannot be understood.

7. Finally, the system reflects continual and direct crises of legitimacy. It is highly funded but left open in every respect to fundamental cultural attacks.

Resolutions

What kinds of changes can one envision that would simplify the organizational system in this domain? Are such changes likely?

One answer would be organizational centralization of mental health to a given collective level—state or, more likely, federal governments. One would then find, for better or worse, a clearly defined and differentiated system of subunit service organizations (Meyer & Scott, 1983b). Such a solution is obviously very unlikely in this country. Both American federalism as an organizational principle and the related diffuse sovereignty of the individual run against such a solution.

A second solution would be the denial of collective authority or responsibility in the matter, and the delegation of authority and responsibility to private actors or their third-party agents. This resort to an earlier individualism, advocated by some on the right, is also very unlikely. The whole organizational fabric of all developed modern societies involves a substantive specification of the meaning and rights of the individual.

A third solution, common in other American domains, is institutional rather than organizational coordination. Education is a classic example here (Meyer & Scott, 1983b). There is the same mixture of complex organizational controls as in the mental health domain. The difference is that there is a national institutionalized definition of education, broadly shared and used in every arena, from which schooling organizations can draw clarity, support, and legitimacy. A chaotic and decentralized organizational system is held together by highly institutionalized definitions of teachers, pupils, curricula, degrees, fields, credit, and so on. The parallel in mental health would be the evolution of standard definitions of the problems, goals, and professions involved. One can expect changes in this direction.

It is unwise to expect too much. The very process by which education and its related occupational credentials became institutionalized in the United States helps militate against the same solution in the mental health field. Organizational expansion in the United States took the form of much technical rationalization rather than a change in myths of sovereignty. It generated an enormous expansion of education and of its utilization as a basis of both productive membership and social allocation. This is in sharp contrast to more corporatist societies (such as Germany) in which modernization involved not only technical elaboration of organizational structure but also a collective organization and control of individuals as persons. In the United States, the latter structure—the definition of the self—was left free for indefinite expansion as an ultimate accounting element in the rationalized world. So many rights and motives remain legitimately embedded in the individual—given their increasing substantive specification but still ultimately located in the sovereign individual—that it is extremely difficult to generate a collectively specified definition of the proper self and its substantive rights.

Nevertheless, this is the dimension on which changes can be expected in the future. We can expect institutional agreements on the definition of treatable problems, of appropriate professionals, of funding responsibility, and so on. As these definitions arise and become consensual, we can expect some simplification of the organizational structures of the domain. There will be fewer and more clearly defined types of mental health organizations. Their vertical and horizontal relations will be more clearly defined. And their stability and survival will be enhanced. There is no way to pass a normative judgment on the value of this, but clearly it will appear more efficient and more just.

11

The Rise of Training Programs
in Firms and Agencies

An Institutional Perspective

W. RICHARD SCOTT

JOHN W. MEYER

MODERN ORGANIZATIONS contain all sorts of components beyond those once considered essential. There are specialized structures to manage safety, environmental impacts, personnel benefits, research, and many other functions.

Training programs in employment organizations are a prevalent structural feature that has been neglected by organizational sociologists. Such

We are happy to acknowledge the assistance of a huge number of graduate student collaborators who have worked with us as we have developed our theoretical ideas, constructed research designs, and collected data relevant to testing and amplifying our arguments. Participating in one or more stages of our work have been Nitza Berkovitch, Patricia Chang, Rene Fukuhara Dahl, Dana P. Eyre, Jingsheng Huang, Karen Bradley, Kelly Massey, David Miyahara, Susanne Monahan, Amy Roussel, JoEllen Shively, and Marc Ventresca.

Scott presented early versions of this paper at the Texas Conference on Organizations near Austin, Texas, April 15-17, 1988; and at a Conference on Computers and Learning sponsored by the Social Science Research Council held in Tortola, British Virgin Islands, from June 26 to July 1, 1989. Participants at these conferences made useful comments, some of which have been incorporated into the chapter. For all of this assistance, we express our gratitude.

Support for this program of research has come principally from the Spencer Foundation. In addition, this chapter was completed while Scott was a Fellow at the Center for Advanced Study in the Behavioral Sciences. He is grateful for financial support provided by the John D. & Catherine T. MacArthur Foundation.

programs were once rare but are now very common. They were once limited in scope but now cover many sorts of training—from remedial education to technical job skills to very broad human relations and management training. Organizations devote substantial resources to the training of personnel. Setting aside informal training, which occurs in all work contexts, and even excluding the semiformalized practices of on-the-job and apprenticeship training—types of training that are clearly the dominant mode within organizations[1]—formal training is very extensive and is growing in magnitude.

In this chapter we examine organizational training, focusing on two general questions. First, why have training programs expanded so much in modern organizations? Second, what accounts for the broadened focus of organizational training?

To answer the first question, we review in the latter half of this chapter, four general types of arguments. First, modern organizations have complex work requirements that call for workers trained in specialized technologies and for managers who can cope with more complex internal systems and external environments. Second, modern organizations obtain increased social control from having participants who carry their own internalized commitments; at the same time participants have increased their control over organizational resources, and one of the benefits they claim is training. Third, in modern organizations, as in modern nation-states, training is increasingly viewed as a right of membership and as a requisite for elevation to an elite position. All of these lines of thought provide explanations for the expansion of training programs and suggest specific hypotheses about organizational settings that are more likely to generate training of one type or another.

Finally, we offer two types of institutional arguments. The first focuses on institutional agencies, such as the state and professional associations, that create legal requirements and professional ideologies that make training seem necessary and rational. The second form of institutional argument stresses a process explanation. Institutional processes operate to diffuse beliefs in the desirability of training so that, increasingly, over time, the value of training in modern organizations is taken for granted. Rules and practices supporting training have become value-laden and widely accepted. More specific lines of argument are ensconced as ideologies in modern organizational belief and practice. As such beliefs diffuse, training spreads throughout organizations over and above the impact of specific causal factors characteristic of particular organizational settings. Considered altogether, the four arguments make up a multilayered explanation of and justification for training.

Institutional arguments are also employed, in the first half of the chapter, to explain the broadening of focus and the reduction in direct controls over training programs. Training programs are viewed as a subtype of a more general, institutionalized form: instruction. The social forms and cultural patterns associated with instruction are widely diffused in modern societies and operate in a wide array of settings. Although there are some distinctive features associated with each of these contexts, the broader institutional pattern exerts strong effects.

Most contemporary perspectives on organizational training emphasize the differences between corporate training and traditional educational programs, seeing the former as a product of specific technical or organizational-level requirements, and as being tightly controlled. There are, to be sure, differences between traditional education and corporate training programs. Chief among these is that educational programs devote more attention and energy toward making their processes and products appear comparable so that the values attained in educational settings can be more easily transferred to other contexts. Corporate training programs are less concerned to ensure—indeed, may take steps to resist—the transferability of their products.

Although there are some discernible differences between the organization of educational and training programs, our observations suggest that the appropriate contrast is not between an institutionalized framework in the traditional educational sector versus organization-specific controls in the corporate settings. Rather, there appear to be two distinct institutional forms: the one supporting education, the other, training. Though distinct from traditional educational systems, training is itself becoming institutionally stylized and legitimated. Corporate training programs appear to be developing their own distinct institutional bases, linked to modern theories of organizational, rather than to societal purposes, and creating somewhat distinctive professional norms, practices, and justifications. The focus of training has been broadened from more specific to more diffuse areas, and they rely on more professionalized controls rather than on arrangements of close inspection and evaluation. As it becomes institutionalized, organizational training has become more extensive, broader in scope, and more indirect in its organizational controls.

The Institutionalization of Training

THE MAGNITUDE OF CORPORATE-AGENCY TRAINING

Little accurate data exists about the pervasiveness of training programs in American organizations. It is difficult to know how to count students (because most are part-time) or courses (which differ greatly in format and duration). Estimates of employer expenditures on training thus vary widely— from $2 billion to $100 billion per year (see Carnevale & Goldstein, 1983; Eurich, 1985; Wagner, 1980). Higher estimates extrapolate from data on expenditures from the largest companies and include trainee wages and foregone production costs. Lower estimates are based on survey data from a wider range of firms and exclude all but direct costs. Still other estimates are based on surveys of individuals who report their involvement in adult education provided or paid for by employers.

Carnevale and Goldstein (1983) provide a relatively well-grounded estimate of number of employees and size of expenditures. They employ data from an industry survey, conducted by Lusterman (1977) for the Conference Board in 1974-1975, that surveyed firms employing 500 or more employees. Carnevale and Goldstein (1983) adjust their estimates for company size, add information on training within governmental agencies, and update the estimates to 1981. They conclude that

> industry and government provided about 17.6 million courses or training
> programs to 11.1 million workers—nearly one of eight employees. About 12
> million courses, or 68 percent of the total, were given in-house and the
> remainder in outside institutions such as schools, colleges, professional
> organizations and companies in the training business. In-house training alone
> was roughly estimated to cost between $5 billion and $10 billion, with a most
> likely estimate at around $7 billion. Adding a rough estimate of the wages and
> salaries of trainees while in training, one gets a range for total in-house
> expenditures of $12 to $17 billion, with a most likely figure of about $14
> billion. To these figures for in-house training should be added the cost of the
> 32 percent of courses that were given by outside institutions. If we were to
> assume the same cost per course, the totals (for both in-house and external
> training) would be $10 billion, excluding trainees' wages and salaries, and
> $21 billion including these items. (p. 36)

By comparison, at roughly the same time all U.S. universities and four-year colleges, public and private, enrolled approximately 7.6 million full-time students and spent just over $60 billion.

In short, it appears that by any criterion training conducted by U.S. work organizations is a sizable enterprise, involving in any given year more than half again as many students as are enrolled in 4-year colleges and universities and consuming from a quarter to a third of all resources expended on traditional higher education programs. Moreover, the evidence is strong that while conventional higher education programs have been and are expected to remain relatively stable, corporate training programs have been expanding.

PREVIOUS APPROACHES TO CORPORATE TRAINING

Corporate training has been examined from several social science per-spectives. Far and away the dominant view is one justifying training in terms of its contributions to productivity. This technical or instrumental view of training has been in ascendance since the work of Taylor (1911) and Munsterberg (1913), both of whom emphasized the importance of worker selection and training. Taylor viewed training as critical for replac-ing the inefficient, casual work habits that employees developed on their own with efficient, parsimonious procedures. This general view of training is embodied in the approaches of most economists and industrial and organization psychologists.

Specifically human capital theorists, primarily labor economists, have examined the relation between education and productivity. They posit that education contributes to human productivity (Becker, 1964) and, more often than not, have "confirmed" their predictions by noting the positive association between education and individual earnings (Schultz, 1961) or between aggregate indices of education and economic development (Denison, 1974). More recent analysts have been skeptical of the direct contribution of education to productivity. They argue that the association reflects primarily the "signaling" or "credentialing" value of education (Berg, 1971; Collins, 1979; Spence, 1973; Thurow, 1975). Although some studies in this tradition have attempted to distinguish between the effects of basic and vocational training, there has been little research attention devoted to exam-ining the direct effects of corporate training programs on productivity.[2]

Also embracing a technical view of training is the large body of work amassed by industrial and organizational psychologists (for example, see, Goldstein, 1986; Laird, 1985; Latham, 1988; Nadler, 1984).[3] Their focus is primarily applied, with much attention given to techniques for assessing the need for training, determining the utility of alternative training techniques, and developing methods for ascertaining the effectiveness of training.

A closely related body of literature on training has been developed by researchers and practitioners in organization development (OD) and applied change (see, e.g., Bennis, Benne, & Chin, 1985; Woodman & Pasmore, 1987). Training is viewed by these analysts as one lever among many others (e.g., survey feedback, team building) for stimulating and supporting change. The primary emphasis in these approaches is on influencing motivations rather than affecting job skills or knowledge—on nonrational rather than rational sources of change (see Chin & Benne, 1985).

Two other approaches to training are more sociological in emphasis. There is, first, a small literature on socialization in organizations (see, e.g.,

Rohlen, 1978; Van Maanen, 1978; Van Maanen & Schein, 1979). While this work addresses the question of how individuals learn to acquire organizational roles, studies have emphasized primarily informal and apprenticeship-type training rather than more formalized training programs. Also, like the OD literature, this work has focused primary attention on the motivational aspects of socialization, stressing the development of commitment to the organization and changes in identity and self-conception.

A second body of sociological theory and research that has emerged in recent years focuses on organizational learning (see, e.g., Argyris & Schon, 1978; Duncan & Weiss, 1979; Hedberg, 1981; Levitt & March, 1988). The work examines whether, how, and under what conditions organizations learn. Learning sometimes refers to the outcomes of adaptive processes in organizations and sometimes to the processes themselves: to the ways in which organizations generalize from their own and others' experiences in the development of rules and practices. Most discussions stress the distinction between organizational and individual learning: the former emphasizing learning as structurally encoded in organizational procedures and rules such that the "lessons of experience are maintained and accumulated within routines despite the turnover of personnel and the passage of time" (Levitt & March, 1988, p. 326). Training conducted by organizations would appear to qualify as one important mechanism linking organizational and individual learning, but few discussions of organizational learning pursue the topic in a systematic fashion.

In sum, there exists very little in the way of a sociological analysis of why training is a prominent and pervasive feature of modern organizational structure. Dominant models are psychological and economic and either assume that training is beneficial to productivity or are involved in assessing and improving its contributions. Most of these analysts argue that training improves the knowledge and skills of performers contributing to their increased productivity. Others have broadened the argument to encompass motivation and commitment as well as technical skills and know-how; but the focus remains largely on the consequences of training for workers and worker performance.

There has been little interest in examining the determinants of training programs in organizational settings, in viewing training as a dependent rather than an independent variable. By contrast, we seek to explain the pervasiveness of training and to ascertain what accounts for its recent rapid growth. In what types of organizations is training likely to develop? Has the definition or scope of training become more diffuse over time, and if so, why is this the case? These and related questions are not adequately addressed by the current literature.

AN INSTITUTIONAL APPROACH TO CORPORATE TRAINING

Institutional Environments and Education

Organizational analysts in recent years have expanded their conceptions of organizations as determined by their technical work environments to include an examination of the impact of wider institutional settings (Meyer & Scott, 1983b; Scott, 1987b). Early research emphasized the effects of technical factors, market forces, and uncertainty on organizational forms (e.g., Child & Mansfield, 1972; Hickson, Pugh, & Pheysey, 1969; Lawrence & Lorsch, 1967; Thompson, 1967; Woodward, 1965).

More recently, thinking has shifted to focus on the importance of institutional forces shaping organizations (e.g., DiMaggio & Powell, 1983; Meyer & Rowan, 1977; Zucker, 1983). Two kinds of institutional arguments have emerged (see Scott, 1987a). The first emphasizes institutionalization as a *process:* the construction over time of a social definition of reality such that certain ways of acting are taken for granted as the "right" if not the only way to do things (Berger & Luckmann, 1967; Meyer & Rowan, 1977; Selznick, 1957; Zucker, 1977). The second emphasizes institutions as a distinctive class of *agencies:* the existence of collective actors empowered to create cognitive and normative symbolic systems that support and constrain organizational behavior through a variety of mechanisms, including coercive sanctions, normative pressures, and mimetic influences (DiMaggio & Powell, 1983). Both types of arguments appear to be relevant to explaining training programs, and both are employed in constructing our arguments.

The shift from technical to institutional perspectives has been particularly influential in the analysis of educational organizations—an arena to which we have devoted much of our own efforts (see, for example, Meyer, Scott, Cole, & Intili, 1978; Meyer, Scott, & Strang, 1987, reprinted as Chapter 8 in this volume; Meyer, Tyack, Nagel, & Gordon, 1979; Meyer, Scott, Strang, & Creighton, 1988, reprinted as Chapter 9 in this volume; Scott & Meyer, 1988, reprinted as Chapter 7 in this volume). We view educational organizations as controlled and sustained primarily by institutional forces. Instructional activities and programs are rarely supported and rewarded directly in response to the quality of their educational outputs; rather, they receive legitimacy and material resources by conforming to widely shared cultural beliefs—concerning, for example, curriculum and instructional practice—and by meeting the requirements of regulatory structures—for example, accrediting bodies and licensing agencies.

In our previous work, we have examined how changes in the institutional environment of education—for example, changes in funding sources or regulatory controls—have affected the range and types of organizations in this arena. Now we ask how educational activities—more broadly conceived—vary depending on the context within which they are conducted. Specifically, what changes occur when education takes place in a business setting rather than within the traditional educational context? To pursue this question, it is necessary to broaden our purview of educational activities.

Instruction as an Institutional Pattern

Education may be usefully viewed as a subtype of a more general institutional pattern: instruction. Instruction connotes a set of activities, arrangements, categories, and cultural forms that supports activities across a wide array of contexts. Whereas "learning" is something one does, "instruction" is something that is done to one. Thus instruction calls up the clear notion of differentiated roles: teacher or instructor versus student or trainee. It suggests a set of activities distinguished from "work" or "play." It implies an outcome—the learning of subject matter or the acquisition of skills—that is expected to occur, an output different from any tangible product that may result from performing the activities. This outcome is often socially constructed to appear to be more tangible: It may be accompanied by the assigning of scores or grades, the specification of credit units, the granting of certificates, or other tangible evidence of successful completion.

Moreover, if we restrict our attention to the more formally structured programs of instruction—versus informal teaching or on-the-job training—then additional features appear. They include the erecting of explicit temporal and spatial boundaries that define and protect the activity, the systematic structuring of program content in the form of some type of curriculum or "program of instruction," and the utilization of a limited set of instructional techniques, such as lectures, discussion, hands-on practice, and exercises.

Such "schools" or instructional programs constitute a set of institutionalized beliefs and practices that have become compulsory for children and adolescents and are universally found in all developed and developing societies (see Meyer, 1977). Virtually every individual in the modern world has experienced this cultural form, is able to readily identify its distinguishing elements, and is likely to quickly adapt to its prescriptions.

The generic schooling or instructional form is found (and created) in the traditional educational sector, where basic socialization and general education are expected to take place. But it is also utilized in many other social contexts. Restricting attention to adult instruction, organized programs of instruction can be observed to operate in many major societal domains, as is illustrated in Figure 11.1. (For another categorization that emphasizes the wide distribution of educational forms, see Wagner, 1980.)

Four social domains are depicted within which the instructional pattern operates: the traditionally defined arena of education, business, the military, and religion. Others (for example, health, leisure) could also be identified. We observe that instructional programs have developed at varying levels— depicted on the vertical axis—in all four domains. There are multiple, somewhat vague criteria for determining levels, but differentiated clusters of programs sharing common features exist in all the domains. In particular, two broad categories of instruction are widely recognized: *education* and *training* (see, e.g., Eurich, 1985; Nadler, 1984).

The top tier of programs depicted in Figure 11.1 is generally labeled the realm of "education": the middle and, particularly, the lower tiers are more likely to be described as "training." Figure 11.2 lists a set of contrasting features commonly thought to be associated with each mode of instruction. Note that differences described relate to ends or goals, to cognitive frames or orientations, to teacher-student roles, and even to student-student relations. The contrasting features associated with the two models are not necessarily assumed to be empirically correct, but are of interest because they suggest that the institutional frames underlying different levels of instruction vary. Indeed, they suggest the possibility that training may represent a distinctive pattern of instruction, different from education.

A major difference between the higher and the lower tiers of instruction—between education and training—is in the extent to which the learning involved is expected to be generalizable across settings. Broadly speaking, education is represented as being less context dependent while training is more embedded in context. This difference in turn gives rise to some of the most important distinguishing features of the institutional context of the conventional education sector: the emphasis on degrees and all the attendant concern with graduation requirements, including credit units, grades, and standardized curricula and major fields of study.

For education to be of value outside of the context in which it is acquired, it must be made palpable, possessable, and portable. Grades and credit units render education ownable; they transform it into a commodity that can be possessed and accumulated in a manner that can be counted and accounted (verified). Accreditation systems allow education to be portable: They act to standardize curricula and requirements sufficiently to enable students to transfer from one educational institution to another and to expect to have their transcripts and diplomas accepted by employers or other educational organizations as evidence of specific work accomplished. These types of mechanisms perform the same function for the educational sector that monetization

Figure 11.1. Adult Instruction: Context and Level

Level	Traditional Education		Business	Military	Religion
	Public	Private			
Degree Programs	Colleges and universities	Colleges and universities	Corporate colleges, e.g., Wang Institute, Rand Graduate Institute	Military academies, e.g., West Point, Annapolis	Religious colleges, e.g., Notre Dame
Certificate, Vocational Programs	Community colleges and vocational high schools	Private training schools	Company-run vocational programs	War colleges	Seminaries
Nondegree Programs	Adult education programs	Specialized training	Corporate training	Basic training	Church schools, catechism classes
Goal	Self-improvement	More selective and specialized	Productivity, human capital	Discipline	Belief, commitment

Education ⟶ Training

237

Education	Training

Goals

Learning as an end in itself	Learning as a means to an end
Future utility	Present utility
Understanding	Results

Cognitive Frames

Theoretical	Practical
Subject-oriented	Problem-oriented
Concepts emphasized	Skills emphasized

Teacher-Student Relation

Teacher active; students passive	Both teacher and students active
Students dependent	Students independent
Student differences minimized	Student differences emphasized

Student-Student Relation

| Cooperation forbidden | Cooperation encouraged |
| Learning only from teacher | Learning from each other |

Figure 11.2. Contrasting Education and Training

performs for the economy. Such elements, however, are less crucial for training within organizations, because instruction is expected to have more immediate utility, and portability is not an issue. Indeed, corporations express concern that employees *not* transport skills acquired in their settings, and at their expense, to other potential competitors.

The values and belief systems associated with instruction appear to vary across the four sectors—depicted along the horizontal axis in the bottom row of Figure 11.1. The principal dimension of variation appears to echo one of the distinctions already noted between education and training; namely, whether the learning involved is viewed as itself an end or as being instrumental to some more ultimate value. In this sense, even the "higher" and more generalized levels of instruction are more likely to be considered as "training" when they operate in the business, military, and other "noneducational" sectors. Thus education is more likely to be linked to and justified by its contribution to productivity in the business domain or by its contribution to deepening faith and commitment in the arena of religion. Although instructional programs are found in abundance in a great variety of domains, it appears that their meaning and the justifications employed to sustain and motivate participants vary significantly by context.

We turn now to briefly describe the nature of instructional programs in business.

INSTRUCTIONAL PROGRAMS IN THE BUSINESS ARENA

As Figure 11.1 suggests, instructional programs exist at all levels within business settings. One of the most interesting developments in recent years has been the rapid growth of corporate colleges. A survey conducted by Eurich reveals that 18 corporate colleges existed in the United States in 1985 with several more in the planning stages. These degree-granting, accredited educational organizations have developed almost entirely since World War II. Although founded by individual companies or by trade associations, all of these programs have "moved toward increasing independence, added academic degree work, broadened the curriculum and programs, and widened their clientele" (Eurich, 1985, p. 97).

Just as we would expect to observe, as these organizations have attempted to survive in a niche largely occupied by traditional colleges and universities, they have, over time, become more isomorphic with these forms. With the attempt to create a more "portable" product, these organizations have shifted away from a training toward an educational pattern. Both ecological arguments emphasizing competition and institutional arguments stressing the mimetic processes of modeling, the normative pressures of professional culture, and the coercive forces of accreditation would predict these results (see DiMaggio & Powell, 1983; Hannan & Freeman, 1989).

Our primary interest, however, is on those instructional programs that remain closely tied to employment settings: on corporate and agency training programs. We have already noted the general magnitude of these programs and now turn to consider their structure and content.

Much of the prevailing discourse concerning organization training programs emphasizes the differences between them and conventional educational programs. Training in employment settings is described as being closely related to the technical and managerial tasks to be performed, conducted by persons experienced in carrying out these tasks, and closely evaluated and controlled. The tone of these accounts is illustrated by Eurich's (1985) description of company training:

> The ambiance is very different from the collegiate setting; there is no leisurely chatting and loitering about campus. Behavior is purposeful, the atmosphere intense and concentrated. . . .
>
> Instructional efficiency characterized corporate training, but it is not obtrusive in a learning atmosphere that offers variety and flexibility. . . . Time is determined by purpose. Teaching in the corporate classroom is by objective, like management by objective: a planned and stated goal, controls, and measurement of performance. Course development . . . follows careful procedures, starting with assessment of need for the instruction. Given that,

close collaboration then follows with operational personnel who know what they want and help determine clear objectives. (pp. 48, 53-54)

Eurich gives illustrations of such practices, but does not attempt to assess their prevalence. Most empirical surveys as well as our own observations of training programs in a diverse sample of organizations[4] suggest, by contrast, that evaluations of individual learning, instructor performance, or course effectiveness on any basis other than student's satisfaction or self-reported improvements are extremely rare (see Chmura, Henton, & Melville, 1987; Saari, Johnson, McLaughlin, & Zimmerle, 1988). Surveys also reveal that rather than being drawn from the workplace and having experience in performing the specific tasks for which training is offered, a large and growing number of organizational trainers have educational degrees and backgrounds (see Lee, 1985, 1986). A movement is underway to develop certification procedures for trainers. The American Society for Training and Development (ASTD), the leading professional association of trainers, is supporting efforts to raise standards and to standardize practice by certifying trainers (American Society for Training and Development, 1983; Galbraith & Gilley, 1986).

Inspection of courses offered indicates that a high proportion are not narrowly technical but more broadly oriented to prepare persons to become better organizational members and leaders. Much of what goes on in organizations relates to the management of people and the management of information. Typical course titles are Time management; Improving communication skills; Motivating subordinates; and Leadership. Such courses involve skills that are readily transferable across organizations.

Thus there is evidence to suggest that while corporate training programs exhibit some distinctive characteristics, they also draw on and embody many of the features of contemporary educational systems. Notions of professionalized teachers, standardized curricula, and transferable skills are appropriated from and legitimated by this source. Contrary to the notion that corporate training operates in a manner quite distinctive to instruction in more conventional educational settings, survey results reveal many similarities as well as some differences.

We consider then some of the factors that may account for both these general and distinctive characteristics.

Explaining the Existence, Nature, and Variety of Organizational Training Programs

Four general types of theoretical approaches can be identified that are intended to account for corporate training programs. The four types of explanations are not necessarily incompatible, although they may produce some inconsistent predictions.

TECHNICAL EXPLANATIONS

The most obvious, widely accepted, and historically earliest explanation for the existence and expansion of training in corporate organizations is a technical or instrumental one; technological advances and environmental challenges require informed decision making and skilled attention. Training is expected to contribute to such qualities in both production workers and managers. Training programs are supported because of their contribution to organizational effectiveness. Arguments and explanations along this line developed with the rise of modern organizational structures and theories and were highly developed by the early decades of this century. They were closely linked to the rise of the personnel profession (see Jacoby, 1985). More recently, they have been reinforced by the development of human capital theory.

These types of arguments can be extended to apply to all levels of the organization and to many if not most types of training. Thus,

1. Organizations forced to employ employees lacking basic educational skills are more likely to establish remedial training programs than organizations confronting better qualified labor pools.

Whereas technical or instrumental arguments were originally used to account for the development of courses designed to provide specialized, advanced skills and knowledge, they have more recently been employed to also explain the development of remedial training.

2. Organizations operating in environments undergoing rapid technological change are more likely to establish (re)training programs for production and sales workers.

Training programs for production workers are common in organizations confronting rapid technological change—such as the computer industry— and often include not only technicians and sales persons but also customers. In some types of environments it is difficult not only to make but also to sell and to buy products without technical training.

3. Organizations with managers that confront diverse employees performing complex tasks are more likely to establish managerial training programs.

4. Organizations with more decentralized decision-making structures are more likely to establish managerial training programs.

The argument here is that in organizations in which discretion is more widely distributed throughout the organizations, training provides a means not only to enhance skills and transfer information but also a mechanism for instilling a shared conception of objectives.

5. Organizations confronting more complex and turbulent environments are more likely to establish executive training programs.

Complex and changing environments reward organizations that increase the information seeking and processing skills of their executives.

6. Organizations routinely evaluate the adequacy and appropriateness of their training programs, including content, methods, and personnel, by assessing the effectiveness of training on personnel skills and knowledge and on work performance and outcomes.

A technical model of corporate training requires that performance and outcome assessment be an integral part of the system. Technical explanations of the existence and nature of such programs are difficult to sustain in the absence of clear assessment and feedback mechanisms. (For an elaboration of the requirements of such a technical model of training, see Eyre, Dahl, & Shively, 1986.)

Although considerable attention is devoted in the literature to the discussion of techniques for evaluating programs, courses, teaching personnel, methods, and students (e.g., Goldstein, 1986; Kearsley, 1982; Latham, 1988; Phillips, 1983), survey results examining actual practice in organizations, as already noted, document their infrequent use. Such findings suggest that technical explanations for organizational training do not fully account for training programs and need to be supplemented.

CONTROL EXPLANATIONS

For many years, instrumental or rational explanations for prevalent features of organizations were unchallenged. Recently, however, alternative arguments have developed to undermine existing consensus. Neo-Marxist theorists argue that many aspects of organizations are better explained by power or control considerations than by efficiency concerns. For example, analysts such as Braverman (1974) and Marglin (1974) propose that the emergence of a division of labor is better explained as a strategy by managers to increase their control over workers—by, for example, deskilling workers or by increasing the need for coordination—than as a device for improving efficiency. Creating, maintaining, and augmenting hierarchical controls are viewed as valued ends in themselves rather than as means to ensuring effectiveness.

Edwards (1979) has proposed a general model of the evolution of control systems in organizations. He suggests that early forms of simple, direct personal systems of subordination are replaced in many organizations by technological controls—controls built in to the design of machines and the flow of work. These, in turn, give way in some organizations to bureaucratic control: control that

> is embedded in the social and organizational structure of the firm and is built into job categories, work rules, promotion procedures, discipline, wage scales, definitions of responsibilities, and the like. Bureaucratic control establishes the impersonal force of "company rules" or "company policy" as the basis for control. (p. 131)

Bureaucratic control represents the formalization of the power structure: the creation of a complex system of rules governing roles, promotions and rewards, the development of an internal labor market (see Althauser & Kalleberg, 1981; Doeringer & Piore, 1971). Training programs in organizations appear to conform to and complement these bureaucratic systems. They provide a systematic basis for distributing responsibilities, wages, and promotion opportunities differentially among employees. Training may be viewed either as a logical component and an extension of existing bureaucratic controls or as a new form of control—the evolution of a fourth level or type of control system. The argument for the latter view is that, to the extent that training is successful, we are no longer dealing with the exercise of external controls regardless of how formalized their manifestation, but with *internalized* controls that are expected to operate in the absence of surveillance or sanction. In interpreting modern organizational mechanisms in this way, neo-Marxian arguments become "critical" versions of the human relations theories they have long challenged.

Irrespective of which view of training is taken, we expect it to flourish under the same kinds of conditions that give rise to more highly bureaucratized systems (or to more highly developed internal labor markets). Following arguments developed by Doeringer and Piore (1971), Williamson (1981), and Pfeffer and Cohen (1984), among others, we would expect to find these associations:

1. Organizations operating in core industrial sectors are more likely to develop training programs than organizations operating in peripheral sectors.
2. Irrespective of sector location, larger organizations are more likely to develop training programs than smaller organizations.

One interpretation of this association is that large organizations are more likely to be formalized, and formalization is associated with bureaucratic controls. However, a second interpretation is that organization size is associated with the development of a differentiated personnel department, and that such a unit is more likely to establish a variety of personnel control mechanisms, including training programs. Thus:

3. Organizations having personnel departments are more likely to develop training programs.

Williamson (1981) argues that the more specific the skills possessed by employees are to their organizations, the greater the costs to the organization of losing those employees, and therefore the more inducements firms provide to reward those who remain.

4. The greater the extent of firm-specific skills among employees, the more likely organizations will provide training.

This type of hypothesis is consistent with technical as well as control arguments.

Students of bureaucratic personnel systems have observed that Marxist views emphasize some functions of these systems but overlook others. From many vantage points, training is not just an obligation imposed on employees but also an important individual benefit. Whether viewed as adding capital value to employees' labor, as enhancing the development of their capacities, or as enabling them to be eligible for advancement—training opportunities are desirable and sought-after benefits under many circumstances. From this perspective, we would expect:

5. Organizations employing more highly educated or more highly skilled workers will offer more training.
6. Organizations confronting more competition in the recruitment of qualified workers will offer more training.
7. Organizations that are more highly unionized will offer more training.

More generally, these predictions are consistent with Tannenbaum's (1968) observation that organizations vary not only in the distribution of power among participants but also in the total amount of power exercised. Some organizations are characterized by high levels of power exercised by both superiors and subordinates: high levels of interdependence and reciprocal controls.

8. Organizations characterized by higher levels of power that is broadly distributed will have more extensive training programs serving multiple levels of participants.

POLITY EXPLANATIONS

In an important but neglected discussion of organizations as political systems, Selznick (1969) argues that organizations are not simply economic or production systems; they are governance structures. Selznick asserts that the concepts of law and the legal order apply to private associations as well as to public structures. Both are systems of governance that "rely for social control on formal authority and rule making" (1969, p. 7). Both are marked by pressures for expanding "legality": developing mechanisms to "reduce the degree of arbitrariness in positive law and its administration" (1969, p. 12). Selznick argues that these concerns give rise—in both public and private governments—to the creation of due-process procedures (see Dobbin, Edelman, Meyer, Scott, & Swidler, 1988).

But more than specific due-process protections are at issue. Selznick argues that individual participants in private associations may not only be said to have acquired *property* rights by virtue of their participation—the sorts of rights that call up due-process considerations; they also possess *membership* rights. These rights are defined by and most fully developed in the public sphere. "Citizenship," Selznick (1969, p. 249) notes, "is a special kind of group membership." When applied to private organizations, membership rights, according to Selznick (1969, pp. 117-118) ideally should include the following:

1. Employees should be treated as competent participants in a civic order.
2. As a condition of civic competence, employees need organizational support.

Such general arguments become of special interest in relation to education and training. Meyer (1977, p. 66) has emphasized the special functions that educational systems perform for the nation-state in rationalizing "the nature and organization of personnel and knowledge in modern society." Mass education makes national citizenship meaningful.

Beyond defining and extending national culture, mass education defines almost the entire population as possessing this culture, as imbued with its meanings, and as having the rights implied by it. . . . It allocates persons to citizenship—establishing their membership in the nation over and above various subgroups. And it directly expands the definition of what citizenship and the nation mean and what obligations and rights are involved.

Mass education is now quite widespread among nation-states of all types, so that there is little variance to be explained by characteristics of regime (see Boli, Ramirez, & Meyer, 1985; Meyer, Tyack, Nagel, & Gordon, 1979). But such characteristics may still explain differences in the prevalence and type of corporate training across national boundaries.

1. Organizations operating in societies that emphasize pluralism, individualism, and democracy are more likely to develop training programs than organizations operating in less democratic societies.
2. Organizations operating in more democratic societies are likely to develop more training programs that emphasize nontechnical, more diffuse forms of employee training (e.g., courses in leadership and human relations skills) than organizations operating in less democratic societies.

Meyer identifies a second, different function of education in the modern state. It not only creates and validates citizens, but also creates and validates elites. Elite cultural knowledge is expanded by education; elite positions are defined and legitimated by education; and persons are allocated to elite positions based on educational attainment. Although certain membership rights are available to all, others are differentially allocated. Mass education legitimates the former; specialized and restricted education legitimates the latter.

These conceptions and arguments may apply to training in corporations. There is considerable evidence to suggest that there has been an expansion in membership rights—for example, from employment security to participation in decision making—and, conversely, in corporate responsibilities for membership welfare. These concerns have expanded from relatively narrow, contractually defined rights to more diffuse notions of entitlements.

We would expect public organizations to lead the way in these developments. They are more likely to embrace an expanded conception of their members and to seek ways to ensure more equal access to elite roles within their administrative structures.

3. Organizations located within the public sector or that are more closely connected to it are more likely to develop training programs.

Some support for this proposition comes from a study by Collins (1974) of a sample of more than 300 organizations in the San Francisco Bay area, although Collins focused on educational requirements rather than on training programs within organizations. Collins reports that "public trust" organizations—those that offer a public service or rely heavily upon public confidence in the standards they uphold—exhibited higher educational requirements than "market" organizations.

4. Organizations located within or near the public sector are more likely to link training programs to promotion to elite positions and are more likely to stress broad access to such positions and programs.

In his analysis of the federal civil service system, DiPrete (1989) emphasizes the continuing efforts of designers and reformers of this system to ensure that opportunities to secure education necessary for promotion be available to all members.

The expanded conception of the facets, needs, and rights of employees is reflected by the widened conception of the role of organizational officials charged with personnel functions. Their responsibilities are being broadened from recruitment, selection, compensation, and dismissal to overseeing a wide variety of benefit packages and programs intended to develop and expand the capacities of employees. Such changes in functions are often accompanied and signaled by a change in the name of the responsible administrative unit.

5. Organizations that have created human resources departments are more likely to develop training programs than organizations that lack departments with such labels.
6. Organizations that have human resources departments are likely to offer more diffuse, nontechnical training than organizations lacking departments with such labels.

INSTITUTIONAL ARGUMENTS

Two related and separable types of arguments emphasize, respectively, the role of institutional agencies and the effect of institutional processes on the rise of training programs.

Institutional Agencies

The first strand of institutional analysis directs attention to the effect on organizational forms and activities of the actions of institutional agencies. These agents have the capacity to generate and enforce more general symbolic frameworks—both cognitive and normative belief systems—

having the power to shape organizations. We include here those collective actors having the power to formulate or influence rules and regulations or to promulgate norms and standards governing practice. Principal among such actors in modern societies are agencies of the state, various legal entities, and professional associations. Organizations are rewarded for conforming to requirements generated by such actors irrespective of whether they support improved performance. (In some cases, compliance by the organizations to the demands of the external agent may serve a technical function in the sense that it leads to improved outcomes. But the outcomes have been defined by and are of interest to the external agency rather than the host organization.)[5]

Institutional agencies operate through a variety of mechanisms (see DiMaggio & Powell, 1983; Scott, 1987a): legal rules backed with sanctions, material incentives, moral suasion. Some types of training requirements are directly imposed by governmental bodies. The Occupational Safety and Health Administration (OSHA), for example, requires that training in safety procedures be regularly provided by employers for selected personnel. Other types of training are directly paid for by federal or state funds. Examples include programs such as the earlier Comprehensive Education and Training Act (CETA) or the current U.S. Job Training Partnership Act that provide incentives to employers to provide basic or remedial training or retraining to unemployed or underemployed workers. The federal government also provides tax incentives to encourage training of all employees by defining training as an appropriate business expense. And, since the 1964 Civil Rights Act, the linkage between training and selection and promotion decisions has been recognized, and access to training affirmed as a right to be upheld by the courts (see Latham, 1988).

1. Organizational training increases with the availability of public funding and tax concessions and with the proliferation of regulations relating to training.

Other types of demands are supported primarily by normative pressures. Professional bodies may lack the power of legal enforcement for their preferred arrangements but command the loyalty of their members—often key participants in organizations—and the respect of client or constituency groups. Professional networks are often observed to stimulate and support innovations in organizations that may not necessarily improve performance. Much training occurs in response to requirements and standards promulgated by professional bodies. Although much of this training targets professionals—e.g., training required for licensure renewal—some is imposed on ancillary personnel—for example, medical technicians—who work under the direction of professionals.

2. Organizations employing professionals are more likely to provide training for their participants, including nonprofessional members, than organizations lacking professional participants.

Trainers within organizations are themselves increasingly organized as a professional community. The largest and most influential association representing training interests in the United States is the American Society for Training and Development.[6] With a current membership of more than 46,000 affiliated with either national or local chapters, ASTD has served as a stimulus for expansion of the training arena and of professional development. Although the ASTD hosts national conferences and workshops, more decentralized activities are emphasized: Local chapters of the society exist in more than 125 cities; and a number of professional practice area networks operate to connect individuals with related interests (see Chalofsky, 1984).

3. Organizations having participants who are members of professional training associations are more likely to develop training programs than organizations lacking such participants.

Recognition of the influence of groups such as ASTD calls attention to the effects occasioned by other suppliers of training. These include educational organizations such as community colleges who, increasingly, are adapting their services to meet the training needs of corporations and companies who are in the business of retailing training—sometimes producing packaged educational materials and sometimes providing standardized or tailorized educational services. Little systematic data exist on these external training units, but informed observers estimate that between 35% and 45% of all corporate training is "contracted out" to external providers (Carnevale & Goldstein, 1983).

4. The larger the number of training firms operating in a particular sector or industry, the more likely that organizations in that sector will offer training to their employees.

An institutional perspective emphasizes that much of the stimulus for training arises in structures and interests external to any given organization. As described, the number and variety of such sources in contemporary societies such as the United States is quite large. Training nodes will arise in varying locations within an organization in response to these diverse external influences.

5. The more diverse and complex the organization's institutional environment, the larger the number of training programs it will offer.

The diversity of sources will also have effects on the coherence or integration of training programs within a specific organization.

6. The more an organization's training programs have developed in response to different external stimuli, the less informed will any organizational respondent be about such programs and the less integrated will these programs be.

Institutional Processes

The second strand of institutional theory emphasizes the processes by which, over time, beliefs and attitudes develop such that certain arrangements and activities come to be taken for granted or valued as ends in themselves. Two variants of this perspective have developed. The first, stemming from the work of Berger and Luckmann (1967), stresses the processes by which interacting individuals construct certain interpretations or "typifications" that become depersonalized over time, appearing to be externalized and objectified. Emphasis is on cognitive processes that construct a shared definition of social reality. The second, emphasized by Selznick (1957) focuses on the processes by which arrangements or procedures that are devised for their instrumental value come over time to be valued ends in themselves. This process by which mechanisms become infused with value emphasizes the motivational aspects of institutionalization: the social construction of value.

Our observations of training programs in firms and agencies lead us to assert that these programs are undergoing institutionalization in both senses. As they become more widespread, they also become more conventional and taken for granted; and as they develop over time, they become more infused with value. Thus technical training, by virtue of its historical success, does not have to be invented or demonstrated over and over again, but becomes a standardized organizational response to changing circumstances. This suggests:

1. As technical training becomes more routinized and legitimate, such training programs will be found in more diverse work settings.

As modern organizations come under a regime in which technical training is a routinely available and valued institution, training itself may become less technical in format and less predictable by technical factors.

Similarly, control and political theories and their justification of training have become standard parts of the modern ideology of organizing. It is widely believed that participants possess multiple capacities and needs and that organizations benefit if participants bring more than a contractual obligation and develop more diffuse commitments to their goals and values.

2. As models of organizations stressing the ideological commitment of participants become more widely held, training programs will expand over time in diverse organizations.

Modern organizational ideologies, given their high legitimacy, may create control-related training programs in varied enterprises, little related to the specific need for strong controls.

These arguments suggest a more general proposition about the changing determinants of training. They imply that as training programs become more highly institutionalized, the types of organization-specific features we have proposed as accounting for training programs—features such as the complexity of work, location in a core industry, publicness—will become less predictive over time.

3. With the rise of the legitimacy of training as an institutional form, organizational characteristics will become less significant as predictors of amount and type of training found in a given setting.

To the extent to which such institutional forms and beliefs are growing in significance with the passage of time, we should also expect to observe differences in training programs related to time of founding. Following Stinchcombe (1965), who was the first to argue that organizations are imprinted with distinctive structural properties at the time of their creation reflecting wider societal beliefs and patterns, we would expect:

4. Organizations that operate within more recently founded industries will offer more training programs to participants than organizations within older industries.

5. Within a given industry, younger organizations will offer more training programs to participants than older organizations.

6. Organizations in newer industries and younger organizations in all industries will offer more nontechnical courses than organizations in older industries or older organizations.

7. Organizations in newer industries and younger organizations will link training and promotion more tightly than organizations in older industries or older organizations.

We noted earlier in this chapter that the prevailing rhetoric of organizational training emphasizes the differences between training and conventional educational programs. The development of training as a profession, however, appears to push in the opposite direction. There is increasing impetus, as discussed, for certification of trainers. Descriptive accounts of training acknowledge that most organizations do not attempt to systematically evaluate the effectiveness of their training by examining its effects on productivity or outputs. Other criteria—primarily employee satisfaction or attendance—predominate. The curriculum of work organizations tends to expand to include more generalized—less work-specific—skills.

In all of these ways, the schooling model presses against the work model: Employee development is separated as a differentiated and legitimate interest from employee training geared exclusively to improving current productivity. The goals of training become more diffuse; the competencies identified become less context specific, the timeline within which relevant effects are expected is extended.

We believe that these trends in training reflect the continuing influence and power of the institutional beliefs and patterns associated with the traditional educational sector. We have already pointed to these same influences operating to affect the evolution of corporate colleges. Although there is some evidence of attempts to differentiate training from educational models, training programs in corporate organizations still tend to draw support and legitimacy from modeling more traditional educational practices. We expect:

8. Training programs in organizations that adopt more of the characteristics associated with conventional educational programs will be more stable—more likely to persist.

Conclusions

We conclude by emphasizing two themes that underlie most of our arguments. The first comes from our descriptive and theoretical examination of the nature of training programs in work organizations. It appears to us that organizational training is already a distinctive and rather highly developed institution. Its ideology, structure, and foci are considerably impacted by the strength of the traditional models of education (themselves highly involved in organizational life and used in many ways), which provide a source of personnel, instructional patterns, and much content. But training is itself an institution and as such readily available to modern organizations as a set of taken-for-granted practices. It exhibits stability and coherence distinct from and independent of the credentialing rules and accreditation devices of the main educational system. It is seen as linked to organizational purposes rather than to societal or individual development; it has distinct content of its own, and it is organizationally and professionally controlled in distinctive ways.

Precisely because training is so heavily institutionalized, however, its structure differs from the rigorous technical model that is widely touted by its advocates. The tightly controlled training system, closely linked to very specific organizational tasks and purposes, is rarely to be found. Organizations tend to copy generally valued models, only loosely linked to their specific tasks and purposes. And they copy them as institutionalized forms, with loose controls and evaluation systems, in ways that are in many respects directly analogous to the operation of the traditional educational system.

A second conclusion follows from our analysis of the factors giving rise to training in modern organizations. Forces ranging from specific task performance demands to requirements for organizational and political control to general societal pressures to develop participants' capacities have cumulated to make for a generalized and multilayered set of pressures and justifications for training. They have not only cumulated, but also become institutionalized, so that the multiple virtues of training come together to support a general package of forms and processes, and also to make this package seem reasonable and appropriate in all sorts of organizational contexts and not just those to which the original justifications and explanations are most forcefully applied. We thus argue that, increasingly over time and with institutionalization, training programs can be expected to develop and flourish across the wide and diverse array of organizations that are to be found in contemporary society.

Notes

1. A study by Carnevale (1986) reported that more than 80% of the training taking place in industry was in the form of on-the-job training.

2. An exception is the study by Carnevale (1984) who examined the consequences of workplace learning on growth in economic output, the latter measured by variation in lifetime earnings. However, Carnevale placed primary emphasis in his study on "informal training" defined broadly as including: supervision, observation of fellow workers, learning from one's mistakes, reading, self-study, and other unstructured ways of acquiring work skills in the course of doing one's job.

3. In addition, much work of this type is published in two journals: *Training* and *Training and Development Journal.*

4. We are currently conducting a survey of training programs in a diverse sample of for-profit firms and public agencies, including local, state, and federal branches, in a county in Northern California.

5. A familiar example is provided by the economists' notion of an externality: a (usually undesirable) outcome produced by an organization for which it does not incur costs—e.g.,

pollution by a chemical plant. In such a case, representatives of those affected may impose regulations to ensure that the organization will take steps to correct the problem or be sanctioned. The pollution-control devices installed may serve to improve the technical performance of the plant, but only in terms of the new goals imposed by the external agency.

6. Other professional associations operating in this arena include: the American Society of Personnel Administrators, the National Society of Performance and Instruction, the American Association for Adult and Continuing Education, the Association for Educational Communications and Technicians, the Organizational Development Network, and the Human Resources Planning Society. Many of these associations contain one or more subgroups focused specifically on corporate training.

12

Employee Training

The Expansion of Organizational Citizenship

SUSANNE C. MONAHAN

JOHN W. MEYER

W. RICHARD SCOTT

IN WHAT IS PROBABLY STILL THE DOMINANT IMAGE, formal organizations are viewed as highly rationalized systems intended to run like clockwork: They operate as closed systems of preplanned and hierarchically coordinated activities and roles. In this model, the smooth functioning of the organization is seen to be at odds with the exercise of individual initiative or judgment: organization is created to eliminate the need for autonomous decision making or action by participants.

This mechanistic model of organizations is, however, increasingly being challenged both theoretically and empirically. Recent theory and research emphasize the openness of organizations to their environments, the loose coupling of their structures, and the quasi-autonomy of their departments and participants. We also observe that the growth of organization goes hand-in-hand with the expansion of education, the proliferation of the

This research is part of the Alternative Education Project, supported by a grant from the Spencer Foundation to W. Richard Scott and John W. Meyer. The chapter benefited greatly from the insights and comments of other participants in the project—Nitza Berkovitch, Karen Bradley, Patricia Chang, David Miyahara, and Marc Ventresca—as well as comments from participants in the Complex Organizations Seminar at Yale University.

professions, and increased emphasis on individual development. In this revised view, organization and individuality are viewed as not only compatible, but also mutually supportive.

In this chapter, we suggest that both of these conceptions of organization have validity but that the former, more mechanistic model was more characteristic of earlier forms of organization, while the latter, more flexible model is more representative of contemporary forms; that is, we offer an historical perspective on the changing nature of organizations. The consideration of this larger transformation constitutes the subtext of our work, but our direct focus is on training programs for employees of organizations. Although such programs are only one facet of organizations, we view them as a particularly sensitive indicator of the changing relation of individuals to organizations. Our discussion is informed by a recent small-scale survey of organizational training programs we conducted with other colleagues in a single, urban county in Northern California (see Miyahara, Monahan, Meyer, & Scott, 1991). The intent here, however, is to develop explanations, not to evaluate evidence.

Three observations, on which we elaborate below, motivate our discussion. First, we are struck by and seek to explain the prevalence of employee-training programs in contemporary organizations. It appears that they have developed and spread rapidly, particularly in the period since World War II. They are now ubiquitous structural features of all but the smallest public and private organizations in this country. Second, we observe that such programs are not reserved for only the top echelons of employees, but reach far down, involving significant numbers of lower-level employees. At the same time, however, current organizations have found new ways, which we describe below, to restrict the population of participants defined as employees. Third and most important: It appears that the scope of training programs has been broadened to encompass not only more types of employees but also more, and more diffuse, types of training. An earlier focus on training to promote technical skills has evolved to embrace a much broader domain—from human relations skills to self-enhancement techniques.

In this chapter, we attempt to characterize and to place in perspective the expansion and broadened character of training programs within organizations in the United States. We begin with a brief review of the evolution of training as an adjunct of the development of corporate personnel systems. Then we interpret these developments as reflections of two broad trends in social models of organization, involving the two main elements of organizational structure: persons and tasks.

The first trend involves shifts in the conception of the ordinary employee from a market commodity to a disciplined—and thus, in a narrow sense,

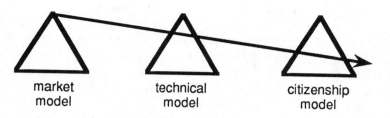

market
model

technical
model

citizenship
model

Figure 12.1. The Evolution of Organization-Participant Relations

partly trainable—participant to a complex person whose motives can be managed and even trained, in a human relations sense. This trend, in our current period, has led to the construction of a surprising number of organizational participants as something like citizens, bringing to the organization a sovereign capacity to manage their own participation in organizational life. Such citizens require and have the capacity for very broad sorts of training in self- and organizational development.

A second trend involves parallel shifts in social models of organizational tasks or work from simple market-driven labor, with little prospect or need for training, to more elaborate technical divisions of labor, with specific tasks for which one may be trained, and finally to more contemporary abstract models of work. In the latter models, all sorts of training make sense, analogous to the faith of all modern societies in mass and massive educational systems (see Ramirez & Boli, 1987): A generalized competence in, for instance, managing one's day, understanding computer or accounting systems, "working with others," or creating either one's job or future organizational changes seems desirable. This trend, too, culminates in very general pictures of organizational employees as abstracted citizens, constrained as with all forms of citizenship by a general investment in civility and in proper organizational culture.

Personnel Systems and Training in Organizations

We begin by describing the evolution of training in U.S. organizations by relating its development to more general changes in the management of human resources. Students of personnel systems and practices do not agree on the precise number of periods or phases but do agree on the general trajectory of development that has occurred since the latter part of the 19th century, by which time the major industrialization movements were well underway in the United States. Somewhat arbitrarily, we distinguish three periods (see Figure 12.1).

THE MARKET MODEL

Lawrence (1985) described the period extending from the early 1800s up to World War I as the market era.[1] It was characterized by the expansion of markets—for resources and customers but more important, as immigrants poured into the country, for laborers. Factories replaced small workshops, and the power of master craftsmen was reduced by the deskilling and task specialization brought about by industrialization. Master craftsmen were succeeded by merchant capitalists with expertise in marketing and finance. In these more complex organizations, turnover of workers was typically high with hiring and firing governed by economic cycles; labor organizing was erratic, and conflict between labor and management was high. As Jacoby (1985, p. 34) observes, "Because the employment relationship was one of weak attachment on both sides, the industrial labor market prior to 1915 was a market of movement, characterized by high rates of mobility." Although the latter part of the 19th century created the seeds for the later development of more technical models of organizing (see Tyack, 1974, on the public sector and Chandler, 1990, on the private side), the dominant models of the period viewed organization simply as a power structure replacing and stabilizing market forces. Both persons and tasks were derived from a fairly raw market system.

Not surprisingly, there was little or no formal training of employees in the typical firm at this time. Indeed, within most industries the earlier occupational-based training associated with craft organization was disrupted as the great majority of jobs required few skills and only minimal on-the-job training. Power and discretion were concentrated in the owner-managers. Because throughout most of the 19th century firms were small, the few top officials could directly oversee labor inputs. After 1880, as firms increased in size, power over workers was increasingly concentrated in the hands of foremen. These individuals were typically given free rein in controlling labor: They hired and fired employees and decided matters of retention and promotion based on their personal likes and dislikes or on the basis of bribes (Jacoby, 1985). Because there were few formalized policies and rules, control tended to be personal and direct (Edwards, 1979).

THE TECHNICAL MODEL

Organization as the simple accumulation, stabilization, and replacement of market forces was a fact of late 19th-century industrial and political development. Nevertheless, the dreams and ideologies of the period went much further. In nearly every contemporary core country, the idea that the organization of both people and tasks would make possible a higher and more technicized social form—indeed society—was endemic. In these dreams, both people and tasks were seen as schoolable, and capable of improvement through training programs. During the period from the late 19th century through World War I, the dreams were realized in practice, as the older arbitrary employment systems underwent a transformation. Thus in a substantial number of industrial firms, military establishments, and state organizations, more explicit, formalized systems and methodologies emerged for managing the work force.

Several factors contributed to the changes. The market system had engendered escalating hardship among workers and conflict with management. Just at the time that the war was creating new production demands and conscription was removing eligible males from the work force, European immigration slackened causing significant labor shortages. Employers were motivated to dampen worker unrest and reduce turnover.

The war period also witnessed a marked increase in governmental involvement in the economy. The state defended the right of workers to join unions and acted to set and enforce industry-wide standards for wages and working conditions (Jacoby, 1985, pp. 140-141). These actions supported and encouraged the development of centralized personnel departments that worked to develop standardized job definitions and to rationalize industrial wage structures. These departments increasingly took over the foreman's functions of selection, assignment, and promotion of employees.

The foreman's role was also being affected by other forces. The development of mass production machinery and assembly-line procedures introduced machine pacing so that substantial work controls were built directly into the technologies (Edwards, 1979). These impersonal controls reduced the need for the supervisory "drive system" characteristic of the market period. Supervisors were encouraged to provide technical assistance to workers, to "troubleshoot," and, increasingly, to properly motivate them to increase productivity (Lawrence, 1985).

Jacoby (1985) summarizes these quite substantial changes:

Looking back on the war years, one is struck by how much was accomplished in a short period of time. A substantial minority of firms had, through personnel management, introduced a more equitable employment relationship, one that encouraged workers to remain with the firm and be loyal to it. Line managers lost their exclusive right to determine corporate labor policies, and foreman gave up some of the power they wielded in their balkanized fiefdoms. New company-wide rules and procedures enmeshed the employment relationship in a web of bureaucratic rationality. (pp. 163-164)

Note that, even many years later, Jacoby's account reflects not only the instrumental powers or efficiencies involved in the change, but also the broader positive organizational vision—indeed, societal vision, in progressive thought—embodied in it. The cultural optimism, almost millennialist in style, indicates the extent to which the organizational changes were embedded as much in a cultural and legitimating matrix as in one of power and interest.

Consistent with these changes in work and supervision, this was also the period during which training was first introduced on a broad scale into organizations. Training was designed with a careful eye to the elaborated technical task—itself highly rationalized and schooled in theories of this period. Taylor's scientific management stressed the importance of finding "the one best way" to perform a task and drove technical training that would imbue workers with superior techniques. But training was also focused on the discipline of the worker, not simply narrow task accomplishment: Training would, it seemed, bring the body and mind of the worker under simple forms of organizational control, and was a social as well as technical ideology. As for supervisors, although they lost their absolute discretion over workers under their charge, they needed to acquire greater knowledge of centralized standards and policies and to master techniques that would assist them to better motivate workers. In short, they needed indoctrination in company-wide policy and practice, and training in leadership skills and human relations techniques.

The literature often treats the human relations period—with its atechnical commitment to a vision of the worker as infused with sentiment and community—as a dramatic reaction to the technicist tradition. The broadening of the psychological conception of the worker, however, may be as much a linear development as a reaction. In any event, the reliance on training of the person, as well as technical training for specific tasks, increased.

Today's organizations continue to emphasize both technical training for rank-and-file workers and human relations training for managers and supervisors. Our survey (as well as those of others—e.g., Carey, 1985; Carnevale, Gainer, & Villet, 1990; U.S. Small Business Administration, 1988; Zemky & Meyerson, 1985) reveals that many types of organizations teach their employees how to do their jobs, or selected aspects of it, and assist them to adapt to technological change. In formal classroom settings, employees learn to use particular computer programs and operate a variety of machines and equipment used in offices and plants.

Organizations also offer many courses intended to apprise supervisors of company policy as it affects their work: employment procedures and record keeping, disability procedures, accounting and administration, overview of financial systems, and payroll and personnel procedures. And organizations offer a large variety of training opportunities targeted toward improving the managerial techniques of supervisory personnel. Courses teach group-building skills (e.g., group action, group process, group dynamics, building teamwork and commitment), leadership techniques (e.g., motivation, delegation, managing authority, staff development), and interpersonal skills (e.g., communication, conflict management).

THE CITIZENSHIP MODEL

A third model has come into existence, beginning during World War II and continuing to develop to the present. Various labels have been proposed to capture these arrangements. Edwards (1979) employs the concept of "bureaucratic" personnel controls; Lawrence (1985) suggests two phases: A "career" system that developed post-World War II has begun to be superseded by a "commitment" system. For reasons we discuss below, and pursuing arguments first enunciated by Selznick (1969), we view the current personnel system as embodying a "citizenship" model.

In many respects, the citizenship model represents an extension of the trends associated with personnel practices initiated in the earlier period. Employment reforms continued in the interwar period in response to the legalization and growth of unions—both as an outcome of collective bargaining and as employer initiatives designed to deter unionism. Most organizations continued to develop stronger ties with their employees, offering more job security, more types of benefits, and more regularized promotion and training opportunities. Internal labor market systems were extended offering more employees not simply a job but a career (Lawrence, 1985, p. 28).

State intervention occurred not only with legislation in the mid-1930s supporting collective bargaining but also even more directly with the return to a wartime economy. As Jacoby (1985) observes:

> Government's impact on the labor market extended far beyond collective
> bargaining. During the war the nation came close to having a command labor
> market, as the President and agencies like the War Manpower Commission
> made important decisions affecting pay and labor allocation within and
> between firms. Government intervention resulted in more standardized
> employment conditions across industry. (p. 261)

Not surprisingly, these pressures greatly enlarged and strengthened personnel departments within organizations (see also Baron, Dobbin, & Jennings, 1986).

Training programs became more elaborate; they incorporated, in addition to technical training for workers and human relations training for supervisors and managers, a widening array of developmental, personal growth, and self-management courses. Courses of this nature include office professionalism, time management, individual contributor programs, intrapreneuring, transacting with people, applying intelligence in the workplace, career management, and structured problem solving. Courses are also offered on health and personal well-being, including safe diets, exercise, mental health, injury prevention, holiday health, stress, and nutrition.

THE CURRENT SITUATION

As noted in our introduction, the current scene is one in which most organizations offer training opportunities of a wide variety to most of their employees. A survey we conducted in 1990 in Santa Clara County targeted a diverse sample of 140 organizations—public and private, manufacturing and service, high and low skill requirements—having at least 25 employees (see Miyahara et al., 1991). We found that 71% of the organizations responding to our survey offered in-house training and that 78% offered assistance to their employees seeking external training. Virtually all of these organizations offered a variety of technical training courses to a wide array of employees (see Table 12.1). Similarly, nearly all offered diverse nontechnical training to these same employees. Lower level employees were only slightly more likely to receive technical training, and upper levels to receive nontechnical training. Thus the organizations surveyed reveal a high probability of offering training of a diverse sort to a broad range of their employees (see also Carnevale, Gainer, & Villet, 1990; Eurich, 1985). One additional finding: Although larger agencies and firms in our sample were more likely to offer training and more types of training, other organization-specific features—for example, unionization, skill level, sector of operation—were not strongly associated with training differences. Most of the organizations in our diverse sample, regardless of specific organizational characteristics, were in the training business. We turn now to develop a more general account of the training phenomenon in organizations.

The Expansion of Employee Competence

TRAINING AS AN INSTITUTION

The fact that it is possible to identify rather clear periods or eras of personnel policies and training regimes suggests that we are dealing here with an institutional phenomenon. First, employee-training programs may

TABLE 12.1 Percent of Organizations With Formal Training That Provide Technical and Nontechnical Training to Selected Categories of Workers ($N = 75$)

Type of Worker	Technical Training	Nontechnical Training
Managerial		
Top-level executives	24	37
Managers and supervisors	53	65
Nonmanagerial		
Technical or professional	77	52
Clerical	60	37

be viewed as buoyed up by wider cultural forms, and particular instances devolve from them. They are not typically created in specific organizations but are taken from a favorable institutional environment. They thus appear where expected from a rational analysis, but also where they would be thought as unlikely to do so. Second, in that training programs are infused with value far beyond the local situation, they are institutional in Selznick's classic vision. Training—often extremely vaguely defined—is dramatically presented as a virtue, as an investment in a highly progressive vision of the future, and as a core ideal. At least symbolic training programs and classrooms appear in corporate headquarters, with assertive spatial locations and occupational titles and formal ties to chief executives, and with much hoopla: Training people are easiest to find and interview.

Organizations adopt institutional packages from their environments (Baron, Dobbin, & Jennings, 1986; Dobbin, Edelman, Meyer, Scott, & Swidler, 1988; Edelman, 1990; Meyer & Rowan, 1977; Tolbert & Zucker, 1983). In the case of training programs, our survey as well as research by others (Chmura, Henton, & Melville, 1987; Saari, Johnson, McLaughlin, & Zimmerle, 1988) reveals that organizations only rarely define specific needs for training and design programs to meet those needs; they rarely evaluate the concrete and local benefits of their training programs or rely on assessment methods that go beyond obtaining survey feedback from course participants. The efficacy of training is taken on faith.

Training, in other words, is an institution in the contemporary organizational environment (Scott & Meyer, 1991; reprinted as Chapter 11, this volume). It is a set of legitimated ideas with virtues that are taken for granted by modern organizers. This view is entirely compatible with the notion that the evolution of training is best seen as a larger historical process, occurring in the wider environment, not a creature of painstaking decision making and rational assessment at the level of particular organizations. The fashionable training packages, with their trendy topics and methods and professional practitioners, are available in the contemporary environment, and can be appropriated with minimal effort. A cultural logic, more than a narrowly organization logic, is at work here and is the focus of our analysis.

The content of corporate training as an institutionalized model has changed over time, indicating the evolving conception of the relation between individuals and organizations. We see this evolution as governed by the two dimensions identified by Meyer (1987) in his discussion of the Western conception of individualism:

> Politically, economically, and culturally, social action is to make social sense but is also to spring from the subjective self and needs of the actor. The tension between the two is a central dialectic in Western history, often discussed as the relation between achievement and equality, or self and society, or human experience and technical development. Our point here is that both poles are institutions and both are institutions of individuality. (p. 244)

In the present context, we view the first pole as the problem of depicting action as rational and technical—seeing the individual actor as skilled to contribute to the attainment of a socially valued goal. The second pole concerns the manner in which the individual actor is constructed so as to be seen as selecting and willing the actions he or she contributes. We view the first wave of training activities in the United States as contributing to both dimensions in a narrowly technicized way—but especially to the first dimension. We see the later and current waves of training as also addressed to both dimensions—but perhaps especially to the second. The focus is less narrowly technical, and its emphasis on the construction of a broader committed person—and concurrently a looser and more open organization—is greater. Armed with this thesis, let us revisit the three historical periods identified earlier through which personnel practices and training ideologies have progressed.

ORGANIZING AS RATIONALIZING COLLECTIVE ACTION

The idea of organizing activities or people in tightly controlled and coordinated structures swept across the world of competitive modern nation-states in the later 19th century and took hold everywhere. These new ventures were part of a struggle to achieve efficiency and progress against an inefficient past and were directly linked to rising national states, expanding educational systems, and industrializing economies. The modern model of collective action gave rise to a form of polity characterized by "a distinctive rule system organizing persons and their activities in terms of universalistically defined resources, and means to collective ends" (Jepperson & Meyer, 1991, p. 207). The broadest embodiment of this polity was, of course, the nation-state, but intermediate forms also developed to serve more limited public (e.g., voluntary associations, non-profits) and private (e.g., corporations) purposes.

All of these forms exhibited, to an increasing extent (a) a unified sovereign, (b) a collective purpose, (c) culturally defined means-ends relations or technologies, and (d) subscription to the notion that the human actors were not only resources but also members having certain rights (Jepperson & Meyer, 1991; Meyer, 1983b). The first two of these elements were already visible during the early stages of corporate development in the United States, described above as the market model. In this early period, sovereignty rested primarily if not exclusively with the owner or entrepreneur. His vision—and it was almost always a male—and his will defined the purposes and prescribed the technologies. He was viewed as having the legitimate right to set objectives; and the corporate objectives were viewed as consistent with and contributing to the larger public welfare. Indeed, at first only selected, but by the early 20th century most private organizations were "chartered" as public corporations (Creighton, 1990; Seavoy, 1982).

Less systematic attention, however, was devoted during this period to the design of and control over work processes in a technical sense, or workers as persons. Standardization of products and procedures was low. If skilled work was required, decisions remained in the hands of craft workers. Rank-and-file workers were viewed as disposable resources to be deployed and fired, as necessary, depending on supply and demand. The concept of employees as "members" of the polity was either missing or very weak during the dominance of the market model.

As corporate organizations became larger, work more complex, and labor more scarce—and, as emphasized above, with encouragement and direction from the state—the market model gave way to the technical model during the second decade of this century. At this time, the emphasis on work organizations as rational frameworks became more explicit and more pronounced. In the initial stages of this period, organizing efforts focused on the design and inculcation of technical activities. Managers, aided by engineers, designed Taylor-type activity schemes for workers, and the first technical training programs were instituted. Workers needed to be trained to perform activities "in the one best way." An ideally technicized task skill was to be installed in the ideally disciplined worker. A narrow picture of a properly organized whole society was building up, with training as an integral part (directly analogous to some of the more fashionable ideals of morally infused, highly disciplined mass education of the period).

Thus early in the 20th century ideas about employee training became prominent in the system of U.S. organizations.[2] The core need was viewed as the promotion of technical skills and social discipline—not diffuse socialization or judgment for broad accomplishment. Broader socialization of both person and diffuse task skills would be supplied by the mass education system, commitment by the labor contract. And above all, broader personal capability and judgment was not required: It was reserved for the upper levels of the organization, in all prevailing organization theory. Workers could be made more efficient if they were trained to do the specific tasks built into the grand rational design. And, because training increased workers' value to the firm, greater efforts were made to retain current employees. It was during this period that technical training came to be viewed as integral to rational organization; and still today, it remains an important component of organizational training programs.

ORGANIZING AS CONSTRUCTING INDIVIDUALISM

The same ideologies of individualism that encouraged the expansion of mass educational systems and extended the boundaries of citizenship to include most adults as members of the wider national polity also penetrated corporate organizations. Although celebrating the extension of rationality, American values raised questions about the legitimacy and ultimate efficiency of a mechanistic view of organization. Impersonal rational organization was increasingly viewed as being in opposition to the natural human needs of employees for social support and approval. As Selznick (1969) notes:

> The man-as-machine conception faded as a new image emerged. The worker came to be recognized as a responsive being whose style of participation was greatly influenced by what he brought to the job and what that job could do for him. In due course, it was also learned that human response is something more than mechanical reaction to determinate stimuli. (p. 99)

By recognizing the social character of human motivation and its effect on performance, organizations could gain in efficiency. Of course, the humanization of organization—and indeed of the "society of organizations"—can easily be criticized as creating a society permeated by standardized social controls, as observers of American society since Tocqueville have noted.

The human relations emphasis had its earliest effects not on rank-and-file workers but on middle managers and supervisors. If the new views were to be acted on, it was these middle-level personnel whose ideas and behavior had to change. Workers received technical training, but supervisors and managers received training in human relations. These officials were increasingly expected to understand and embrace the organization's mission so as to be able to control and motivate not only their own but also their subordinate's contributions. In this sense, these middle-level officials were allowed to share in the role of organizational sovereign: They participated in, if not the setting, at least the interpretation and the implementation of the organization's goals.

The right to interpret organizational goals, however, obviously builds a pervasive cultural responsibility to fall in line with them. Indeed, critics of organizational training programs argue that these programs—rather than broadening opportunity for expanded sovereignty—in fact enforce diffuse social controls of a broadened kind on participants. And in some instances, organizational training programs have clearly violated ordinary principles of civil liberties—as has historically been an occasional feature of American civic culture generally.

With the coming of the technical model and its associated view of a more complex participant who needed to be motivated as well as directed, a new wave of human relations training programs were instituted within organizations—programs that still form a prominent layer in the archaeology of corporate training programs.

Throughout the 1930s and 1940s in the United States, again through the intervention of the nation-state, the political—or, in keeping with our thesis, the membership— rights of workers received increased recognition and protection. Reformers saw that corporate organizations were not simply economic systems but also systems of governance, and took steps during this period to "reduce the degree of arbitrariness in positive law and its administration" (Selznick, 1969, p. 12) and to institute mechanisms for securing the rights of workers to organize and to receive due-process protections against arbitrary exercise of corporate power. These developments, Selznick cogently argues, may be viewed as attempts to secure and extend citizenship rights to rank-and-file members of organizations. Even though the union movement has lost ground in recent years, many of these types of employee protections have been preserved and gradually extended (Dobbin, Sutton, Meyer, & Scott, 1993; reprinted as Chapter 13, this volume).

The contemporary period has seen great expansions in the number of domains in which organizations attempt to function and in the range of roles and educational qualifications they incorporate. Organizations now undertake more kinds of tasks and more complex tasks. These developments have been accompanied by a further decline in conceptions of organizations as preplanned rationalized structures set in place by central sovereigns. Organizations are now more often seen as abstract entities (e.g., financial interests) whose actual structures are expected to be fluid and worked out in practice. There is much celebration of adaptability, flexibility, and ongoing evolution as opposed to stability, fixity, and clarity of structure. More complex arrangements are made possible (e.g., matrix structures) as are highly decentralized and volatile forms (e.g., network structures) (see Davis, 1987; Eccles & Crane, 1988; Handy, 1989). Such structures place great demands on individual participants. In addition, it should be noted that the creating of so much organizational culture, and its enactment in training programs, can obviously constrain as much as construct autonomy for individual participants.

Concurrently with these organizational changes, a new wave of federal policies has extended protections to various categories of disadvantaged and handicapped employees, including those disadvantaged by earlier discrimination based on ethnicity or gender.

All of these changes embrace an expanded conception of employees as citizens of the organization: Citizens not only in the sense of enhanced welfare rights (e.g., to health and retirement benefits), but also in the sense of sovereign members in the classic American political vein. With increased membership rights go increased responsibilities. Organ (1988, 1990) emphasizes this aspect of the process in his conception of "organizational citizenship." Organ views citizenship behavior as an elaboration of Barnard's (1938) emphasis on the "willingness" of the participant to contribute to achieving organizational goals. Whether they use the labels "altruism," "conscientiousness," or "commitment," Organ argues that modern organizations rely for their effectiveness on employees going beyond their narrow, contractual obligations.

Employees are increasingly expected to exercise judgment and initiative and, in some cases, are allowed to create and modify their own job definitions (see Miner, 1987). More corporations are experimenting with increased employee involvement in organizational decisions through such mechanisms as quality circles, job enrichment and redesign, self-managing work teams, and minienterprise units. And it is entirely in the American tradition that such expanded conceptions of persons should be accompanied by enhanced corporate training programs: programs designed to train individuals for more active and effective participation as full-fledged members of the polity. Whether in the broader national polity or in its many more limited versions, the expansion of membership rights in the modern world has always been accompanied by an increase in educational opportunities.

Many of the new courses are designed to enhance interpersonal and communications skills as more work, of all types, involves increased interdependence. Hence the courses on "maximizing your communication skills to get results," "effective written communication," "group decision making," and "team building skills."

Other additions to the training program—and the major arena of growth at this time—represent attempts to train employees to be proactive sovereigns. The effort is to get employees to manage and modify their own contributions to suit the changing needs of the corporation. Thus organizations offer courses in self-assessment and career development, in "managing yourself for excellence," "assertiveness training," "pathways toward personal progress," "practical smarts—applying intelligence in the workplace," and "intrapreneuring." But even beyond this, many more types of employees than in the past are being prepared to manage and modify the organizational structures around them. The "learning organization" requires attentive, engaged, empowered participants.

Note that these enlarged conceptions of individual members focus on an expanded self, but a self that is an organizational member, not a private entity. Participation in a collective rationality and enhancement and elaboration of individuality are seen as complementary, not opposing, developments. The expanded self is not inconsistent with an organizationally competent self. Thus many of the new types of training emphasizes instruction in corporate culture and socialization in corporate values. One effect of such changes overall may be to lower our theoretical concern that the society of organizations, acting as Leviathan, is so oppressive. And to increase our theoretical concern that the society of organizational culture, rather than the iron cage, may constrain individuality and diversity.

Our general thesis is summarized in Figure 12.1, which depicts the changing nature of training as reflecting the extension of sovereignty to more, and more varied, participants within the organization. Broadened citizenship rights have been extended in many corporate polities to encompass rank-and-file workers, and these rights have been accompanied by expanded types of training programs.

Caveats and Summary

In many respects, the shift to the citizenship model of organization reflects constitutive structures in American society; and because of that, it resonates as a highly legitimate extension of rights and discretion to workers. The recognition and nurturing of individual judgment in the work world seems a positive development; but the exercise of discretion is directed toward a collective goal over which the worker still has little influence. Thus, for example, the training that organizational citizens receive is more broad than in earlier organizational models, but the development of the worker is still mainly focused toward the ultimate benefit of the organization. American structures of this kind have often been criticized as extending participation in a cooptive way.

In the market model of organization, the worker supplied labor to complete a task, and the organization structured that labor; such was the extent of the employer-employee relation. In the citizenship model, however, more facets of the worker are incorporated and drawn upon in organizational life. Perhaps more important, control of the worker no longer rests solely in the technical structuring of the work but extends to the shaping and redirecting of individual will by organizational culture. The worker may gain rights and accumulate responsibilities, but he or she is also more completely drawn in by the employing organization.

Finally, as membership rights have devolved deeper in organizations incorporating more members as responsible citizens, these developments have been countered by a move to redraw and restrict organizational boundaries. As membership becomes more meaningful, an increasing number of participants are defined as nonmembers. Recent years have seen a broad trend among U.S. organizations toward the "externalization of workers": in particular, using part-time workers whose rights and benefits are truncated or using "temporary" workers on contract who are entirely excluded from the rights and responsibilities of full-fledged membership (see Pfeffer & Baron, 1988). Citizenship rights within employment organizations may lead to redrawing the organizational boundaries to exclude some categories of participants in a way that parallels the evolution of Japanese organizations.

It remains to be seen whether the rights that workers have accumulated during the modern era can survive in the face of slower economic growth. It seems likely that at least some of the rights associated with organizational citizenship have been institutionalized and will survive economic downturns. Other rights may eventually be taken over by the state—health care, for example. But still others may disappear or become ritualized, or currently protected groups may be disenfranchised as the pool of resources available to support rights and citizens shrinks.

In sum, the notion of organizational citizenship offers an explanation for the expansion and development of the employee-training project in organizations. More generally, however, it provides a framework for understanding the emergence of a diverse set of organizational structures and arrangements that reflect the changing nature of the relationship between employees and organizations. The development of personnel systems, the expansion of due process in organizations, the diffusion of bottom-up quality-improvement and management programs, and the growth in diffuse forms of employee training in organizations are all indications of an emerging conception of employees as contributing to collective organizational rationality, but in a purposeful and willful manner.

Notes

1. Lawrence identifies a period prior to this—extending from the beginning of this nation up to 1820 as characterized by the "craft" system: one in which the production of industrial goods and services was dominated by small workshops operating under the control of master craftsmen.

2. In other types of polities, different means have been developed to construct rational systems. For example, some European systems have vested such rights in collectivities, such as strong occupational associations, who then are held accountable for the dimensions of work under their control. (For a discussion of alternative forms of polity, see Jepperson & Meyer, 1991.)

13

Equal Opportunity Law and the Construction of Internal Labor Markets

FRANK DOBBIN

JOHN R. SUTTON

JOHN W. MEYER

W. RICHARD SCOTT

INTERNAL LABOR MARKETS have been explained with efficiency and control arguments; however, retrospective (1955-1985) event-history data from 279 organizations suggest that federal Equal Employment Opportunity (EEO) law was the force behind the spread of formal promotion mechanisms after 1964. The findings highlight the way in which American public policy, with its broad outcome-oriented guidelines for organizations, stimulates managers to experiment with compliance mechanisms with an eye to judicial sanction. In response to EEO legislation and case law, personnel managers devised and diffused employment practices that treat all classes of workers as ambitious and achievement-oriented in the process of formalizing and rationalizing promotion decisions.

The research reported here was supported by the National Science Foundation (grant SES-8511250). We are grateful to Lauren Edelman and Ann Swidler for their participation in an earlier study on which this project draws, and to Keith Allum, Jessica Torres, and Roberta Stich for helping us conduct the survey and code the data. Paul Burstein, Yinon Cohen, Paul DiMaggio, Lauren Edelman, Matthijs Kalmijn, Peter Marsden, Stephen Mezias, and Debra Minkoff provided useful suggestions.

Do the policies of America's notoriously "weak" federal state have any effect on organizational practices at all? Until recently organizational theorists seemed to agree that they only affected management behavior at the margins. Lately, that belief has come under scrutiny. Organizational analysts have come to the conclusion that common management practices do not arise through spontaneous combustion in thousands of different locations at once; rather they are socially constructed by networks of managers who are attentive to signals and incentives that emanate from the state, the legal system, and the wider political culture. Many practices we think of as motivated by strict efficiency concerns, such as merger and acquisition strategies, can be traced to an iterative process in which the state creates broad rules about corporate behavior and then organizations experiment to find practical strategies that will be acceptable to the courts (Edelman, 1992; Fligstein, 1990). In this article we chart the roles of equal employment opportunity law, personnel managers, and the courts in designating internal labor market (ILM) practices as appropriate means to the prevention of discrimination and to the efficient allocation of human capital. We review arguments made by rationalist organizations theorists and labor economists about why managers adopt ILM practices, and we show that of the variables these theorists point to, changes in EEO law have a marked effect on the incidence of these practices.

Before the 1930s, firms were organized to recruit almost exclusively from the external labor market, and they seldom promoted current employees to fill open positions (Jacoby, 1985). Public organizations were more likely to use civil service practices that facilitated internal promotion, but civil service systems were far from universal in the public sector (DiPrete, 1989; Tolbert & Zucker, 1983). By the 1950s internal promotion systems had become widespread: William Whyte's *The Organization Man* (1956) characterized them as emblematic of the modern organization and as the driving force behind corporate careerism. Under what circumstances do organizations adopt practices that facilitate the recruitment of existing employees to fill open positions? Below we use event-history techniques to analyze the adoption of six bureaucratic personnel practices that are integral to ILMs: formal job descriptions, performance evaluations, salary classification systems, job ladders, employment tests, and promotion tests. Our focus is not on whether firms *practice* internal promotion, but on whether they employ the bureaucratic rules associated with ILMs (Stark, 1986, p. 493).

Perspectives on Internal Labor Markets

Since the time of Max Weber (1968, p. 957), who saw career-oriented employment structures as part and parcel of bureaucracy, most analysts have made efficiency arguments to explain formal internal promotion systems. Recent rationalist works suggest that increases in organizational size lead to differentiation and specialization and, in turn, to the formalization of a wide range of activities, including personnel activities (Blau, Falbe, McKinley, & Tracy, 1976). Blau and Schoenherr (1971) and Pugh, Hickson, and Hinings (1969) have found that, indeed, large organizations are more likely to adopt personnel practices, such as formal job descriptions, that are associated with ILMs. Large organizations have also been found to offer better promotion opportunities than small ones (Phelps Brown, 1977), which may suggest that they are more likely to use internal promotion schemes.

Peter Doeringer and Michael Piore's (1971) seminal *Internal Labor Markets and Manpower Analysis* sought to reconcile the existence of ILMs with neoclassical economic views, which suggest that free competition in open labor markets is ultimately efficient, by arguing that ILMs help companies to retain firm-specific skills and reward workers for developing such skills. In technologically advanced sectors, employees must learn complex skills on the job and employers use the carrot of promotions to persuade such workers to stay with the firm. Oliver Williamson's (1975) transaction costs approach offers a similar hypothesis: Employers with complex technologies will pursue long-term employment arrangements in order to escape the high cost of training new workers. These arguments suggest that ILMs should be found in technologically advanced industries that depend on firm-specific skills. Neo-Marxists emphasize control over the work force rather than efficiency, but they predict that ILMs will appear in these very sectors (Edwards, 1979; Gordon, Edwards, & Reich, 1982). These approaches also suggest that labor-intensive, service-sector industries that do not utilize firm-specific skills will be unlikely to adopt ILMs.[1]

Another sort of efficiency argument suggests that firms will adopt formal ILM practices in response to competitive pressures from the external labor market. When internal promotion schemes are provided by competing organizations, managers will implement them to retain existing workers and attract new ones. This suggests that the prevalence, or density, of a practice in the sample should be positively related to the likelihood of adoption.

By contrast, conflict approaches point to struggles over the terms of employment between personnel professionals and labor leaders. In a cross-sectional analysis of data collected in the late 1960s, Pfeffer and Cohen (1984; Cohen & Pfeffer, 1986) find that factors associated with efficiency do not predict ILMs. Instead, ILMs depend on the relative power of personnel managers, who favor ILMs because they expand personnel activities, and unions, who oppose ILMs because they undermine union authority over jobs. The presence of a personnel department should increase the likelihood an organization will install ILM practices; the presence of a union should decrease the likelihood.

Equal Employment Law and Internal Labor Markets

We stress wider institutional forces that operate through public policy, the courts, and personnel professionals. In recent decades American law and public institutions have elaborated rights for diverse categories of individuals and have developed standard organizational models for incorporating such rights. We see these general institutional processes as creating widespread adaptations in all sorts of organizations over time.

Strict, ahistorical, efficiency explanations of the proliferation of ILMs have been challenged by recent historical studies that examine the role of such institutional factors in the changing construction of efficiency. In 1935 the Wagner Act legitimized industrial unions and established mechanisms to protect union organizing efforts. In response employers began to hire personnel professionals who advocated ILM mechanisms to counter unionism (Jacoby, 1985). During World War II the War Production Board, the War Labor Board, and the War Manpower Commission exercised controls over labor mobility, employment practices, and wages in order to ensure stability in sectors that contributed to the war effort. Personnel professionals responded by promoting ILM mechanisms to facilitate federal accountability and rationalize the use of human resources (Baron, Dobbin, & Jennings, 1986). Michael Burawoy (1985, p. 142) offers a slightly different argument about the role of federal policy: The Wagner Act (1935), the National War Labor Board (1942-1946), and the Taft-Hartley Act (1947) narrowed the scope of union bargaining, which led unions to guard member prerogatives by pushing for formal rules governing wage rates, job duties, promotions, and seniority. Such rules became key to ILMs. Data from the 1930s and 1940s support these arguments and show that ahistorical efficiency arguments poorly predict where ILM practices will appear (Baron et al., 1986). We find that in more recent years, public policy changes associated with civil rights and equal employment opportunity have had a similarly profound impact on the growth of the personnel function (Kochan & Cappelli, 1984, p. 146).

Broadly speaking, we believe the institutional forces—in the polity, the legal system, and personnel doctrine—that supported ILM mechanisms between the 1960s and the 1980s reflect a general expansion in the social construction of the individual (Thomas, Meyer, Ramirez, & Boli, 1987).

This expanded conception of the individual—embodied in public concern and legislation about the status of women, minorities, the handicapped, and disadvantaged groups generally—contrasts distinctly with previous organizational constructions of the individual. In particular, the creation of formal ILM mechanisms for all categories of employees symbolically transformed people who were traditionally disadvantaged into ambitious, occupationally mobile individuals. Thus ambition and self-actualization came to be represented as characteristics of *all individuals,* not just white males.

This new managerial conception of worker and individual was distinctly different from the conceptions Bendix (1956), and others, charted in early management practices. At the turn of the century the Darwinist "drive system" suggested that human motivation was a matter of short-term reward and punishment (Slichter, 1919). Later Taylor's (1911) rationalist logic made it the duty of managers to optimize the match between employee and job through testing and training: "The worker came to be viewed as an embodiment of aptitudes" (Bendix, 1956, p. 308). The labor strife of the 1910s and 1920s led to a paternalistic managerial strategy, based on welfare work and on company unions, that represented the worker as capable of devotion to the organization that could win his heart and mind with benevolence (Brandes, 1976). The subsequent growth of unions led to the institutionalization of a new and highly contractual "industrial relations" regime by the end of the 1940s, in which motivation came to depend on the long-range incentives embodied by seniority practices (Edwards, 1979; Baron et al., 1986; Burawoy, 1985).

Between the mid-1960s and the early 1980s, public policy, case law, and prevailing personnel ideology emphasized employment practices that carried a new vision of the individual and a new logic of human motivation. The personnel practices that symbolized the employee as motivated by reward and punishment (the drive system), as a self-interested cog in the wheel of production with a limited capacity to learn (Taylorism), as a malleable political entity (welfare work), or as member of an oppositional interest group whose actions demanded legal restraint (the industrial relations approach), gave way to practices that represent the individual as self-actualizing, future-directed, and psychologically complex (Cole, 1989). Some trends in employment practices were conspicuously oriented to this conception of the individual and individual rights. Organization development (OD) programs offered a management approach based firmly in psychology (Kochan & Cappelli, 1984, p. 150). Sexual harassment policies aimed to protect the physical and psychological integrity of the employee. Employment-at-will clauses were designed to protect firms from employee claims to a newly articulated right to lifelong employment

(Sutton, Dobbin, Meyer, & Scott, in press). The quality-of-work-life movement promoted collective decision making, in part to improve employee morale, and advocated the "enrichment," "enlargement," or "humanization" of jobs by reversing the trend toward job simplification (Cole, 1989). In this article we show that even ILM mechanisms diffused in response to the elaboration of this new logic. In particular, organizations installed formal ILM mechanisms to protect the rights of all classes of employees to self-actualizing, career-oriented employment in response to shifts in the legal environment. Those legal changes led managers to view formal hiring and promotion practices not merely as means to promote equity, but also as means to promote efficiency by depersonalizing decisions about the use of human resources and thereby (a) matching employees with jobs based on their abilities rather than on ascribed characteristics and (b) creating incentives for all classes of employees to excel.

THE TRANSFORMATION OF THE LEGAL ENVIRONMENT

Because America's "weak" federal state seldom dictates behavior to private actors—even corporate actors—analysts have tended to assume that it has little effect on the institutions of civil society (Hamilton & Sutton, 1989). Although the federal government rarely mandates the use of particular organizational practices, public policies frequently lead to clear models of organizational compliance. Federal law typically establishes broad guidelines for behavior, and corporate actors respond by designing practical compliance strategies that are in turn reviewed by courts and administrative agencies. Once approved, organizationally devised solutions act as prescriptions for legal compliance (Abzug & Mezias, 1993; Edelman, 1992; Hamilton & Sutton, 1989). For instance, Neil Fligstein (1990) shows that organizations responded to antimonopoly policies by experimenting with vertical integration and diversification and that the courts then approved these solutions. While the creation of compliance mechanisms is iterative and haphazard in the United States, the mechanisms that emerge from this process become powerful institutional models, not unlike the solutions directly mandated by "strong" states (Meyer & Scott, 1983b). We suggest that the effects of U.S. policy on organizations are interesting precisely because compliance mechanisms are often worked out between organizations and the state.

In support of our hypotheses outlining the salience of the legal environment, crossnational studies suggest that nation-state characteristics are excellent predictors of organizational employment practices, whereas neoclassical economic variables have little predictive power. In a study of 12 matched companies in Germany and France, Maurice, Sellier, and Silvestre

(1984) show that size, product, and technology explain little about how job hierarchies will be structured; instead, national historical differences explain much of the variance (see also Dore, 1973; Lincoln & Kalleberg, 1985; Maurice, Sorge, & Warner, 1980).

We will argue that equal employment opportunity law led organizations to formalize promotion mechanisms to undermine managerial discrimination. How do we know that organizations did not simply adopt these measures in response to the civil rights and women's movements? Of course these movements were important, but their broad effects do not explain the fact that organizational antidiscrimination policies converged on a set of personnel practices that were isomorphic with the procedurally oriented, quasi-judicial administrative configuration of the federal government—formal, merit-based employment and promotion conventions complete with an internal system of grievance adjudication (see Scott & Meyer, 1988). Once sanctioned by the courts, this approach eclipsed all competing strategies for redressing discrimination. It is clear that, even if social movements encouraged organizations to end discrimination, public policy shaped the particular approach organizations would embrace.

Equal Employment Opportunity Law

We hypothesize that two major changes in the legal environment increased the popularity of internal labor market mechanisms. First, the passage of the Civil Rights Act of 1964 prompted employers to experiment with various antidiscrimination approaches, including (a) formal hiring and promotion procedures to depersonalize employment decisions, (b) sophisticated employment and promotion tests to create objective selection criteria, and (c) numerical quotas for the employment of disadvantaged groups. Second, in the early 1970s legislative changes and court decisions required more employers to be attentive to the issue of discrimination, but discouraged the testing and quota solutions while reinforcing the ILM strategy. More generally, because ILM procedures operate on a classificatory logic in which certain categories of employees are afforded specified protections against firing and promises of consideration for promotion (Stark, 1986, p. 494), they were particularly well suited to protecting rights for new classifications based on gender and minority status.

Title VII of the Civil Rights Act of 1964 made it illegal for employers with 25 or more employees to discriminate on the basis of race, color, religion, sex, or national origin. These protections were extended to persons between the ages of 40 and 65 in 1967 and to the physically and mentally impaired in 1973 (Farley, 1979, p. 12). The new Equal Employment Opportunity Commission (EEOC) was charged with overseeing Title VII of the act. In September 1965 President Johnson issued Executive Order (EO) 11246, which required federal agencies as well as major federal contractors and subcontractors, and unions covering employees who work for them, to take what came to be called "affirmative action" to redress inequality. Employers associated with contracts of more than $10,000 were required to practice affirmative action, and those associated with contracts of more than $50,000 were required to write affirmative action plans. EO 11246 was to be enforced by the Department of Labor's Office of Federal Contract Compliance (OFCC), later named the OFCC Programs (OFCCP) (see Burstein, 1985; Edelman, 1990). Although federal enforcement was notoriously weak during this period (Ashenfelter & Heckmann, 1976, p. 46), the threat of private litigation compelled corporate actors to be attentive to the law. Thus many organizations responded to Title VII and EO 11246 by designating affirmative action officers, and establishing affirmative action offices, between 1964 and 1970 (Edelman, 1990).

In the early 1970s several judicial and administrative clarifications of EEO compliance criteria discouraged the use of tests and quotas and encouraged the adoption of formal ILM mechanisms. First, in *Griggs v. Duke Power Company* (401 U.S. 424, 1971), the Supreme Court outlawed employment tests that were not demonstrably related to the work to be performed if those tests had the effect of excluding blacks. In ruling that employment tests must be relevant to job tasks the Supreme Court spurred firms to specify job prerequisites, in written job descriptions, and discouraged them from using general employment tests. In 1974 EEOC guidelines explicitly stated that education, experience, and test scores could not be used as selection criteria unless they could be shown to be related to job performance (U.S. Equal Employment Opportunity Commission, 1974, pp. 35-40). Few employers were able to convince the courts that their tests could predict job performance (Burstein & Pitchford, 1990) and, as a result, many ceased using testing to achieve EEO goals.

Second, in the early 1970s, discrimination and reverse-discrimination suits increased in number. Between 1965 and 1970 only three reverse-discrimination suits reached appellate courts, yet in the next 6-year period 24 such suits were heard (Burstein, 1990; Burstein & Monaghan, 1986, p. 380). These suits made employers reluctant to follow compliance strategies, such as quotas, that explicitly gave an edge to disadvantaged groups. Voluntary quotas (i.e., those not mandated by courts) had never been the favored EEO compliance strategy (Burstein, 1985), and now several well-publicized judgments found them to be illegal (Leonard, 1985). In addition, the General Accounting Office's interpretation of the Equal Employment Opportunity Act of 1972 rejected the use of quotas in the federal civil service on the grounds that quotas would undermine the merit system (DiPrete, 1989, p. 199). This interpretation caused both public and private employers to retreat from voluntary quotas and to expand the formalization of hiring and promotion.

Third, in December 1971 the OFCCP issued Revised Order 4, which set out specific affirmative action guidelines for federal contractors. The order required federal contractors to file annual EEO reports detailing employment in each job category by gender, race, and ethnicity. The order also called for affirmative action plans to identify areas of minority and female "underutilization," to develop numerical goals and timetables for enlarging job opportunities in those areas, and to specify mechanisms for evaluating program effectiveness (Leonard, 1985).

Fourth, the 1972 Equal Employment Opportunity Act gave the EEOC the authority to bring suit in federal court under Title VII; the act also extended Title VII coverage to private employers with 15 or more employees, to educational institutions, and to state and local governments. This legislation simultaneously expanded the scope of federal EEO law and strengthened the capacity for active enforcement. Finally, the EEOC's 1974 guidebook for employers, *Affirmative Action and Equal Employment,* suggested that employers could avoid litigation by formalizing hiring and promotion procedures and expanding personnel record keeping so that they would be able to prove that they did not discriminate (Benokraitis & Feagin, 1977).[2]

PERSONNEL PROFESSIONALS

Personnel professionals played a central role in constructing formal ILM practices as EEO compliance mechanisms. Personnel departments typically implement and administer ILMs, and they have promoted ILMs to serve a series of management problems since early in this century (Jacoby, 1984). We argue that personnel departments provided the path through which ILM mechanisms diffused in the years after the Civil Rights Act.

Personnel professionals responded to the ambiguity of the 1964 legislation by developing the three principal antidiscrimination strategies we have discussed: quota systems, tests designed to objectively evaluate the qualifications of job candidates, and rules to formalize hiring and promotion. The personnel and business management journals published articles advocating all three strategies between the mid-1960s and mid-1970s (e.g., Bassford, 1974; Bell, 1971). Personnel managers also came to extol affirmative action-related formalization as a way to rationalize personnel allocation: Open bidding for jobs would undermine favoritism and periodic, written performance evaluations would encourage promotions based on objective criteria (*Harvard Law Review* Note, 1989, p. 669). Personnel managers sold their bosses on formal evaluation and promotion systems with two arguments: These systems thwarted discrimination and, at the same time, rationalized the allocation of human resources. Their rhetoric coupled the ideas of equity and efficiency.

Job Descriptions, Performance Evaluations, and Salary Classification

In the early 1970s, in response to the OFCCP's Revised Order 4 and the 1972 expansion of the EEOC's authority, the major practitioner journals began publishing articles that promoted a specific set of ILM practices to improve federal accountability and to redress discrimination. For instance, in 1974 the *Harvard Business Review* published "Make Your Equal Opportunity Program Court-Proof," which emphasized "the need for positive action against the risk of prolonged and serious litigation or crippling financial judgments." It specifically encouraged firms to establish nondiscriminatory job descriptions and salary classification systems and to "ensure that prescribed qualifications and pay scales can be justified on business grounds and that inadvertent barriers have not been erected against women and minorities" (Chayes, 1974, p. 81; see also Kochan & Cappelli, 1984, p. 147). In the same year, the journal *Personnel* published "A Total Approach to EEO Compliance" (Giblin & Ornati, 1974), which argued that affirmative action programs must begin with a census of minority and women employees in each department and within each major job classification—which required having a salary classification system in place—and encouraged employers to implement periodic performance evaluations for all categories of employees to make all employees eligible for promotion. Written performance evaluations were also thought to be essential to the successful defense of discrimination suits involving promotions. In brief, the personnel journals promoted salary classification systems, job descriptions, and formal performance evaluations as EEO compliance mechanisms.[3] These articles noted that salary classification systems, and expanded record keeping in the areas of hiring and promotion, were now virtually mandatory for federal contractors who were required to file annual EEO reports. Evidence that federal contractors expanded black male employment in response to federal oversight (Ashenfelter & Heckmann, 1976; Leonard, 1984b) leads us to predict that these contractors were also likely to adopt ILM mechanisms.

Many of these articles treated EEO law as an opportunity to increase the efficiency of personnel decisions. Executives soon recognized that by requiring middle managers to justify hiring and promotion decisions, they could undermine favoritism and ensure that jobs would be filled by the best-qualified applicants. As R. J. Samuelson argued in 1984, "Many firms have overhauled personnel policies. . . . Promotions are less informal. When positions become open, they are posted so anyone (not just the boss's favorite) can apply. Formal evaluations have been strengthened so that, when a manager selects one candidate over another . . . there are objective criteria" (in *Harvard Law Review* Note, 1989, p. 669). By 1979 some two thirds of top corporate executives favored government efforts to increase female and minority participation in the labor force, and a decade later the *Harvard Law Review* (1989) argued that managerial support for EEO had become widespread because EEO was seen as a force promoting rational personnel practices. Alternative economic analyses reinforce this view by suggesting that EEO encourages employers to match employees with jobs on the basis of their abilities rather than on the basis of irrelevant ascribed characteristics (Donohue, 1986; Lundberg, 1991). Thus although neoclassical economists argued that antidiscrimination laws were inefficient because they disrupted market mechanisms and unnecessary because discriminatory practices would eventually die under the weight of their own inefficiency (Becker, 1971; Friedman, 1962), business executives came to see EEO as a source of increased efficiency.

Job Ladders, Testing, and Quotas

By contrast, personnel journals suggested that formal job ladders, testing, and quota schemes could lead to problems with the EEOC and OFCCP. Formal job ladders had not been part of any of the three main EEO compliance strategies devised in the 1960s, and in the 1970s they were found to produce unnecessary barriers to advancement by making only certain groups of employees eligible for promotion. Giblin and Ornati (1974) counseled that firms should examine whether their promotion ladders "create unwarranted restrictions to minority mobility" and, in particular, whether "women or minorities are concentrated in certain jobs *outside* any line of progression or in jobs that dead-end" (p. 40). DiPrete (1989, p. 197) argues that the problem with job ladders was quite simple: Most organizations had different, discontinuous, upper- and lower-tier job ladders. Employees in the lower tier, frequently dominated by women and minorities, were generally ineligible for promotion to upper-tier jobs even if they held the necessary educational qualifications (see also Halle, 1984). Federal agencies responded to EEO legislation by creating bridges between job ladders in different tiers (DiPrete, 1989), but the personnel journals urged private employers to switch to open bidding systems that allowed any employee to bid for a vacant job—such systems had already substituted for formal job ladders in several industries (Burawoy, 1985, p.

138).[4] Thus after about 1973 job ladders were incorporated into some government EEO programs, but were less likely to be used in private-sector programs.

Many personnel administrators initially believed that employment and promotion testing could solve their EEO problems. Since the time of Frederick Taylor, testing had been viewed as a way to ensure that workers would be allocated to "the highest class of jobs" that they were capable of performing, thereby maximizing both their own rewards and their utility to the organization (Bendix, 1956, p. 279; Taylor, 1911). Personnel managers reacted to the 1971 *Griggs* decision, which required them to demonstrate the relevance of tests, in two ways: Some saw this ruling as a chance to expand their departments by developing more sophisticated tests that would predict job performance and stand up to EEOC guidelines (Campbell, 1973; Gavin & Toole, 1973; Gorham, 1972; National Civil Service League, 1973; Slevin, 1973), while others advocated the abandonment of testing. The second camp came to prevail. A study conducted in 1973 and reported in *Personnel* found that 15.1% of sampled firms had already abandoned employment tests in reaction to the *Griggs* decision (Peterson, 1974).[5] Similarly, in our sample, 15% of the organizations using employment tests abandoned them during the period under study, and 11% of the organizations using promotion tests abandoned them. By contrast, no other practice was abandoned by more than 2% of the organizations using it.

The reverse-discrimination suits of the early 1970s led personnel managers to repudiate schemes, such as quotas, that explicitly advantaged protected groups. While court orders and consent decrees had required some companies to conform to specific black-white or female-male hiring ratios, the voluntary establishment of quotas had led to many legal fights (Burstein & Monaghan, 1986; *Harvard Law Review* Note, 1989; Leonard, 1984a). By 1974 personnel experts were advising their colleagues that voluntary quotas could "render them liable to legal attack" (Chayes, 1974, p. 87). In 1978 the widely publicized Bakke case led personnel managers who had not yet done so to excise the word *quota* from their personnel guidelines.

Finally, public and nonprofit organizations were most susceptible to these trends because these organizations (a) depend on public opinion for legitimacy and resources and (b) are subject to evaluation on the basis of their use of up-to-date procedures and structures because they cannot, in most cases, be judged on the basis of profitability (Meyer & Rowan, 1977; Meyer & Scott, 1983b; Scott, 1987; Zucker, 1983). Other studies (e.g., Dobbin, Edelman, Meyer, Scott, & Swidler, 1988) have shown such organizations to be most likely to install formal affirmative action offices and procedures. To the extent that organizations adopt ILM mechanisms to symbolize their commitment to equality, rather than to retain firm-specific skills as labor economists suggest, we should find that the likelihood of adoption is highest among public and nonprofit organizations, rather than among technically complex organizations.

In sum, we suggest hypotheses about the spread of ILM mechanisms that challenge traditional arguments. First, whereas neoclassical and rationalist arguments treat separate ILM practices as integral parts of a whole and predict incremental increases in their popularity as firm size and complexity increase, our arguments suggest that EEO law should affect adoption of these practices differently and that two broad shifts in the legal environment should produce dramatic, stepwise changes in the likelihood of adoption. The personnel profession came to reject two early solutions to employment discrimination, testing and quotas, in reaction to case law. As a result, the likelihood of adopting tests should increase in the period between 1964 and about 1973, but should not increase thereafter. After 1964, personnel managers began using job descriptions, performance evaluations, and salary classification systems to codify and depersonalize employment and promotion decisions. When case law reinforced these solutions in the early 1970s, personnel professionals pursued them with new vigor; thus adoption should rise after 1964 and again in the early 1970s. Initially personnel managers saw no EEO benefits in the formal job ladders that had traditionally been part of ILMs, but because job ladders were included in government EEO programs in the early 1970s, we expect their incidence to rise from 1973. Second, personnel professionals and affirmative action officers helped to develop and diffuse these compliance strategies, both individually and through their professional associations. Thus organizations with personnel departments and affirmative action offices should be susceptible to adoption. Third, public policy required federal contractors and some other organizations to file annual EEO reports. Such organizations should be likely to adopt ILM mechanisms. Fourth, public sector and nonprofit organizations have been especially attentive to personnel procedures that confer legitimacy, and we expect they will prove susceptible to the adoption of ILM mechanisms.

Data and Methods

THE SAMPLE

We selected a stratified random sample of public, for-profit, and nonprofit organizations in 1985-1986, collecting retrospective data from 279 organizations on the history of their personnel practices. We generated the sample in three states—California, New Jersey, and Virginia—that have varying legal environments (Edelman, 1990; Sutton, Dobbin, Meyer, & Scott, in press). We concentrated on a limited number of sectors, which represent different parts of the economy, so that we would be able to examine arguments about sectoral effects. In each state we selected an equal number of organizations from each of 13 sectors.

The difficulties associated with sampling organizations have been well documented (Kalleberg, Marsden, Aldrich, & Cassell, 1990). We chose the most complete published list of organizations available for each sector. Our source for firms in publishing, banking, chemicals, machinery, electrical manufacturing, retail trade, and transportation was Dun's *Million Dollar Directory*, which lists all publicly traded firms with assets of at least $500,000. We sampled hospitals from the 1983 directory of the American Hospital Association and nonprofits from the 1985 *Encyclopedia of Associations*. To sample organizations in the public sector we used commercial telephone directories as well as official state and federal government directories. We sampled randomly from each source. We had only four criteria for inclusion in the study: that the organization was currently operating, that it was located in one of the three states selected, that it operated in one of the 13 sectors, and that it employed at least 50 persons. Smaller organizations were excluded because previous studies suggested that very few of them would use formal employment practices. We contacted selected organizations to ascertain whether they met these four criteria.

Response Rate

We contacted 620 organizations that met the inclusion criteria, and we received completed questionnaires from exactly 300 of them—a response rate of 48%.[6] Despite the fact that we telephoned respondents, and other members of their organizations, in order to clarify responses and fill in blanks, we had to exclude 21 of the 300 questionnaires from the analysis because of the poor quality of the data. This brings the successful completion rate down to 45%, which compares favorably with other organizational studies: Blau, Falbe, McKinley, and Tracy (1976) report a rate of 36%, Lincoln and Kalleberg (1985) a rate of 35%, and Edelman (1992) reports 54% for a telephone interview and a net of 33% for a mailed follow-up questionnaire. We believe that our sample exaggerates the use of ILM practices because having a personnel office may increase the likelihood of adopting ILM practices and of participating in our survey. This points to a possible problem with sample selection bias; however, the event-history framework we use minimizes this problem. That is, the data set includes many cases (annual organizational spells) without personnel departments, particularly in the early years. Bias may also result from the fact that our retrospective data-collection effort necessarily excludes failed organizations. The only realistic remedy would be longitudinal data collection which, if begun in 1985, would have prevented us from examining the historical processes of interest.

MEASUREMENT AND MODEL SPECIFICATION

Dependent Variables

We examine the rate of adoption of six personnel practices: job descriptions, performance evaluations, salary classification systems, job ladders, employment testing, and promotion testing. Formal *job descriptions* outline the work to be performed in each job and the prerequisites for job applicants; they thereby enable the organization to identify a pool of internal candidates for each vacant position. Periodic, written *performance evaluations* are conducted by supervisors and results are kept on record for use in promotion decisions. *Salary classification systems* arrange jobs in a series of hierarchical wage categories based on requisite duties and skills; the creation of categories that are consistent across departments enables managers to determine which job shifts constitute lateral moves and which constitute vertical moves. Each formal *job ladder* specifies a succession of jobs in a sequence that constitute an expected promotion pattern. Written *employment tests* are designed to evaluate applicants' intelligence, experience, and personal character in order to match them with jobs, and *promotion tests* are used to judge current employees for promotion. Again, it is important to note that formal ILM procedures may be poor indicators of whether organizations practice internal promotion, because organizations that lack these procedures may nonetheless routinely promote from within and organizations with these procedures may routinely hire from the external labor market.

To code each practice in event-history format, we asked respondents whether their organization had ever used the practice. For each affirmative response, we coded the year in which the practice was first used; if the practice had been abandoned we coded the year in which that occurred.

Independent Variables

Table 13.1 lists the independent variables. All vary over time, and all but the time periods, time trend, and density are measured at the organiza-

TABLE 13.1 Variable List

Variable	Description
Log employment	Natural logarithm of the number of employees reported in the current year
Personnel office	Binary variable for presence of a personnel office in the current year
Member personnel association	Binary variable for membership in a personnel association in current year
Period 2	Binary variable for spells occurring between 1964 and 1973, inclusive
Period 3	Binary variable for spells occurring between 1974 and 1985, inclusive
Time trend	Linear variable representing years since 1954 (1-30)
Chemicals, machinery, electrical, nonprofit	Binary variable for organization operating in the sector
City, county, federal government	Binary variable for government agency
Density (for each ILM practice)[*]	Percentage of firms in the sample reporting the use of the practice in current year
Federal contractor[*]	Binary variable for federal contracts in current year (limited to private organizations)
EEO reporting status[*]	Binary variable for organizations that filed an EEO report with the EEOC or the OFCCP in current year (limited to private organizations)
AA office/officer[*]	Binary variable for presence of affirmative action office, or designated officer, in current year
Union contract[*]	Binary variable for presence of union contract in current year

[*]These variables are excluded from the results reported in Tables 13.3 through 13.7 because they showed no effects in multivariate analyses.

tional level. Our predictions about the effects of policy shifts vary. The omitted period is 1955-1963 (c_1), the first phase of EEO law is 1964-1973 (c_2), and the second phase is 1974-1985 (c_3). For job descriptions, performance evaluations, and salary classification we predict that $c_1 < c_2 < c_3$. For employment and promotion tests we predict that $c_1 < c_2 > c_3$. We predict that the rate of adoption of job ladders will rise only in the third period and principally for public organizations. The sectoral variables represent neoclassical arguments about firm-specific skills (i.e., chemical, machinery, electrical equipment industries) and institutional arguments about what types of employers are susceptible to new procedural norms (nonprofit and government organizations).

TABLE 13.2   Average Annual Hazard Rate for Each Internal Labor Market Practice

ILM Practice	Period 1 (1955-1963)	Period 2 (1964-1973)	Period 3 (1974-1985)
Job descriptions	.015	.036	.095
Performance evaluations	.011	.039	.099
Salary classification	.013	.031	.061
Job ladders	.005	.009	.017
Employment testing	.009	.024	.023
Promotion testing	.006	.007	.004

ESTIMATION

Before turning to methods and modeling, we show changes in the prevalence of the six personnel practices. Figure 13.1 reports the proportion of existing organizations that used each of the practices in each year. Changes are dramatic over time. Although a small proportion of organizations used performance evaluations, job descriptions, and salary classification systems in 1955, a majority of sampled firms used these three practices by 1985. It is evident that these first three practices grew more quickly between 1964 and 1973 than they did before 1964; they grew even more quickly between 1974 and 1985. By contrast, employment tests, which were at first more prevalent than any other practice, diverge notably from the first three practices after the early 1960s. Promotion tests and job ladders rise very slowly in absolute terms. Table 13.2 reports the average annual hazard rate for each of the six outcomes, in each of the three policy periods. These figures tell a similar story about the positive effects of legal changes on the first three variables in both periods 2 and 3. They also support our hypothesis that job ladders should increase in period 3 and that employment testing should increase between periods 1 and 2 but not between periods 2 and 3.

Tables 13.3 through 13.7 present log-linear event-history models, estimated with Tuma's RATE program, for five of the six ILM practices. Over the 30-year time frame we cover, the 279 organizations sampled yield 6,701 annual spells of observation. In the models, organizations are excluded from the at-risk pool before their birth and after they have adopted a practice. The number of at-risk spells ranges from 3,400 to 5,396 for the five modeled outcomes. The number of transitions modeled ranges from 61 to 164. We treat as left censored organizations that adopted the modeled practice before 1955 as well as those founded after 1955 that started out with the modeled practice. For each outcome we present equations that include, in addition to other variables, (a) the two binary time-period

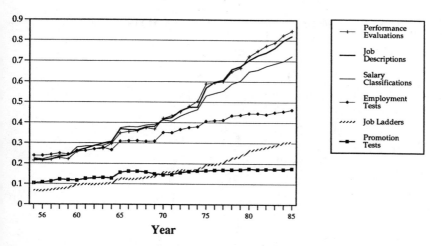

Figure 13.1. Proportion of Sample With ILM Practices

variables representing changes in EEO law, (b) a time-trend variable, and (c) the time-period variables as well as the time trend. Our aim here is to discern either a linear increase in the likelihood of adopting ILM practices, which might be caused by any number of factors, or stepwise increases that correspond to legal changes. We also report the effects of the two time-period variables and the time-trend variable separately because they are multicollinear.

Findings

Rationalist arguments are weakly supported by our analyses. Contrary to rationalist arguments that size is the most important cause of the formalization of organizational personnel practices, employment size shows significant effects for only two of the outcome variables. Neoclassical economic arguments that organizations employ ILMs to guard firm-specific skills in capital-intensive, modern sectors receive some support. In accord with those predictions, electrical equipment industries showed positive effects on two outcomes and chemical industries showed an effect on one. Machinery produced no significant effects. Parenthetically, we tested all other sectors for significant positive effects and found none. On the whole, public and nonprofit organizations were most likely to adopt these practices, as institutional theory predicts. The density measures representing the proportion of the sample with the specified practice in the

(Text continued on page 295)

TABLE 13.3 Estimates of Factors Affecting the Adoption of Job Descriptions, 1956-1985

Equa-tion	Intercept	Log Employ-ment	Presence of a Personnel Office	Member of a Personnel Asso-ciation	Period 2 (1964-1973)	Period 3 (1974-1985)	Time Trend	Sector[a] Chemicals	Machin-ery	Electrical	Non-profit	City Govern-ment	County Govern-ment	Federal Govern-ment	χ^2
(1)	-5.704**	.165*	.460*	.303	1.059**	2.164**		.285	.129	.079	1.171**	.899**	1.540**	.252	136.92
	(.439)	(.068)	(.186)	(.240)	(.301)	(.291)		(.326)	(.277)	(.306)	(.271)	(.319)	(.274)	(.719)	
(2)	-5.962**	.160*	.457*	.216			.099**	.291	.093	.106	1.242**	.974**	1.599**	.198	134.05
	(.423)	(.068)	(.187)	(.244)			(.011)	(.325)	(.277)	(.307)	(.274)	(.322)	(.277)	(.719)	
(3)	-5.958**	.168*	.449*	.248	.653	1.288**	.046	.294	.112	.091	1.236**	.949**	1.603**	.219	149.69
	(.465)	(.068)	(.187)	(.243)	(.373)	(.549)	(.025)	(.326)	(.277)	(.307)	(.274)	(.321)	(.277)	(.720)	

NOTE: Number of cases at risk = 223; left-censored cases = 56; number of transitions = 164. SEs are shown in parentheses. $N = 3,436$ spells.
[a]Omitted sectors are publishing, banking, retail trade, transportation, hospitals, and state government.
*$p \leq .05$.
**$p \leq .01$.

290

TABLE 13.4 Estimates of Factors Affecting the Adoption of Performance Evaluations, 1956-1985

| Equation | Intercept | Log Employment | Presence of a Personnel Office | Member of a Personnel Association | Period 2 (1964-1973) | Period 3 (1974-1985) | Time Trend | Sector[a] | | | | | | | χ^2 |
								Chemicals	Machinery	Electrical	Non-profit	City Government	County Government	Federal Government	
(1)	-5.906**	.150*	.467*	.091	1.382**	2.326**		.753*	.179	.938*	1.047**	.483	1.214**	.398	136.78
	(.457)	(.065)	(.188)	(.234)	(.334)	(.327)		(.299)	(.268)	(.299)	(.269)	(.330)	(.285)	(.517)	
(2)	-5.950**	.152*	.452*	.013			.097**	.789**	.166	.959**	1.128**	.560	1.262**	.413	131.09
	(.420)	(.066)	(.188)	(.237)			(.011)	(.299)	(.268)	(.300)	(.271)	(.330)	(.288)	(.517)	
(3)	-6.134**	.155*	.456*	.041	1.036*	1.590**	.040	.779**	.171	.950**	1.092**	.521	1.265**	.405	139.19
	(.485)	(.066)	(.188)	(.237)	(.403)	(.578)	(.026)	(.299)	(.268)	(.299)	(.271)	(.331)	(.288)	(.517)	

NOTE: Number of cases at risk = 215; left-censored cases = 64; number of transitions = 162. SEs are shown in parentheses. N = 3,400 spells.
[a]Omitted sectors are publishing, banking, retail trade, transportation, hospitals, and state government.
*$p \leq .05$.
**$p \leq .01$.

291

TABLE 13.5 Estimates of Factors Affecting the Adoption of Salary Classification, 1956-1985

Equation	Intercept	Log Employment	Presence of a Personnel Office	Member of a Personnel Association	Period 2 (1964-1973)	Period 3 (1974-1985)	Time Trend	Sector[a]							χ^2
								Chemicals	Machinery	Electrical	Non-profit	City Government	County Government	Federal Government	
(1)	-5.906**	.135	.750**	.460	.970**	1.680**		.132	.504	1.078**	1.049**	.996**	1.768**	.870	118.58
	(.471)	(.072)	(.207)	(.240)	(.323)	(.315)		(.382)	(.315)	(.301)	(.282)	(.366)	(.301)	(.725)	
(2)	-5.667**	.121	.763**	.465			.058**	.118	.509	1.080**	1.047**	.987**	1.704**	.844	104.40
	(.433)	(.071)	(.208)	(.243)			(.012)	(.382)	(.315)	(.301)	(.283)	(.367)	(.303)	(.725)	
(3)	-5.710**	.133	.763**	.506*	1.324**	2.436**	-.040	.132	.507	1.083**	1.017**	.980**	1.715**	.894	120.67
	(.487)	(.071)	(.206)	(.241)	(.404)	(.609)	(.028)	(.382)	(.315)	(.301)	(.283)	(.367)	(.302)	(.725)	

NOTE: Number of cases at risk = 220; left-censored cases = 59; number of transitions = 132. SEs shown in parentheses. $N = 3,600$ spells.
[a] Omitted sectors are publishing, banking, retail trade, transrotation, hospitals, and state government.
$*p \leq .05.$
$**p \leq .01.$

TABLE 13.6 Estimates of Factors Affecting the Adoption of Job Ladders, 1956-1985

| Equation | Intercept | Log Employment | Presence of a Personnel Office | Member of a Personnel Association | Period 2 (1964-1973) | Period 3 (1974-1985) | Time Trend | Sector[a] | | | | | | | χ^2 |
								Chemicals	Machinery	Electrical	Non-profit	City Government	County Government	Federal Government	
(1)	-6.778**	.151	.404	.164	.589	.114*		.601	.571	.781	.672	.646	1.508**	1.434*	36.97
	(.650)	(.096)	(.323)	(.328)	(.481)	(.455)		(.553)	(.508)	(.509)	(.399)	(.551)	(.388)	(.628)	
(2)	-6.628**	.146	.422	.194			.366*	.591	.578	.787	.673	.658	1.481**	1.420*	32.98
	(.608)	(.095)	(.323)	(.334)			(.173)	(.553)	(.508)	(.509)	(.399)	(.551)	(.388)	(.629)	
(3)	-6.549**	.147	.419	.229	1.025	2.090*	-.049	.595	.579	.794	.657	.635	1.480**	1.417*	38.42
	(.671)	(.095)	(.322)	(.322)	(.600)	(.901)	(.041)	(.553)	(.509)	(.509)	(.399)	(.551)	(.388)	(.629)	

NOTE: Number of cases at risk = 257; left-censored cases = 22; number of transitions = 61. SEs are shown in parentheses. $N = 5,396$ spells.
[a] Omitted sectors are publishing, banking, retail trade, transportation, hospitals, and state government.
*$p \le .05$.
**$p \le .01$.

TABLE 13.7 Estimates of Factors Affecting the Adoption of Employment Tests, 1956-1985

| Equation | Intercept | Log Employment | Presence of a Personnel Office | Member of a Personnel Association | Period 2 (1964-1973) | Period 3 (1974-1985) | Time Trend | Sector[a] | | | | | | | χ^2 |
								Chemicals	Machinery	Electrical	Non-profit	City Government	County Government	Federal Government	
(1)	-5.596**	.097	.080	-.073	1.113**	1.112**		.196	.384	.403	-.165	1.353**	1.045**	.212	26.49
	(.524)	(.083)	(.285)	(.347)	(.395)	(.249)		(.488)	(.365)	(.454)	(.434)	(.402)	(.357)	(.610)	
(2)	-5.195**	.102	.061	-.121			.029*	.211	.395	.437	-.160	1.369**	1.022**	.202	19.03
	(.474)	(.082)	(.284)	(.347)			(.015)	(.488)	(.365)	(.453)	(.434)	(.402)	(.358)	(.700)	
(3)	-5.460**	.095	.096	-.036	1.366*	1.661*	-.028	.190	.381	.397	-.172	1.336**	1.029**	.214	27.10
	(.549)	(.082)	(.285)	(.349)	(.509)	(.803)	(.036)	(.488)	(.365)	(.454)	(.434)	(.402)	(.357)	(.610)	

NOTE: Number of cases at risk = 233; left-censored cases = 46; number of transitions = 81. SEs are shown in parentheses. $N = 4,104$ spells.
[a]Omitted sectors are publishing, banking, retail trade, transportation, hospitals, and state government.
*$p \le .05$.
**$p \le .01$.

current year, which operationalize the argument that organizations install ILM mechanisms to compete for labor, performed well in bivariate analyses, but their effects disappeared in multivariate models. For parsimony we omit the density measures from the reported results, as well as several other variables that showed no significant effects in multivariate models.

Conflict arguments do not receive support here. Pfeffer and Cohen (1984) suggest that personnel departments have positive effects and unions have negative effects. Their argument hinges on the struggle between these two interests; the theory depends on our finding both effects. We found strong positive effects of personnel departments, but no effects of union contracts in either bivariate or multivariate models.

Legal changes show strong effects. The time periods, which represent changes in the legal environment, were important in all of our models. In accord with our predictions, the period effects are consistently positive, and the period 3 coefficients exceed the period 2 coefficients for job descriptions, performance evaluations, and salary classification systems. In equation (1) of Table 13.3, for instance, the constant, which represents the baseline rate for the period 1955-1963, is -5.704. To calculate the change in the rate of adoption between periods we add the parameter for period 2 (1.059) to the constant, and the sum (-4.645) shows that, between c_1 and c_2, the rate increases by about 19%. Similarly, when we add the parameter for period 3 to the constant, the sum (-3.540) shows that the rate increases by approximately 38% between c_1 and c_3. Very similar findings are presented for performance evaluations and salary classification. For job ladders, only period 3 shows a significant effect; this supports DiPrete's (1989) argument that civil service systems bridged job ladders to conform to EEO guidelines after the early 1970s. For employment tests, the parameters for the two later periods are roughly equal, which supports our argument that personnel professionals responded to the Civil Rights Act by encouraging adoption of such tests but that the legal precedents of the early 1970s made testing difficult to support in court. Some organizations undertook studies to demonstrate that tests predicted job performance, but many avoided testing altogether.

We introduce a time-trend variable to evaluate whether the period variables actually tap a steady secular increase in adoption rather than the discontinuous effects of policy shifts. If the former is the case, the time-trend variable, coded from 1-30, should wash out the effects of the binary time-period variables. This is not what happens. In constrained models the period variables produce better results than the time trend variable for all five outcomes. In unconstrained models that include all three variables, the time trend uniformly fails to achieve significance. For four of the outcomes, the time-period variables that show significant effects in equation (1) remain significant. For job descriptions, only period 2 shows significant effects. These results suggest that increases in the likelihood of adoption were stepwise and dramatic rather than incremental. While these general measures of legal change show robust effects, the direct measures of whether organizations come under federal EEO scrutiny—federal contractor status and EEO report filing status—showed weak effects that did not hold up in multivariate models, hence we omit them from the tables.

The presence of a personnel office shows a positive effect on the adoption of job descriptions, performance evaluations, and salary classification, which were ultimately approved by the personnel profession and the courts as EEO compliance strategies, but not on job ladders or employment tests, which were generally discouraged by the profession and the courts. For one outcome, salary classification, membership in a personnel association also shows a weak net effect. In bivariate analyses the presence of an affirmative action office or officer showed a significant positive effect for four of the outcomes, but the fact that this measure washed out in multivariate analyses suggests that personnel networks, not affirmative action networks, were the most important interorganizational conduits of these practices.

Location in the "institutional" (nonprofit and government) sector showed an effect for every outcome despite the fact that many state and federal agencies used civil service systems, which incorporate our outcome variables, before 1955; the at-risk group includes relatively few state or federal agencies. By examining the constant (−5.704) and parameters in equation (1) of Table 13.3 we find that nonprofits (1.171) were 21% more likely to adopt job descriptions than organizations in the reference group, city agencies (.899) were 16% more likely, and county agencies (1.540) were 27% more likely. The nonprofit sector shows significant positive effects in four of the equations; county governments show up in five; city governments show up in three; and the federal government shows up in one. In accord with DiPrete's argument that government agencies used bridged job ladders to achieve EEO compliance from the mid-1970s, we find that only county and federal governments show positive effects on job ladders, and only the 1974-85 time period shows an effect.

We do not present a table for promotion testing because only one factor had a significant bivariate effect. Personnel association membership produced a log-likelihood chi-square statistic of 4.71, with a coefficient of .894 and a standard error of .387. The practice of promotion testing showed the slowest growth over the period and was the least prevalent of all of these practices by 1985; this supports our hypothesis that EEO case law discouraged employers from using tests to evaluate employees.

We believe that, taken together, these results demonstrate that since 1955 particular ILM practices diffused largely in response to shifts in the legal environment. They diffused through networks of personnel professionals who collectively devised organizational formulas for inoculation against EEO litigation. Organizations subject to public scrutiny were more likely to adopt these practices. Organizations subject to direct federal oversight in view of their contractor status were no more likely to adopt these practices than were other organizations because the process by which the practices spread is diffuse and normative rather than specific and coercive.

Conclusion

Organizational analysts have traditionally explained management practices by tracing their origins. This has been our strategy as well, and the process has led us to be skeptical about the very terms *internal, labor,* and *market.* Between the 1960s and 1980s, as in the 1930s and 1940s, organizations adopted formal promotion mechanisms in response to external changes as much as, or more than, in response to *internal* imperatives. They installed these mechanisms in reaction to the elaboration of employee rights, as well as to deal with problems associated with the management of *labor* (i.e., human capital). And they adopted these practices to conform to legal requirements, as well as to effect interior *market* mechanisms. We found that organizations adopt ILM practices less in response to internal imperatives than in response to changes in the general model of organizing offered by the environment.

Our findings concern the relationship between the state and organizations. In the United States, public policy governing organizational practices seldom takes the form of direct mandates; policies create broad rules about outcomes rather than specific rules about means to those outcomes. As a result, specific organizational means are worked out in the nexus between organizations and the state. Ambiguous public policies invite organizations to experiment with solutions that will withstand legal tests, and in turn the courts and Congress affirm certain strategies and veto others (Edelman, 1992). This process contributed to the evolving understanding of what constitutes discrimination and how to guard against it (see Burstein, 1990). In the case of EEO law, the courts discouraged the use of formal testing and made it clear that organizations that used voluntary quotas would open themselves up to reverse-discrimination litigation. But they approved the formalization of hiring and promotion through the use of traditional ILM practices. This procedural strategy became the favored approach to pursuing nondiscrimination. The process was diffuse and normative, rather than targeted and coercive, and this showed up in our finding that being a federal contractor, or coming under EEOC or OFCCP scrutiny, had no net effect. In short, public policy helped to create broad models of organizing that were embraced as just and rational by all sorts of organizations; it did not force a narrow range of targeted organizations to adopt specified practices in order to avoid sanctions.

These findings are entirely consistent with the idea that ILM mechanisms got their first push from federal labor legislation of the 1930s and 1940s (Jacoby, 1985) and wartime labor market controls (Baron, Dobbin, & Jennings, 1986), both of which helped to designate ILM practices as solutions to problems of unionism, turnover, and motivation. Since 1964 federal EEO law has caused personnel managers to view formal selection and promotion practices as ways to protect employee rights and, simultaneously, rationalize the allocation of workers. One result is that management came to see affirmative action in a positive light—as a force for equity and efficiency (*Harvard Law Review* Note, 1989). Legal changes also encouraged managers to treat all employees as career-oriented and self-actualizing by creating organizational structures that would allow all classes of employees to pursue promotions, including groups employers previously took to have naturally low aspirations and weak needs for ego gratification (e.g., minorities and women).

It appears that legal changes have altered the meaning of ILM mechanisms since the 1960s (see Pfeffer & Cohen, 1984); as a result, union attitudes have changed. Pfeffer and Cohen found strong evidence that, for personnel managers and unions, ILM mechanisms represent an effort to maximize management control. But since 1964, ILM practices have come to represent a means to achieve equity. Personnel managers continued to promote ILMs because it was in their interest to do so. And ILM mechanisms have continued to exemplify garbage-can theory's solution-in-search-of-a-problem, for EEO is just the latest in a series of problems personnel managers have sought to solve with ILMs (Cohen, March, & Olsen, 1972). Yet the evidence suggests that once ILM mechanisms had taken on a different meaning, unions stopped opposing them. Our findings reinforce the idea that interest group goals are not primordial and unwavering; rather they change over time in response to shifts in the environment (DiMaggio, 1988; Dobbin, 1992).

We have suggested that organizational employment practices are driven by evolving conceptions of the individual, and of individual rights, that become institutionalized in public policy. Employment practices, in turn, feed back in to these conceptions. To wit, ILM practices that make promotion available to all categories of employees portray ambition and achievement orientation as characteristics of *all* individuals—as inherent in individualism. These practices also democratize organizational representations of human motivation by breaking down the distinction between managers and employees Bendix (1956) identified in early thought and practice; in contemporary management doctrine even the lowest-level employees are driven by the same desire for mobility as their bosses. Of course, management practices designed to achieve efficiency have always been oriented to current ideas about human nature, and in turn they have always helped to construct beliefs about human nature. This was as true in the heyday of Taylorism as it is today. We view the legal and organizational concern with guarding the integrity of workers (e.g., sexual harassment policies), with participative management and work-group identification (e.g., quality circles), and with transforming all jobs into rungs on career ladders to make advancement available to all (e.g., open job bidding and formal promotion mechanisms) as integral to today's organizational representation of the individual. However, evidence that, since the mid-1980s, firms have moved away from long-term employment and toward short-term contracting suggests that the future of the organizational embodiments of individualism that we have depicted is uncertain (Hirsch, 1991; Pfeffer & Baron, 1988).

Although prevailing rationalist theorists treat organizational structure as mainly responsive to economic imperatives that transcend time and locale, we have shown the impact of particular institutions found in the environment. Those institutions reflect and embody the expanding Western conception of the individual that is central to the project of modernity. Institutional attention to the individual has intensified and produced new organizational practices in recent decades; this process has been fueled by pressures to achieve equity by extending the rights of occupational mobility and expanded organizational membership to all of society's members (Selznick, 1969). The new organizational model for promoting equity incorporates practices that, at the same time, advance the project of rationalization by contributing to the efficient allocation of "human capital." Future studies could usefully set aside the premise that organizational practices are structured by extrasocietal principles of efficiency and attend to how the evolving institutional constructions of individualism and efficiency affect organizational practices.

Notes

1. We also operationalized labor economists' arguments with a number of sector-level variables that are thought to tap firm-specific skills and labor-market characteristics: capital-labor ratio (capital expenditures—labor expenditures) and percentages of managerial employees, professional employees, black employees, and female employees. These factors

showed no effects in multivariate models, but we hesitate to draw conclusions because they are measured at the sectoral level.

2. The report argued that if an EEO survey shows that women and minorities are not employed in an organization "at all levels in reasonable relation to their presence in the population data and the labor force, the burden of proof is on . . . [the employer] to show that this is not the result of discrimination, however inadvertent" (Farley, 1979, p. vi).

3. One article in the *Harvard Business Review* not only advocated performance evaluations, but also recommended separate performance evaluations to assess managers' affirmative action performance (Purcell, 1974).

4. A 1973 how-to article on affirmative action for women thus advocated the "institution of a method of job posting so that all employees are aware of vacancies as they occur and that promotion into these vacancies is based on qualifications, not sex" or prior position (Slevin, 1973, p. 30).

5. Small firms were most likely to abandon testing, in part because they could not produce sufficient data to demonstrate that tests predicted job performance (Walsh & Hess, 1974).

6. We were never able to contact 86 of the nonrespondents to determine whether they met the sampling criteria. To calculate the response rate we assume that this entire group would have met the criteria.

References

Abramowitz, S., & Tenenbaum, E. (1978). *High school '77: A survey of public secondary school principals.* Washington, DC: National Institute of Education.

Abzug, R., & Mezias, S. (1993). The fragmented state and due process protections in organizations: The case of comparable worth. *Organization Science, 4,* 433-453.

Alchian, A. A., & Demsetz, H. (1972). Production, information costs, and economic organization, *American Economic Review, 62,* 777-795.

Alexander, J. C. (1983). *Theoretical logic in sociology. Vol. 3: The classical attempt at theoretical synthesis, Max Weber.* Berkeley: University of California Press.

Alexander, J. C. (1987). *Twenty lectures: Sociological theory since World War II.* New York: Columbia University Press.

Althauser, R. P., & Kalleberg, A. L. (1981). Firm, occupations, and the structure of labor markets: A conceptual analysis and research agenda. In I. Berg (Ed.), *Sociological perspectives on labor markets* (pp. 119-149). New York: Academic Press.

American Society for Training and Development. (1983). *Models for excellence: The conclusions and recommendations of the ASTD Training and Development Competency Study.* Washington, DC: Author.

Anderson, P. (1974). *Lineages of the absolutist state.* New York: Schocken.

Argyris, C., & Schon, D. (1978). *Organizational learning.* Reading, MA: Addison-Wesley.

Arthur, W. B. (1983). *On competing technologies and historical small events: The dynamics of choice under increasing returns.* Unpublished manuscript, Stanford University, Stanford, CA.

Ashenfelter, O., & Heckmann, J. (1976). Measuring the effect of an antidiscrimination program. In O. Ashenfelter & J. Blum (Eds.), *Evaluating the labor-market effects of a social program* (pp. 46-84). Princeton, NJ: Princeton University, Industrial Relations Section.

Axelrod, R. (1984). *The evolution of cooperation.* New York: Basic Books.

Bankston, M. (1982). *Organizational reporting in a school district: State and federal programs* (Rep. No. 82-A10). Stanford, CA: Stanford University, Institute for Research on Educational Finance and Governance.

Bardach, E. (1977). *The implementation game: What happens after a bill becomes a law.* Cambridge: MIT Press.

Barley, S. R. (1986). Technology as an occasion for structuring: Evidence from observations of CT scanners and the social order of radiology departments. *Administrative Science Quarterly, 31,* 78-108.

Barley, S. R., & Kunda, G. (1992). Design and devotion: Surges of rational and normative ideologies of control in managerial discourse. *Administrative Science Quarterly, 37,* 363-399.

Barnard, C. I. (1938). *The functions of the executive.* Cambridge, MA: Harvard University Press.

Baron, J. N. (1984). Organizational perspectives on stratification. *Annual Review of Sociology, 10,* 37-69.

Baron, J. N., & Bielby, W. T. (1980). Bringing the firm back in: Stratification, segmentation, and the organization of work. *American Sociological Review, 45,* 174-188.

Baron, J. N., Dobbin, F. R., & Jennings, P. D. (1986). War and peace: The evolution of modern personnel administration in U.S. industry. *American Journal of Sociology, 92,* 350-383.

Baron, J. N., Mittman B., & Newman, A. (1991). Targets of opportunity: Gender integration in the California civil service, 1979-1985. *American Journal of Sociology, 96,* 1362-1401.

Barrett, D. (1992). *Reproducing persons as a global concern: The making of an institution.* Unpublished doctoral prospectus. Stanford University, Stanford, CA.

Barth, F. (Ed.). (1969). *Ethnic groups and boundaries: The social organization of culture difference.* Boston: Little, Brown.

Bartholomew, D. J. (1982). *Stochastic models for social processes.* New York: John Wiley.

Bartunek, J. M. (1984). Changing interpretive schemes and organizational restructuring: The example of a religious order. *Administrative Science Quarterly, 29,* 355-372.

Bassford, G. L. (1974). Job testing—alternative to employment quotas. *Business Horizons, 17,* 37-50.

Becker, G. (1964). *Human capital.* New York: Columbia University Press.

Becker, G. (1971). *The economics of discrimination* (2nd ed.). Chicago: University of Chicago Press.

Becker, M. H. (1970). Sociometric location and innovativeness: Reformulation and extension of the diffusion model. *American Sociological Review, 35,* 267-282.

Bell, D., Jr. (1971). Bonuses, quotas, and the employment of black workers. *Journal of Human Resources, 6,* 309-320.

Bellah, R. N. (1964). Religious evolution. *American Sociological Review, 29,* 358-374.

Benavot, A. (1983). The rise and decline of vocational education. *Sociology of Education, 56*(2), 63-76.

Bendix, R. (1956). *Work and authority in industry.* New York: John Wiley.

Bendix, R. (1964). *Nation-building and citizenship.* New York: John Wiley.

Bendix, R. (1978). *Kings or people: Power and the mandate to rule.* Berkeley: University of California Press.

Bennis, W. G., Benne, K. D., & Chin, R. (Eds.). (1985). *The planning of change* (4th ed.). New York: CBS College Publishing.

Benokraitis, N., & Feagin, J. (1977). *Affirmative action and equal opportunity.* Boulder, CO: Westview.

Berg, I. (1971). *Education and jobs: The great training robbery.* Boston: Beacon.

Berger, P. L., Berger, B., & Kellner, H. (1973). *The homeless mind: Modernization and consciousness.* New York: Random House.

Berger, P. L., & Kellner, H. (1981). *Sociology reinterpreted: An essay on method and vocation.* Garden City, NY: Doubleday.

Berger, P. L., & Luckmann, T. (1967). *The social construction of reality.* New York: Doubleday.

Berger, S. (Ed.). (1981). *Organizing interests in Western Europe: Pluralism, corporatism, and the transformation of politics.* Cambridge, UK: Cambridge University Press.

Bergesen, A. J. (Ed.). (1980). *Studies of the modern world system.* New York: Academic Press.

Berke, J. S., & Kirst, M. W. (1975). The federal role in American school finance: A fiscal and administrative analysis. In F. M. Wirt (Ed.), *The polity of the school* (pp. 15-23). Lexington, MA: Lexington Books.

Berkovitch, N. (1993). *From motherhood to citizenship: The world-wide incorporation of women into the public sphere in the twentieth century.* Unpublished dissertation prospectus, Stanford University, Stanford, CA.

Berman, P., & McLaughlin, M. W. (1975-1978). *Federal programs supporting educational change* (Vols. 1-8). Santa Monica, CA: Rand Corporation.

Blau, P. M. (1970). A formal theory of differentiation in organizations. *American Sociological Review, 35,* 201-218.

Blau, P. M., Falbe, C. McH., McKinley, W., & Tracy, P. K. (1976). Technology and organization in manufacturing. *Administrative Science Quarterly, 21,* 20-40.

Blau, P. M., & Schoenherr, R. A. (1971). *The structure of organizations.* New York: Basic Books.

Blaug, M. (Ed.) (1968, 1969). *Economics of education* (Vols. 1 and 2). New York: Penguin.

Boeker, W. (1989). The development and institutionalization of subunit power in organizations. *Administrative Science Quarterly, 34,* 388-410.

Boland, R. J. (1982). Myth and technology in the American accounting profession. *Journal of Management Studies, 19,* 109-127.

Boland, R., & Pondy, L. (1983). Accounting in organizations: A union of national and rational perspectives. *Accounting, Organizations and Society, 8,* 223-234.

Boli, J. (1979). The ideology of expanding state authority in national constitutions, 1870-1970. In J. W. Meyer & M. T. Hannan (Eds.), *National development and the world system* (pp. 222-237). Chicago: University of Chicago Press.

Boli, J. (1987a). Human rights or state expansion? Cross-national definitions of constitutional rights, 1870-1970. In G. M. Thomas, J. W. Meyer, F. O. Ramirez, & J. Boli (Eds.), *Institutional structure: Constituting state, society, and the individual* (pp. 133-149). Newbury Park, CA: Sage.

Boli, J. (1987b). World polity sources of expanding state authority and organization, 1870-1970. In G. M. Thomas, J. W. Meyer, F. O. Ramirez, & J. Boli (Eds.), *Institutional structure: Constituting state, society, and the individual* (pp. 71-91). Newbury Park, CA: Sage.

Boli, J. (1989). *New citizens for a new society.* Elmsford, NY: Pergamon.

Boli, J., Ramirez, F. O., & Meyer, J. W. (1985). Explaining the origins and expansion of mass education. *Comparative Education Review, 29,* 145-170.

Boli-Bennett, J., & Meyer, J. W. (1978). Ideology of childhood and the state. *American Sociological Review, 43,* 797-812.

Brandes, S. D. (1976). *American welfare capitalism, 1880-1940.* Chicago: University of Chicago Press.

Braverman, H. (1974). *Labor and monopoly capital: The degradation of work in the twentieth century.* New York: Monthly Labor Press.

Bridges, E. M. (1982). Research on the school administrator: The state of the art, 1967-1980. *Educational Administration Quarterly, 18,* 12-33.

Brim, O. G., & Kagan, J. (Eds.). (1983). *Constancy and change in human development.* Cambridge, MA: Harvard University Press.

Brunsson, N. (1989). *The organization of hypocrisy: Talk, decisions and actions in organizations.* New York: John Wiley.

Burawoy, M. (1985). *The politics of production.* London: Verso.

Burlingame, M., & Geske, T. G. (1979). State politics and education: An examination of selected multiple-state case studies. *Educational Administration Quarterly, 15* (Spring), 51-75.

Burstein, P. (1985). *Discrimination, jobs, and politics: The struggle for equal employment opportunity in the United States since the New Deal.* Chicago: University of Chicago Press.

Burstein, P. (1990). Intergroup conflict, law, and the concept of labor market discrimination. *Sociological Forum, 5,* 459-476.

Burstein, P., & Monaghan, K. (1986). Equal employment opportunity and the mobilization of law. *Law and Society Review, 16,* 355-388.

Burstein, P., & Pitchford, S. (1990). Social-scientific and legal challenges to education and test requirements in employment. *Social Problems, 37,* 243-257.

Burt, R. S. (1987). Social contagion and innovation: Cohesion versus structural equivalence, *American Journal of Sociology, 92,* 1287-1335.

Burt, R. S., & Minor, M. J. (Eds.). (1983). *Applied network analysis.* Beverly Hills, CA: Sage.

Campbell, J. T. (1973). Tests are valid for minority groups too. *Public Personnel Management, 2,* 70-73.

Campbell, J. L., Hollingsworth, J. R., & Lindberg, L. N. (Eds.). (1991). *Governance of the American economy.* New York: Cambridge University Press.

Campbell, J. L., & Lindberg, L. N. (1991). The evolution of governance regimes. In J. L. Campbell, J. R. Hollingsworth, & L. N. Lindberg (Eds.), *Governance of the American economy* (pp. 319-355). New York: Cambridge University Press.

Carey, M. L. (1985). *How workers get their training.* Washington, DC: Department of Labor, Bureau of Labor Statistics.

Carley, K. (1990). Structural constraints on communication: The diffusion of the homomorphic signal analysis technique through scientific fields. *Journal of Mathematical Sociology, 15,* 207-246.

Carnevale, A. P. (1984). *Jobs for the nation: Challenges for a society based on work.* Alexandria, VA: American Society for Training and Development.

Carnevale, A. P. (1986). The learning enterprise. *Training and Development Journal, 40.*

Carnevale, A. P., Gainer, L. J., & Villet, J. (1990). *Training in America: The organization and strategic role of training.* San Francisco: Jossey-Bass.

Carnevale, A. P., & Goldstein, H. (1983). *Employee training: Its changing role and an analysis of new data.* Washington, DC: American Society for Training and Development Press.

Carroll, G. R., Delacroix, J., & Goodstein, J. (1988). The political environments of organizations: An ecological view. In B. M. Staw & L. L. Cummings (Eds.), *Research in organizational behavior* (Vol. 10, pp. 359-392). Greenwich, CT: JAI.

Carroll, G. R., Goodstein, G., & Gyenes, A. (1988). Organizations and the state: Effects of the institutional environment on agricultural cooperatives in Hungary. *Administrative Science Quarterly, 33,* 233-256.

Cawson, A. (Ed.). (1985). *Organized interests and the state: Studies in meso-corporatism.* Beverly Hills, CA: Sage.

Chalofsky, N. (1984). Professional growth for HRD staff. In L. Nadler (Ed.), *The handbook of human resource development* (pp. 13.1-13.18). New York: John Wiley.

Chambers, J. G., & Lajoie, S. (1983). A comparative study of private and public schooling organizations: A descriptive summary. *Report to the National Institute of Education.* Stanford, CA: Stanford University, Institute for Research on Educational Finance and Governance.

Chandler, A. D., Jr. (1990). *Scale and scope: The dynamics of industrial capitalism.* Cambridge, MA: Belknap Press.

Charles, M. (1992). Cross-national variation in occupational sex segregation. *American Sociological Review, 57,* 483-502.

Chayes, A. H. (1974). Make your equal opportunity program court-proof. *Harvard Business Review, 52,* 81-89.

Child, J., & Mansfield, R. (1972). Technology, size, and organization structure. *Sociology, 6,* 369-393.

Chin, R., & Benne, K. D. (1985). General strategies for effective change in human systems. In W. G. Bennis, K. D. Benne, & R. Chin (Eds.), *The planning of change* (4th ed.) (pp. 22-45). New York: CBS College Publishing.

Chmura, T. J., Henton, D. C., & Melville, J. G. (1987). *Corporate education and training: Investing in a competitive future* (Rep. No. 753). Menlo Park, CA: SRI International.

Cicourel, A. V. (1968). *The social organization of juvenile justice.* New York: John Wiley.

Cohen, A. (1969). *Custom and politics in urban Africa: A study of Hausa migrants in Yoruba towns.* Berkeley: University of California Press.

Cohen, E. G., Deal, T. E., Meyer, J. W., & Scott, W. R. (1979). Technology and teaming in the elementary school. *Sociology of Education, 52,* 20-33.

Cohen, M. D., March, J. G., & Olsen, J. P. (1972). A garbage can model of organizational choice. *Administrative Science Quarterly, 17,* 1-25.

Cohen, Y., & Pfeffer, J. (1986). Organizational hiring standards. *Administrative Science Quarterly, 31,* 1-24.

Cole, R. E. (1985). The macropolitics of organizational change: A comparative analysis of the spread of small-group activities. *Administrative Science Quarterly, 30,* 560-585.

Cole, R. E. (1989). *Strategies for learning: Small-group activities in American, Japanese, and Swedish industry.* Berkeley: University of California Press.

Coleman, J. R. (1974). *Power and the structure of society.* New York: W. W. Norton.

Coleman, J. R. (1982). *The asymmetric society.* Syracuse, NY: Syracuse University Press.

Coleman, J. R. (1990). *Foundations of social theory.* Cambridge, MA: Belknap Press.

Coleman, J. R., Katz, E., & Menzel, H. (1966). *Medical innovation.* Indianapolis: Bobbs-Merrill.

Collier, D., & Messick, R. (1975). Prerequisites versus diffusion: Testing alternative explanations of social security adoption. *Americal Political Science Review, 69,* 1299-1315.

Collins, R. (1974). Where are educational requirements for employment higher? *Sociology of Education, 47,* 419-442.

Collins, R. (1979). *The credential society: An historical sociology of education and stratification.* New York: Academic Press.

Collins, R. (1980). Weber's last theory of capitalism: A systematization. *American Sociological Review, 45,* 925-942.

Covaleski, M., & Dirsmith, M. (1983). Budgeting as a means for control and loose coupling. *Accounting, Organizations and Society, 8,* 323-340.

Creighton, A. L. (1990). *The emergence of incorporation as a legal form for organizations.* Unpublished doctoral dissertation, Stanford University, Stanford, CA.

Crozier, M. (1964). *The bureaucratic phenomenon.* Chicago: University of Chicago Press.

D'Andrade, R. G. (1984). Cultural meaning systems. In R. A. Shweder & R. A. LeVine (Eds.), *Culture theory: Essays on mind, self, and emotion* (pp. 88-119). Cambridge, UK: Cambridge University Press.

D'Andrade, R. G. (1986). Three scientific world views and the covering law model. In D. W. Fiske & R. A. Schweder (Eds.), *Metatheory in social science* (pp. 19-41). Chicago: University of Chicago Press.

D'Aunno, T., Sutton, R. I., & Price, R. H. (1991). Isomorphism and external support in conflicting institutional environments: A study of drug abuse treatment units. *Academy of Management Journal, 14,* 636-661.

David, P. A. (1985). Clio and the economics of QWERTY. *American Economic Review, 75,* 332-337.

David, P. A. (1988). *Path-dependence: Putting the past into the future of economics* (Tech. Rep. No. 533). Stanford University, Institute for Mathematical Studies in the Social Sciences.

Davis, M., Deal, T. E., Meyer, J. W., Rowan, B., Scott, W. R., Stackhouse, E. A. (1977). *The structure of educational systems: Explorations in the theory of loosely coupled organizations.* Stanford, CA: Stanford University, Center for Research and Development in Teaching.

Davis, S. M. (1987). *Future perfect.* Reading, MA: Addison-Wesley.

Deal, T. E., & Kennedy, A. A. (1982). *Corporate cultures.* Reading, MA: Addison-Wesley.

Demsetz, H. (1967). Toward a theory of property rights. *American Economic Review, 57,* 347-359.

Denison, E. (1974). *Accounting for United States economic growth, 1929-1969.* Washington, DC: Brookings Institution.

Dill, W. R. (1958). Environment as an influence on managerial autonomy, *Administrative Science Quarterly, 2,* 409-443.

DiMaggio, P. J. (1982). Cultural entrepreneurship in nineteenth-century Boston: The creation of an organizational base for high culture in America. *Media, Culture and Society, 4,* 33-50.

DiMaggio, P. J. (1983). State expansion and organization fields. In R. H. Hall & R. E. Quinn (Eds.), *Organization theory and public policy* (pp. 147-161). Beverly Hills, CA: Sage.

DiMaggio, P. J., (1986). Structural analysis of organizational fields: A blockmodel approach. In B. M. Staw & L. L. Cummings (Eds.), *Research in organization behavior* (Vol. 8, pp. 355-370). Greenwich, CT: JAI.

DiMaggio, P. J. (1988). Interest and agency in institutional theory. In L. G. Zucker (Ed.), *Institutional patterns and organizations: Culture and environment* (pp. 3-21). Cambridge, MA: Ballinger.

DiMaggio, P. J. (1991). Constructing an organizational field as a professional project: U.S. art museums, 1920-1940. In W. W. Powell & P. J. DiMaggio (Eds.), *The new institutionalism in organizational analysis* (pp. 267-292). Chicago: University of Chicago Press.

DiMaggio, P. J., & Powell, W. W. (1983). The iron cage revisited: Institutional isomorphism and collective rationality in organizational fields. *American Sociological Review, 48,* 147-160.

DiMaggio, P. J. & Powell, W. W. (1991). Introduction. In W. W. Powell & P. J. DiMaggio (Eds.), *The new institutionalism in organizational analysis* (pp. 1-38). Chicago: University of Chicago Press.

DiMaggio, P. J., & Stenberg, K. (1985). Conformity and diversity in the American residential stage. In J. Balfe & M. Wyszonirski (Eds.), *Sociology and the arts.* New York: Praeger.

DiPrete, T. A. (1989). *The bureaucratic labor market: The case of the federal civil service.* New York: Plenum.

Dobbin, F. R. (1992). The origins of private social insurance: Public policy and fringe benefits in America, 1920-1950. *American Journal of Sociology, 97,* 1416-1450.

Dobbin, F. R. (in press). *Forging industrial policy: The United States, France and Britain in the railway age*. New York: Cambridge University Press.

Dobbin, F. R., Edelman, L., Meyer, J. W., Scott, W. R., & Swidler, A. (1988). The expansion of due process in organizations. In L. G. Zucker (Ed.), *Institutional patterns and organizations: Culture and environment* (pp. 71-100). Cambridge, MA: Ballinger.

Dobbin, F. R., Sutton, J. R., Meyer, J. W., & Scott, W. R. (1993). Equal opportunity law and the construction of internal labor markets. *American Journal of Sociology, 99,* 396-427.

Doeringer, P. B., & Piore, M. J. (1971). *Internal labor markets and manpower analysis.* Lexington, MA: D. C. Heath.

Donohue, J. J., III. (1986). Is Title VII efficient? *University of Pennsylvania Law Review, 134,* 1411-1431.

Dore, R. (1973). *British factory—Japanese factory.* Berkeley: University of California Press.

Douglas, M. (1966). *Purity and danger.* London: Penguin.

Douglas, M. (1986). *How institutions think.* Syracuse, NY: Syracuse University Press.

Doyle, D. P., & Finn, C. E., Jr. (1984). American schools and the future of local control. *Public Interest, 77* (Fall), 77-95.

Duesenberry, J. (1960). Comment on "An economic analysis of fertility." In Universities–National Bureau Committee for Economic Research (Ed.), *Demographic and economic change in developed countries* (pp. 230-240). Princeton, NJ: Princeton University Press.

Duncan, R., & Weiss, A. (1979). Organizational learning: Implications for organizational design. In B. Staw (Ed.), *Research in organizational behavior* (Vol. 1, pp. 75-123). Greenwich, CT: JAI.

Eccles, R. G., & Crane, D. B. (1988). *Doing deals: Investment banks at work.* Boston: Harvard Business School Press.

Edelman, L. (1990). Legal environments and organizational governance: The expansion of due process in the American workplace. *American Journal of Sociology, 95,* 1401-1440.

Edelman, L. (1992). Legal ambiguity and symbolic structures: Organizational mediation of civil rights law. *American Journal of Sociology, 97,* 1531-1576.

Edwards, R. (1979). *Contested terrain: The transformation of the workplace in the twentieth century.* New York: Basic Books.

Ellul, J. (1973). *The new demons.* New York: Seabury.

Elster, J. (1983). *Explaining technical change: A case study in the philosophy of science.* Cambridge, UK: Cambridge University Press.

Encarnation, D. J. (1983). Public finance and regulation of non-public education: Retrospect and prospect. In T. James & H. M. Levin (Eds.), *Public dollars for private schools* (pp. 175-195). Philadelphia: Temple University Press.

Erickson, D. (1983). *Public schools in contemporary perspective* (Rep. No. TTC-14). Stanford, CA: Stanford University, Institute for Research on Educational Finance and Governance.

Eurich, N. P. (1985). *Corporate classrooms: The learning business.* Princeton, NJ: Carnegie Foundation for the Advancement of Teaching.

Evans, P. B., Rueschemeyer, D., & Skocpol, T. (Eds.). (1985). *Bringing the state back in.* Cambridge, UK: Cambridge University Press.

Evans, P. B., & Stephens, J. D. (1988). Development and the world economy. In N. J. Smelser (Ed.), *Handbook of sociology* (pp. 739-773). Newbury Park, CA: Sage.

Eyre, D. P., Dahl, R. F., & Shively, J. (1986). *The organization of schools outside the traditional educational sector: An exploratory study* (Proj. Rep. No. 86-SEPI-10). Stanford, CA: Stanford University, Stanford Educational Policy Institute.

Farley, J. (1979). *Affirmative action and the woman worker.* New York: AMACOM.

Feld, W. (1972). *Nongovernmental forces and world politics: A study of business, labor, and political groups.* New York: Praeger.

Fiala, R., & Gordon-Lanford, A. (1987). Educational ideology and the world educational revolution, 1950-1970. *Comparative Education Review, 31,* 315-332.

Finnemore, M. (1990). *International organizations as teachers of norms: UNESCO and science policy.* Unpublished doctoral dissertation, Stanford University, Stanford, CA.

Fishlow, A. (1966). Levels of nineteenth century investment in education: Human capital formation or structural reinforcement? *Journal of Economic History, 26,* 418-436.

Fligstein, N. (1985). The spread of the multidivisional form among large firms, 1919-1979. *American Sociological Review, 50,* 377-391.

Fligstein, N. (1990). *The transformation of corporate control.* Cambridge, MA: Harvard University Press.

Fligstein, N. (1991). The structural transformation of American industry: An institutional account of the causes of diversification in the largest firms, 1919-1979. In W. W. Powell & P. J. DiMaggio (Eds.), *The new institutionalism in organizational analysis* (pp. 311-336). Chicago: University of Chicago Press.

Foucault, M. (1965). *Madness and civilization: A history of insanity in the age of reason* (R. Howard, Trans.). New York: Pantheon.

Frank, D. (1992). *Global environmentalism: International treaties and nation-state participation.* Unpublished dissertation prospectus, Stanford University, Stanford, CA.

Frank, D., Miyahara, D., & Meyer, J. W. (1992). *The scientized self: Cross-national variation in the prevalence of psychology.* Paper presented at annual meeting of the American Sociological Association, Pittsburgh.

Freeman, J., Hannan, M. T., & Hannaway, J. (1978). *The dynamics of school district administrative intensity: Effects of enrollments and finance in five states.* Cambridge, MA: ABT Associates.

Freeman, J., & Kronenfeld, J. E. (1974). Problems of definitional dependency: The case of administrative intensity. *Social Forces, 52,* 108-121.

Friedland, R., & Alford, R. R. (1991). Bringing society back in: Symbols, practices, and institutional contradictions. In W. W. Powell & P. J. DiMaggio (Eds.), *The new institutionalism in organizational analysis* (pp. 232-263). Chicago: University of Chicago Press.

Friedman, M. (1962). *Capitalism and freedom.* Chicago: University of Chicago Press.

Frost, P., Moore, L. F., Louis, M. R., Lundberg, C. C., & Martin, J. (1991). *Reframing organizational culture.* Newbury Park, CA: Sage.

Fuhrman, S., & Rosenthal, A. (Eds.). (1981). *Shaping education policy in the states.* Washington, DC: Institute for Educational Leadership.

Galaskiewicz, J., & Burt, R. S. (1991). Interorganizational contagion in corporate philanthropy. *Administrative Science Quarterly, 36,* 88-105.

Galbraith, J. (1973). *Designing complex organizations.* Reading, MA: Addison-Wesley.

Galbraith, M., & Gilley, J. (1986). *Professional certification: Implications for adult education and HRD.* (Information Series No. 307). Columbus: Ohio State University, ERIC Clearing House on Adult, Career, and Vocational Education.

Garfinkel, H. (1967). *Studies in ethnomethodology.* Englewood Cliffs, NJ: Prentice Hall.

Gavin, J. F., & Toole, D. L. (1973). Validity of aptitude tests for the "hardcore unemployed." *Personnel Psychology, 26,* 139-146.

Geertz, C. (1973). *The interpretation of cultures.* New York: Basic Books.

Geertz, C. (1980). *Negara: The theatre state in nineteenth-century Bali.* Princeton, NJ: Princeton University Press.

Gerschenkron, A. (1962). *Economic backwardness in historical perspective.* Cambridge, MA: Harvard University Press.

Giblin, E. J., & Ornati, O. (1974). A total approach to EEO compliance. *Personnel, 51,* 32-43.

Giddens, A. (1984). *The constitution of society.* Berkeley: University of California Press.

Gilliland, E. M., & Radle, J. (1984). *Characteristics of public and private schools in the San Francisco Bay Area: A descriptive report.* Stanford, CA: Stanford University, Institute for Research on Educational Finance and Governance.

Goettel, R. J. (1976). Federal assistance to national target groups: The ESEA Title 1 experience. In M. Timpane (Ed.), *The federal interest in financing schooling* (pp. 173-208). Cambridge, MA: Ballinger.

Goffman, E. (1974). *Frame analysis.* New York: Harper & Row.

Goldstein, I. L. (1986). *Training in organizations: Needs assessment, development and evaluation* (2nd ed.). Belmont, CA: Brooks/Cole.

Gordon, D. M., Edwards, R., & Reich, M. (1982). *Segmented work, divided workers.* Cambridge, UK: Cambridge University Press.

Gorham, W. A. (1972). New answers on employment tests, *Civil Service Journal, 13,* 8-12.

Granovetter, M. (1985). Economic action and social structure: The problem of embeddedness. *American Journal of Sociology, 91,* 481-510.

Grodzins, M. (1966). *The American system.* Chicago: Rand McNally.

Guillen, M. (1993). *Models of management: Work, authority and organization in comparative perspective.* Chicago: University of Chicago Press.

Habermas, J. (1975). *Legitimation crisis* (T. McCarthy, Trans.). Boston: Beacon Press.

Hagerstrand, T. (1967). *Innovation diffusion as a spatial process.* Chicago: University of Chicago Press.

Hall, J. (1985). *Powers and liberties.* New York: Penguin.

Hall, P. A. (1992). The movement from Keynesianism to monetarism: Institutional analysis and British economic policy in the 1970s. In S. Steinmo, K. Thelen, & F. Longstreth (Eds.), *Structuring politics: Historical institutionalism in comparative analysis* (pp. 90-113). Cambridge, UK: Cambridge University Press.

Halle, D. (1984). *America's working man.* Chicago: University of Chicago Press.

Hamilton, G., & Biggart, N. W. (1988). Market, culture, and authority: A comparative analysis of management and organization in the Far East. *American Journal of Sociology, 94* (Supplement), S52-S94.

Hamilton, G. G., & Sutton, J. R. (1989). The problem of control in the weak state: Domination in the United States, 1880-1920. *Theory and Society, 18,* 1-46.

Handy, C. (1989). *The age of unreason.* Boston: Harvard Business School Press.

Hannan, M. T., & Carroll, G. (1992). *Dynamics of organizational populations: Density, legitimation, and competition.* New York: Oxford University Press.

Hannan, M. T., & Freeman, J. (1977). The population ecology of organizations. *American Journal of Sociology, 82,* 929-964.

Hannan, M. T., & Freeman, J. (1989). *Organizational ecology.* Cambridge, MA: Harvard University Press.

Hannaway, J., & Sproull, L. S. (1978-1979). Who's running the show? Coordination and control in educational organizations. *Administrator's Notebook, 27*(9), 1-4.

Hargrove, E., Scarlett, G., Ward, L. E., Abernethy, V., Cunningham, J., & Vaughn, W. K. (1981). School systems and regulatory mandates: A case study of the implementation of the Education for all Handicapped Children Act. In S. B. Bacharach (Ed.), *Organizational behavior in schools and school districts* (pp. 97-123). New York: Praeger.

Harvard Law Review Note. (1989). Rethinking Weber: The business response to affirmative action. *Harvard Law Review, 102,* 658-671.

Hayek, F. A. (1973). *Law, legislation, and liberty. Vol 1: Rules and order.* Chicago: University of Chicago Press.

Hecter, M. (1990). The emergence of cooperative social institutions, in M. Hecter, K.-D. Opp, & R. Wippler (Eds.), *Social institutions: Their emergence, maintenance and effects* (pp. 13-33). Hawthorne, NY: Aldine.

Hecter, M., Opp, K.-D., & Wippler, R. (Eds.). (1990). *Social institutions: Their emergence, maintenance and effects.* Hawthorne, NY: Aldine.

Hedberg, B. (1981). How organizations learn and unlearn. In P. C. Nystrom & W. H. Starbuck (Eds.), *Handbook of organization design* (Vol. 1, pp. 3-27). Oxford, UK: Oxford University Press.

Hickson, D. J., Pugh, D. S., & Pheysey, D. C. (1969). Operations technology and organization structure: An empirical reappraisal. *Administrative Science Quarterly, 14,* 378-397.

Hirsch, P. M. (1985). The study of industries. In S. B. Bacharach & S. M. Mitchell (Eds.), *Research in the sociology of organizations* (Vol. 4, pp. 271-309). Greenwich, CT: JAI.

Hirsch, P. M. (1991). *Undoing the managerial revolution? Needed research on the decline of middle management and internal labor markets.* Paper presented at annual meeting of the American Sociological Association, Cincinnati, OH.

Hodgson, G. (1988). *Economics and institutions.* Cambridge, MA: Polity.

Hofstede, G. (1980). *Culture's Consequences: International Differences in Work-related Values.* Beverly Hills, CA: Sage.

Homans, G. C. (1964). Bringing men back in. *American Sociological Review, 29,* 809-818.

Huefner, K., Naumann, J., & Meyer, J. W. (1987). Comparative education policy research: A world society perspective. In M. Dierkes, H. Weiler, & A. Antal (Eds.), *Comparative policy research* (pp. 188-243). Aldershot, UK: Gower.

Inkeles, A., & Sirowy, L. (1983). Convergent and divergent trends in national educational systems. *Social Forces, 62,* 303-334.

Inkenberry, G. J. (1989). *Explaining the diffusion of state norms: Coercion, competition, and learning in the international system.* Paper presented at annual meeting of the International Studies Association, London.

Jacoby, S. M. (1984). The development of internal labor markets in American manufacturing firms. In P. Osterman (Ed.), *Internal labor markets* (pp. 23-69). Cambridge: MIT Press.

Jacoby, S. M. (1985). *Employing bureaucracy: Managers, unions, and the transformation of work in American industry, 1900-1945.* New York: Columbia University Press.

James, T., & Levin, H. (Eds.). (1988). *Comparing public and private schools. Vol. 1: Institutions and organizations.* Philadelphia: Falmer Press.

Jepperson, R. L. (1991). Institutions, institutional effects, and institutionalization. In W. W. Powell & P. J. DiMaggio (Eds.), *The new institutionalism in organizational analysis* (pp. 143-163). Chicago: University of Chicago Press.

Jepperson, R. L., & Meyer, J. W. (1991). The public order and the construction of formal organizations. In W. W. Powell & P. J. DiMaggio (Eds.), *The new institutionalism in organizational analysis* (pp. 204-231). Chicago: University of Chicago Press.

Kaestle, C., & Vinovskis, M. (1976). *Education and social change: Nineteenth century Massachusetts: Quantitative studies* (Final Research Rep., Proj., No. 1-3-0825). Washington, DC: National Institute of Education.

Kalberg, S. (1980). Max Weber's types of rationality: Cornerstones for the analysis of rationalization processes in history. *American Journal of Sociology, 85,* 1180-1201.

Kalleberg, A. L., Marsden, P. V., Aldrich, H. E., & Cassell, J. W. (1990). Comparing organizational sampling frames. *Administrative Science Quarterly, 35,* 658-688.

Karpik, L. (Ed.). (1978). *Organization and environment: Theory, issues, and reality.* Beverly Hills, CA: Sage.

Katz, D., & Kahn, R. L. (1966). *The social psychology of organizations.* New York: John Wiley.

Kearsley, G. (1982). *Costs, benefits and productivity in training systems.* Reading, MA: Addison-Wesley.

Kerr, C., Dunlop, J. T., Harbison, F., & Meyers, C. A. (1964). *Industrialism and industrial man* (2nd ed.). New York: Oxford University Press.

Kirp, D. L., & Jensen, D. N. (Eds.). (1986). *School days, rule days: The legalization and regulation of education.* Philadelphia: Falmer.

Kirst, M. W. (1978). The state role in regulating local schools. In M. F. Williams (Ed.), *Government in the classroom: Dollars and power in education* (pp. 45-56). New York: Academy of Political Science.

Kitschelt, H. (1991). Industrial governance structures: Innovation strategies, and the case of Japan: Sectoral or cross-national comparative analysis? *International Organization, 45,* 453-493.

Knoke, D. (1982). The spread of municipal reform: Temporal, spatial, and social dynamics, *American Journal of Sociology, 87,* 1314-1339.

Knudsen, C. (1993). Modelling rationality, institutions and processes in economic theory. In B. Gustafsson, C. Knudsen, & U. Maki (Eds.), *Rationality, institutions and economic methodology.* London: Routledge.

Kochan, T. A., & Cappelli, P. (1984). The transformation of the industrial relations and personnel function. In P. Osterman (Ed.), *Internal labor markets* (pp. 133-162). Cambridge: MIT Press.

Krasner, S. D. (Ed.). (1983). *International regimes.* Ithaca, NY: Cornell University Press.

Krasner, S. D. (1988). Sovereignty: An institutional perspective. *Comparative Political Studies, 21,* 66-94.

Laird, D. (1985). *Approaches to training and development* (2nd ed.). Reading, MA: Addison-Wesley.

Lammers, C. J., & Hickson, D. J. (1979). A cross-national and cross-institutional typology of organizations. In C. J. Lammers & D. J. Hickson (Eds.), *Organizations alike and unlike: International and interinstitutional studies in the sociology of organizations* (pp. 420-434). London: Routledge & Kegan Paul.

Land, K. C., Deane, G., & Blau, J. R. (1991). Religious pluralism and church membership: A spatial diffusion model. *American Sociological Review, 56,* 237-249.

Langlois, R. N. (1986a). The new institutional economics: An introductory essay. In R. N. Langlois (Ed.), *Economics as a process: Essays in the new institutional economics* (pp. 1-25). New York: Cambridge University Press.

Langlois, R. N. (1986b). Rationality, institutions and explanations. In R. N. Langlois (Ed.), *Economics as a process: Essays in the new institutional economics* (pp. 225-255). New York: Cambridge University Press.

Latham, G. P. (1988). Human resource training and development. *Annual Review of Psychology, 39,* 545-582.

Lave, C. A., & March, J. G. (1975). *An introduction to models in the social sciences.* New York: Harper & Row.

Lawrence, P. R. (1985). The history of human resource management in American industry. In R. E. Walton & P. R. Lawrence (Eds.), *Human resource management: Trends and challenges* (pp. 15-34). Boston: Harvard Business School Press.

Lawrence, P. R., & Lorsch, J. W. (1967). *Organization and environment: Managing differentiation and integration.* Boston: Harvard University, Graduate School of Business Administration.

Leblebici, H., Salancik, G. R., Copay, A., & King, T. (1991). Institutional change and the transformation of interorganizational fields: An organizational history of the U.S. radio broadcasting industry. *Administrative Science Quarterly, 36* (September), 333-363.

Lee, C. (1985). Trainers' careers. *Training, 22*(10), 75-80.

Lee, C. (1986). Training profiles: The view from ground level. *Training, 23*(10), 67-84.

Leonard, J. S. (1984a). The impact of affirmative action on employment. *Journal of Labor Economics, 2,* 439-463.

Leonard, J. S. (1984b). Antidiscrimination or reverse discrimination: The impact of changing demographics, Title VII, and affirmative action on productivity. *Journal of Human Resources, 19,* 145-174.

Leonard, J. S. (1985). What promises are worth: The impact of affirmative action goals. *Journal of Human Resources, 20,* 3-20.

Levin, B. (1977). *The courts as educational policy makers and their impact on federal programs.* Santa Monica, CA: Rand Corporation.

Levitt, B., & March, J. G. (1988). Organizational learning. *Annual Review of Sociology, 14,* 319-340.

Lincoln, J. R., & Kalleberg, A. L. (1985). Work organization and workforce commitment: A study of plants and employees in the U.S. and Japan. *American Sociological Review, 50,* 738-760.

Lindberg, L. N., Campbell, J. L., & Hollingsworth, J. R. (1991). Economic governance and the analysis of structural change in the American economy. In J. L. Campbell, J. R. Hollingsworth, & L. N. Lindberg (Eds.), *Governance of the American economy* (pp. 3-32). New York: Cambridge University Press.

Lindblom, C. (1977). *Politics and markets.* New York: Basic Books.

Lowi, T. (1969). *The end of liberalism.* New York: W. W. Norton.

Lundberg, S. J. (1991). The enforcement of equal opportunity laws under imperfect information: Affirmative action and alternatives. *Quarterly Journal of Economics, 106,* 309-326.

Lusterman, S. (1977). *Education in industry.* New York: Conference Board.

McCarthy, J. D., & Zald, M. N. (1977). Resource mobilization and social movements: A partial theory, *American Journal of Sociology, 82,* 1212-1243.

McDonnell, L. M., & McLaughlin, M. W. (1982). *Educational policy and the role of the states.* Santa Monica, CA: Rand Corporation.

McNeely, C. (1989). *Cultural isomorphism among nation-states.* Unpublished doctoral dissertation. Stanford University, Stanford, CA.

MacPherson, C. B. (1962). *The political theory of possessive individualism.* Oxford, UK: Oxford University Press.

Mann, M. (1984). The autonomous power of the state: Its origins, mechanisms, and results. *Archives Europeanes de Sociologie, 25,* 185-213.

March, J. G., & Olsen, J. P. (1976). *Ambiguity and choice in organizations.* Bergen, Norway: Universitetsforlaget.

March, J. G., & Olsen, J. P. (1984). The new institutionalism: Organizational factors in political life. *American Political Science Review, 78,* 734-749.

March, J. G., & Olsen, J. P. (1989). *Rediscovering institutions: The organizational basis of politics.* New York: Free Press.

March, J. G., & Simon, H. A. (1958). *Organizations.* New York: John Wiley.

Marglin, S. (1974). What do bosses do? The origins and functions of hierarchy in capitalist production. *Review of Radical Political Economics, 6,* 60-112.

Market Data Retrieval. (1980). Unpublished tabulations of educational personnel by state. Westport, CT.

Marsden, P. V., & Lin, N. (Eds.). (1982). *Social structure and network analysis.* Beverly Hills, CA: Sage.

Marsden, P. V., & Podolny, J. (1990). Dynamic analysis of network diffusion processes. In H. Flap & J. Weesie (Eds.), *Social networks through time.* Utrecht, Netherlands: Rijksuniversiteit Utrecht.

Marsh, C. P., & Coleman, A. L. (1956). Group influences and agricultural innovations: Some tentative findings and hypotheses. *American Sociological Review, 61,* 588-594.

Marshall, T. H. (1948). *Citizenship and social class.* Garden City, NY: Doubleday.

Marshall, T. H. (1964). *Class, citizenship and social development.* Garden City, NY: Doubleday.

Masten, S. E. (1986). The economic institutions of capitalism: A review article. *Journal of Institutional and Theoretical Economics, 142,* 445-451.

Maurice, M., Sellier, F., & Silvestre, J.-J. (1984). The search for a societal effect in the production of company hierarchy: A comparison of France and Germany. In P. Osterman (Ed.), *Internal labor markets* (pp. 231-270). Cambridge: MIT Press.

Maurice, M., Sorge, A., & Warner, M. (1980). Societal differences in organizing manufacturing units: A comparison of France, West Germany, and Great Britain. *Organizational Studies, 1,* 59-86.

Mead, G. H. (1934). *Mind, self and society.* Chicago: University of Chicago Press.

Menger, C. (1963). *Problems of economics and sociology* (F. J. Nock, Trans.). Urbana: University of Illinois Press.

Menzel, H. (1960). Innovation, integration, and marginality: A survey of physicians, *American Sociological Review, 25,* 704-713.

Meyer, J. W. (1977). Effects of education as an institution. *American Journal of Sociology, 83,* 55-77.

Meyer, J. W. (1980). The world polity and the authority of the nation-state. In A. J. Bergesen (Ed.), *Studies of the modern world system.* New York: Academic Press.

Meyer, J. W. (1983a). Centralization of funding and control in educational governance. In J. W. Meyer & W. R. Scott (1983b), *Organizational environments: Ritual and rationality* (pp. 179-197). Beverly Hills, CA: Sage.

Meyer, J. W. (1983b). Conclusion: Institutionalization and the rationality of formal organizational structure. In J. W. Meyer & W. R. Scott (1983b), *Organizational environments: Ritual and rationality* (pp. 261-282). Beverly HIlls, CA: Sage.

Meyer, J. W. (1983c). Organizational factors affecting legalization in education. In J. W. Meyer & W. R. Scott (1983b), *Organizational environments: Ritual and rationality* (pp. 217-232). Beverly HIlls, CA: Sage.

Meyer, J. W. (1987). Self and life course: Institutionalization and its effects. In G. M. Thomas, J. W. Meyer, F. O. Ramirez, & J. Boli (Eds.), *Institutional structure: Constituting state, society, and the individual* (pp. 242-260). Newbury Park, CA: Sage.

Meyer, J. W. (1989). Conceptions of Christendom: Notes on the distinctiveness of the West. In M. Kohn (Ed.), *Cross-national research in sociology* (pp. 395-413). Newbury Park, CA: Sage.

Meyer, J. W., Boli, J., & Thomas, G. M. (1987). Ontology and rationalization in the Western cultural account. In G. M. Thomas, J. W. Meyer, F. O. Ramirez, & J. Boli (Eds.), *Institutional structure: Constituting state, society, and the individual* (pp. 2-37). Newbury Park, CA: Sage.

Meyer, J. W., & Gordon-Lanford, A. (1981). *Socialization theory: Institutional and ideological bases of modern childhood.* Unpublished paper presented at annual meeting of the Pacific Sociological Association.

Meyer, J. W., & Hannan, M. T. (1979). *National development and the world system.* Chicago: University of Chicago Press.

Meyer, J. W., Kamens, D., Benavot, A., Cha, Y.-K., & Wong, S.-Y. (1992). *School knowledge for the masses: World models and national primary curriculum categories in the twentieth century.* London: Falmer Press.

Meyer, J. W., Ramirez, F. O., Rubinson, R., & Boli-Bennett, J. (1977). The world educational revolution, 1950-1970. *Sociology of Education, 50,* 242-258.

Meyer, J. W., Ramirez, F. O., & Soysal, Y. (1992). World expansion of mass education, 1870-1980. *Sociology of Education, 65,* 128-149.

Meyer, J. W., & Rowan, B. (1977). Institutionalized organizations: Formal structure as myth and ceremony, *American Journal of Sociology, 83,* 340-363.

Meyer, J. W., & Rowan, B. (1978). The structure of educational organizations. In M. Meyer et al. (Eds.), *Environments and organizations* (pp. 78-109). San Francisco: Jossey-Bass.

Meyer, J. W., & Scott, W. R. (1983a). Centralization and the legitimacy problems of local government. In J. W. Meyer & W. R. Scott (1983b), *Organizational environments: Ritual and rationality* (pp. 199-215). Beverly Hills, CA: Sage.

Meyer, J. W., & Scott, W. R. (1983b). *Organizational environments: Ritual and rationality.* Beverly Hills, CA: Sage.

Meyer, J. W., & Scott, W. R. (1992). *Organizational environments: Ritual and rationality* (rev. ed.). Newbury Park, CA: Sage.

Meyer, J. W., Scott, W. R., Cole, S., & Intili, J. K. (1978). In M. Meyer (Ed.), *Environments and organizations* (pp. 233-263). San Francisco: Jossey-Bass.

Meyer, J. W., Scott, W. R., & Deal, T. E. (1983). Institutional and technical sources of organizational structure. In J. W. Meyer & W. R. Scott (1983b), *Organizational environments: Ritual and rationality* (pp. 45-67). Beverly Hills, CA: Sage.

Meyer, J. W., Scott, W. R., & Strang, D. (1987). Centralization, fragmentation, and school district complexity. *Administrative Science Quarterly, 32,* 186-201.

Meyer, J. W., Scott, W. R., Strang, D., & Creighton, A. L. (1988). Bureaucratization without centralization: Changes in the organizational system of U.S. public education, 1940-80. In L. G. Zucker (Ed.), *Institutional patterns and organizations: Culture and environment* (pp. 139-168). Cambridge, MA: Ballinger.

Meyer, J. W., Tyack, D., Nagel, J., & Gordon, A. (1979). Public education as nation-building in America. *American Journal of Sociology, 85,* 591-613.

Meyer, M. (Ed.). (1978). *Environments and organizations.* San Francisco: Jossey-Bass.

Mezias, S. J. (1990). An institutional model of organizational practice: Financial reporting at the Fortune 200. *Administrative Science Quarterly, 35,* 431-457.

Miller, P., & O'Leary, T. (1993). Accounting expertise and the politics of the product. *Accounting, Organizations and Society, 18*(2-3), 187-206.

Mills, C. W. (1940). Situated actions and vocabularies of motive. *American Sociological Review, 5,* 904-913.

Miner, A. S. (1987). Idiosyncratic jobs in formalized organizations. *Administrative Science Quarterly, 32,* 327-351.

Mischel, W. (1971). *Introduction to personality.* New York: Holt, Rinehart & Winston.

Miyahara, D., Monahan, S. C., Meyer, J. W., & Scott, W. R. (1991). *A survey of organizational training.* Unpublished manuscript, Stanford University, Stanford, CA.

Moe, T. (1990a). Political institutions: The neglected side of the story. *Journal of Law, Economics and Organizations, 6,* 213-253.

Moe, T. (1990b). The politics of structural choice: Toward a theory of public bureaucracy. In O. E. Williamson (Ed.), *Organization theory: From Chester Barnard to the present and beyond* (pp. 116-153). New York: Oxford University Press.

Mohr, L. B. (1982). *Explaining organizational behavior.* San Francisco: Jossey-Bass.

Morris, V. C., Crowson, R. L., Hurwitz, E., Jr., & Porter-Gehrie, C. (1981). *The urban principal: Discretionary decision-making in a large educational organization.* Chicago: College of Education, University of Illinois at Chicago Circle.

Munsterberg, H. (1913). *Psychology and industrial efficiency.* Boston: Houghton Mifflin.

Murphy, J. T. (1981). The paradox of state government reform. *Public Interest, 64,* 139-149.

Nadler, L. (Ed.). (1984). *The handbook of human resource development*. New York: John Wiley.

Naroll, R. (1965). Galton's problem: The logic of cross-cultural analysis. *Social Research, 32,* 429-451.

National Civil Service League. (1973). *Training and testing the disadvantaged.* Washington, DC: Consortium.

National Education Center. (1931). *Studies in state educational administration* (No. 9). Washington, DC: National Education Association, Research Division.

North, D. C. (1986). The new institutional economics. *Journal of Institutional and Theoretical Economics, 142,* 230-237.

North, D. C. (1989). Institutional change and economic history. *Journal of Institutional and Theoretical Economics, 145,* 238-245.

North, D. C. (1990). *Institutions, institutional change and economic performance.* Cambridge, UK: Cambridge University Press.

Oliver, C. (1991). Strategic responses to institutional processes. *Academy of Management Review, 16,* 145-179.

O'Malley, C. J. (1981). Governance of private schools. *Private School Quarterly* (Summer), 12-15.

Organ, D. W. (1988). *Organizational citizenship behavior: The good soldier syndrome.* Lexington, MA: Lexington Books.

Organ, D. W. (1990). The motivational basis of organizational citizenship behavior. In B. M. Staw & L. L. Cummings (Eds.), *Research in organizational behavior* (Vol. 12, pp. 43-92). Greenwich, CT: JAI.

Orru, M., Biggart, N. W., & Hamilton, G. G. (1991). Organizational isomorphism in East Asia. In W. W. Powell & P. J. DiMaggio (Eds.), *The new institutionalism in organizational analysis* (pp. 361-389). Chicago: University of Chicago Press.

Orton, J. D., & Weick, K. E. (1990). Loosely coupled systems: A reconceptualization. *Academy of Management Review, 15,* 203-223.

Parsons, T. (1951). *The social system.* New York: Free Press.

Perrow, C. (1967). A framework for the comparative analysis of organizations. *American Sociological Review, 32,* 194-208.

Perrow, C. (1979). *Complex organizations: A critical essay* (2nd ed.). Glenview, IL: Scott, Foresman.

Perrow, C. (1986). *Complex organizations: A critical essay* (3rd. ed.). New York: Random House.

Perrow, C. (1991). A society of organizations. *Theory and Society, 20,* 725-762.

Peterson, D. (1974). The impact of Duke power on testing. *Personnel, 51,* 30-37.

Pfeffer, J., & Baron, J. N. (1988). Taking the workers back out: Recent trends in the structuring of employment. In B. M. Staw & L. L. Cummings (Eds.), *Research in organizational behavior* (Vol. 10, pp. 257-303). Greenwich, CT: JAI.

Pfeffer, J., & Cohen, Y. (1984). Determinants of internal labor markets in organizations. Administrative Science Quarterly, 29, 550-572.

Pfeffer, J., & Salancik, G. (1978). *The external control of organizations.* New York: Harper & Row.

Phelps Brown, H. (1977). *The inequality of pay.* Oxford, UK: Oxford University Press.

Phillips, J. J. (1983). *Handbook of training evaluation and measurement methods.* Houston, TX: Gulf.

Porter, M. E. (1980). *Competitive strategy.* New York: Free Press.

Powell, W. W. (1991). Expanding the scope of institutional analysis. In W. W. Powell & P. J. DiMaggio (Eds.), *The new institutionalism in organizational analysis* (pp. 183-203). Chicago: University of Chicago Press.

316 INSTITUTIONAL ENVIRONMENTS AND ORGANIZATIONS

Powell, W. W., & DiMaggio, P. J. (Eds.). (1991). *The new institutionalism in organizational analysis.* Chicago: University of Chicago Press.

Pressman, J. L., & Wildavsky, A. (1973). *Implementation.* Berkeley: University of California Press.

Pugh, D. S., Hickson, D. J., & Hinings, C. R. (1969). An empirical taxonomy of structures of work organizations. *Administrative Science Quarterly, 14,* 115-126.

Purcell, T. V. (1974). How G.E. measures managers on fair employment. *Harvard Business Review, 52,* 99-104.

Rabinow, P., & Sullivan, W. M. (1987). The interpretive turn. In P. Rabinow & W. M. Sullivan (Eds.), *Interpretive social science: A second look* (pp. 1-30). Berkeley: University of California Press.

Ramirez, F. O. (1987). Global changes, world myths, and the demise of cultural gender. In T. Boswell & A. J. Bergesen (Eds.), *America's changing role in the world system* (pp. 257-273). New York: Praeger.

Ramirez, F. O., & Boli, J. (1987). Global patterns of educational institutionalization. In G. M. Thomas, J. W. Meyer, F. O. Ramirez, & J. Boli (Eds.), *Institutional structure: Constituting state, society, and the individual* (pp. 150-172). Newbury Park, CA: Sage.

Ramirez, F. O., & Meyer, J. W. (1980). Comparative education: The social construction of the modern world system. *Annual Review of Sociology, 6,* 369-399.

Ramirez, F. O., & Rubinson, R. (1979). Creating members: The political incorporation and expansion of public education. In J. W. Meyer & M. T. Hannan (1979) (Eds.), *National development and the world system* (pp. 128-160). Chicago: University of Chicago Press.

Ramirez, F. O., & Weiss, J. (1979). The political incorporation of women. In J. W. Meyer & M. T. Hannan (Eds.), *National development and the world system* (pp. 238-249). Chicago: University of Chicago Press.

Riddle, P. (1989). *University and state: Political competition and the rise of universities.* Unpublished doctoral dissertation. Stanford University, Stanford, CA.

Rogers, D., & Whetten, D. (Eds.). (1981). *Interorganizational coordination.* Ames: Iowa State University Press.

Rogers, E. M. (1983). *Diffusion of innovations.* Detroit, MI: Free Press.

Rohlen, T. P. (1978). The education of a Japanese banker. *Human Nature, 1,* 22-30.

Rokkan, S. (1975). Dimensions of state formation and nation-building: A possible paradigm for research on variations within Europe. In C. Tilly (Ed.), *The formation of national states in Western Europe* (pp. 562-600). Princeton, NJ: Princeton University Press.

Roth, G., & Schluchter, W. (1979). *Max Weber's vision of history: Ethics and methods.* Berkeley: University of California Press.

Rowan, B. (1981). The effects of institutionalized rules on administrators. In S. B. Bacharach (Ed.), *Organizational behavior in schools and school districts* (pp. 47-75). New York: Praeger.

Rowan, B. (1982). Instructional management in historical perspective: Evidence on differentiation in school districts. *Educational Administration Quarterly, 18,* 43-59.

Saari, L. M., Johnson, T. R., McLaughlin, S. D., & Zimmerle, D. M. (1988). A survey of management training and education practices in U.S. companies. *Personnel Psychology, 41,* 731-743.

Scherer, F. M. (1970). *Industrial market structure and economic performance.* Chicago: Rand McNally.

Schluchter, W. (1981). *The rise of Western rationalism: Max Weber's developmental history.* Berkeley: University of California Press.

Schmitter, P. (1974). Still the century of corporatism? In F. B. Pike & T. Stritch (Eds.), *The new corporatism: Social-political structures in the Iberian world* (pp. 85-131). South Bend, IN: University of Notre Dame Press.

Schmitter, P. (1990). Sectors in modern capitalism: Models of governance and variations in performance. In R. Brunetta & C. Dell-Aringa (Eds.), *Labour relations and economic performance* (pp. 3-39). London: Macmillan.

Schotter, A. (1981). *The economic theory of social institutions.* New York: Cambridge University Press.

Schotter, A. (1986). The evolution of rules. In R. N. Langlois (Ed.), *Economics as a process: Essays in the new institutional economics* (pp. 117-134). New York: Cambridge University Press.

Schultz, T. (1961). Investment in human capital. *American Economic Review, 51,* 1-17.

Scott, M. B., & Lyman, S. M. (1968). Accounts. *American Sociological Review, 33,* 46-62.

Scott, W. R. (1981). *Organizations: Rational, natural and open systems.* Englewood Cliffs, NJ: Prentice Hall.

Scott, W. R. (1983). The organization of environments: Network, cultural, and historical elements. In J. W. Meyer & W. R. Scott (1983b), *Organizational environments: Ritual and rationality* (pp. 155-175). Beverly Hills, CA: Sage.

Scott, W. R. (1987a). The adolescence of institutional theory. *Administrative Science Quarterly, 32,* 493-511.

Scott, W. R. (1987b). *Organizations: Rational, natural and open systems* (2nd ed.). Englewood Cliffs, NJ: Prentice Hall.

Scott, W. R. (1992). *Organizations: Rational, natural and open systems* (3rd ed.). Englewood Cliffs, NJ: Prentice Hall.

Scott, W. R. (in press). Conceptualizing organizational fields: Linking organizations and societal systems. In U. Gerhardt, H.-U. Derlien, & F. W. Scharpf (Eds.), *Systems rationality and partial interests.* Baden-Baden, Germany: Nomos-Verlag.

Scott, W. R., & Black, B. (Eds.). (1986). *The organization of mental health services: Society and community systems.* Beverly Hills, CA: Sage.

Scott, W. R., & Meyer, J. W. (1983). The organization of societal sectors. In J. W. Meyer & W. R. Scott (1983b), *Organizational environments: Ritual and rationality* (pp. 129-153). Beverly Hills, CA: Sage. Revised version in W. W. Powell & P. J. DiMaggio (Eds.) (1991), *The new institutionalism in organizational analysis* (pp. 108-140). Chicago: University of Chicago Press.

Scott, W. R., & Meyer, J. W. (1988). Environmental linkages and organizational complexity: Public and private schools. In T. James & H. M. Levin (Eds.), *Comparing public and private schools. Vol 1: Institutions and organizations* (pp. 128-160). Philadelphia: Falmer.

Scott, W. R., & Meyer, J. W. (1991). The rise of training programs in firms and agencies: An institutional perspective. In B. M. Straw & L. L. Cummings (Eds.), *Research in Organizational Behavior, 13,* 297-326. Greenwich, CT: JAI.

Searle, J. R. (1969). *Speech acts: An essay in the philosophy of language.* Cambridge, UK: Cambridge University Press.

Seavoy, R. E. (1982). *The origins of the American business corporation, 1784-1855: Broadening the concept of public service during industrialization.* Westport, CT: Greenwood.

Selznick, P. (1949). *TVA and the grass roots.* Berkeley: University of California Press.

Selznick, P. (1957). *Leadership in administration.* New York: Harper & Row.

Selznick, P. (1969). *Law, society, and industrial justice.* New York: Russell Sage.

Sergiovanni, T. J., Burlingame, M., Coombs, F. D., & Thurston, P. (1980). *Educational governance and administration.* Englewood Cliffs, NJ: Prentice Hall.

Shepsle, K. A., & Weingast, B. (1987). The institutional foundations of committee power. *American Political Science Review, 81,* 85-104.

Sherman, R. (1974). *The economics of industry.* Boston: Little, Brown.

Simon, H. A. (1957). *Administrative behavior* (2nd ed.). New York: Macmillan.

Singh, J. V. (Ed.). (1990). *Organizational evolution: New directions.* Newbury Park, CA: Sage.

Skocpol, T. (1979). *States and social revolutions.* Cambridge, UK: Cambridge University Press.

Skocpol, T. (1985). Bringing the state back in. In P. B. Evans, D. Rueschemeyer, & T. Skocpol (Eds.), *Bringing the state back in* (pp. 3-43). Cambridge, UK: Cambridge University Press.

Skog, O.-J. (1986). The long waves of alcohol consumption: A social network perspective on cultural changes. *Social Networks, 8,* 1-32.

Skowronek, S. (1982). *Building a new American state: The expansion of national administrative capacities, 1877-1920.* Cambridge, UK: Cambridge University Press.

Slevin, D. (1973). Full utilization of women in employment: The problem and an action program. *Human Resource Management, 12,* 25-32.

Slichter, S. (1919). *The turnover of factory labor.* New York: Appleton.

Smircich, L. (1983). Organizations as shared meanings. In L. Pondy, P. J. Frost, G. Morgan, & T. C. Dandridge (Eds.), *Organizational symbolism* (pp. 55-65). Greenwich, CT: JAI.

Smith, A. (1957). *Selections from The Wealth of Nations* (G. J. Stigler, Ed.). New York: Appleton-Century-Crofts.

Solmon, L. (1970). Estimates of the costs of schooling in 1800 and 1890. *Explorations in Economic History, 7* (supplement), 531-581.

Spence, M. (1973). Job market signaling. *Quarterly Journal of Economics, 87,* 355-374.

Stackhouse, E. A. (1982). *The effects of state centralization on administrative and macrotechnical structure in contemporary secondary schools* (Project Rep. No. 82-A24). Stanford, CA: Stanford University, Institute for Research on Educational Finance and Governance.

Stark, D. (1986). Rethinking internal labor markets: New insights from a comparative perspective. *American Sociological Review, 51,* 192-204.

Statistics of State School Systems (1938-1980). From 1940 to 1956 published in the biennial survey of education in the United States.

Staw, B., & Cummings, L. L. (Eds.). (1991). *Research in organizational behavior* (Vol. 13). Greenwich, CT: JAI.

Stinchcombe, A. L. (1965). Social structure and organizations. In J. G. March (Ed.), *Handbook of organizations* (pp. 142-193). Chicago: Rand McNally.

Strang, D. (1987). The administrative transformation of American education: School district consolidation, 1938-1980. *Administrative Science Quarterly, 32,* 352-366.

Strang, D. (1990). From dependency to sovereignty: An event history analysis of decolonization. *American Sociological Review, 55,* 846-860.

Strang, D. (1991). Adding social structure to diffusion models: An event history framework. *Sociological Methods and Research, 19,* 324-353.

Strang, D., & Tuma, N. B. (1990). *Spatial and temporal heterogeneity in diffusion.* Paper presented at the World Congress of Sociology, Madrid.

Strayer, J. (1970). *On the medieval origins of the modern state.* Princeton: NJ: Princeton University Press.

Streeck, W., & Schmitter, P. C. (Eds.). (1985). *Private interest government: Beyond market and state.* Beverly Hills, CA: Sage.

Suchman, M. C. (1991). *On advice of counsel: Legal and financial firms as information intermediaries in the structuration of Silicon Valley.* Unpublished doctoral prospectus, Stanford University, Stanford, CA.

Sugden, R. (1986). *The economics of rights, cooperation and welfare.* Oxford, UK: Basil Blackwell.

Sullivan, D. J. (1974). *Public aid to non-public schools.* Lexington, MA: Lexington Books.

Sutton, J. R., Dobbin, F. R., Meyer, J. W., & Scott, W. R. (in press). The legalization of the workplace. *American Journal of Sociology.*

Swanson, G. B. (1971). An organizational analysis of collectivities. *American Sociological Review, 36,* 607-623.

Swidler, A. (1986). Culture in action: Symbols and strategies. *American Sociological Review, 51,* 273-286.

Tannanbaum, A. S. (1968). *Control in organizations.* New York: McGraw-Hill.

Taylor, F. W. (1911). *The principles of scientific management.* New York: Harper & Row.

Thoits, P. A. (1989). The sociology of emotions. *Annual Review of Sociology, 15,* 317-342.

Thomas, G. M., Boli, J., & Kim, Y. (1993). *World culture and international nongovernmental organization.* Paper presented at annual meeting of the American Sociological Association, Miami, FL.

Thomas, G. M., & Meyer, J. W. (1984). The expansion of the state. *Annual Review of Sociology, 10,* 461-482.

Thomas, G. M., Meyer, J. W., Ramirez, F. O., & Boli, J. (Eds.). (1987). *Institutional structure: Constituting state, society, and the individual.* Newbury Park, CA: Sage.

Thompson, E. P. (1963). *The making of the English working class.* New York: Vintage.

Thompson, J. D. (1967). *Organizations in action.* New York: McGraw-Hill.

Thurow, L. (1975). *Generating inequality.* New York: Basic Books.

Tilly, C. (1975). *The formation of national states in Western Europe.* Princeton, NJ: Princeton University Press.

Tilly, C. (1978). *From mobilization to revolution.* Reading, MA: Addison-Wesley.

Tilly, C. (1984). *Big structures, large processes, huge comparisons.* New York: Russell Sage.

Timpane, M. (Ed.). (1976). *The federal interest in financing schooling.* Cambridge, MA: Ballinger.

Tocqueville, A. de (1947). *Democracy in America.* New York: Oxford University Press. (Originally published 1835)

Tolbert, P. S., & Zucker, L. G. (1983). Institutional sources of change in the formal structure of organizations: The diffusion of civil service reform, 1880-1935. *Administrative Science Quarterly, 30,* 22-39.

Tushman, M. L., & Anderson, P. (1986). Technological discontinuities and organizational environments. *Administrative Science Quarterly, 31,* 439-465.

Tyack, D. (1974). *The one best system: A history of American urban education.* Cambridge, MA: Harvard University Press.

Union of International Associations. (1992 and previous years). *Yearbook of international organizations.* Munich: K. G. Sauer.

U.S. Equal Employment Opportunity Commission. (1974). *Affirmative action and equal employment: A guidebook for employers* (2 vols.). Washington, DC: Author.

U.S. Small Business Administration. (1988). *Job training in small and large firms.* Washington, DC: Government Printing Office.

Van de Ven, A. H., & Garud, R. (1989). A framework for understanding the emergence of new industries. In R. S. Rosenbloom (Ed.), *Research on technological innovation, management and policy* (Vol. 4, pp. 195-225). Greenwich, CT: JAI Press.

Van Maanen, J. (1978). People processing: Major strategies of organizational socialization and their consequences. In J. Papp (Ed.), *New directions in human resource management.* Englewood Cliffs, NJ: Prentice Hall.

Van Maanen, J., & Barley, S. R. (1985). Cultural organization: Fragments of a theory. In P. J. Frost, L. F. Moore, M. R. Louis, C. C. Lundberg, & J. Martin (Eds.), *Organizational culture* (pp. 31-54). Beverly Hills, CA: Sage.

Van Maanen, J., & Schein, E. H. (1979). Toward a theory of organizational socialization. In B. M. Staw (Ed.), *Research in organizational behavior* (Vol. 1, pp. 209-264). Greenwich, CT: JAI.

Wagner, A. P. (1980). *An inventory of post-compulsory education and training programs in the U.S. and sources of support* (Proj. Rep. No. 80-A14). Stanford, CA: Stanford University, Institute for Research on Educational Finance and Governance.

Walker, J. (1969). The diffusion of innovation among the American states. *American Political Science Review, 63,* 880-899.

Wallerstein, I. (1974). *The modern world-system. Vol I: Capitalist agriculture and the origins of the European world economy.* New York: Academic Press.

Wallerstein, I. (1980). *The modern world-system. Vol. II: Mercantilism and the consolidation of the European world economy.* New York: Academic Press.

Walsh, R. J., & Hess, L. R. (1974). The small company, EEOC, and test validation alternatives: Do you know your options? *Personnel Journal, 53,* 840-845.

Warren, R. (1967). The interorganizational field as a focus for investigation. *Administrative Science Quarterly, 12,* 396-419.

Weatherley, R. A. (1979). *Reforming special education: Policy implementation from state level to street level.* Cambridge: MIT Press.

Weber, M. (1927). *General economic history.* New York: Greenberg.

Weber, M. (1930). *The Protestant ethic and the spirit of capitalism.* New York: Scribner's. (Originally published 1904-1905)

Weber, M. (1946). *From Max Weber: Essays in sociology* (H. H. Gerth & C. W. Mills, Eds.). New York: Oxford University Press. (Originally published 1906-1924)

Weber, M. (1968). *Economy and society: An interpretive sociology* (3 vols.) (G. Roth & C. Wittich, Eds.). New York: Bedminister. (Original work published 1924)

Weick, K. E. (1976). Educational organizations as loosely coupled systems. *Administrative Science Quarterly, 21,* 1-19.

Weingast, B. R., & Marshall, W. (1988). The industrial organization of Congress. *Journal of Political Economy, 96,* 132-163.

Weir, M., & Skocpol, T. (1985). State structures and the possibilities for "Keynesian" responses to the great depression in Sweden, Britain, and the United States. In P. B. Evans, D. Rueschemeyer, & T. Skocpol (Eds.), *Bringing the state back in* (pp. 107-163). Cambridge, UK: Cambridge University Press.

Wendt, A. (1992). Anarchy is what states make of it: The social construction of power politics. *International Organization, 46,* 391-425.

Westney, D. E. (1987). *Imitation and innovation: The transfer of Western organizational patterns to Meiji Japan.* Cambridge, MA: Harvard University Press.

Whitley, R. (1992). The social construction of organizations and markets: The comparative analysis of business recipes. In M. Reed & M. Hughes (Eds.), *Rethinking organizations: New directions in organization theory and analysis* (pp. 120-143). Newbury Park, CA: Sage.

Whyte, W. H., Jr. (1956). *The organization man.* New York: Simon & Schuster.

Wilensky, H. L. (1976). *The "new corporatism," centralization, and the welfare state.* Beverly Hills, CA: Sage.

Williamson, O. E. (1975). *Markets and hierarchies: Analysis and antitrust implications.* New York: Free Press.

Williamson, O. E. (1981). The economics of organization: The transaction cost approach. *American Journal of Sociology, 87,* 548-577.

Williamson, O. E. (1985). *The economic institutions of capitalism.* New York: Free Press.

Williamson, O. E. (1991). Comparative economic organization: The analysis of discrete structural alternatives. *Administrative Science Quarterly, 36,* 269-296.

Williamson, O. E. (1992). *Transaction cost economics and organization theory.* Unpublished manuscript, University of California, Berkeley.

Wirt, F. (1978). School policy culture and state decentralization. *Policy Studies Review Annual, 2,* 458-481.

Wolcott, H. F. (1973). *The man in the principal's office.* New York: Holt, Rinehart & Winston.

Woodman, R. W., & Pasmore, W. A. (Eds.). (1987). *Research in organization change and development* (Vol. 1). Greenwich, CT: JAI.

Woodward, J. (1965). *Industrial organization: Theory and practice.* New York: Oxford University Press.

Wrong, D. (1961). The oversocialized conception of man in modern sociology. *American Sociological Review, 26,* 183-193.

Wuthnow, R. (1980a). The world economy and the institutionalization of science in seventeenth-century Europe. In A. J. Bergesen (Ed.), *Studies of the modern world system* (pp. 25-55). New York: Academic Press.

Wuthnow, R. (1980b). World order and religious movements. In A. J. Bergesen (Ed.), *Studies of the modern world system* (pp. 57-75). New York: Academic Press.

Wuthnow, R. (1985). State structures and ideological outcomes. *American Sociological Review, 50,* 799-821.

Wuthnow, R., Hunter, J. D., Bergesen, A. J., & Kurzwell, E. (1984). *Cultural analysis: The work of Peter L. Berger, Mary Douglas, Michel Foucault, and Jurgen Habermas.* Boston: Routledge & Kegan Paul.

Zald, M. N. (1970). Political economy: A framework for comparative analysis. In M. N. Zald (Ed.), *Power in organizations* (pp. 221-261). Nashville, TN: Vanderbilt University Press.

Zald, M. N. (1984). The sociology of enterprise, accounting and budget rules: Implications for organization theory. *Accounting, Organizations and Society, 11,* 327-340.

Zemky, R., & Meyerson, R. (1985). *Training practices: Education and training within the American firm.* Philadelphia: University of Pennsylvania, Philadelphia Higher Education Finance Research Institute.

Zimmerman, D. (1969). Record keeping and the intake process in a public welfare agency. In S. Wheeler (Ed.), *On record: Files and dossiers in American life.* New York: Russell Sage.

Zucker, L. G. (1977). The role of institutionalization in cultural persistence. *American Sociological Review, 42,* 726-743.

Zucker, L. G. (1983). Organizations as institutions. In S. Bacharach (Ed.), *Research in the sociology of organizations* (Vol. 2, pp. 1-47). Greenwich, CT: JAI.

Zucker, L. G. (1987). Institutional theories of organization. *Annual Review of Sociology 13,* 443-464.

Zucker, L. G. (Ed.). (1988a). *Institutional patterns and organizations: Culture and environment.* Cambridge, MA: Ballinger.

Zucker, L. G. (1988b). Where do institutional patterns come from? Organizations as actors in social systems. In Zucker (Ed.), *Institutional patterns and organizations: Culture and environment* (pp. 23-49). Cambridge, MA: Ballinger.

Index

About the Editors

John W. Meyer is Professor of Sociology at Stanford University. His research interests include macrosocial environments and their effects on structure, the rise and impact of the institutional system of modern world society, and the impact of world educational models on modern national societies. He is the coauthor of *Organizational Environments: Ritual and Rationality* (with W. R. Scott), *National Development and the World System* (with M. T. Hannan), *Institutional Structure: Constituting State, Society, and the Individual* (with G. M. Thomas, F. O. Ramirez, and J. Boli), and *School Knowledge for the Masses* (with D. Kamens et al.).

W. Richard Scott is Professor of Sociology at Stanford University, where he also holds courtesy appointments in the schools of business, education, and medicine. He also acts as director of the university's Center for Organizations Research. He is the author of *Organizations: Rational, Natural and Open Systems* (3rd ed.) (1992) and is currently working on a book on institutional theory and organizations and conducting research on the changing character of organizations and interorganizational ties in the health care arena.

About the Contributors

John Boli is Assistant Professor of Sociology at Emory University. A graduate of Stanford University, he has published extensively on world culture and organization, the sociology of education, citizenship, and state power and authority in the world polity. His books include *New Citizens for a New Society: The Institutional Origins of Mass Schooling in Sweden* and the forthcoming *Cream of the Crop: The Educational Elite Comes of Age* with Herant Katchadourian. His current projects include a longitudinal study of international nongovernmental organizations and a prognostic study of millennial movements at the end of the 20th century.

Andrew L. Creighton is Assistant Professor of Sociology at the University of Washington and a visiting Assistant Professor at the University of California at Berkeley. He has conducted research on legal environments and organizations and is currently working on a manuscript on the origins of legal incorporation.

Frank Dobbin teaches sociology at Princeton University. His research interests include the historical construction of rationality in national industrial policy paradigms and in management theory and practice, rational industrial strategies, rational business strategies, and rational tactics for managing personnel. His forthcoming *Forging Industrial Policy: The United States, Britain, and France in the Railway Age* charts the emergence of distinct national industrial policy strategies during the 19th century.

327

Susanne C. Monahan (Ph.D., Stanford University) has conducted research in the organization of work in churches and the institutionalization of the U.S. nonprofit sector. She is also involved in a meta-analytic review of the alcoholism treatment literature for the Center for Health Care Evaluation at the Veterans Administration hospital in Palo Alto, California.

David Strang (Ph.D., Stanford University) is Assistant Professor of Sociology at Cornell University. His research focuses on institutional analyses of change in organizational populations and state policy. His current research includes studies of health maintenance organizations and the global diffusion of educational, environmental, and welfare policies across nation-states in the 20th century (with John Meyer and Nancy Tuma).

John R. Sutton is Associate Professor of Sociology at the University of California at Santa Barbara. He is conducting research on the legalization of the employment relationship, the population dynamics of American Protestant denominations, and the relationship between imprisonment and social welfare policies in Western democratic societies.

George M. Thomas is Professor of Sociology at Arizona State University. His research interests include recent religious trends in the United States, religious liberty and religious nationalism, the concept of world culture, and the rise of nongovernmental organizations. He is author of *Revivalism and Cultural Change: Christianity, Nation Building, and the Market in the Nineteenth-Century United States* and coauthor of *Institutional Structure: Constituting State, Society, and the Individual.*